# ISRAEL

Building a New Society

# Jewish Political and Social Studies

*General Editors*
Daniel J. Elazar     Steven M. Cohen

# ISRAEL

## Building a New Society

Daniel J. Elazar

INDIANA UNIVERSITY PRESS • Bloomington

Manufactured in the United States of America

Library of Congress Cataloging-in-Publication Data

Elazar, Daniel Judah.
  Israel: building a new society.

  (Jewish political and social studies)
  Bibliography: p.
  Includes index.
    1. Israel—Politics and government—Philosophy—
Addresses, essays, lectures. I. Title. II. Series.
JQ1825.P3E39 1986      320.95694      84-48648
ISBN 0-253-338184-6

1   2   3   4   5   90   89   88   87   86

*This book is dedicated to the memory of my grand-parents, Hakham Yehudah and Naama Elazar, of Jerusalem, whose lives began in the days of the old Sephardic yishuv and spanned the Zionist transformation from its beginning until the reestablishment of the State of Israel.*

# CONTENTS

# PART 4 *Futures*

# PREFACE

This study constitutes another extension of my continuing effort to understand the difference between new and traditional societies, the role of the frontier in shaping new societies, the place of convenantal or federal principles and arrangements in the frontier process and the constitution of new societies, and how the frontier concretizes the generational rhythm of political affairs. My principal studies to date have dealt with the United States and the Jewish people: the first, the epitome of territorial democracy, and the second, the epitome of a people minimally bound by territory. In this volume, territorial democracy and peoplehood come together in a way that enables us to examine elements of both.

This book developed out of a series of studies undertaken since 1968. The kernels of part 1 appeared in my monograph *Israel: From Ideological to Territorial Democracy*, originally prepared for presentation at a seminar at the Harvard University Center for Near Eastern Studies, and later published by General Learning Press. Many of the ideas and themes of part 2 were presented initially in "The Compound Structure of Public Service Delivery Systems in Israel," in Vincent Ostrom and Francis Pennell Bish, eds., *Comparing Urban Service Delivery Systems* (Beverly Hills: Sage Publications, 1977): "Israel's Compound Polity," in Howard R. Penniman, ed., *Israel at the Polls: The Knesset Elections of 1977* (Washington, D.C.: American Enterprise Institute for Public Policy Research, 1977); "The Local Elections: Sharpening the Trend toward Territorial Democracy," in Asher Arian, ed., *The Elections in Israel, 1973* (Jerusalem: Jerusalem Academic Press, 1975); and "Local Government as an Integrating Factor in Israeli Society," in Michael Curtis and Mordecai S. Chertoff, eds., *Israel: Social Structure and Change* (New Brunswick, N.J.: Transaction Books, 1973), parts of which were included, in turn, in a monographic essay on "State and Society in Israel" prepared for the 1976 summer institute of the Kotlar Institute for Judaism and Contemporary Thought.

Chapter 7 is derived in part from an earlier work coauthored with Janet Aviad, *Religion and Politics in Israel*, published by the American Jewish Committee, and a *Jerusalem Letter* entitled "Jewish Religion and Politics in Israel." The ideas in chapter 8 originally were presented in two articles, one of which appeared in *Midstream*, entitled "A New Look at the 'Two Israels,'" and the other in *The American Sephardi*, entitled "Israel's Sephardim: The Myth of the 'Two Cultures.'" They later were refined in papers prepared for the Kotlar Institute, entitled "Sephardim and Ashkenazim: The Classic and

Romantic Traditions in Jewish Civilization," and for the New York Council on Foreign Relations Middle East Study Group, entitled "Israel's New Majority." Chapter 9 is an expansion of themes first developed in "Israeli Attitudes toward the Palestinians," which appeared in George Gruen, ed., *The Palestinians in Perspective* (New York: Institute of Human Relations Press, 1982).

Chapter 10 is an expansion of ideas first developed in *Israel: From Ideological to Territorial Democracy* supplemented by extensive subsequent research. Chapter 11 develops themes initially presented in "Local Government as an Integrating Factor in Israeli Society," in Curtis and Chertoff, *Israel: Social Structure and Change*, while chapter 12 had its origins in a combination of the foregoing essays. Thus, on one hand, the ideas and themes presented in the following pages have accompanied me since the beginning of my work. On the other hand, in this book they have gone through serious expansion and revision, based upon up to two decades of additional research.

I have learned a great deal from many people in preparing to write this book. My academic colleagues are almost without exception acknowledged in the footnotes and bibliography that follow. In particular, I have learned much from my colleagues and associates at the Jerusalem Center for Public Affairs, especially Janet Aviad, Eliezer Don Yehiya, Hillel Frisch, Moshe Hazani, Orli Ha Cohen, Paul King, Jacob Landau, Charles S. Liebman, Moshe Sanbar, Schmuel Sandler, Eliezer Schweid, Dan Segre, Tzippozah Stein, Ernest Stock, Efraim Torgovnik, and Alex Weingrod.

I have learned at least as much from my students, going back to my first teaching experience in Israel in 1968 and continuing through to the present. My graduate students, including Yosef Lanir and Nezer Menuhin, and Avraham Lantzman and Nissim Mishaal, who completed their doctorates and master's theses respectively under my supervision, were particularly helpful. My understanding of local government rests heavily on my colleagues at the Bar Ilan University Institute of Local Government, particular Arye Hecht, Haim Kalcheim, Moshe Gat, Shlomo Revital, and Israel Peled.

Much of what I know about the old Yishuv and the pioneering efforts of the Ottoman period I have learned from my father, Albert Elazar, and my uncle, Yaakov Elazar, whose direct experiences and witnessing, as well as their studies, of the period have made it live for me. Other veterans of those days from whom I have learned much include the late Eliahu Eliachar, the late Yaakov Yehoshua, and Avraham Elhanani, all chroniclers of the Sephardic dimension of both the old and new yishuvim.

My principal research assistant on this project was Alysa M. Dortort of the Jerusalem Center for Public Affairs, who has contributed to this book in uncounted ways. Among those who assisted us were Edward Miller and Robert Bash. As always, my secretarial staff at both the Jerusalem Center and the Center for the Study of Federalism at Temple University made a crucial difference in the production of the manuscript. Mary Duffy and Desiree Mueller of the Center for the Study of Federalism played a particularly important role in this regard, as did Judy Cohen, Barbara Lahav, and Sarah Lemann at the Jerusalem Center for Public Affairs. I also learned much about Israel from Clara Feldman, first my secretary and then my associate at the Bar Ilan Institute of Local Government.

Part of the research for chapter 10 was supported by a grant from the Ford Foundation, received through the Israel Foundation Trustees.

As I reread this manuscript, I see how much I have not said. On one hand that is reassuring, since one never should write a book in which one has to tell all that he knows. On the other hand, I send this off to the publisher for the final time with reluctance, knowing the details, nuances, complexities, and subtleties that are missing. Israel is a state of nuances, complexities, and subtleties because it is compounded of so many details. Its human and social landscapes are even more diverse than its physical landscape, which may be the most diverse in the world for a country of its size. (Geographers have identified forty different physiographic regions in all of the United States, and, using the same measures, twenty-six different regions in tiny Israel.) All I can do is assure my readers that I am aware of what is missing, and hope for the best.

Daniel J. Elazar

# ISRAEL

Building a New Society

# INTRODUCTION

# A Prismatic View of the Israeli Polity

The State of Israel is, in many respects, sui generis. In its own self-image an old-new polity that continues and, indeed, reinvigorates the more than three millennia of Jewish national existence, it also sees itself as one political unit, albeit the central one, in a nation that embraces organized communities in nearly ninety countries around the world. At the same time, Israel is one of the handful of "new societies" that were consciously created in the modern epoch by pioneers with a mission that could be achieved only in a sociopolitical order created "from scratch," and it can be understood in comparison to its "sisters" in that group. Finally, Israel is a polity compounded along several lines: ethnic (Jews and Arabs); religious (Jews, Moslems, several varieties of Christians, Druse, and various other minority sects); and ideological (the range of Zionist ideological movements, plus one or two non-Zionist ones).

This study looks at Israel's political system from the prismatic perspectives offered by these several images, applying paradigms developed by this writer to understand new societies as a group and Jewish society in particular. It is the product of the writer's research in Israel since 1968. While the research has encompassed all aspects of the Israeli polity, from the historical development of the pre-Zionist *yishuv* (Jewish community) to the problems of peace between Israel and her neighbors, its emphasis has been on local government and politics in Israel, intergovernmental relations, and the provision of public services. Consequently, this study gives special emphasis to the local dimension in Israeli politics. There is good reason for doing so. Israel's state political institutions suffer from being foreign implantations within a political culture that renders them increasingly dysfunctional in their original form and has given rise to a range of informal modifications that often work at cross purposes to the formal structures. On the other hand, it is precisely in the local arena that a new shape of Israeli politics is beginning to emerge and Israel is beginning to devise indigenous ways of approaching political matters and organizing power.

Much of the emphasis in this volume is on the founding of Israel. That is because of the author's belief—following that of the ancients, both Jewish and Greek—that foundings are especially significant and that they shape politics

1

long after the founders themselves have passed from the scene. This approach is at variance with much of contemporary political science, which looks upon regimes as evolving out of prepolitical bases and has focused on their developmental aspects, rather than on their foundings. New societies are preeminently founded societies, so much so that even contemporary political science has been unable to avoid the fact of their founding. Israel is no exception, and Israelis are at least as conscious as any classical philosopher would be of the importance of the founding in their own history.

Yet the matter is not as simple as it may seem at first glance. Contemporary Israel has an accepted founding myth developed by the Labor camp that was in power from the mid-1920s until 1977, or for over fifty years, and which led in the establishment of the state itself. That myth leaves out or rearranges certain crucial elements, thereby distorting the actual founding. The myth itself was the product of certain events of the 1920s that gave rise to Labor hegemony. Now it is being challenged in many quarters as the hegemony itself passes. In fact, Israel went through three foundings, a revolution, and then a fourth founding, each of which sought to make its own constitutional choices with regard to the form of the Jewish entity it sought to build: traditional, liberal, socialist, collectivist, and statist, in turn. This study explores the actual founding and some of the consequences of the distortions.

Like the United States, Israel is an extension of the great European frontier, but with a special twist. Founded "from scratch" as the result of the migration of self-selected populations to "virgin" territories (that is, territories perceived by the migrants to be essentially uninhabited at the time of their settlement), its settlers underwent a frontier experience as a major part of the process of settlement and consciously had to covenant or contract with one another in order to create social and political institutions. At the same time, it is a new society whose founders did not come from the British Isles or the other regions of Europe bordering on the North Sea (the Netherlands, northwest Germany, and southeast Scandinavia), as did those of most of the other new societies extant in the world today. The great majority of Israel's settlers came from the eastern peripheries of Europe, including Eastern Europe, Western Asia, and North Africa, thus bringing with them very different cultural baggage. Israel is the only new society founded by people of those cultural backgrounds and, as such, offers an unusual opportunity to gain another perspective on the great frontier.

The Jewish community of prestate Israel actually was referred to as a new society by its members and was built through a series of interlocking covenants and compacts in the manner of all such new societies. The construction of the modern Israeli polity can be said to have begun in the middle and last generations of the nineteenth century. The Jews became the largest population group in Jerusalem, the country's major city, by 1845, at the beginning of the middle generation, and began to build the new city outside the old walls in 1860. The first modern Jewish agricultural settlement was established in 1878, at the beginning of the century's last generation. By

World War I, when that generation came to an end, the well-known Second Aliyah of 1903-1914 had begun to give form to the Zionist enterprise, and the Zionist movement had created the first national institutions within the country that were to give the future state much of its tone.

Because of the particular background of the founders, whether rooted in traditional patterns of Jewish life, committed to the shared religious life of the *kollel* (a scholarly community committed to perpetual Torah study), influenced by the cooperative and single-tax movements, or socialists imbued with the ideologies dominant in the socialist circles of Central and Eastern Europe, those covenants and contracts were oriented toward a cooperative rather than an individualistic model of social and political organization, at times with a strong collectivist tinge. This orientation was reinforced by the Jewish political culture of the founders (see below). As a result, when the State of Israel was established as an outgrowth of the Jewish yishuv of the prestate period, it assumed very extensive responsibilities within the polity, touching most aspects of the lives of the citizenry. Today Israel's polity consists of a society extensively permeated by governmental activity. Thus, Israel may be the only new society developed on the basis of cooperative and socialist principles.

As a still-emergent society, Israel has an emergent political culture that contains a number of conflicting elements, yet to be integrated. Three such elements, or strands, are particularly evident. One is a continental European *statist* political culture, which, in its original form, implicitly accepts the concept of a reified state existing independently of its citizens and views political organization as properly centralized, hierarchical, and bureaucratic in character. It has influenced the vast majority of those Israelis who come from Europeanized backgrounds. The statist strand replaced an eastern *subject* political culture, which viewed government as the private preserve of an elite, functioning to serve the interests of that elite and hence a potentially malevolent force in the lives of ordinary citizens, to be avoided as much as possible. This political culture was shared by perhaps the great majority of the Israeli population, those coming from Eastern Europe and the countries of the Middle East and North Africa, where such was the reality of political life. Today the subject political culture survives in vestigial ways only. Alongside both strands there exists a Jewish political culture, *civic* and republican in its orientations, which views the polity as a partnership of fundamentally equal citizens. Under the terms of reference of this Jewish political culture, all are entitled to equal benefits emerging as a result of the pooling of common resources within a framework that combines both a high level of citizen participation and a clear responsibility on the part of the governing authorities to set the polity's overall direction. It is shared to a greater or lesser degree by the 83 percent of the population of the state which is Jewish, who inherited it from the patterns of Jewish communal life in the diaspora.

These three political cultures exist in somewhat uneasy tension with one another, a tension that is manifested in the great gap between the formal institutional structure of the polity, which is an expression of continental European statism, and the actual political behavior and informal institutional arrangements that make it work, which are closer to the Jewish civic culture. Thus, formally Israel is a highly centralized, hierarchically structured, bureaucratic state on the model of France, whereas in fact the state and its institutions function on the basis of myriad contractual obligations (literally referred to as such in the colloquial Hebrew in which the day-to-day business of government is conducted). These agreements assume widespread power sharing on a noncentralized basis and are enforced themselves only through a process of mutual consultation and negotiation, in which every individual party to the agreement must be conciliated before he (or it) will act.

What seems to be emerging in Israel is a national-civic political cultural synthesis whose precise character cannot yet be forecast. Nor have Israeli political institutions reached a stage of crystallization, despite a rather intense conservatism on the part of Israelis in matters of political change. While there has been strong resistance to institutional change in the state arena, in 1975 the proportional-representation, party-list electoral system, which is a feature of modern Israel and was a feature of the Jewish yishuv before that, since the beginning of the Zionist effort, was modified to provide for the direct election of mayors independently of their city councils and to endow them with a modest veto power over council actions. This radical departure from the existing system has had repercussions in the distribution of power within the political parties and is one of several developments that represent a step away from continental European parliamentarism toward a separation-of-powers model that is more consonant with Jewish political culture.

Israel is also an exceptional phenomenon in the world of modern territorial states, in that it is linked intimately to the Jewish people, an entity possessing certain distinctly political as well as religious and ethnic characteristics, a polity that is not confined to a particular territory and that has spanned thousands of years of recorded history. For the present, at least, Israel itself has indeterminate territorial boundaries, a condition that is presented to the world as a product of momentary circumstances but that really has been characteristic of the entire Middle East since the dawn of civilization. Moreover, a great part of Israel's political life is not territorially based but is rooted in confessional, consociational, and ideological divisions at least as permanent as the territorial boundaries, if not more so (again, a common Middle Eastern phenomenon). It is not that Israel is a-territorial— quite to the contrary; it was brought into being precisely because of Jews' desire for a territorial state of their own—but, rather, that territory is but one of the dimensions that its people and institutions use in organizing space and time for political purposes.

Finally, many students of the Israeli political system have been misled by the apparent simplicity of the state's governmental apparatus, built as it is on classical European models, which have their origin in the hierarchical simplicity of Napoleonic France or the Prussia of Frederick the Great. For those familiar with Western European and American institutions, where polities are almost exclusively territorially based, government is organized fairly simply on two or three levels, or planes (state and local, or federal, state, and local), and the greatest complexity may be found in the overlapping of local governments, the Israeli political system is complex indeed, in that it typifies the region in which it is located and the people it serves. It is of particular interest to note that *leharkiv*, the Hebrew word used to describe the organization of a polity or government, means "to compound," and the same word is used to describe complexity. It offers etymological testimony regarding the expectations inherent in the kind of environmental and cultural matrix in which the Jewish people always has been embedded and in which Israel must function today. The fundamentally contractual character of Jewish political life is reflected in the idea that bodies politic are compounded from different entities that retain their respective integrities even in the larger whole. That carries over into the shaping of the Israeli polity.

The State of Israel must be understood not simply as a Jewish state but as one that is compounded in a variety of ways. Thus, it is also compounded of several different ethnoreligious minorities, in addition to the Jewish majority: Muslim Arabs; Christians, mostly Arab, divided into various churches; Druse, Bahai, Circassians, and Samaritans, each with its own socioreligious structure and legal status. Following the Middle Eastern pattern, all of these groups seek to preserve their corporate identity, and Israel has granted them legal status, institutional frameworks, and government support through which to do so. Each of the several communities represents a further compound within its ranks. Every Arab locality is a compound of extended families—really clans—so much so that voting and political officeholding, not to speak of decision making and the distribution of political rewards, are dependent upon the competition or cooperation among the extended families in each locality.

The Jewish population in Israel is a compound of communities of culture and communities of interest, both of which manifest themselves through ideological movements and territorial settlements. Today, as in the past, the country fairly well divides into three "camps": Labor; Liberal, or center (known in Hebrew as the *ezrahi*, or civil, camp); and Religious. The remarkable stability of voting patterns in Israel between 1948 and 1977 (and in reality since the 1930s when the elections to the governing bodies of the prestate Jewish community are included) was a reflection of this basic division. Even the masses of post-1948 immigrants who tripled the population of the state were settled, employed, educated, and politically absorbed on the basis of the "party key," through which the relative strength of the various parties within the three camps was maintained.

The 1977 elections brought an unprecedented change in the Israeli electoral scene, in that for the first time since the 1920s, power passed from the Labor to the Liberal camp. Whatever the long-range consequences of this shift, the election itself can be said to mark the beginning of a new generation, the second of Israeli statehood and the fifth of the modern Jewish return to the land. Even so, much of the success of the victorious Likud was due to a split within the Labor camp, which gave the Democratic Movement for Change, an offshoot of the Labor party, fifteen seats in the Knesset, thereby depriving the Labor Alignment (in Hebrew, *Maarach*) of its plurality.

Still, the results were not merely the consequences of the split in the Labor camp. A trend toward the center and away from Labor on the part of the new voters and Sephardim had been in progress since the mid-1960s. Other than that, however, such electoral shifts as have taken place rarely have crossed the boundaries of the camps, reflecting only changes within each. The very fact that control of the government passed from one party to another in 1977 and was retained in the 1981 elections has had a profound impact on the Israelis' political perceptions and behavior. There are now two major parties in Israel capable of forming a government. Thus, Israel may well be on the threshold of a new era in its politics, one that will also see the revision of Israelis' perceptions of themselves and their polity in other ways, as well.

In sum, Israel cannot be understood simply by applying the conventional categories of political and social analysis characteristic of contemporary social science. It must be viewed in the larger context of Jewish peoplehood, on one hand, and as one of a handful of new societies, on the other. At the same time, it is a state of, as well as in, Western Asia, or the Middle East, and shares many of the characteristics of its region. When viewed from these perspectives, the Israeli system offers special and unique opportunities for extending the comparative study of new societies, political culture, political development, and what may be the new trends in the political organization of space in the postmodern era.

# PART 1 *Foundings*

# ONE

# The Covenantal Foundations of a New Society

## ISRAEL AS A NEW SOCIETY

Israel is one of the handful of "new societies" in the world, in the select company of the United States, Canada, the Republic of South Africa, Australia and New Zealand, Iceland, and perhaps two or three others.[1] "New societies" are, most immediately and simply, those founded "from scratch" as a result of migrations to "virgin" territories (i.e., territories perceived by the migrants to be essentially uninhabited, whose settlers underwent a frontier experience as a major part of the process of settlement). Most of the new societies were founded since the beginning of the modern era in the mid-seventeenth century. Each in its own way was founded as a modern society from its very beginning. Among other things, the new societies stand out in sharp contrast to both traditional societies and those that have undergone modernization, whether from a traditional or feudal base, by virtue of that fact. The key to their birth as modern societies from the first lies in the migration of their members to new "frontier" environments where builders could create a social order with a minimum amount of hindrance by the entrenched ways of the past, whether traditional or feudal, or by existing populations needing to be assimilated.

Societies with traditional or feudal backgrounds are rooted in what are perceived to be organic linkages between men, communities, or estates, whose origins are lost in the proverbial "mists of history" or are the results of conquest in one form or another. New societies are constructed upon conscious (and historically verifiable) contractual or covenantal relationships established between individuals and groups, based on some sense of common purpose or need that binds them together. In most cases, the founders of the new societies, in creating their new institutions in frontier territories unencumbered by existing institutions that could significantly influence their development, were motivated by a common sense of vocation based on ideologies or commitments they brought with them and forged in the process of nation building: a sense of vocation that continues to serve as a shared mystique (a future-oriented myth) to inspire or justify their heirs' efforts at national development.[2] The actual founding of their civil societies

9

almost invariably was manifested through some kind of constituting act, usually one that was concretized in documentary form. Even if there was no single compact involved, their social and political organization was based on many "little" compacts or contracts necessitated by the realities of having to create new settlements and institutions overnight on virgin soil.

While the founders of the new societies obviously brought with them a cultural heritage derived from their societies of origin, their motivation in migrating was almost invariably a revolutionary one. That is to say, they sought to create a better society (or, at the very least, better lives for themselves) than the one they left and, indeed, were motivated to leave because they did not believe it possible to build the society they wanted within the framework of their original homelands. Usually they took what they believed to be the most significant ideas (and institutions) from their homelands and transplanted them, with appropriate adaptations, to their new lands as part of their effort.

The United States is the paradigmatic new society. Its first settlements were founded in the seventeenth century on a continent that not only was relatively empty of population but whose indigenous inhabitants were not considered by the settlers to be serious factors in the pioneering process. Using covenants such as the charters of the great London trading companies, the Mayflower Compact, the Fundamental Orders of Connecticut, and, ultimately, the Declaration of Independence and the Constitution of 1787, as well as the myriad little compacts that created towns, congregations, and commercial enterprises, those settlers created new social and political institutions to meet their needs "from scratch." They did so by reorganizing, as it were, the cultural "baggage" they brought with them in accordance with a new sense of common purpose or vocation, which in turn was developed out of a combination of the frontier experiences they passed through and the ideological grounding (essentially religious in origin) they brought with them. The mystique they created has continued to serve as the basis for national consensus and as a major stimulus for national action ever since.[3]

Israel falls squarely within the "new society" model, though, like the other new societies, it departs from the American paradigm in those particulars that reflect its own unique historical experience. The settlement by the Zionist pioneers of those provinces of the Ottoman Empire known in the west as Palestine, and to them as Eretz Israel, was, for them, the settlement of new and vacant territories open to the construction of a new society without any locally entrenched encumbrances. Though the Palestine area in the nineteenth century was not an empty land, not even as empty as North America in the early seventeenth century, for the Zionist *halutzim* (pioneers) it was effectively empty, in that they did not expect to model the society they intended to build upon anything provided by the indigenous population. No matter how much they romanticized certain aspects of the local Arab culture and even affected certain Bedouin modes of dress or behavior, that was never even remotely a possibility for them.[4]

The Jews of "old yishuv"—those who had settled in the country's cities in pre-Zionist days—were rejected as models, to no less a degree, even though they obviously would be included within any new Jewish society and, in fact, had prepared the groundwork for the Zionist enterprise by establishing a major Jewish presence in the land. Indeed, the stated goal of the pioneers was to replace the traditional way of life that those Jews represented—especially the Ashkenazim among them—with a new one that, while in harmony with the highest Jewish ideals, would be fully modern, i.e., socialist or liberal democratic. The halutzim actually developed a myth based on a partial truth about the "old yishuv" to the effect that its members all lived on the *halukah* (charitable) funds collected for their support from abroad and hence were nonproductive. In their eyes that was a cardinal sin, since it was their explicit intention to work the land—in their slogan, "to build and be built in it."\* Later, when religiously orthodox Jews entered into the pioneering arena, they, too, showed their modernism by embracing socialism though within the four ells of traditional Judaism. Moreover, the very essence of the Zionist idea was that Jews could redeem themselves and build their new society only by leaving the lands of the diaspora and migrating to a new land, or, more accurately, by "returning" to their "old-new land."[5]

But it was not only the Zionist pioneers who saw themselves as building a new society. The bulk of the members of the Ashkenazic old yishuv had come to the land between 1840 and 1880 to create what they also saw as a kind of new society, in the sense of implanting a version of the Eastern European *yeshiva* world in the holy land. They rejected the indigenous Sephardic Jewish community as fully as they were to be rejected by the Zionist pioneers, for similar reasons, and fought with them as intensely when they could not simply ignore them. Needless to say, the ways of the Arab population were utterly irrelevant to them.

The Sephardim themselves also had sought to develop their version of a new society in the land of Israel in their time. There had been regular Sephardic *aliyot* to the land since the time of Nachmanides in the late thirteenth century, each of which had as its avowed purpose the reestablishment or expansion of organized Jewish life in the country. These *aliyot* intensified in size, scope, and frequency after the Jewish expulsion from Spain (1492) and Portugal (1497). The final pre-Zionist Sephardic *aliyah* came

---

\*While most of the Ashkenazic Jews from Eastern Europe had come to study Torah and did live on the halukah, that was not true of the Sephardic majority, which was gainfully employed. The Sephardim prided themselves on the fact that even their rabbis supported themselves. They, indeed, were responsible for preparing the way for the Zionist pioneers, even though their efforts were not recognized for what they were. Even at the time, the Sephardim were distinguished from the old yishuv by most of those who used that term, which was applied to the Ashkenazim who had come to Eretz Israel in the nineteenth century. See Yehoshua Kaniel, "The Terms 'Old *Yishuv*' and 'New *Yishuv*' in Contemporaneous Usage (1882–1914) and in Historiographical Usage" (Hebrew), *Cathedra* 6 (December 1977): 3–19.

in the mid-nineteenth century and was linked to the reconstitution of the Jewish community in the land under Sephardic leadership in 1840.

The commonwealth that the Zionist pioneers hoped to build was based upon modern ideologies and technologies long since separated from either traditional or feudal principles. Indeed, the Zionists, whatever their ideological persuasions, quite explicitly and consciously intended to build in their own land the kind of society advocated for their countries of origin by those of their European peers sharing the same modern ideologies, whether liberal or socialist. In the process of implanting their settlements and institutions in the new territory, the Zionist pioneers shaped a sense of national vocation that has become, with appropriate modifications, the Israeli mystique.[6]

While most Zionist theories were based on the ideas of organic nationhood fashionable in nineteenth-century Europe, the organizations and settlements of the pioneers themselves were based quite literally on compacts or covenants linking the dedicated individuals who took upon themselves the burdens of the founding. Thus, at every turn, Jewish resettlement was tied intimately and directly to the idea of founding or refounding a new society.

The Zionists were heirs to this tradition as much as they were its inventors. Israel's character as a new society is additionally shaped by factors that transcend its origins. As the Jewish state, Israel is an extension of the Jewish people, the world's oldest "new society" and the first identifiable one in history. While the United States has been called the first new nation and, indeed, is the first new society of the modern world, the first new society recorded in ancient history was that of the Israelites, who, in their migration to Canaan and settlement there under the aegis of the Abrahamic and Sinai covenants, represented the same phenomenon approximately three millennia before the opening of the modern epoch.[7]

There is now reasonable historical evidence to confirm this fact, whether the Biblical account is exactly accurate or not. Perhaps more important, the Israelite experience as it is described in the Bible is paradigmatic of all subsequent new societies. Indeed, the Bible devotes considerable space to discussing and emphasizing precisely those elements that are here identified as being essential to the definition of new societies—migration to new territory, covenanting to form a new polity, and pioneering on a frontier—in its explanation of the origins of the Jewish people.[8]

Both the covenantal nature of Jewish political organization and the future-oriented mystique of the Jewish people were institutionalized within Jewish society in the course of time, passing through various permutations in the land and in the diaspora as conditions demanded, to reappear in new form in modern Israel as part of the overall thrust of the Zionist pioneering experience.[9] One consequence was that even those Jews who came from distinctly premodern environments had, to some degree, internalized a political culture with "new society" characteristics that, however latent, could be made manifest upon their settlement in the new territory and relocation in the new society.

Consequently, the understanding of Israel's political and social system is to be found not in the study of modernization in the conventional sense, which relates to the transformation of a traditional society into a modern one, but in the recognition of the fact that Israel is one of a unique handful of countries, made doubly unique by its position as the Jewish state. The crucial questions to be confronted in the study and improvement of Israel's society and politics, then, are those that revolve around the actualization of a new society: the problems of political cultural continuity and change, or how the particular cultural baggage brought by Jews coming ("returning") to their old-new land was subsequently modified by the experience of nation building in the new territory; the impact of the new territory and the confrontation with it; what has been called in the United States the frontier experience; and the constitutional problems (in Israel's case, problems of reconstitution) that necessarily accompany the creation of a new society.

## ISRAEL AS AN IDEOLOGICAL DEMOCRACY

Zionism was an effort at refounding the Jewish people. As such it had to develop at least partly in relation to earlier refoundings and a much earlier founding. That in itself has dictated many of the parameters and paradoxes of the Zionist movement and much of the dynamic which has animated it. Two basic sets of relationships that lie at the core of Zionism have had a particularly profound effect on Israel as state and society: the relationship between those who required an ideological basis for their Zionism and those who approached Zionism and Israel nonideologically, and the relationship between the major trends or camps within the Zionist movement. Each of these sets of relationships has been present from the founding, and the patterns of interaction that have animated them have given life to the Zionist enterprise.

As in the cases of the founders of other new societies, the organizing principles that most of the Zionist pioneers brought with them were ideological.* First of all, as Zionists they were committed to the idea of the existence of a Jewish nation with national rights of survival and self-determination. While from the first there were various Zionist schools, or trends, some of which emphasized cultural, religious, or socialist approaches, all perforce accepted the political basis of Zionism and the need to express themselves politically through settlement activities. Only those people committed to the particular national ideology of Zionism cared to participate in the venture.[10] Membership in the community of halutzim was contingent

---

*Ideology* as used here refers to a coherent, systematic, and complete body of ideas designed to shape the thinking of large publics by providing them with explicit guidelines of the kind formerly provided in implicit ways by tradition.

upon acceptance of the Zionist ideology in one of its several versions. Thus the fundamentals of Zionism were established at the very founding of the movement and remained embedded within it, shaping its subsequent development at every turn. Although the modes of concrete expression of those fundamentals may be changing for the second or third time, the principles and relationships that constitute them remain as firm as ever.

The founding of the new Jewish society in the land of Israel was manifested in three ways: the mainstream Zionist effort of the World Zionist movement, embodying the Zionist consensus; the varying visions of the new society developed by Zionist thinkers and spokesmen for the movements that federated together to create the World Zionist Organization; and the on-the-spot efforts of the founders of the yishuv prior to World War I.

Theodore Herzl's *The Jewish State* is the classic manifesto of the Zionist movement, the catalyst that led to the bringing together of the various Zionist societies that had been developing in Eastern Europe for several decades and the emancipated Jewish leaders of the West to hold the First Zionist Congress in Basle in 1897 and to establish the World Zionist Organization. Herzl was both the common prophet for all Zionists and the bearer of a Zionist vision of his own.

In *The Jewish State*, Herzl spoke for all those who were to be awakened to the Zionist dream of a renewed Jewish society in the land of their forefathers.[11] Already in that book, his seminal work on the subject, Herzl considered the character of the Jewish state-to-be, and not simply the necessity for it to be. All the signs are present that he saw himself as designing a whole new society, to which he later gave expression in his diaries, and especially in his utopian novel *Altneuland*. He even created a legitimate role for himself as founder—as the gester of the Jews, presenting a theory of the origins of the state that could accommodate his initiative.

The constitution of the World Zionist Organization, initially adopted under Herzl's direction, was the first comprehensive constitution for the new Jewish society in the making. While it was essentially a diaspora instrument, many of the elements within it, particularly its structure as a federation of Zionist movements and the system of elections that guaranteed that federation, became basic to the governance of the new society as it unfolded. These elements can be traced through to the contemporary Israeli polity.

While Herzl was organizing a worldwide "society of the Jews" to seek a charter for Jewish resettlement in the land of Israel anchored in public law, other Zionists were engaged in the more prosaic work of actually settling the land on a piecemeal basis. Their view, most forcefully expressed by David Ben-Gurion, the other towering figure of Israel's founding, was that the land and the redemption its resettlement was to bring could be achieved only by direct action—"a dunam here and a dunam there," in the words of a popular song of the time.[12]

The Zionist movement was built out of the tension between these two views, a tension that continues to echo in the State of Israel today. The

Knesset debate of September 1978 regarding the evacuation of Jewish settlements in the Sinai Peninsula was the most recent expression of that tension. Menachem Begin, who considered himself and his Herut Party to be the heirs of the Herzlian view, was willing to withdraw the settlements for peace, while even the most "dovish" members of the settlement sector of the Labor camp were opposed to the very idea of abandoning settlements on the grounds that such an action would undercut the very basis of the Zionist vision. Subsequently, the shoe was transferred to the other foot, with Gush Emunim gaining a certain measure of support across party lines because of its settlement activity in Judea and Samaria while being opposed by those who were willing to forego settlement activity in part of Eretz Israel in order not to foreclose on the possibility of a formal peace treaty with Jordan.

## VARYING VISIONS OF THE NEW SOCIETY

Zionism represented both a break with the Jewish past and a continuation of Jewish tradition. One element of the break was in the suggestion advanced by various Zionist theorists and pioneers that traditional Judaism be replaced by new secular—usually socialist—forms. One aspect of the continuity was the degree to which Zionism itself represented a messianic movement and, as in all cases of Jewish messianism, involved varying visions of what the messianic goals should be and how they should be achieved. Another involved the emphasis on transforming traditional Judaism into what social scientists have denominated a civil religion for the new society.

All of these visions shared a common ambivalence toward European society and culture. On one hand, they were heavily indebted to then-current European philosophic systems, ideologies, and modes of thought. On the other, as Jews and revolutionaries, these theorists and pioneers rejected Europe with its antisemitic and feudal dimensions in their quest for a new society.

Herzl's vision was expressed more fully in his political novel *Altneuland* (Old-New Land), which presents his late-nineteenth-century synthesis of liberalism and progressivism. [13] In the novel, Herzl's hero, Dr. Friedrich, very nearly a self-portrait, is a disillusioned Viennese Jewish intellectual. In the throes of this disillusionment, he comes into contact with the misanthropic Baron Koenigshoff, or Kingscourt, who is planning to abandon the world by voyaging on his yacht to the South Seas. Friedrich joins him, and on the way they stop to visit the still-desolate Palestine. After twenty years away from almost all human contact, the two decide that it is time to pay a visit to civilization. On their way back to Europe, they once again stop in Palestine, to find an amazing transformation, in which Herzl's plan set forth in *The Jewish State* has been fulfilled. This new society, a cooperative commonwealth rather than a state, is led by David Litwak, a young man whom Dr. Friedrich had first encountered in Vienna twenty years earlier, when Litwak was a poverty-stricken Jewish boy from Eastern Europe.

Herzl's expectation was that the Jewish people, following their Jewish vocation, would construct an exemplary new society, capitalist but cooperative, Jewish but pluralist, European but serving the Middle East.

Herzl's rather a-Jewish vision was opposed by Ahad Ha'am (the pseudonym of Asher Ginsberg, literally "One of the People"), the founder of cultural Zionism, who sought to anchor the Jewish national revival in fully Jewish cultural modes. He developed his ideas in the diaspora but settled in Eretz Israel after World War I. During Herzl's lifetime, the two men stood at opposite poles of the Zionist spectrum, with Ahad Ha'am often attacking the founder of political Zionism for being unconcerned with the Jewish cultural dimension. In the end, Ahad Ha'am's views not only animated those concerned with the revival of Hebrew culture but also became part of the mainstream of the Zionist effort to rebuild Jewish culture along modern lines in tandem with various political visions.[14]

Modern Israel was built through a series of aliyot, literally "goings up to settle in the land." There were five numbered "official" Zionist aliyot. The first began in 1882 and lasted until the mid-1890s and led to the founding of the first string of Jewish agricultural settlements in the country. The second, between 1904 and 1914, established the beginnings of socialist Zionism.

A. D. Gordon was the spokesman for the mainstream of the Second Aliyah. His combination of Tolstoyan and Jewish mysticism offered a most appealing synthesis to young Russian Jews who were trying to build a new tradition out of both aspects of their heritage and who sought to express that synthesis through the building of a new cooperative society in the land of their forefathers.[15]

While the efforts of those halutzim later were canonized as part of the myth of the Second Aliyah—as the founding force of the state in the making—and they did provide many of the leaders of the Labor camp that emerged after World War I, their vision was substantially replaced by the more ideologically militant socialism of the Third Aliyah in the course of the 1920s. The two articulators of the socialist ideology that became dominant in that period were Berl Katznelson, the spokesman for the more moderate wing of the Labor camp and the chief ideologist of what was to become Mapai and later the Israel Labor party, and Ber Borochov, who earlier had articulated a strong Marxist Zionist position. Katznelson emphasized the dilemmas of the socialist Zionist revolutionaries who were nonetheless thoroughly committed to Jewish self-expression. On one hand, he rejected the Jewish condition; on the other, he valued Jewish historical consciousness and the humanity inherent in the Jewish religious calendar and sought to reorient it in terms of his socialist-messianic goals. In a sense he was the first to try to articulate what was to become Israel's civil religion.[16]

Borochov was the classic Marxist of the Zionist movement. He tried to bring ideas of Marx and Engels into line with revolutionary Zionist nationalism, emphasizing the class struggle within a restored Jewish polity. Borochov had a greater immediate influence than Katznelson—his views shaped the vision of the Third Aliyah—but subsequently faded as Marxian socialism was abandoned by all but a few.[17]

A very different view was presented by Valdimir (Ze'ev) Jabotinsky. He continued the Herzlian vision in both its political and social aspects, laying the foundations for the "civil," or Liberal, camp of the Zionist movement.[18] His version of Zionism found expression in the Revisionist party and is now continued by Herut, and in many respects by the Likud (which unites Herut and the old Herzlian General Zionists—now the Liberal party) as a whole. Jabotinsky's Zionism was propelled by his sense of the impending doom of European Jewry. Therein lies his greatness as a prophet, albeit one with little honor in the Zionist movement in his own day. His emphasis on large-scale migration from Eastern Europe to Palestine on the eve of the Holocaust has a particular poignancy. His emphasis on a plan, or blueprint, for development of historic Eretz Israel as a whole and of a Jewish self-defense force is directly in line with Herzl's. Jabotinsky's uncompromising attitude led him and his Revisionist party to leave the world Zionist Organization in the 1930s, the only Zionist group to break the basic federative consensus of Zionism in that way.

Religious Zionism had a variety of articulators of its vision in its various forms. Two of the foremost were Yehiel Michael Pines, one of the leaders of the Hovevei Tzion (Lovers of Zion) movement, the predecessor of the World Zionist Organization, and later a major theoretician of the Mizrachi movement, now the backbone of the National Religious party; and Rabbi Abraham Isaac Kook, the first Ashkenazic chief rabbi of Israel and the spiritual mentor of Zionists of all persuasions. Both men sought to build bridges between religious and secular Zionists on behalf of their common goal, while firmly asserting their own religious visions.[19]

Pines settled in Jerusalem in 1878, where he became a leader and spokesman for the First Aliyah, perhaps the most eminent visionary of that effort, which, unlike later aliyot, tended to combine pioneering with a commitment to Jewish tradition. Kook, a kabbalist with a mystical view of the land and people of Israel, had the task of holding the yishuv together in the difficult 1920s, in the face of the Marxian socialist Third Aliyah. His mystical sense of the special character of the Jewish people stood him in good stead in that task.

A very different Zionist vision was that of Judah L. Magnes, the first president of the Hebrew University. With Martin Buber and others, he was one of the spokesmen for a kind of pacifist Zionism that ultimately took the form of opposition to separate Jewish statehood. His approach did not succeed in attracting many advocates in Israel but was nevertheless a force in certain intellectual circles in the founding period. Magnes, an American Reform rabbi by training, born in San Francisco, brought with him to Jerusalem many of the ideas of American Reform Judaism and the turn-of-the-century Progressive movement, including a belief in the goodness of humanity and of democracy as a way of life, and a denigration of political sovereignty. As an American, he was also the most diasporist of the Zionist visionaries and the least concerned about antisemitism as a motivating force for Zionism. Consequently, his vision stands in stark contrast to Borochov's class struggle or Jabotinsky's clarion call for the evacuation of European Jewry and reliance on arms if necessary to establish a state.[20]

## THE FIRST FOUNDING: TRADITION PLUS MODERNIZATION

In the last analysis, however, the most important manifestations of the new society were to be found in the concrete efforts of its founders and builders. Conventional Zionist history has it that those founders and builders made their first appearance beginning in 1882, with the coming of the First Aliyah, and did not really become significant until after 1904, during the course of the Second. In fact, however, the foundations for the Zionist enterprise already were being laid a full generation earlier, as thousands of Jews came to settle in the country after 1840, and the combination of Ottoman, European, and Jewish efforts began to build a modern infrastructure, which was then available to make possible the settlement and absorption of the Zionist pioneers.

It was in this generation between 1840 and 1882 that the land of Israel acquired communications links with Europe; was given a more or less stable government, including more institutionalized provisions for Jewish communal autonomy and the establishment of the first local governmental institutions; acquired a basic internal transportation network; witnessed the founding of the first modern educational and social institutions, both Jewish and non-Jewish; and saw the first steps in the development of a modern Jewish culture through newspapers and printing establishments, linked to the beginnings of the revival of the Hebrew language. Finally, new Jewish settlements, both urban and rural, emerged in this period as the vanguard of later Zionist efforts.[21] The members of this pre-Zionist generation and their children remained the dominant forces in the yishuv until World War I and did not finally lose their dominant position until the late 1920s, when internal divisions within their own ranks allowed the Labor representatives of the new yishuv to gain power.

The first years of the nineteenth century witnessed the nadir of the Ottoman government in the country. Then, between 1840 and 1880, the land began to move ahead. The former year saw a restoration of direct Turkish rule after eight years of occupation by Mehmet Ali, the quasi-independent governor of Egypt. Rather than return to the old system of feudal-style control, the Turks instituted an effort at centralized administration and also regularized the status of the Jewish community under the leadership of the *Rishon-le-Zion* (literally; the First of Zion), the Sephardic chief rabbi, referred to by the Turks as the *Hakham Bashi*. The latter, in turn, was part of a more sophisticated system of internal self-government devised by the Jews themselves, based upon a council of notables sitting in Jerusalem. Jewish self-government was more firmly established in Sephardic hands by *firman* (the Sultan's proclamation), although it soon was to be weakened by attempts by the newly arrived Ashkenazim to erect their own separate institutions under the protection of their respective consuls.

The number of Jews in Eretz Israel had doubled between 1800 and 1840—from 5,000 to 10,000. The community, responding to outside pressures, on one hand, and increased immigration, on the other, began to expand its activities. These efforts were embraced within the framework of a traditional society seeking just enough modernization to be part of the modern world without abandoning traditional institutions or ways. While there were a few modest experiments with agricultural settlement in this generation, most of the expansion of the yishuv was urban in character, with new Jewish neighborhoods—almost invariably self-contained—being founded in Jerusalem, Jaffa, Haifa, and Tiberias, by other Jews drawn from the selfsame groups: Sephardim and Ashkenazim from the old yishuv; their brethren from the Balkans, Syria, and the Russian Empire; plus Bukharans, Moroccans, and Yemenites, who received the call from emissaries sent out to them by the Jews of Jerusalem.[22]

Most of those neighborhoods were founded as cooperative enterprises or mutual housing societies, through which the actual residents-to-be covenanted together to embark upon a common enterprise and, often, to maintain in their neighborhoods a common way of life. The Bukharan Quarter and Mea Shearim are two of the best-known examples of this arrangement, but, in fact, until the British conquest of the city, all new neighborhoods were founded as separate associations—some as mere arrangements of convenience, while others were openly dedicated to preserving a very specific and concrete way of life, as much as the collective settlements were.[23]

Substantial efforts were made to settle outside the walls of the old cities, and the first quarters of the new city of Jerusalem were built. The first agricultural settlements were founded (Pardess Montefiore near Jaffa in the 1850s, Mikveh Israel and Motza in the early 1870s, and Petah Tikvah in 1878). The Jewish population increased to 24,000 by 1880. Jews became the majority in Jerusalem, spreading beyond the Jewish Quarter into the other three quarters of the city. In the process, Jerusalem again became the largest city in the country. Jews also increased in numbers in Tiberias, Hebron, and Jaffa and established a new presence in Haifa and Nablus.

Meanwhile, the country as a whole also was beginning to wake up. In 1838, Britain was permitted to open a regular consulate in Jerusalem, something that European states had been prohibited to do earlier. By 1858 every major power had a consulate in the country, most with the authority to protect their citizens or subjects resident in the land under capitulation agreements. The arrival of Protestant missionaries in substantial numbers led to the development of modern health, education, and welfare services for the first time and actually stimulated the emergence of parallel services under

Jewish auspices to counter the missionaries' work. Two hospitals and the first modern schools were established by the Jewish community in that generation. Steamboat connections were established with Europe in the 1830s and 1840s, a regular postal service was instituted by the Turkish authorities in mid-century, and telegraphic connections between the country's major cities, Constantinople, and the Western world were inaugurated in 1865. In 1868, the country's first road suitable for four-wheeled vehicular traffic was completed between Jerusalem and Jaffa. That was the beginning of a real communications infrastructure for the country, which would be expanded in the next generation by the construction of a network of roads and railroads, the latter linked to the famous Hejaz Railway and, through it, to the European rail network. Local Jews had a hand in much of this effort.

These first founders initiated the revival of the Hebrew language through Hebrew newspapers and journals, plays, and schools, to complement other aspects of Jewish life, not to replace the tradition with the kind of cultural "Hebraism" of a later time. The first two Hebrew journals (*HaLevanonim* in 1863 and *Havatzelet* in 1870) were inaugurated. Of the three pioneers of modern Hebrew, Eliezer Ben-Yehuda came to the country at the outset of the First Aliyah, while David Yellin and Nissim Behar were native-born participants in the work of the previous one.[24] Nevertheless, that was in the way of a false start. Although the Jewish community developed new social institutions, it was unable to develop an economic base capable of supporting the rapidly increasing population. Thus, dire poverty increased alongside progress in other fields, leading to growing reliance upon the halukah, or the distribution of funds from abroad for the support of indigents. While general use of the halukah was an Ashkenazic rather than a Sephardic phenomenon, the great increase in the Ashkenazic population made possible by the progress of that generation served, in fact, to weaken the community by increasing its dependency beyond anything known earlier.

To make matters worse, the Ashkenazim were unwilling to accept the jurisdiction of the Sephardic-dominated communal structure. They set up subcommunities of their own and, through the mechanism of the *kollel*, sought to create independent institutions of communal governance. As foreign subjects, they sought to enlist the support of their consular protectors in this effort. At first the consular authorities refused, as they were unwilling to come into conflict with the Ottoman authorities, who supported the indigenous communal structure sanctioned by the sultan, but by the end of the generation, the *kollelim* were well on their way to achieving their goal with consular assistance. The autonomous power of the Jewish people in the land was fragmented, which added political weakness to the community's economic woes.

Regular interventions on behalf of local Jewries by European and even American Jewish leaders, such as Moses Montefiore and Baron Edmond de Rothschild, became the rule in this period, leading to the founding of the first modern diaspora-sponsored institutions to serve the growing Jewish

FIGURE 1-1

### The First Founding

| Jewish Settlements Existing before 1870 | Jewish Population | | | |
|---|---|---|---|---|
| | 1870 | 1914 | 1983 | |
| Jerusalem | 16,000 | 45,000 | 304,200 | |
| Safed | 4,000 | 2,800 | 16,900 | |
| Tiberias | 2,500 | 4,000 | 29,300 | |
| Tel Aviv—Jaffa | 1,000 | 15,000 | 316,700 | |
| Hebron | 800 | 700 | 4,500 | (Kiryat |
| Haifa | 300 | 1,400 | 209,400 | Arba) |

*Jewish Settlements Founded by Local Jews* (date of founding in parentheses)

Motza (1859)  Bat Shelomo (1889)
Petah Tikvah (1878)  Menahemiyyah (1902)
Rosh Pina (1878)

*Jewish Settlements Founded by First Aliyah* (date of founding in parentheses)

Rishon-le-Zion (1882)  Rehovot (1890)
Zikhron Yaakov (1882)  Haderah (1890)
Nes Ziyonah (1883)  Metullah (1896)
Mazkeret Batya (1883)  Be'er Tuviyyah (1887)
Yesud Ha-Ma'alah (1883)  Kefar Tavor (1901)
Gederah (1884)

population. For the first time in centuries, suggestions for reestablishing a Jewish state became common among Jews and non-Jews alike. It was in this generation that the "grandfathers" of the modern Zionist idea—Rabbi Judah Alkalai, Zvi Hirsch Kalischer, and Moses Hess– developed and expounded the first systematic expositions of Zionism. Each was a product of one of the three major segments of the modern Jewish world: Alkalai of the Sephardic east; Kalischer of the Ashkenazic east; and Hess of the West. Together they symbolized the simultaneous emergence of an idea whose time was about to come.

## THE FIRST ALIYAH

The first aliyah consciously initiated pioneering efforts in the last generation of the nineteenth century, essentially between 1878 and 1914. During the first half of that generation, the first successful agricultural settlements of modern Israel were established, by young men and women of the established Sephardic population, the Ashkenazic old yishuv, their counterparts who came from Russia as part of the First Aliyah, and several groups of Jews from Yemen who heeded the appeals of both to participate in rebuilding the land. All of these groups saw themselves as the vanguard of a new society— indeed, they were the ones who first applied the term to their endeavors.[25] But for them the new society was to be an extension of the continuing flow of

Jewish history on the basis of a revival of ancient ways. They were protected in their autonomy to no small degree by the Rishon-Le-Zion and the Sephardic authorities responsible for governing the Jewish millet.

While the first founders considered themselves to be engaged in revolutionary actions, they saw themselves not as revolting against the bonds of Jewish tradition but as fulfilling a traditional hope. Thus, they founded their colonies using the same legal and institutional bonds that had been used in the founding of Jewish communities for a millennium or more, adapting those forms to modern needs. They built synagogues in their settlements, and while rarely, if ever, Orthodox Jews in an ideological sense, they accepted the principles of Jewish religious observance as natural for them. Indeed, they turned to the Sephardic rabbinate for guidance in matters of *halachah* (Jewish law), especially those associated with agriculture in Eretz Israel.

It would not be inaccurate to portray the underlying constitutional principles of this founding as liberal in character. There was a transformation in the thrust of modernization, from simply adding modern elements to a traditional society to one in which the goal was a modern society in which those aspects of tradition not incompatible with modernity would be preserved.[26]

The institutions of the First Aliyah reflected the forms of Jewish autonomy that their founders had known in their own experience, coupled with a commitment to modern agriculture and social organization. The First Aliyah introduced federal principles as a basis for building the new society on a broad scale, first through individual covenants, which served as charters in the case of many of the colonies that they founded and later in the federations of colonies in Judea and the Galilee that they established, and in their efforts, somewhat less successful, to create a countrywide federation of Jewish colonies and institutions. These written covenants established the allocation of land, the responsibilities of the colonizing families, and the institutions of governance (usually a "general meeting" of all householders and a small executive committee). The style and terminology of those documents indicate a direct connection with the pattern of Jewish communal government in the diaspora, even to the point of specifying the commitment to public piety on the part of the new entity. The founding covenant of the original Petah Tikvah colony (initiated in 1878 by Jerusalemites representing the founders of the previous generation but made viable only as a result of the First Aliyah) is typical and prototypical of the founding documents that were used to establish the new Jewish colonies and give them a constitutional basis.[27]

*Altneuland*, Theodore Herzl's utopian vision of the Zionist commonwealth-to-be, in many respects summarizes the vision of the First Aliyah. If it has a clear resemblance to contemporary reality in some ways, as it does, that in itself is a reflection of the important founding role of the First Aliyah, which continued to influence a majority of those who came to settle the land in subsequent decades and generations as much as, if not more than, the Second and Third aliyot.

The settlers of the First Aliyah suffered from being in a poor country whose ruling authorities were in many respects hostile to the Zionist enterprise. As a result, they survived only through the support of the Baron Edmond de Rothschild, who, operating in the true French manner, imposed his authority on them in a hierarchical way, in opposition to the budding federative arrangements preferred by the colonists themselves. For some twenty years, the baron was successful, and the effects of his success persisted even after he transferred his direct control to Pica, the institutionalized expression of Rothschild interests established in 1903.

In the course of the next decade, the federative impulses of the First Aliyah settlers reasserted themselves, culminating in the intercolony federations and a countrywide organization built upon federal principles established in 1913, all of whose activities effectively were suspended during World War I. The conflict between the two approaches has remained in one guise or another and represents one of the basic tensions of the contemporary Israeli polity. In the meantime, however, the arrival of the Second Aliyah began to have its impact.

## TIIE SECOND ALIYAH

The Second Aliyah represented a third founding. In part it was stimulated by those in the land who were dissatisfied with the progress of the First Aliyah, and in part it was a reaction to the Russian Revolution of 1905. Its cutting edge was utopian socialist, a back-to-the-land movement based upon the brotherhood and sisterhood of humanity, rejecting capitalist exploitation in favor of small communities of toilers who would be redeemed through their labors.

During the decade allocated to it, the Jewish population of the country increased by tens of thousands, to reach 85,000 in 1914, or 12 percent of the country's total. An estimated 35–40,000 Jews immigrated to the land of Israel between 1904 and 1914. Relatively few of those thousands fit what was to become the mythic mold of the young Eastern European Zionist socialist revolutionaries come to the land to fulfill the ideals of Russian-style Marxism, Zionist version. Few, indeed, even were utopian socialists. Most came for a mixture of traditional and modern Zionist reasons, and a very high percentage were from the other countries of the Middle East. Even among the agricultural colonists who constituted the heart of the *halutzic* (pioneering in the Zionist sense) movement in those years, nearly half were of Sephardic and Oriental backgrounds, and clearly did not represent the socialism of the class warriors.[28]

Even fewer of those who did fit the myth managed to stay in the country. In fact, most of those who did stay came to join the urban and First Aliyah settlements rather than the Second Aliyah revolutionaries. The Yemenite Jews, for example, ended up settling or being settled in villages alongside the Ashkenazi colonies, where they could continue to work as laborers on the farms of the First Aliyah. Consequently, they attracted the attention of the Ashkenazim. The Sephardic Jews from the Balkans, Western Asia, and North Africa, who kept coming in numbers out of proportion to their share of the total world Jewish population throughout all this period, and, subsequently, most of whom settled in the cities, did not attract the same attention; and since they were a minority and politically inactive, the picture of the Zionist enterprise as an exclusively Ashkenazic one has become as entrenched as the myth of the Second Aliyah.

The Ashkenazic Jews had a rather patronizing attitude toward their non-Ashkenazic brethren, particularly the Jews from Yemen, who were exploited by those from Russia. A story more complete than the conventional myth would indicate that the first call to the Yemenite Jews to join in the rebuilding of the land came from the Sephardic community of Jerusalem in the 1870s and early 1880s, more or less at the same time that the Jerusalem Sephardic community sent an emissary to Bukhara to encourage Jews from there to settle in the land. Moreover, of the Yemenites who responded, it has been said that for every ten who came, nine remained, in contrast to the Russian and Polish Jews, of whom nine out of every ten left. More recently, this lack of balance in the recounting of the past has come back to haunt Israel, as neither the Ashkenazic Jews nor the Sephardic, who now constitute a majority of the total Jewish population of the state, are aware of the role of their contribution to the earlier foundings.

Nevertheless, there is no gainsaying the fact that the halutzim of the Second Aliyah did leave the principal imprint on the period, and, as is well known, an even greater one on the subsequent history of the Zionist enterprise. They are given credit for the establishment of the precursors of all the major institutions that were to shape the yishuv in the British mandatory period, and, as a result, the state after 1948. In fact, their success in this respect came to fruition only in the course of the Third Aliyah, the most left-wing of all the waves of settlement.

The Second Aliyah introduced the *kvutzah*, the first of Israel's collective settlements. The *kvutzah* was a covenanted community in the fullest sense of the word. Its members voluntarily bound themselves to the collective life through covenantlike agreements.[29] It established *HaShomer* (the watchman), the first organized Jewish self-defense, and introduced the principle of exclusively Jewish labor in Jewish settlements. Unquestionably, the commitment of the Second Aliyah to exclusively Jewish labor was of first importance for the later history of the yishuv. At the same time, as David Ben-Gurion himself indicated, only with the Third Aliyah, when Jewish labor was able to organize sufficiently, was the Second Aliyah's goal accomplished.[30] What was not clear at the time, and has become clear only more recently, is how much this insistence on Jewish labor contributed to the alienation of the Arabs, who viewed what the Jews saw as a great victory for the normalization of the Jewish people as an attempt to rob them of the opportunity to share in the prosperity of the country's development. Thus, the effort became an unwitting step toward fostering the gulf between Arab and Jew, even as it made the Jews a more productive element.

The Second Aliyah was sharply divided against itself in matters of socialist doctrine. Its leading figure, A. D. Gordon, the guiding light of the most successful of the settlers during the actual course of the decade, taught a doctrine that synthesized Tolstoyan and kabbalistic elements.[31] Indeed, most of the halutzim were nonrevolutionary, and many were politically unaffiliated.

Yosef Gorni has summarized the situation as follows:[32]

1. Toward the end of World War I, there were 1,279 agricultural workers in the Jewish colonies, some 750 of whom were Ashkenazim, and approximately 530 Sephardim.

2. In 1918, 5,695 Jews who had settled in the land between 1904 and 1914 remained, or some 15 percent of the total who attempted settlement in that period.

3. Even among the halutzim in the strict sense of the word (i.e., rural and urban laborers with Zionist commitments), 33 percent were not affiliated with any political party or movement before their aliyah, and no more than 30 percent belonged to socialist parties. After their arrival in Israel, some 20 percent opted for the Poalei Tzion (Workers of Zion), the Marxist social-revolutionary party that emphasized the class struggle and links with the international workers' movement; some 24 percent opted for HaPoel HaTzair (the Young Workers), which explicitly rejected these social revolutionary doctrines; less than 3 percent opted for General Zionist, or Mizrachi (religious Zionist), ties; and over 41 percent were politically unaffiliated.

## ZIONIST FEDERATIONS

From the first, the Zionist organizations in the diaspora were organized on a federal basis. Before the First Zionist Congress in 1897, the local Zionist societies were confederated in the Hovevei Tzion (Lovers of Zion) society. As the World Zionist Organization took form, it, too, developed along federal lines. At first it was built around countrywide federations of Zionist societies, but almost immediately, ideological differences led to the emergence of the various Zionist trends—socialist, liberal, religious. These trends became movements, and by 1902 they already had institutionalized themselves as parties, each with its own vision of the Zionist enterprise. The religious Zionist Mizrachi movement actually antedated the first Zionist congress by four years. In 1902, it was restructured as a party within the WZO. The

Labor Zionist Poalei Tzion (Workers of Zion) emerged at the same time out of the same eastern European milieu, although in this case from among the Jewish socialists.

In Eretz Israel itself, the emergence of these divisions coincided with the Second Aliyah, the climax of the second generation of the return. By 1906, David Ben-Gurion, Yitzhak Ben-Zvi (later the second president of Israel), and their followers could issue a full-blown platform emphasizing all the elements of radical Russian socialism in a Zionist context. They already had come into conflict with the First Aliyah farmers of the *moshavot*, who earlier had formed associations of their own. Several Labor Zionist bodies emerged in those early years, each following its own ideologist.

The WZO provided the closest thing to a common framework in Eretz Israel in this period, locally through the Jewish Colonial Trust, its agent for land purchase and the stimulation of urban and rural settlement. The latter encouraged cooperative arrangements of all kinds to cope with the harsh local conditions, including marketing cooperatives for the moshavot, building cooperatives in the cities, and cooperative settlement of the land by the Second Aliyah halutzim. Since there is a close affinity and even overlap between federative and cooperative principles, those efforts served to reinforce the emerging federal structure of the yishuv.

In the course of the development of the Zionist myth, the role of the pre-Zionist yishuv was denigrated or ignored. It was harder to ignore the First Aliyah, considering that its participants founded the first string of successful agricultural colonies that represented the first fruits of Russian Zionism. Nevertheless, their role also has been denigrated in conventional Zionist history, along with that of the pre-Zionist settlers. If the latter represented a kind of proto-founding, the First Aliyah represented a first Zionist founding, and the Second Aliyah a second. Thus, in the course of two generations, three successive foundings succeeded in laying the foundations for the new Jewish society.

The principal tensions of contemporary Israel also emerged during these first foundings. They include the tension between Ashkenazim and Sephardim and within each of those groups, between traditional and modern religion and secularism, between socialism and liberalism, and between hierarchical and federal principles as the basis for political organization. The first, based on the principal division in Jewish life for the previous millennium, was exacerbated when Sephardim and Ashkenazim began to migrate to the same lands. The other two were modern, even contempory to the late nineteenth century, in their origins. All took on a special character in the land of Israel when the Zionist enterprise was inaugurated and have continued to reflect that special character within the Jewish state.

The conflict between Ashkenazim and Sephardim emerged in the generation between 1840 and 1880 as Eastern European Jews, who had been notably absent from the country for the previous two generations, flooded in and soon outnumbered the Sephardim. They displayed the kind of domineering presence for which their Zionist brethren were to become notable in the twentieth century, demanding their own separate institutions, introducing their standards of religiosity in an intolerant way, and emphasizing their right to exemption from everyday toil in order to study Torah.

Ashkenazic dominance did not become truly feasible, however, until the Zionists came from Eastern Europe in the next generation, bringing with them a more acceptable ideology as well as great vigor in pursuing it. Their coming sharpened the struggle between traditionalism and modernism that had reared its head in the previous generation, but that was only sharpened when the Zionists brought a truly secular option into the picture. That, too, was to become a permanent point of tension. Initially, the struggle was between those who wanted to modernize traditional Judaism but to stay within the shared ethnoreligious framework, and those who were digging in their heels in the face of the pressures of modernity, reinterpreting traditional Judaism to be more rigid than it ever was in the past. The former group was heavily but not exclusively Sephardic, since it also included the Ashkenazi pioneers of the new yishuv who had been born and raised in the old. The latter consisted of almmost exclusively of Ashkenazim who had come to the country to establish the various forms of nineteenth-century Orthodoxy in Jerusalem. Most of the halutzim of the First Aliyah fell into the modern traditionalist group. The Second Aliyah brought in secular Zionism with a vengeance, thereby creating the basis for a far sharper polarization, one that persists in contemporary Israel.

The same group introduced socialism into the yishuv, attacking both the nineteenth-century liberalism of the First Aliyah and the traditional small-scale capitalism of the old yishuv. While the conflict between socialism and capitalism was not to take on its full flowering until after World War I during the Third Aliyah, the basis for the conflict was established. It, too, is one that has yet to be resolved.

Finally, there was the conflict between federal and hierarchical principles of organization. The natural inclination of virtually all the Jews who came to settle in the land was to utilize federal principles in their organizational efforts, following traditional Jewish models. These natural inclinations were subject to challenge from three sources. The first, and perhaps the most benign, was the kind of quasi-oligarchical class system that prevailed in the Sephardic community in the pattern of the Mediterranean world, whereby the Sephardic Jews essentially were divided into patricians and plebians, the former consisting of a small group of families of notables and the latter of the vast majority of the poor working-class Sephardim. While the lines between these two groups were fairly clear-cut, the community was too small for sharp separation of their respective interests.

The second challenge came from the authoritarian structures of modern Eastern European Jewry, whether in the form of the Hassidic court dominated by its *rebbe* or the *yeshiva* headed by its *rosh yeshiva*. Both the Hassidic court and the yeshiva had emerged in the late eighteenth and early nineteenth centuries as hierarchical institutions imposed upon older federal patterns. Both were imported to Eretz Israel after 1840 and became rooted in the country after 1860.

The third challenge came from the hierarchical and authoritarian approach of Baron Edmond de Rothschild and his agents in their efforts to save settlements of the First Aliyah. Theirs was also a modern hierarchical approach, born out of the combination of Jacobin and imperialist centralism characteristic of nineteenth-century France. By World War I, the three hierarchical approaches had managed to impose an institutional framework on both the old and new *yishuvim*. However, it was a framework that had to function side by side with a federalist political culture and constitutional orientation, generating a gap between the institutional structure and political culture reflected in the differences in the political behavior of the establishment and the general public. This gap persists to this day, with all the resultant tensions therein.

This last tension was almost as old as the Jewish people itself, although it took on a particularly virulent form in the modern epoch. Prior to modernity, the problems were usually those of reconciling oligarchic with federal principles. Modernity introduced real issues of hierarchy. These tensions and contradictions have led Israel to send double messages to its people, in essence suggesting that all of the foregoing are legitimate, even when they contradict one another.

# TWO

## Foundings and Revolutions

The domestic structure of the State of Israel that emerged in 1948 was the direct product of a veritable "Bolshevik Revolution" within the yishuv, which took place between 1919 and 1927. That revolution shifted the thrust of the *halutz* movement from utopian socialism to collectivism and completely shifted power from the hands of the old yishuv and its allies to those of the new yishuv and, most particularly, the Labor camp. The history of this revolution is of utmost importance to understanding the ideological democracy of the prestate period and the way it has shaped the present state of Israel, even though the very fact of it has been obscured in the accepted view of the building of the third Jewish commonwealth.

According to the conventional myth of the Zionist revolution, the true founding of modern Israel dates from the Second Aliyah (1904–1914), the first wave of true socialists who came as young men and women from Russia and Russian Poland to revolutionize the Zionist enterprise. Their work was disrupted by World War I but was resumed after the war with the help of the Third Aliyah (1919–1923), during whose time a more elaborate institutional structure was erected on the foundations laid earlier. That led, in a natural way, to the emergence of the socialist Labor camp as the majority and dominant force in the yishuv.[1]

As indicated in the previous chapter, the true situation was at once more complex and different. The new Jewish society had three foundings and a revolution before 1948, or, perhaps more accurately, was founded on two separate tracks, whose immediate relationship was resolved through the revolution. Figure 2-1 charts the history of the Jewish rebuilding of Eretz Israel.

World War I nearly destroyed the work of the previous generation. The Jewish population was halved, principally as a result of Turkish expulsions, and those who remained were destitute. Yet the war also brought with it the British conquest of Palestine, the Balfour Declaration, and the League of Nations affirmation of the Jews' right to Palestine as their national home.[2]

In the wake of those momentous developments, Jewish immigration resumed after the war, spurred on and shaped by the Bolshevik Revolution in Russia. The result was the Third Aliyah, which represented simultaneously

**29**

FIGURE 2-1

Five Generations of Constitutional Choice in Israel

| Generation | Form of Constitutional Choice |
|---|---|
| 1840–1878 | Traditional: Ottoman Firman (1839–1840) consolidates traditional Sephardic community as classic millet. |
| 1878–1917 | Liberal: Introduction of modern forms of local government in cities and villages. Breakdown of united community. Plural authorities, traditional and modern, under the protection of various external powers.<br>Utopian Socialist: Struggle among various traditional orthodoxies, various Socialist orthodoxies, and between both and liberalism. |
| 1917–1948 | "Bolshevik Revolution" introduces collectivist political effort.<br>Collectivist: Reunification of the community under the Knesset Israel Law (1927), establishing a state within a state. |
| 1948–1977 | Statist: Declaration of Independence outlines new state's constitutional principles. Piecemeal enactment of basic laws defines outlines of state constitution under Labor dominance, increasingly pragmatic and statist in character. |
| 1977–? | Rejection of Labor dominance; challenges to statism. |

substantial success and great disappointment. In the first decade under the British mandate, the Zionists were successful in establishing the Jewish community as a state within a state, with a complete range of political, economic, and social institutions on the local and countrywide planes, rural and urban, whose status was firmly defined in law. At the same time, no mass immigration of Jews materialized, Arab opposition to the Zionist enterprise stiffened, and the British succumbed to Arab pressures and began the process of crippling the Zionist efforts to redeem the land.[3]

The Third Aliyah initiated the generation between the wars, a generation that saw the rise and fall of British rule and that culminated in the establishment of the state. In the four years between 1919 and 1923, the Jewish population of the land of Israel rose from 57,000 to 90,000. The Third Aliyah itself brought in some 35,000 immigrants, not all of whom stayed, by any means. Other thousands came in less organized fashion from the Sephardic communities of the Middle East.

The concretization of the work of the Second Aliyah took place in the Third. Its representatives brought with them the more sophisticated socialist ideas of revolutionary and postrevolutionary Russia: highly secularist, militant, collectivist, "scientific" rather than mystical, and dedicated to the building of large organizations rather than small communes. During the Third Aliyah, the kibbutz, or large collective, replaced the kvutzah as the vanguard of agricultural settlement; the mass political party replaced the intimate pioneering movement as the means of mobilizing political power; and the large labor organization (the Histadrut), with its large holding company (Hevrat Ovdim) through which it sought to create a labor economy, replaced the intimate working groups of the prewar period. There is no question as to the necessity to move into larger-scale enterprises if the Zionist effort was to be more than the reclamation of "a dunam here and a dunam there." Nor were these enterprises so large in their early days. But the shift did mark a sea change in the organization of the yishuv, one that ultimately was to lead to the bureaucratic structures and systems that emerged after 1948 and to the alienation of the Histadrut, the political parties, and the Histadrut enterprises from the citizenry and even their own membership.

The driving force behind the Third Aliyah was the *Hechalutz* movement, a Second Aliyah-inspired product of the upheavals of World War I and the Russian Revolution. Fifty-three percent of all Third Aliyah immigrants came from Russia proper, while only 800 came from Western and Central Europe. Most of the remainder, over 40 percent of the total, came from Poland, Lithuania, and other Eastern European countries that had been part of the Russian Empire up until the time of the revolution. Thus, the coloration of the Third Aliyah was clear. Moreover, this coloration was decidedly radical.[4]

To a great extent, the Third Aliyah consisted of people who had placed great hopes in the Russian Revolution and who had been disappointed with the rise of the Bolsheviks and their negative attitude toward Jewish national existence. These immigrants transferred their radicalism to the Palestinian scene. In doing so, they brought about a strengthening of the Marxian socialist elements in socialist Zionism, a stronger commitment to class consciousness and to the class struggle, and a much more militant attitude toward nonsocialists, including nonsocialist Zionists.

So extreme was the radicalism of the Third Aliyah that, among other things, it gave birth to the Communist party in Palestine. During the course of the 1920s, a significant number of Third Aliyah pioneers actually returned to Russia, especially after the economic situation in Palestine deteriorated. (One of the sad footnotes to contemporary Jewish history is to be found in the repatriation of a small number of the survivors to Israel in the 1950s and 1960s. Every one of them had tales of concentration camps, executions of close comrades, and the like.)[5]

Thus, it was the Third Aliyah that galvanized the ambivalences of the Second, to create the framework for the Labor camp and Israeli socialism in its most radical form. Significantly, such Second Aliyah figures as David Ben-Gurion, Moshe Sharett, Yitzhak Ben-Zvi, and Zalman Shazar, hailed later as the founding fathers of Israel, constituted a minority in those years, in that they refused to accept this radicalization (except occasionally on a tactical basis in order to maintain their political leadership) and constantly tried to move the Labor camp toward the center, away from Marxian principles and the class struggle.

In December 1920, the leaders of the Third Aliyah joined with the survivors of the Second to establish the Histadrut, which was to be the foundation for a comprehensive Labor-centered society within the framework of the Zionist enterprise. Since the Histadrut preceded the reorganization of the yishuv itself, its leaders set as their goal the domination of a reorganized yishuv, and they devoted the next decade to securing both the reorganization and the dominant place within it.

The links with Jewish tradition that had been so prominent a dimension of the First Aliyah and had persisted during the Second were sharply assaulted in the 1920s by these Third Aliyah revolutionaries, who succeeded in breaking most of the bonds between those in the Labor camp and that tradition. It is an open question how fully they sought to break those bonds, or whether they sought to redesign them along secularist lines. For example, it was during the 1920s that the idea of a secular *haggadah*, omitting references to God and the miraculous deliverance of the Jews from Egypt, spread in the *kibbutzim*, along with other secularized expressions of traditional phenomena. The three pilgrimage festivals were reinterpreted along strictly agricultural lines; the Bible was desanctified on one level and re-sanctified as the basic book of Jewish nationalism on another.[6]

Since the revolutionaries who fostered these changes were steeped in Jewish tradition themselves, the effects of their efforts did not become immediately apparent. It was not until their sons and daughters grew up that the vacuum that they created became apparent. Thus it was that in the late 1950s, when the grandchildren of the revolutionaries were discovered to have almost no sense of Jewish tradition, demands were made to have the school system foster Jewish identity. (Experience has shown that that is easier said than done, and the problem continues to plague Israeli society.) The results became easily visible in the first generation of sabra leadership of the Israeli polity, people such as Yigal Allon, Moshe Dayan, and Yitzhak Rabin, born at the time of the revolution and raised during the 1920s, when it was at its height—people who grew up utterly ignorant of every aspect of Jewish tradition and who even had to learn how to wear a *kipa* (skullcap) once they achieved political power and were required to publicly demonstrate some links with that tradition.

The revolution was not accomplished that easily, as the histories of that period attest. (It should be noted that until very recently most of the histories were written from the perspective of the revolutionaries and thus substantially distorted the overall picture.) The Jewish community of the immediate postwar period consisted predominantly of members of the old yishuv and their children, settlers from the First Aliyah and theirs, and those who came to the country sharing the outlook of one or the other. The situation was reflected in the political competition of the interwar generation.

The first elections in the newly reconstituted Jewish community were held on April 19, 1920. Seventy-seven percent of the qualified electors participated to elect a total of 314 seats to the Asefat HaNivcharim (Elected Assembly). Of the total, Labor won 111 and representatives of the old yishuv

136, while the remaining 67 mainly reflected the orientation of the First Aliyah.[7]

In the second elections, held on December 6, 1925, the proportion of eligible voters who participated dropped to 57 percent, in part a reflection of the growing alienation of certain Orthodox elements. Of the 221 delegates elected, 90 were from the Labor camp. The representation of the old yishuv dropped to 59, because the ultra-Orthodox boycotted the elections, while 72 reflected the civil camp, which was an extension of the First Aliyah.

The ultra-Orthodox continued their boycott through the 1931 elections (January 5, 1931), where the turnout was 56 percent. A much smaller assembly was elected, consisting of only 71 delegates—34 from the Labor camp, 14 representing the old yishuv, and 23 from the civil camp. It was in this election that Labor crossed the 40 percent mark to become the dominant political force in the Jewish community.

The high point of Labor electoral power came in the August 1, 1944 elections, where, with a 67 percent turnout (the ultra-Orthodox and the Revisionists boycotted the election), Labor won 103 out of 171 seats, a reflecting the full triumph of the revolution. The next elections were held after the establishment of the state, when the combination of full participation of all of the camps and the mass aliyah of the poststatehood period served to diminish the Labor tide.

The division of the Jewish community into three camps was already apparent in the first meeting of the Asefat HaNivcharim in October 1920. The two Labor parties, Ahdut HaAvodah and HaPoel HaTzair, which had contested the election, joined to form the Labor camp. The former, with seventy delegates, was the largest single party. This ability of the left wing of the Labor movement to unify itself while representatives of the other camps were fragmented among eighteen different lists was what gave it the political power to achieve far more than its gross numerical strength would have indicated. At the same time, the fact that HaPoel HaTzair, which was the major representative force of the Second Aliyah, stayed out of the new united party because of its opposition to Ahdut HaAvodah's self-identification as a "branch of the socialist labor movement in the world" gives us an additional clue as to who the real revolutionaries were. While its forty-one delegates were more or less dragged along in the wake of the larger party to preserve some kind of unity in the Labor camp, the separation of the two parties persisted until the late 1920s.

A second camp was composed of an alliance among the Sephardic and Oriental Jews, on one hand, and the Ashkenazic religious groups, on the other. It was, for all intents and purposes, the camp of the old yishuv. The Sephardim elected fifty-four delegates, to become the second-largest party, while the other Oriental communities elected an additional eighteen (if they could have united, they would have formed the largest party in assembly). The ultra-Orthodox elected fifty-one delegates, the religious Zionists eleven, and other religious groups two. That was the high point of their strength. The

Sephardim declined precipitously in subsequent elections, in part because the younger generation went over into the Zionist camps. The ultra-Orthodox never again participated in an election for the Asefat HaNivcharim and did not resume an active role in the country's political life until after the state was established.[8] In the 1925 elections, this camp already was divided almost equally among Sephardim, other Oriental communities, and the religious Zionists, although it was not until the 1944 elections that the latter succeeded in becoming fully dominant and transforming the camp into the totally religious one it is today.

The remaining delegates formed themselves into a camp that was to become known as the civil *(ezrahi)* camp. In 1920, its dominant element was the Farmers' List, which spoke for the First Aliyah settlements. In the 1925 elections, they were replaced by the Revisionists, who remained dominant through 1931. Then they, too, dropped out, as a result of the split in the World Zionist Movement, in the process reducing the civil camp to third place among the three, a position that would persist for another generation.

In general, the political history of the 1920s was one of increasing Labor unity and growing fragmentation in the other camps. Most of the younger generation or the new nonsocialist immigrants viewed the latter as reflecting the past and turned elsewhere. Mot important, vital elements rejected the Zionist consensus and refused to participate within it. In that respect, the socialist revolutionaries' triumph in the course of that critical decade was deserved.

The final triumph of Labor was brought about by the 1930 merger of Ahdut HaAvodah and HaPoel HaTzair to form Mapai (*Mifleget Poalei Eretz Israel*, or the Party of the Workers of the Land of Israel). Only the left Poalei Tzion and the HaShomer HaTzair remained outside this new force. This merger, which followed on the heels of the formal recognition by the British of Knesset Israel, the Jewish community of Israel (1928), made possible the critical elections of 1931. Mapai clearly emerged as the largest party, while the Sephardim were split, with four Sephardic delegates supporting Labor and five the Revisionists. The Farmers' party boycotted the elections, thus virtually terminating the voice of the First Aliyah. The ultra-Orthodox continued their boycott, leaving only the still-relatively weak Mizrahi-HaPoel Mizrahi, which won five delegates. When the Revisionists refused to join the Vaad Leumi, the executive body of the assembly, the way was cleared for Labor control of the Jewish Agency, the operating arm of the yishuv. The consolidation of Labor's position came in 1935, when David Ben-Gurion became chairman of the Jewish Agency Executive, the Revisionists left the World Zionist Organization, and the General Zionists split into two factions, one led by Chaim Weizmann, which was willing to cooperate with Labor, and the other remaining in the opposition.[9]

Meanwhile, the revolution was manifesting itself throughout the social structure of the yishuv. In the 1920s, in addition to the still-fledgling Histadrut, the settlers of the Third Aliyah formed the *gedudei haavodah*, or labor battalions, collectives of workers who traveled around the country to engage in construction projects wherever needed by the Zionist movement. It was in these wandering collectives that the most radical elements of the Third Aliyah gathered, a goodly number of whom later were to found the Israeli Communist Party and constitute the returnees to the Soviet Union.

At the same time, HaShomer HaTzair, the most clearly Marxist of the Zionist socialist movements, began to found kibbutzim and to articulate an ideology of the kibbutz in opposition to the ideology of the kvutzah that had emerged out of the Second Aliyah. The agrarian socialists of the Second Aliyah had envisaged a collective life built around small groups of compatible people who would form what were, in effect, extended families engaged in agricultural pursuits. Their kvutzot were confined to a maximum of a few hundred members, so that they would not lose their intimacy. That was the vision of A. D. Gordon, the spiritual mentor of the Second Aliyah. HaShomer HaTzair, on the other hand, saw this approach as too slow a process of collectivization. They envisaged collective settlements without any size limit, where intimacy would give way to collectivism in the fullest sense of the word. Thus, from the first, they sought to build large kibbutzim. Even the name *kibbutz* (borrowed from the Hassidic lexicon) signified the difference. Thus, while Degania, the first kvutzah of the Second Aliyah, actually spun off a Degania Bet (or Degania 2) when its settlers thought that it had become too large, the new kibbutzim were in time to grow and grow, in some cases to over 3,000 people. Although the two trends created separate roof organizations in the 1920s, in fact the kibbutz won out as a form, as witnessed by the fact that its name became the common term for collective settlements.[10]

Not only did the revolution of the 1920s succeed in imposing a new pattern on the yishuv, but it also created a mythology of the rebuilding of Zion, which persists to this day and which remains entrenched in the hearts, minds, and schoolbooks of the country. That myth focused on the Labor camp as the true source of Zionist ideals and the only legitimate vehicle for their realization. It is difficult to underestimate the degree to which this myth has become all-pervasive, to the point where for years either no mention was made of the other forces within the Zionist movement and the yishuv or, if mention was made, it was invariably negative. We already have suggested that the old yishuv was written off as being recipients of the halukah, that is to say, as living off the dole of the Jews of the diaspora without any productive effort on their own part. Entirely ignored was the Sephardic element in the old yishuv, who lived by the sweat of their brows, or the fact that the Zionist enterpise was and is equally dependent upon diaspora aid. Similarly, the contribution of members of the other camps was simply written off. Recognizing that the Revisionists were their chief rivals, every effort was made by the Labor camp to discredit them. They were called fascists at every turn and remained labeled as such in many of the history books used in the schools, even after Herut became a legitimate opposition party in every respect.

In addition, the Third Aliyah created the myth of the Second Aliyah. Seeking legitimation for their revolutionary efforts, the leaders of the Third Aliyah projected their outlook and doctrines back to the Second, making the Second the founding fathers of socialist Israel. In the process, the First Aliyah was dismissed as consisting of bourgeois reactionaries who came only to exploit Arab labor, and the Second Aliyah was transformed into a collection of doctrinaire socialists. Recent historiography has demonstrated the mythic character of this projection. But since it also met the needs of those of the Second Aliyah who had become the leaders of the new Labor movement, giving them added legitimacy in their struggle for power, both groups were willing to foster the myth, and so it became entrenched in Zionist history.

While the Third Aliyah built up the myth of the Second, the members of the latter actually were withdrawing from political life as a result of the revolution. There was widespread depolitization of the surviving Second Aliyah members in the 1930s and 1940s, i.e., after the revolution wrought by the Third Aliyah and the subsequent synthesis in the form of Mapai. After 1930, only 7.4 percent were active in political life, and only a third were even affiliated with Mapai. Nearly 60 percent were entirely unaffiliated. Although sixteen of the twenty members of the Mapai Central Committee in 1930 had arrived in the country in the years of the Second Aliyah, they were there as individuals, not as representatives of a particular group or generation. Significantly, it was only then that the myth of the Second Aliyah was given full form. [11]

## IDEOLOGICAL CONFLICT AND FEDERAL UNITY

While conflict between proponents of the various ideologies was often intense on the intellectual level, in practice the pioneers worked out concrete ways of cooperating with one another virtually from the first, containing their conflict within a growing set of ideologically rooted proto-governmental institutions that soon became a "state within a state." They were able to do that by judicious use of federal principles and techniques. The strong commitment of each group to applying its own special ideological principles in practice, coupled with the need for unity in the face of the obstacles placed in their way, led them to seek federal solutions that allowed them to preserve significant elements of both concerns. [12]

As individuals, the Zionist pioneers covenanted or federated with one another to form collective settlements, cooperative organizations and institutions, and political parties reflecting their various ideological differences. Then, through their settlements and other institutions, they sought to federate with one another to create countrywide frameworks. The ties linking individuals to institutions and the institutions with one another were essentially voluntary and predicated on the mutuality of their relations with one another. These voluntary compacts were sustained by the objective situation in which the pioneers found themselves and by the overall mystique forged by the Zionist movement.[13]

Most of the cities of the yishuv were created neighborhood by neighborhood, with most of the neighborhoods—whether Mea Shearim in Jerusalem or Kiryat Haim in Haifa—originally organized by the would-be settlers as joint stock companies, associations of shareholders, or cooperative building ventures. These neighborhoods were then combined into cities that were themselves unions (Jerusalem, Tel Aviv) or federations (Haifa) of neighborhoods. Even smaller cities, such as Rehovot and Petah Tikvah, developed on this union-of-neighborhoods basis.[14]

Despite the shift to the kibbutz, the agricultural colonies remained covenanted communities. In the late 1920s, after the number of kvutzot and kibbutzim grew, they organized themselves into countrywide federations to undertake common marketing functions, handle the founding of new settlements, and provide common educational and cultural services. They were organized on an ideological basis, including the highly centralized federation of HaKibbutz HaArtzi (the Countrywide Kibbutz); HaKibbutz HaMeuhad (the United Kibbutz), which shared the ideological predispositions of the first but allowed autonomy in the individual kibbutzim within the federation on other than ideological matters; and Hever HaKvutzot, a loose, nonideological federation.[15] Standardized articles of association were developed by each of the movements reflecting their own approach to kibbutz building, which the members of each new kibbutz would adopt as their own.

The Third Aliyah also contributed the *moshav ovdim* to the range of rural settlement types. It was the most clearly federative of all, since it represented a linkage of individual family farms for cooperative purposes under formal and binding articles of agreement that served as the constitution of the *moshav*. Its founders, who sought to bring the family farm to Israel as an element in the pioneering enterprise, understood that under local conditions, family farms could be made operative only if federated with one another in cooperative villages. Ultimately the *moshavim* also developed an umbrella confederation to handle certain common economic, technical, and educational tasks.

Beginning in the 1930s, adjacent settlements began to federate into regional councils to develop common public services and economic enterprises on an areal basis. While these federations linked settlements of the same ideological persuasions, they also represented a step toward territorially based political organization.

Still, the main trend was in the other direction. As the ideologically based party, or movement, federations became institutionalized, they became tighter and more all-embracing. Each developed its own settlements, schools, press, cultural institutions, industries, and sports clubs, and even its own paramilitary formation. In prestate days that was particularly functional, not only as a way of mobilizing energy for the pioneering tasks but as the basis for organizing the incipient Jewish commonwealth within the political context set by the colonial authorities, who were opposed to or ambivalent about relinquishing real governmental powers to the Jewish community.

Since the land in which the pioneers were building their new structure had long been organized on the basis of the millet system, a form of political and social organization that had existed throughout the Middle East for centuries, if not millennia, this tendency was reinforced by the external environment as well. The millet system provided for the maintenance of quasi-autonomous ethnic communities organized on the basis of ethnoreligious ties within the framework of whatever empire was holding overall power at any particular time. The system reached the peak of its development in the days of the Ottoman Empire, when the ruling authorities left even the provision of basic common public services to the discretional control of the individual millets. Since imperial policy under the millet system was to limit the internal activities of the ruling power severely and to allow each millet to determine the extent of local services to be provided to its members, the system made it possible for the Jewish community to provide such governmental or quasi-governmental services as it wished, without too much reference to the formal government structure. Every Jew, simply by virtue of being Jewish, was assigned to the Jewish community as a matter of "citizenship" and was required to adjust himself and his life within the framework of that community, just as Muslims and various Christian groups did in their respective communities.

Under the British, the name *millet* was dropped and the system was given a quasi-republican character (that is to say, those individual communities that chose to were reorganized on republican principles); otherwise it continued to shape the country's sociopolitical form. The system made it both easy and natural for the British colonial authorities to allow the Jewish community to function as what was, in effect, the Jewish millet. This status was formalized by legislation promulgated by the British high commissioner in 1927 as the Knesset Israel Law (Law of the Assembly of Israel), the first Zionist constitution of modern Israel. [16] The law itself was the product of some seven years of negotiation and conflict within the Jewish community regarding the distribution of power and authority. As such, it was the expression of the communal consensus that dominated the mandatory period between the Balfour Declaration in 1917 and the establishment of the state in 1948. The law created a classic *kehillah*, or autonomous Jewish community, in modern dress, perhaps the last of its kind in the age of the citizen-state. Many of the elements included within it were transferred afterward to the institutions of the state.

## ISRAEL AS A FEDERATION OF PARTIES

Thus, the post-World War I generation, through (or despite) its internal conflicts, produced the federation of parties that became the foundation of the organized yishuv and, after 1948, the state. This federal arrangement followed patterns that contemporary political scientists have described as consociational; that is to say, the links were based upon ideological camps rather than territorial divisions. Since territorial divisions had very little meaning in interwar Palestine, while ideological divisions were of the essence, that could be considered a natural development. In light of the revolution wrought by the Third Aliyah, however, the emergence of this federation of parties can be seen as a triumph of a different sort.

Given the intensity of ideological conflict, every possibility existed for the unity of the Zionist movement to crumble. We have noted how certain groups did indeed secede from the yishuv's political structure. The introduction of federal arrangements as a basis for accommodating the various factions, giving each representation more or less in proportion to its strength within the overall community, offered a means for accommodating every group willing to accept even a modicum of national discipline. At the same time, it offered each group a means of self-expression within the community, a chance to gain some share of the benefits provided collectively by the Zionist movement, and an opportunity to bargain with the other groups so as to improve its position.

To accomplish that, the purest possible system of proportional representation was introduced. Under it, each party submitted a list of candidates of its own choosing, appropriately ranked by the party itself; voters cast their ballots for the party of their choice; and each party received the number of seats equal to its percentage of the total vote, allocating those seats to the candidates in the order in which they appeared on its list. Moreover, all appointive positions, allocations of funds, and other benefits were divided according to the election results or the coalition negotiations (since no party was likely to win a majority under such a situation, or has) among the victors. This form of distribution became known as the party key.

The effort worked. While various groups did boycott the elections to the elected assembly from time to time, and conflicts persisted with what seemed to all to be great intensity, only the ultra-Orthodox actually tried to secede from the overall structure. How the Zionist founders arrived at this scheme is yet to be studied properly, but the role of Jewish political culture, which emphasizes federative arrangements, at least in part because Jewish history has been consistently marked by conflict between different sets of messianic expectations (see below), should not be underestimated.[17]

The Jewish source of the origins of the federative system of the yishuv gains further credence when it is recalled that the overwhelming majority of the Zionist pioneers came from the countries of Eastern Europe, where socialist, Communist, and other movements dedicated to radical social change flourished in an atmosphere of the most extreme ideological intensity, an atmosphere that brooked of no compromise, as history was to reveal. They brought with them a strong predisposition toward making ideology the measure of all things, coupled with a tendency toward ideological hairsplitting. Indeed, so intensely ideological were they that it is possible to argue that only their common Jewishness, which led them to certain perceptions about the necessity for unity at some point and which gave them a useful cultural inheritance for the promotion of the requisite unity, kept them from going the divisive or repressive way of their non-Jewish peers from the same Eastern European milieu.

From the first, the strongest and most successful of these transterritorial parties, or "movements," functioned as all-encompassing civil societies, providing their members with virtually all the domestic services normally provided by governments. These services ranged from the utterly all-embracing life of the kibbutz, on one hand, and the ultra-Orthodox kollel, on the other, through less intense manifestations such as job placement, banking, and education, which in the cities became the principal points of contact between individuals and the party system. Within the Israeli political system, membership in, or at least some relationship with, a political party became the sine qua non of existence, so that it was virtually impossible to receive any social benefits or to function as a citizen in any meaningful way without being associated with one party or another.

Understood in this context, the electoral system introduced in this period, using proportional representation, was quite appropriate, since it provided each constituent unit in the federation with representation according to its strength as a unit. It was no different, in essence, from other kinds of federal arrangements in which the territorial units are represented as such in the federal legislature, leaving the choice of the representatives themselves to the unit to determine internally. As long as the great majority of potential citizens could find a home within one of the parties, this system was able to represent the yishuv adequately, provide a proper arena for bargaining among the various interests within it, and promote the adoption of policies and courses of action appropriate to the needs of the overall community.

That was the situation inherited by the new state in 1948. The history of its vicissitudes since then is the essence of the constitutional history of Israel. In essence, it is the history of a growing conflict between the original ideological basis of Israeli civil society and the new demands of a poststatehood generation. The Israelis' growing perception of the need to modify the existing political order is a response to a convergence of forces that have combined to greatly weaken the degree of commitment to the specific ideologies of the prestate period while increasing the functionality of territorial units at the expense of existing institutions with ideological roots.

# THREE

## Toward Territorial Democracy

The State of Israel formally came into existence at 12:01 A.M. on Saturday, May 15, 1948, having been proclaimed some hours earlier, before sunset on May 14 (in the twilight beginnings of the fifth of Iyar 5708 by the Jewish calendar), to avoid profaning the Sabbath. It was proclaimed by the People's Council, "representatives of the Jewish community of Eretz Israel, and the Zionist movement," a wall-to-wall coalition including everyone from the Communists on the political left to Agudath Israel on the religious right. The Declaration of the Establishment of the State of Israel, through which the state was proclaimed on that occasion, represented the ultimate comprehensive covenant of the Zionist enterprise. The history of its preparation and acceptance is a history of the negotiations that took place to achieve general consent across the entire spectrum of the Jewish community in Eretz Israel, with the exception of a few hundred ultra-Orthodox extremists, to the new state's terms of reference.[1]

The state itself was the culmination of the Zionists' decade-long struggle for political sovereignty under international law. The original founders of the Zionist enterprise at the end of the nineteenth century were of two minds about political sovereignty. Even Herzl, the champion of statehood, was prepared to accept an autonomous Jewish national home within the framework of the Ottoman Empire: in the manner of late-nineteenth-century liberals, he had at least a latent interest in a world order that would transcend politically sovereign states, and he was willing to see the Jewish state as a harbinger of that order, if that was the best way to bring it about. This commitment to a world order of semisovereign national homes was certainly part of the socialist ideology of the pre-World War I generation, and it, too, functioned to retard clear-cut demands for statehood.

It was only in the late 1930s, after the rise of Nazism and the divergence of Jewish and British interests in the Middle East, that the tide turned in favor of full politically sovereign statehood, even within the Zionist movement. The issue was more or less settled for the Zionists as a result of the debate over the proposals of the British Peel Commission (1937) to partition western Palestine into Jewish and Arab ministates (with the bulk of the country to remain permanently in British hands). After that the die was cast, and the only remaining issue was whether to accept the partition of western Palestine or to hold out for the entire cis-Jordanian region, on the understanding that the separation of Transjordan from the Jewish national home in 1922 was partition enough.

World War II and the Holocaust brought general acceptance of statehood as a goal by world Jewry, and, in the aftermath of the war, the partitionists won out for lack of a feasible alternative. A United Nations commission recommended partition in 1947, and the UN General Assembly accepted that recommendation on November 29 of that year. What remained was the most difficult part, namely, the struggle of the yishuv to actually implement the UN resolution in the face of the military opposition of their Arab neighbors within Palestine and the five Arab states surrounding the country.

Israel's War of Independence began on November 30, 1947 and continued for nearly a year and a half. Out of it emerged the State of Israel with boundaries somewhat better than the impossible division of the land called for in the UN Resolution. Jordan (the official name of the newly independent Transjordan) occupied the remaining Arab territories immediately west of the river, and Egypt, the Gaza Strip.

The first step taken by the government of the new state was to repeal all British restrictions on Jewish immigration and land acquisition; that had been the principal bone of contention that brought the final rupture between Britain and the Jewish people. The Law of Return became a fundamental part of the state's constitution, no less than the declaration of its establishment, which guaranteed the right of every Jew to settle freely in the land of Israel. At the same time, the gates of the new state were opened wide, and hundreds of thousands of Jews flooded in: first the survivors of the Holocaust from Europe, followed by Jewish refugees from the Arab lands. Between May 15, 1948 and the end of 1951, 687,000 Jews were brought into the country, or 150,000 more than had come in between 1882 and 1948.

## DECLARATION OF THE ESTABLISHMENT
## OF THE STATE OF ISRAEL

ERETZ-ISRAEL (Land of Israel) was the birthplace of the Jewish people. Here their spiritual, religious and political identity was shaped. Here they first attained statehood, created cultural values of national and universal significance and gave to the world the eternal Book of Books.

After being forcibly exiled from their land, the people kept faith with it throughout their Dispersion and never ceased to pray and hope for their return to it and for the restoration in it of their political freedom.

Impelled by this historic and traditional attachment, Jews strove in every successive generation to re-establish themselves in their ancient homeland. In recent decades they returned in their masses. Pioneers, immigrants and defenders, they made deserts bloom, revived the Hebrew language, built villages and towns, and created a thriving community, controlling its own economy and culture, loving peace but knowing how to defend itself, bringing the blessings of progress to all the country's inhabitants, and aspiring towards independent nationhood.

In the year 5657 (1897), at the summons of the spiritual father of the Jewish State, Theodor Herzl, the First Zionist Congress convened and proclaimed the right of the Jewish people to national rebirth in its own country.

This right was recognised in the Balfour Declaration of the 2nd November, 1917, and re-affirmed in the Mandate of the League of Nations which, in particular, gave international sanction to the historic connection between the Jewish people and Eretz-Israel and to the right of the Jewish people to rebuild its National Home.

The catastrophe which recently befell the Jewish people—the massacre of millions of Jews in Europe—was another clear demonstration of the urgency of solving the problem of its homelessness by re-establishing in Eretz Israel the Jewish State, which would open wide to every Jew the gates of the homeland and confer upon the Jewish people the status of a fully-privileged member of the family of nations.

Survivors of the Nazi holocaust in Europe, as well as Jews from other parts of the world, continued to immigrate to Israel, undaunted by difficulties, restrictions and dangers, and never ceased to assert their right to a life of dignity, freedom and honest toil in their national homeland.

In the Second World War, the Jewish community of this country contributed its full share to the struggle of freedom- and peace-loving nations against the forces of Nazi wickedness and, by the blood of its soldiers and its war effort, gained the right to be reckoned among the peoples who founded the United Nations.

On the 29th November, 1947, the United Nations General Assembly passed a resolution calling for the establishment of a Jewish State in Eretz-Israel; the General Assembly required the inhabitants of Eretz-Israel to take such steps as were necessary on their part for the implementation of that resolution. This recognition by the United Nations of the right of the Jewish people to establish their State is irrevocable.

This right is the natural right of the Jewish people to be masters of their own fate, like all other nations, in their own sovereign State.

ACCORDINGLY WE, MEMBERS OF THE PEOPLE'S COUNCIL, REPRESENTATIVES OF THE JEWISH COMMUNITY OF ERETZ-ISRAEL AND OF THE ZIONIST MOVEMENT, ARE HERE ASSEMBLED ON THE DAY OF THE TERMINATION OF THE BRITISH MANDATE OVER ERETZ-ISRAEL AND, BY VIRTUE OF OUR NATURAL AND HISTORIC RIGHT AND ON THE STRENGTH OF THE RESOLUTION OF THE UNITED NATIONS GENERAL ASSEMBLY, HEREBY DECLARE THE ESTABLISHMENT OF A JEWISH STATE IN ERETZ-ISRAEL, TO BE KNOWN AS THE STATE OF ISRAEL.

WE DECLARE that, with effect from the moment of the termination of the Mandate, being tonight, the eve of Sabbath, the 6th Iyar, 5708 (15th May, 1948), until the establishment of the elected, regular authorities of the State in accordance with the Constitution which shall be adopted by the Elected Constituent Assembly not later than the 1st October, 1948, the People's Council shall act as a Provisional Council of State, and its executive organ, the People's Administration, shall be the Provisional Government of the Jewish State, to be called 'Israel'.

THE STATE OF ISRAEL will be open for Jewish immigration and for the Ingathering of the Exiles; it will foster the development of the country for the benefit of all its inhabitants; it will be based on freedom, justice and peace as envisaged by the prophets of Israel; it will ensure complete equality of social and political rights to all its inhabitants irrespective of religion, race or sex; it will guarantee freedom of religion, conscience, language, education and culture; it will safeguard the Holy Places of all religions; and it will be faithful to the principles of the Charter of the United Nations.

THE STATE OF ISRAEL is prepared to cooperate with the agencies and representatives of the United Nations in implementing the resolution of the General Assembly of the 29th November, 1947, and will take steps to bring about the economic union of the whole of Eretz-Israel.

WE APPEAL to the United Nations to assist the Jewish people in the upbuilding of its State and to receive the State of Israel into the family of nations.

WE APPEAL—in the very midst of the onslaught launched against us now for months—to the Arab inhabitants of the State of Israel to preserve peace and participate in the upbuilding of the State on the basis of full and equal citizenship and due representation in all its provisional and permanent institutions.

WE EXTEND our hand to all neighbouring states and their peoples in an offer of peace and good neighbourliness, and appeal to them to establish bonds of cooperation and mutual help with the sovereign Jewish people settled in its own land. The State of Israel is prepared to do its share in a common effort for the advancement of the entire Middle East.

WE APPEAL to the Jewish people throughout the Diaspora to rally round the Jews of Eretz-Israel in the tasks of immigration and upbuilding and to stand by them in the great struggle for the realization of the age-old dream—the redemption of Israel.

PLACING OUR TRUST IN THE ROCK OF ISRAEL, WE AFFIX OUR SIGNATURES TO THIS PROCLAMATION AT THIS SESSION OF THE PROVISIONAL COUNCIL OF STATE, ON THE SOIL OF THE HOMELAND, IN THE CITY OF TEL-AVIV, ON THIS SABBATH EVE, THE 5TH DAY OF IYAR, 5708 (14TH MAY, 1948).

| | | |
|---|---|---|
| DAVID BEN-GURION | HERZL VARDI | DAVID ZVI PINKAS |
| DANIEL AUSTER | RACHEL COHEN | AHARON ZISLING |
| MORDEKHAI BENTOV | RABBI KALMAN KAHANA | MOSHE KOLODNY |
| YITZCHAK BEN ZVI | SAADIA KOBASHI | ELIEZER KAPLAN |
| ELIYAHU BERLIGNE | RABBI YITZCHAK MEIR | ABRAHAM KATZNELSON |
| FRITZ BERNSTEIN | LEVIN | FELIX ROSENBLUETH |
| RABBI WOLF GOLD | MEIR DAVID | DAVID REMEZ |
| MEIR GRABOVSKY | LOEWENSTEIN | BERL REPETUR |

YITZCHAK GRUENBAUM      ZVI LURIA              MORDEKHAI SHATTNER
DR. ABRAHAM            GOLDA MYERSON          BEN ZION STERNBERG
  GRANOVSKY           NACHUM NIR             BEHOR SHITREET
ELIYAHU DOBKIN         ZVI SEGAL              MOSHE SHAPIRA
MEIR WILNER-KOVNER     RABBI YEHUDA LEIB      MOSHE SHERTOK
ZERACH WAHRHAFTIG          HACOHEN FISHMAN

## THE PERSISTENCE OF IDEOLOGICAL INSTITUTIONS

The federation of parties was perpetuated even during the period of mass immigration following the establishment of the state through the device of allocating new immigrants to the various parties in proportion to the parties' existing strength. The parties then would provide the immigrants with the requisite services and facilities needed for their absorption into the country. In return, the immigrants became enmeshed in the parties' own institutional structures and became faithful voters for "their" party in Knesset elections, more often than not, thus contributing to the virtually undeviating record of electoral stability that Israel maintained until the 1977 elections.[2] Their loyalty also contributed to insuring the perpetuation of the status quo in public policy making, more often than not by allowing the same people to remain in office for long periods of time and discouraging the introduction of young people (or new faces of any age, for that matter) into the higher levels of political decision making.[3]

Furthermore, because most of the immigrants lacked familiarity with popular government, their willingness to conform to the models set before them by the parties contributed to the growth of the power of the party professionals. Even in the years before statehood, the parties and their subsidiary institutions had been growing more centralized, partly because of the exigencies of the objective situation in which the pioneers found themselves, and partly because of their original socialization into the political life of Eastern Europe, where centralization of power was the norm. Still, in those years, when the yishuv was small and relatively homogeneous and face-to-face interpersonal relations were still possible among most party members, the impact of the centralizing tendencies was reduced substantially.

The mass immigration changed the scale of political organization in the country and opened up new possibilities for professional politicians to concentrate party decision-making powers into their own hands. For most of the first two decades of statehood, their success in doing just that was virtually unlimited. Thus, within their respective spheres, the parties remained the basic decision makers, and the decision making was concentrated increasingly in the hands of the party leaders.

On the other hand, the role of the parties or their institutional agents (including the Histadrut) in the provision of normal public services was progressively reduced. Ben Gurion deliberately embarked on a program to consolidate the state by transferring those public services from party to government auspices.

Though the parties continued to provide some services that in other political systems are provided by governments, the transfer to the state of others, particularly their military units, elementary schools, and the labor exchanges, had the effect of substantially reducing the dependence of the citizenry upon those services once they had passed through the initial stages of settlement and absorption. That was particularly true in the case of urban dwellers. The parties' role in their daily lives was shifted to the management of "influence" *(protektzia)* rather than the direct provision of services, with the control of ostensibly neutral enterprises (housing projects, industries, and business enterprises, in particular) and government departments the key to their power.[4]

With the passing of the period of the great mass immigration, the divergences between the political and social structures of the country began to develop in earnest. While party governments of the old style remained dominant, especially at the state level, the parties themselves began to lose their meaning. Not only were they losing responsibility for functions, but their ideological bases were deteriorating.

The Labor camp suffered most in this regard. The lessening in importance of rural pioneering (see chapter 5), the changes in the world situation (particularly the growing antagonism of the Soviet Union and its satellites toward Israel and the concomitant increase in Israeli ties with the United States, and the disappointments with socialist orthodoxies at home and abroad growing out of their evident inability to stimulate economic development and their frequent antidemocractic manifestations, combined to move all but the most hardened ideologues out of old grooves.[5]

Moreover, the great bulk of the population was becoming more or less settled and developing ties both to the land and to the state that were independent of those fostered by the parties and their ideologies. That was particularly true among the young, whether native-born or raised from early childhood in the country. To them, Israel was "home," in a way that it could not be to their immigrant parents.[6]

The civil camp stood to benefit most from this decline of ideological commitment. It had been the least ideological from the first and, indeed, had done less than any of the other camps to provide comprehensive services for its adherents. Its supporters always looked to either individual initiative or state action to undertake social tasks, emphasizing the former but expecting the latter where individual initiative was not sufficient. Thus, its people wholeheartedly supported the transfer of functions from the parties to the state in the 1950s and urged even more transfers than actually were made. (Among Israel's other paradoxes is that, in its political situation, the liberals advocate national health insurance, while the socialists want to preserve the status quo so that they will retain control over Kupat Holim, the General Sick Fund of the Histadrut.) While in the short run they may have lost out because of their stance, in the long run they have probably gained, as the state has taken over responsibilities that in the past had served to strengthen adherents to the Labor camp simply for lack of choice.

Only the religious camp can boast a continued ideological momentum, principally because it is grounded in a set of beliefs that transcend modern ideological considerations. There are even those who argue that the ideological basis of the religious parties has been strengthened as a new generation has been produced by the religious schools, whose commitment to Orthodox Judaism is no longer simply a matter of inertia growing out of a traditional background but a matter of real choice and firm ideological grounding. Were it not for the religious camp's ideological strength, there is little doubt but that the trend away from the ideological and territorial democracy would have moved at an even more accelerated pace.

In any case, the situation in Israel today parallels that of other new societies when the initial ideology of the founders ceased to be all-encompassing. In the United States, for example, Puritan New England underwent a very similar transformation. The Pilgrims and Puritans who settled Massachusetts in the 1620s and 1630s were united by a great idea and their desire to transform that idea into concrete social realities. Puritanism, their religious ideology, was also the basis for their attempt to create a holy commonwealth in North America. To become a citizen of that commonwealth, one had to accept the Puritan covenant, to join a Puritan congregation, and to accept the doctrines of Puritanism. Leadership in that first generation of Puritan New England was vested in the hands of men who were considered to be the best representatives of the common religious ideology, and, if they represented constituencies at all, that role was truly subordinate to their role as spokesmen for and interpreters of the Puritan idea. Moreover, they were accorded full legitimacy by their peers and constituents on that basis. Even those who disagreed with their interpretations did not dispute their right to lead but, rather, moved away to other territories to create congregations or sects (the religious equivalents of the ideological settlements and parties of Israel) of their own, in which they could replicate the same political patterns to implement their conceptions of the holy commonwealth abuilding.

By the second generation, however, the old ideology was no longer a sufficiently binding force to hold Massachusetts together. An increasing number of sons and daughters of Massachusetts by birth did not share in the ideological fervor of their parents. Even those who still stood well within the framework of Puritanism were not necessarily prepared to fully accept its dogmas. Even more important, because they had been born within the Puritan framework rather than called to it, their relationship to its vision was necessarily different. Ultimately, they had to be accommodated within a political order that was not prepared to deny them citizenship but could not grant them full status as citizens without modifying its own ideologically based organization.[7]

The evidence strongly suggests that Israel today is in a similar transitional stage. The clear-cut moral committments of the halutzim could not be transmitted to their successors once the objective situation had changed. As in the Puritan case, the essence of the transformation lies in the movement from ideological to territorial democracy.

## MANIFESTATIONS OF TERRITORIAL DEMOCRACY

If ideological democracy places a premium on doctrinal faithfulness (or what passes for it) for the attainment of full citizenship and political rights, territorial democracy places a premium for their attainment on simply living some *place* by right. In one sense, the entire Zionist endeavor is a reflection of the Jewish people's movement from ideological to territorial democracy. Zionism is a recognition of the vital importance of territoriality—that every people needs a territory of its own to survive in the contemporary world.

Territoriality is not the same as territorial democracy, however. As we have seen, the initial Zionist efforts were based upon the notion that location in the chosen territory would be a minor factor in determining Jewish public policy, far less important than the various ideologically based visions of the new society in the making. Nevertheless, even these ideological movements found it necessary to develop territorially based means of expression in order to develop bases of operations from which to attempt to influence the whole society. The two best examples are the kibbutz and the religious neighborhood. Like the towns of Puritan Massachusetts, both reflect that face of territorial democracy that allows people with strong common beliefs to settle together and, through the governance of the territory upon which they are settled, to assure that their beliefs will be sufficiently dominant locally to protect a common way of life.

The kibbutz is a particularly good example because the one effort within Eretz Israel to utterly do away with the territorial component, the *gedudei haavodah* (labor battalions) of the early and mid-1920s, was based upon that model. The *gedudim* were designed to be mobile kibbutzim, collectives of halutzim who would not have any fixed homes but would move around the country in response to the work needs of the Zionist movement. They held together for a few years while their members were still in their teens or early twenties, and then disintegrated as those same members reached the age where they began thinking about establishing families and needed to support family units. The urban kibbutz, which came much later, represented a second, modified effort to diminish the importance of territory, in this case by establishing a collective in a particular urban setting that would have a fixed locale, but not sufficiently separated from the nonkibbutz environment. To date, the several efforts at establishing urban kibbutzim have all come to naught.

Kibbutzim and religious neighborhoods not only reflect this face of territorial democracy by their very existence but go beyond that. The kibbutzim are divided among several movements, each of which has its own particular vision to protect. Similarly, religious neighborhoods tend to fall into sectarian patterns, although there more of a mixture may be tolerated. For both, there has been tacit recognition by the state and society of the legitimacy of their utilization of the first face of territorial democracy, and they are allowed much greater leeway than other territorial units in protecting their way of life. For example, kibbutzim maintain their own schools, which are nominally part of the state education system but are left fairly well to their own devices. Residents of religious neighborhoods not only maintain their own schools in one way or another but also are allowed to close off their streets to vehicular traffic on the Sabbath and holidays so as to preserve their particular religious way of life, even though there are no laws to that effect.

Territorially based polities of the first kind began to develop as a matter of course as the pioneers settled in and staked claims to "turfs" of their own. The moshavot, kibbutzim, and moshavim came to conceive of themselves as virtually autonomous communities in the prestate days. Their "natural" territorialism remained within and substantially compatible with the existing system of ideological democracy as long as the territories were populated exclusively by people with the same professed ideological commitments, who viewed the world in the appropriate ideological categories, and who were satisfied to function within the overall ideological structure of the society, i.e., as members of movement and party federations.

Territorial democracy has another, more prevalent, face. It can be used in a very neutral way to secure political power or influence for any groups that happen to be resident in a particular area at a particular time. In this respect territorial democracy is the form of the areal division of power that is particularly associated with popular government. It is instituted as a means to strengthen democratic government by providing fixed bases within which public decisions can be made democratically on an appropriate scale. It may be that it is a form particularly associated with new societies, since the territorial units in a new society of necessity reflect the same general goals as the society as a whole. At most, they seek to provide expression for specific facets of those goals. [8]

Israel's cities embody this face of territorial democracy. Indeed, though they long were submerged within the framework of ideological democracy, which continues to hold sway at the state level, their origins lie in the origins of the modern yishuv itself. As noted earlier, they began their development even before the first agricultural settlements. The first of them were founded as syntheses of the two faces, consisting of neighborhoods created as virtually autonomous communities within the city by like-minded householders contracting together to found new settlements within an urban context.

The first city consciously founded as an urban settlement without an ideological base other than the general ideology of Zionism was Tel Aviv, significantly enough founded in the same year (1909) as Degania. Tel Aviv represented, from the first, territorial democracy in its most neutral sense.

Whoever settled within the city limits was entitled to the rights of local citizenship and could participate in political life to the extent and in the way he or she desired (within the context and opportunities offered by the political system in general), without having to subscribe to any particular ideological or religious doctrines or formulas. One result was that Tel Aviv, for years, went counter to the countrywide trend toward socialism to become a stronghold of the General Zionists, though, as the city grew larger, its population became more mixed and diversified and the city lost any particular ideological tinge it might have had.[9]

Tel Aviv became at one and the same time the paradigm and the caricature of the Israeli city as a neutral, democratic, territorial political unit. In the 1920s and 1930s, and then at an accelerating rate after 1948, other cities followed its lead. As the country's Jewish population expanded, many of the original moshavot, the agricultural colonies founded in preideological days, were transformed into just such neutral territorial units as they became citified. After 1948, these were supplemented by over twenty new towns, founded to absorb the new immigrants. Today they represent the cutting edge of the upthrusts of territorial democracy, trying to break through the crust of the highly centralized Israeli polity.

The power of the Zionist back-to-the-land movement was such that urban pioneering was ignored or denigrated until well into the first generation of statehood.[10] At the same time, a majority of the Jews who came to settle in the land of Israel settled in cities. At its height in the 1930s, the agricultural sector did not quite reach a third of the total Jewish population in the country. Thus, urban pioneering remained an important factor in the Zionist enterprise, whether recognized as such or not. The first pioneering sector dating back to the first founding, it continued to be important in the interim, and became the dominant pioneering sector once again after the state was declared. Taken together, these cities, which in 1985 encompassed approximately 90 percent of the country's total population, have become the major vessels for the assimilation of the waves of mass immigration that came into the country beginning in the 1930s.[11]

## THE LOCAL ROOTS OF MODERN ISRAEL

In many respects, local communities have been the vanguard of political development in the country and have become, at the very least, a meaningful starting point for the almost inevitable movement toward greater territorial democracy. Indeed, it is in the local arena that most of the creative and innovative developments in Israeli government and politics have taken place since the early 1960s. Consequently, it is to local government and politics that we must look to understand the direction Israeli political life is likely to take.[12]

Historical exigencies led to the development of contemporary Israel out of local roots. Given the facts of imperial control, first under the Ottomans and then under the British, the Jews could expand their presence only on a local basis, by many local efforts or national efforts expressed locally. Both rural and urban settlement patterns reflected this reality. In both, small groups of settlers came together and organized themselves locally to undertake pioneering tasks.

The local role was stimulated further by the fact that the Ottoman authorities, who governed the land until 1917, saw their functions as essentially custodial and oriented to maintaining minimum security; all else was left to the religioethnic communities to develop as they saw fit. The British authorities who came after the Turks (between 1917 and 1948) did not depart from this pattern, except to make it more honest and efficient. It was left to the individual religioethnic communities within the country to determine the kind of public infrastructure they wanted for themselves. For the ruling powers, that was a natural and highly functional way to deal with the problem of differing ethnic groups with widely differing styles of internal organization and highly divergent expectations from the public sector.

With regard to the Arab villages, this policy meant that they remained almost unchanged until the establishment of the State of Israel. The Israeli authorities encouraged them to acquire municipal status and the services and facilities that went with such status. As a result, the Arab villages have been undergoing modernization, even with regard to basic municipal functions, for no more than a generation.

The Jewish sector, on the other hand, wished to push ahead rapidly with the development of a modern, Western-style society, with all that entailed. Indeed, because of their socialist bent, the Jewish pioneers wished to provide even more services than many individualistic societies in the West. Since neither the Turkish nor the British mandatory authorities were interested in meeting their needs, and, for that matter, the Jews were not interested in having others do for them what they believed that they should do for themselves, the Zionist institutions undertook the task of providing those services. Even within the framework of the federation of parties, the execution of this task, to no small extent, fell upon the Jewish-sponsored local authorities that served most of the Jewish population.

Even local governmental law in the country was generally enacted by the British mandatory regime after the fact, that is to say, after Jewish settlers had created local institutions that then somehow had to be formalized. The regional councils—a basic element in all rural local governments in Israel—are good examples. In the late 1920s and throughout the 1930s in those areas where there were sufficient numbers of Jewish colonies to create contiguous bands of Jewish settlement, the territorial democracy of the pioneers took on an additional form. The leaders of the various kibbutzim and moshavim in the Jordan Valley, the eastern end of the Jezreel Valley, and the Huleh Valley—the three areas with both the requisite concentration of settlements and the need for cooperative action—found it useful and necessary to join together to cooperate with one another for the provision of common regional

services. Several such clusters—two on the coastal plane, two in the Jordan
Valley, and two in the Jezreel Valley—began to do so in the 1930s, creating
councils on a federative basis, i.e., one representative from each settlement,
and possessing only such powers as were delegated to them by the constituent settlements, which retained most powers for themselves. At first they
had no legal status, but in 1941 the mandatory government took note of those
councils and promulgated a law providing for their recognition as formal local
governmental bodies, and for the establishment of others. The yishuv utilized these regional federations of settlements to create small Jewish republics (their terminology) as a form of autonomous space within the
framework of the mandate, something that could be done only with a
territorial base.[13]

The regional council idea spread, particularly after 1948, to become one
of Israel's major contributions to the theory and practice of local government.
Appropriately, regional federations combined the principles of territorial and
ideological democracy to unite settlements within the same or similar political movements.

The regional councils, particularly the older ones among them, have
retained a far greater degree of local autonomy than any other governments
in Israel—partly because a number of them antedate the establishment of
the state and had the experience of being virtually autonomous at a time
when the legitimacy of the colonial government was being challenged by the
indigenous inhabitants of Palestine, and partly because of the special place
their component units (especially the kibbutzim, but also agricultural settlements in general) occupy in Israeli society. As the embodiments of the Israeli
mystique, they have a vital place in Israeli society, which tends to reinforce
their position as self-governing communities.

Simultaneously, cities such as Tel Aviv created statelike service systems
for their residents under the permissive British rule and with the blessings of
the Vaad HaLeumi (Jewish National Committee). Thus, even the state services of the new society had local roots to no small degree and were
pyramided into countrywide programs through various kinds of contractual
and federal arrangements established by the parties.

After the establishment of the state, Israel's cities and townships (known
officially as local councils) became the first line of political integration in the
country. They provided the first opportunities for nonideological participation in Israeli political life, which means, in effect, the first steps toward
opening political participation to younger people, political "amateurs," and
immigrants from the Afro-Asian countries or their children. Two points will
suffice to illustrate this trend. Until very recently, one of the most notable
features of politics in Israel was the great disproportion in the percentage of
leaders drawn from Eastern Europe or their children, particularly from the
*kibbutzim*. Sephardim were drastically underrepresented in every sphere of
public life but one—local government. That was the case even though
Sephardic Jews constituted nearly 50 percent of the Jewish population of

Israel by the mid-1960s (today they exceed half). By 1965, however, approximately 47 percent of the political leaders and public officials in the local arena were Sephardim. Moreover, by that year they constituted 37 percent of the deputy mayors and mayors.[14] Since then, many of those local officials have advanced politically in the state arena, including David Levy, now minister of housing and deputy prime minister; Moshe Katzav, minister of social welfare; and numerous Knesset members. Today, over 70 percent of all mayors are Sephardim.

By any of the measures available to us, local government, by applying the principles of territorial democracy, willy-nilly has served as a channel for recruitment of the othrwise excluded groups into the political process. Even where attempts were made to send political veterans into new towns to assume positions of responsibility in the early days of their development, these people soon were overwhelmed by the rise of local leaders who were able to move ahead simply by virtue of their being who they were, vis-à-vis their reference groups, where they were. Ultimately, the parties had to accommodate them and seek to coopt them, making certain necessary concessions in the process. Not the least of these concessions was an almost total ignoring of ideology in the recruitment of new local leadership, so that now one even finds local members of Mapam who are observant Jews, and members of the Labor party who do not have even the beginnings of a commitment to socialism. In sum, local politics has become far more pragmatic than ideological.

Second, as an outgrowth of this situation, there have developed the beginnings of an independent spirit on the local plane, most overtly manifested in the emergence of local parties (or, more correctly, local lists) in the municipal elections.[15] These local lists have had some substantial success at the polls. Even where they have not emerged, the very suggestion of organizing a local list has caused the regular parties to make substantial concessions in an effort to coopt local leaders who otherwise might be encouraged to go the independent route.

That is particularly important, since one major aspect of the centralization of party government in the post-1948 years was the consolidation of central control over the designation of party candidates for local office. By the mid-1960s, central party intervention was the norm. Then a new breed of local candidates arose who began to challenge that control. In the 1973 elections, for example, the popular incumbent mayors of Rehovot and Rishon-le-Zion refused to accept the dictates of their party headquarters. In the first case, the party gave in. In the second, the mayor left the party and at the last moment filed an independent slate, which then swept the elections. In 1978, Teddy Kollek, the popular mayor of Jerusalem, inaugurated his own independent list, which swept the local election, as did the Eliahu Nawi, the mayor of Beersheba, whose party wanted to drop him. Since then, central party intervention has become virtually extinct.

The impact of this new independence has been felt throughout the political system. It was a major factor in the rise of the Likud to power in 1977 and the transformation of the country's politics into a competitive two-party system. And it has produced the only Knesset members with independent power bases of their own.

The existence of limited territorial democracy has offered voters the opportunity to make distinct choices between local and Knesset tickets and for parties other than the Labor party, even before May 1977. Ticket splitting of the first kind is a growing phenomenon, and has been since the 1969 elections. Where and when it has occurred, it usually has been a significant expression of local political concerns. The introduction of the direct election of mayors in 1978 has served to intensify all of these trends, in addition to making the mayors the most directly representative elected officials in Israel.

In sum, the existence of territorial democracy in the cities has widened the possibilities for participation and the exertion of political influence in several directions. Moreover, the process is still in its early stages. All indications are that Israel's political order is at the beginning of a period of change induced by the continuing process of "settling in" in a new society. While the trend right now is away from the ideological patterns of the first generations of pioneers and toward political paticipation on a territorial basis, in the last analysis, democracy in Israel, as in the other new societies, must develop out of a synthesis between the ideological and territorial dimensions. By their very nature, such societies require the maintenance of a national mystique (with its ideological overtones) as the basis for the consensus that holds them together, while at the same time, the sheer passage of time tends to promote the expression of certain aspects of that mystique through territorial units.

Here, too, the Biblical precedent is paradigmatic. According to the Biblical account, the Israelite tribes relied exclusively upon the Mosaic covenant to unite them only until they reached Canaan. Then, as soon as possible, they very purposely grafted their ideologically rooted polity onto a territorial base that was endowed with a sacred character of its own. [16]

## A NEW ZIONIST IDEOLOGY?

Until June of 1967, it seemed that, in their rejection of the specific ideologies of the prestate era, the new generation of Israelis also were rejecting the basic premises of Zionism, seemingly abandoning it as the country's mystique. [17]

The Six Day War and its aftermath laid that possibility to rest, as the Isarelis rediscovered the nature and importance of their ties with world Jewry. More specifically, the 1967 experience made it possible for Israelis to separate the larger mystique of the Zionist enterprise from the specific ideologies of Zionism and to begin the process of redefining the mystique itself. [18] At the same time, there is no longer the firm belief in particular ideologies of the kind that existed until the establishment of the state. Those ideologies have lost their ability to compel. If today there is a search on the part of many Israelis for new ideological underpinnings, the very fact of the search is in itself a reaffirmation of the importance of ideology to them.

The day-to-day business of maintaining the Jewish state is such that those responsible for conducting its business are not likely to be particularly interested in or concerned with development of a new ideology. The most that can be said is that, coming out of ideologically oriented traditions, they pay lip service to the principle of ideological thought and would like to see ideologies exist for aesthetic reasons. It would make them feel that the world is somehow better put together. Thus, they often are willing to fund ideological conferences and publications, but, in fact, the relevance of those conferences and publications to their own endeavors is very slight. The rebuilding of the Zionist vision will have to be on the basis of a new synthesis of ideological and territorial elements. The way in which that will be done and its effects on Israel's political system will depend upon other factors, to be considered below.

## TERRITORIAL DEMOCRACY: THE MINORITIES

Before turning to those other factors, two more aspects of territorial democracy in Israel need to be considered, both of which are lineal descendants of the old millet system. While that system no longer exists in a formal way in Israel, the Israeli government has made some effort to accommodate the legitimate demands of non-Jewish minorities for local autonomy by applying its principles in the local government sphere. Thus, most Israeli Arabs, Muslim or Christian, and the Israeli Druse have a substantial amount of cultural autonomy maintained through their own local councils, which serve to concretize the rights secured them in Israeli basic law and also provide a basis for implementing services provided by the state through the appropriate departments in the ministries of Religions and Education.

In 1948, there was one Arab local council in Israel, and only 27 percent of all Arabs were located within municipal governments of any kind. During the years following the attainment of statehood, the Israeli authorities made a conscious and concentrated effort to give Arab and Druse villages municipal status and thereby provide them with the political basis for a substantial amount of local self-determination, particularly in the cultural and religious spheres. By 1968, there were forty-two Arab and Druse local councils, one regional council composed exclusively of Druse villages, and eighteen villages within mixed regional councils, so that some three-fourths of the non-Jewish population had its own local government.[19]

Significantly, under the mandatory regime, the Arab villages, as premodern institutions standing outside the new society being built by the Jews, had resisted British efforts to give them modern municipal status, preferring to retain their traditional local governmental system, with its pattern of domination by leading families and lack of popular participation or control. Take, for example, the Druse village of Hurfeish in the upper Galilee (present population approximately 2,200). Originally a Jewish settlement until the fourth century, after a six-hundred year hiatus it was resettled during the Crusades (which in terms of the history of the land of Israel is a relatively late date). Its Druse residents claim residence there since then, under traditional institutions. The village did not acquire formal municipal status until 1967, when the Israeli Ministry of the Interior convinced the local mukhtars (the traditional Arab leaders) to take that step.

The first important public service of a local character to reach the village was its connection to the national water network in 1957, so that its residents no longer had to rely upon local wells. The first paved roads came in 1962, and only in 1975 were the rest of the village's streets paved and, in some cases, widened. The city was linked to the countrywide electrical grid in 1969, and street lights were installed a year later, all as a result of the introduction of municipal government. Since, by and large, the traditional Arab leadership resisted municipalization for fear that it would interfere with their traditional dominance, it came about only when a more educated generation emerged.[20]

For the Arab and Druse, the introduction of formal local governmental institutions became the means for attaining an increasing amount of control over their own immediate destinies. While they are not required to do so, most Israeli Arabs and Druse remain residents of their villages even when they commute to work in Jewish cities, so that they can remain members of the sociocultural system which their village local government protects and sustains; hence, local government is a meaningful way to provide them with the means to do just that.

Israeli policy in this regard has been conscious and deliberate. That is evidenced by the establishment of separate Jewish cities adjacent to principal Arab cities and villages wherever the Israeli government felt the need to do so for security reasons. With two exceptions, no effort was made to create mixed municipalities. Thus, Upper Nazareth (Natzeret Ilit) was created from scratch for Jews alongside Arab Nazareth, and new towns for Jews were established in the middle of western Galilee, in areas with many Arab villages. In all of these cases, the municipal institutions were kept separate, so that each group could preserve its local autonomy through judicious use of the first face of territorial democracy.[21]

A different kind of neomilletization has been developed for those members of the old Jewish yishuv and the immigrants who have joined with them to preserve an ultra-Orthodox way of life outside the Israeli mainstream. Their territorial base tends to be confined to neighborhoods or quarters of major cities, though in at least one case—B'nei Brak—they have developed municipal institutions to support their way of life. By and large, they maintain their separatism through separate government-recognized institutions, primarily schools and rabbinical courts, which receive government subsidies and are given a great deal of autonomy. These, of course, function within the "neighborhood" territories that these groups have staked out for themselves.

# PART 2 Commonwealth

# FOUR

## The Compound Structure of the Israeli Polity

The fundamentally covenantal character of Jewish political life is reflected in the idea that bodies and polities are compounded from different entities that retain their respective integrities even in the larger whole. That carries over into the shaping of the Israeli polity, along the lines of other new societies. The technical terminology of government in Israel implicitly reflects this sense of "compoundedness" (I use the term *implicit* advisedly, since the Israelis themselves are unaware of the implications of their own terminology.) The Hebrew term *medina* (state) is used for the collectivity of Israel, but not for any single institution. While the term is used today in the sense of the sovereign state, its meaning in classical Hebrew is more akin to that of a state in compound polity, a territorial political unit with its own governmental apparatus and autonomy but not possessing sovereignty in and of itself. Sovereignty lies elsewhere—traditionally, in the hands of God; in a modern state, in the hands of the people. The classical usage also implies a constituent state in a compound polity, which squares with Israel's self-understanding as the state of the Jewish people.

The Knesset (the term means assembly) is the state's legislature. It functions in many respects more as a continuing constituent assembly than as a traditional legislative body, having delegated many of its routine legislative powers to the government ministries, in some cases subject to the consent of appropriate Knesset committees, and spending much of its time in debate over symbolic issues. The term *Knesset* reflects this reality. It was chosen deliberately to reflect the historical continuity of the Jewish people in their land from the days of Ezra and Nehemiah, who reconstituted the Jewish medina in Judea 2,500 years ago and established the Anshei Knesset HaGedolah (Men of the Great Assembly), consisting of 120 members— whence the number in today's Knesset—equivalent to 10 from each of the twelve tribes of Israel, to symbolize the body's comprehensive character representing all the people of Israel and national unity. (Under Jewish law, 10 adult males who covenant with one another to do so constitute a community empowered to apply and interpret the laws of the Torah, so $12 \times 10 = 120$.) The ancients, in turn, took the term from the Aramaic *kenishta*, a translation of *edah,* the Hebrew term for assembly used in the Bible to describe the equivalent repository of popular authority in ancient Israel.[1]

The Knesset as an institution originally was designed along the lines of continental European parliaments—in other words, as a quasi-Rousseauian body designed to embody the general will of a state too large for its citizens to come together to decide every issue. Following the Rousseauian model, the Knesset's primary task was to indicate the general will to the government, not to participate in governance. In this respect, it differed from the classic British parliamentary model, whose Whiggish character made participation in governance a crucial element of parliamentary life. Nevertheless, the Knesset has acquired many of the characteristics of a Whiggish institution. That has added meaning when we recall that the term *Whig* is from *Whiggamore,* which meant a seventeenth-century Scottish covenanter. The emergence of a strong committee system in the Knesset, which not only participates in lawmaking through considering and amending draft laws proposed by the government and in legislative oversight of government departments, but actually has powers to approve, modify, or reject ministerial acts, further strengthened this aspect of the Knesset's role. As time passed, the Knesset also acquired something of the character of a Jewish representative institution: that is to say, one operating according to the principles of the Jewish political tradition, namely, as a body in which the people of Israel are represented as a community, and not only with respect to their various interests. That is particularly so in connection with issues such as "Who is a Jew?" and the maintenance of Jewish traditional in the state.[2]

The executive is called the *memshala* (government), derived from the classical Hebrew term for rule among equals. The departments that constitute the executive branch are known as *misradim* (offices—quite a neutral term) and are headed by *sarim* (ministers). The term *sar* in classical Hebrew is clearly applied to a senior officer whose authority has been delegated to him and who possesses no inherent authority of his own. The courts, civil and religious, are known as *batei mishpat* (houses of judgment) in the former case, and *batei din* (houses of law) in the latter. The individual units of both state and local government are known as *reshuyot* (authorities), from the word *reshut,* which, like its English counterpart, implies that is powers are delegated ones, not inherent. Significantly, the term *shilton,* which means government in the sense of a body with sovereign powers, as distinct from government in the sense of a body with delegated powers, is not used anywhere in Israeli law. It may be used in everyday and academic discourse, principally in connection with local government that does not have sovereign powers under present constitutional arrangements.[3] Israel's basic governmental structure is presented in figure 4-1.[4]

STATE INSTITUTIONS
*The President*
The president of the state is elected by the Knesset for a period of five years, and may be reelected for one further term. He has the prerogative of pardon

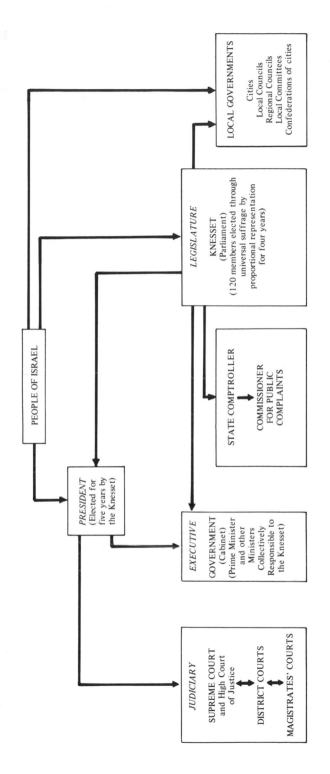

FIGURE 4-1
State Institutions

SOURCE: *Facts about Israel* (Jerusalem: Ministry of Foreign Affairs, 1979)

and of commuting sentences. He accepts the accreditation of foreign ambassadors and ministers, appoints Israel's ambassadors and ministers, judges, and the state comptroller, and signs all laws except those concerning the presidential powers.

When a new government is to be formed, the president consults with representatives of the parties and then calls on a member of the Knesset to undertake the task.

## The Legislature: The Knesset

Israel is a parliamentary democracy. Supreme authority rests with the Knesset, a unicameral legislative body of 120 members.

The Knesset is elected by universal suffrage under proportional representation for four years, but may, by specific legislation, decide on new elections before the end of its term. Electors choose between national lists of candidates, and seats are allocated in proportion to the number of votes obtained by each list.

The Knesset's consent is required before the installation of a new cabinet, which must resign if confidence in it is lost. It approves the annual budget and keeps cabinet policy under constant survey by means of questions to ministers and public debates in the plenary and discussions in its committees, which hear reports from ministers and senior officials.

Any member may propose that a subject of public importance be debated in the House or submitted to a committee for consideration. A motion of no confidence in the government may be proposed at any time and takes precedence over all other business.

Debates, which are conducted in Hebrew, are open to the public and periodically broadcast on radio and television. The proceedings are translated simultaneously into Arabic for Arab members, who may address the House in that language.

## Constitution and Legislation

The Transition Law (1949) prescribed in general terms the powers of the president, the legislature, and the cabinet. In June 1950, the Knesset resolved not to enact a formal constitution but to adopt basic laws, which eventually, taken together, will form a constitution. These eight basic laws are: The Knesset (1958); Israel Lands (1960); The President of the State (1964); The Government (1968); The State Economy (1975); The Army (1976); Jerusalem. Capital of Israel (1980); and the Judicature (1984). A basic law of human rights is before the Knesset. The Declaration of Independence of the State of Israel has been recognized by the courts as having at least quasi-constitutional status.

In addition, certain ordinary legislative acts have constitutional import, including the Law and Administration Ordinance (1948); the Law of Return (1950), recognizing the right of Jews to settle in Israel; the Equal Rights for Women Law (1951); the Nationality Law (1952); the Judges Law (1953); the Courts Law (1957); the State Comptroller Law (1958); the Knesset Elections Law (1969); and the Contracts (Remedies for Breach) Law (1970). The service of an ombudsman (commissioner for complaints) was established in 1971 as an amendment to the State Comptroller Law.

Universally recognized human and civil rights and freedoms, even if not yet laid down in the form of explicit enactments, form part of the law of Israel, much as in Britain, and are safeguarded by the courts through the utilization of the Declaration of Independence and traditional writs such as *habeas corpus* and *mandamus*. They include the freedoms of religious worship, speech, association, assembly, and the press, and the free exercise of any profession, trade, or business: all without any discrimination on the basis of sex, religion, or race. The right to hold property is also assured, subject to law and to the state's power to acquire land for public purposes, on payment of compensation assessed by a district court.

Full legislative competence rests with the Knesset, and the courts cannot, generally, invalidate any law that the Knesset has passed unless they determine that it was enacted improperly. Israel is well on the way to revising and replacing old laws of Ottoman origin, and English law introduced during the mandatory period, replacing both with indigenous law based on the principles of right and justice derived from Hebrew law. It also has enacted much labor legislation, free and compulsory elementary and secondary education laws, and an extensive national insurance system. Capital punishment has been abolished, except for treason in wartime and collaboration with the Nazis. (It has been applied only once in Israel's history—in the case of Adolph Eichmann.)

Bills generally are presented by the cabinet, drafted by the Ministry of Justice, and introduced to the Knesset by the minister concerned. They also may be proposed by one of the Knesset committees or by a member of the Knesset.

A bill requires adoption in three readings to become law. After the first reading, the bill is assigned to the appropriate Knesset committee. Amendments put forward in the committee are reviewed by the full House at the second reading, and the bill then is voted on as a whole at the third.

*The Government*

The government, headed by the prime minister, is collectively responsible to the Knesset. It takes office on receiving a vote of confidence from that body, and continues in office until—after resignation (or death) of the prime minister, or upon a vote of no confidence—a new cabinet is constituted. Ministers are usually, but not necessarily, members of the Knesset. As no party so far has commanded an absolute majority, all cabinets have been based on coalitions.

In September 1984, at the time of the formation of the National Unity government, the cabinet consisted of 25 ministers, divided into the following portfolios:

Prime Minister
Alternative Prime Minister and Foreign Affairs

Deputy Prime Minister and Construction and Housing
Deputy Prime Minister and Education and Culture
Defense
Economic Planning
Health
Energy
Police
Immigrant Absorption
Agriculture
Finance
Industry and Trade
Transport
Labor and Social Affairs
Justice
Tourism
Science and Development
Interior
Religious Affairs
Communications
Minister in the Prime Minister's Office
Without Portfolio (3)

## ISRAEL AS A JEWISH SOCIETY AND
## A MULTIETHNIC STATE

Quite properly, the emphasis in most discussions about Israel is on the
Jewish character of the state. Israel was brought into existence as a Jewish
state, a national home for the Jewish people and the place where a Jewish
majority would be able to build a creative life for itself and a haven for Jews
suffering from persecution and worse. At the same time, reality being what it
is, Israel, like over 90 percent of all of the world's independent states, is in
fact multiethnic in character, with a substantial non-Jewish minority, principally Arab by nationality and Muslim or Christian by religion. As a multiethnic state, it is committed to one of the several variants of pluralism that
democratic polities have developed to accommodate such differences.

Even more than that, the Jewish majority itself is divided in matters of
religion and, to some extent, even custom. The religious divisions reflect the
conditions of modern Jewish life, where normative Judaism no longer embraces all Jews, while the differences in custom reflect the ingathering of the
exiles from over one hundred countries around the world, in many of which
Jews had lived for thousands of years and developed their own syntheses of
Jewish and local cultures.

With regard to the multiethnic character of Israel, there is general
agreement on the part of all parties involved that it is to be retained, and

every effort is made to enable the non-Jewish minorities to preserve their own cultural and religious heritages. The attitude with regard to the differences within the Jewish majority is quite different. At the very least, it generally is agreed that the Jews of Israel must strive for greater integration, and even those who would preserve certain customs from their diaspora countries of origin see these customs as enriching the common Israeli Jewish society, not as enabling them to remain separate within it. Matters on the religious front are somewhat more complex. The Orthodox establishment also seeks to bring all Jews within the religious fold, and, indeed, even the secularists have cooperated to give normative Judaism special status. At the same time, there are voices calling for the legitimation of pluralistic modes of religious expression within the Jewish community. A proper understanding of Israel as a polity requires the exploration of these various dimensions of Israeli society and the ways in which Israel is a Jewish state even beyond conventional conceptions of religious attachment.[5]

## ISRAEL AS A JEWISH STATE

The State of Israel can be seen as a republic compounded in a variety of ways. First of all, it is, by self-definition, a Jewish state. That means not only a state with a Jewish majority but one in which the Jewish people as a corporate entity can express its particular culture, personality, and values and that seeks to foster the expression of that triad as perhaps its principal task. It is in this respect that many Israelis, including the leadership, consider the state a part of a larger entity known as the Jewish people. While it is the only politically sovereign state within that entity and as such occupies a unique position, it is also for certain purposes a Jewish community and maintains relationships with other Jewish communities on what could be considered a federal basis. The Jews of Israel, particularly the most articulate elements among them, see the fostering of this relationship as one of the tasks of the state, and, indeed, a task that does not escape local government, either.[6]

The principal institutional manifestations of this special relationship between Israel and the Jewish people are to be found in the "national institutions" functioning within the state's territory. These institutions are so named because they are considered to belong to the entire Jewish people (in Zionist terminology, nation) ad not to the State of Israel, although their major purpose may be to carry out projects or perform certain functions within the state. Among them are the Jewish Agency for Israel and the World Zionist Organization (WZO), which are responsible for settlement of the land and the Zionist education of Jews in Israel and outside, and the Jewish National Fund (JNF), which is responsible for land purchase and reclamation through the country.[7]

Originally established by the World Zionist Organization in 1922 to represent world Jewry in mandatory Palestine, the Jewish Agency for Israel became the governing body of the Jewish "state within a state" prior to 1948. Its status as the arm of world Jewry was reaffirmed by the Israeli Knesset in 1952 through legislation that was formalized through a covenant between the World Zionist Organization and the State of Israel. Its principal responsibility under the covenant was to handle the mass immigration of Jews into Israel and their absorption. Essentially an instrument of the WZO from 1939 to 1971, it was then reconstituted to include representatives of the diaspora communities and their fund-raising arms as equal partners. The 1952 covenant was revised further in 1979 to strengthen the JA as an instrumentality of the Jewish people and the diaspora role within it. The JA functions in the fields of education, housing, immigration, settlement, and urban rehabilitation, and provides certain social services. It remains closely tied to the WZO, which is, in many respects, its alter ego for work in the diaspora. It is governed by an Assembly of several hundred members drawn from throughout the Jewish world, a Board of Governors of 74, and an Executive of 19.

The WZO was founded at the First Zionist Congress (1897) to attain a "legally secured, publicly recognized national home for the Jewish people." That goal was reached when the Balfour Declaration became part of the League of Nations Mandate for Palestine (1922). The WZO was acknowledged by Britain as the "Jewish agency" charged with representing the world Jewish interest in the implementation of the mandate.

In 1971, when the Jewish Agency was reconstituted, the WZO resumed its independent status. It is charged with implementing the "Jerusalem Program" of 1968, defining as one of the aims of Zionism "the Unity of the Jewish People and the Centrality of Israel in Jewish life; . . . the Preservation of the Identity of the Jewish People through the Fostering of Jewish and Hebrew Education and of Jewish Spiritual and Cultural Values; the Protection of Jewish Rights Everywhere." That makes explicit the WZO's new role as a diaspora-oriented body, where its original purpose had been to harness world Jewry's efforts on behalf of the yishuv. Its functions are ideology- or diaspora-oriented, or deal with areas that cannot be subsumed under the headings for which tax-exempt philanthropic funds in the United States and elsewhere are being allocated. For example, although agricultural settlement work on behalf of new immigrants is the domain of the Jewish Agency, it is the WZO that finances agricultural projects in the administered territories, since tax-exempt philanthropic funds cannot be used for that purpose. The WZO retains a 50 percent partnership in the Jewish Agency, thereby preserving for itself the legitimacy that comes with responsibility for the practical work of immigration and absorption. It also was given exclusive responsibility for encouraging and implementing immigration from the countries of the free world.

Structurally, the WZO is a federation of countrywide Zionist organizations. Most of these constituent bodies are, in effect, extensions or affiliates of Israeli parties, whose ideologies, however, became frozen at a certain point and, as a rule, do not reflect the evolution, mergers, and splits occurring in the Israeli party system.

It should be noted that lands purchased by the Jewish National Fund are deemed to be the permanent possession of the entire Jewish people, for whom the JNF serves as trustee. They cannot be alienated through sale, but only through long-term lease to those who work them or who develop them for useful purposes. Virtually all Jewish agricultural settlements, the kibbutzim (communes) and moshavim (smallholders' cooperatives), are located on JNF land that they hold by lease. The terms of the leases include social provisions with regard to the proper land use and require the observance of the Sabbath in matters connected with the property on the part of the leaseholder (the latter has proved legally unenforceable but retains some moral authority). The leases are for forty-nine years, in recognition of the Biblical Jubilee law.[8]

The Hebrew University is formally designated a national institution, as is its principal library, which is a separate corporate entity, established as the national library of the Jewish people, and is so named. The reality of this designation is manifested in the university's board of governors, which is drawn from the Jewish community worldwide, and the fact that a major share of its budget comes from world Jewish sources other than the State of Israel.

While the Hebrew University is the only one formally designated by law as a national institution, all the other universities in the country have the same status, de facto, since they have the same arrangements for governance and funding. In addition, two of them, the universities of Tel Aviv and Haifa, were founded by their respective municipalities, which continue to make their contribution, as well. The others also get some support from the budgets of the local governments in whose jurisdictions they are located.[9]

It is interesting to note that budgeting and policy-making powers for Israel's universities are shared by the state's Council for Higher Education, each university's "national" governing board, and the university senate, composed of all full professors on full-time appointment. These are roughly the equivalent of state, federal, and local bodies, if one were to translate them into modern political terminology.

In addition to these highly structured institutions, the Israeli government seeks to institutionalize relationships between Israel and the diaspora Jewish communities through common organizations and associations structured along functional, professional, ideological, social, and interest lines. Through the WZO, it sends emissaries to Jewish communities overseas to work with them in strengthening Jewish life. It also encourages study programs in Israel. Many of the study programs involve diaspora Jews' having personal experiences on kibbutzim. Indeed, some kibbutzim, in particular, have developed the servicing of groups and individuals from the diaspora into an "industry"; Kibbutz Kfar Blum, for example, sponsors a high-school year for English-speaking Jews. Many kibbutzim sponsor three-month intensive language programs *(ulpanim)*, which combine half a day's Hebrew study with half a day's work on the land, for which the kibbutzim are compensated by the WZO.[10]

Similar study programs in the country's universities and institutes for higher religious study *(yeshivot)* usually are subsidized directly by both the Jewish Agency and the WZO. The cities themselves subsidize the latter. The local governments do so in line with the political culture of the state that one of the tasks of local government is to foster the culture, personality, and values of the particular national population within it.

Through the Jewish Agency and its related organizations, the Jewish people as a whole undertakes numerous settlement, social, and educational projects throughout the land of Israel, in both rural and urban areas and often in cooperation with the local authorities. The various bodies have regional offices in different parts of the country, and in some cases local ones, as well, which serve local populations in their spheres of authority as if they were governmental agencies. In addition, the Jewish Agency is principally responsible for the construction of such local facilities as high schools and community centers, with funds raised outside Israel.[11]

Finally, the Law of Return, which guarantees virtually every Jew (except those fleeing criminal prosecution of certain kinds) the right of entry into Israel and more rapid naturalization than non-Jewish immigrants, in effect obligates the state and local governments of Israel to provide all services to every Jewish immigrant from the moment of his or her settlement in the country. There is a great deal of misunderstanding regarding the Law of Return. Israel has immigration laws similar to those of other Western countries, with permits issued upon application and naturalization following in due course. However, since Israel is considered the state of the Jewish people, Jews enter almost as if they were engaging in interstate migration within a federal system and are entitled to claim Israeli citizenship from the moment they arrive. It should be noted that similar laws hold true in other countries with regard to those considered their nationals, even if those people are born outside their borders. In fact, because of the dominant political culture, public services and most of the benefits of citizenship extended to all those accepted as residents of the state, without regard to ethnic, national, or religious distinctions.

## ETHNORELIGIOUS PLURALISM IN ISRAEL

On another level, the State of Israel is compounded of several different ethnoreligions, minorities in addition to the Jewish majority: Muslim Arabs (552,000); Christians, mostly Arab (97,000), divided into various churches; Druse (65,000); Bahai (300); Circassians (2,500); and Samaritans (350), each with its own socioreligious structure and legal status. Following the Middle Eastern pattern, all of these groups seek to preserve their corporate identity, and Israel has granted them a legal status and institutional framework through which to do so. While the legal status and institutions of each are adapted to its particular situation, all have certain basic institutions and government support for their activities as corporate entities, as well as the normal services provided to all citizens. Israel is also the world center of the Bahai religion, the headquarters of which are located in Haifa. There are nineteen recognized Christian denominations of varying sizes, and there is a small community of Samaritans that exists separately.[12] The situation is further complicated by the less formally recognized divisions among Muslims and Jews.

Because of the particular pattern of settlement common in the rural Middle East, whereby villages either are ethnically homogeneous or are shared by perhaps two ethnoreligious groups, local government becomes a major vehicle for the expression of these corporate interests, so much so that permanent residents are entitled to participate in local elections whether or not they are citizens of the state. Since the establishment of the state, the Israeli government has made great efforts to encourage the villages housing these minorities to acquire full-fledged municipal status and to utilize the instrumentalities of local government not only to provide standard local services but also as a basis for the expressionof the cultural personalities and values of the groups within them.[13] In this respect, Israel is but a somewhat more enlightened example of a general phenomenon among Middle Eastern governments, all of which have ethnic minorities that must be accommodated in this way (as was true in Labanon before the civil war) or severely repressed (as in the case of the Kurds in Iraq). In a sense, that represents a partial adaptation to the realities of what in the period of the Ottoman Empire was known as the millet system, whereby every such group was constituted as a millet, with its own internal autonomy.

It must be emphasized that the separations that result are by choice and not by law. While Arabs can go to any school in Israel, they prefer to maintain their own schools, where the principal language of instruction is Arabic rather than Hebrew and the curriculum reflects Arabic culture and either Muslim or Christian religious beliefs and practices. For example, the Israeli government recently increased the satisfaction of the two Circassian villages in Israel by completing the development of textbooks in the Circassian language, thereby making it possible for the Circassians to have schools in which Hebrew and Circassian are taught, rather than requiring them to go to Arabic schools, where their children were assimilating into a different culture.

Since in Israel personal status matters are by law the province of the religious communities (that, too, is a common Middle Eastern pattern that is followed in most of the countries of the region), every person must be a member of some religious community if he or she hopes to get married, divorced, or buried in the country. Of course, while an individual may choose to avail himself of only these minimal services from his or her religious community, the communities themselves provide many more, and are expected to do so by the community of the faithful attached to each.

Among the minorities, religious belief and practice are quite high, and even among the Jewish majority, religion is significant, with perhaps one-third of the population quite religious in practice and another 40 percent selective observers of Jewish tradition. Even the so-called secular 25 percent has certain expectations with regard to the institutional activity of the Jewish religious establishment that they see as befitting a Jewish state. There are very few people in any of the communities who are opposed to the present arrangement.

As a result, the various religious communities have substantial institutional structures of their own, recognized in law, and in some cases governed by bodies chosen under state law because they provide state-supported services and thus must follow certain standard procedures with regard to selection and representation (not to speak of accountability and proper administrative procedures). Thus, each religious community has its own religious courts (local and countrywide), whose judges are supported by the state, hold commissions from the state on the basis of qualifications determined by each religious community, and are selected by the appropriate bodies of each religious community under procedures provided for under state law. These courts administer the religious laws of their respective communities, each of which has its own legal system, for matters within their competence. Religious laws and courts in relationship to the secular laws and courts of Israel roughly as state law stands in relationship to federal law in a federation with a dual legal system.[14]

The principal administrative organs of the religious communities vary from community to community. The Christian communities have no separate ones other than the church hierarchies, which also handle matters of religious law, because they are essentially in the Catholic tradition and also play a more limited role in the lives of their citizens.[15] The religious functions of the Muslim communities are administered through the Wakfs, the Muslim religious trusts.[16] In the Jewish communities, every locality with a Jewish majority has a local religious council consisting of laymen and rabbis elected through a complex formula and supported by the local and state governments.[17] All of these bodies are in some respects responsible to the Ministry of Religions, whose minister is a member of the cabinet and which is the channel through which state funds reach the various religious groups.

While from the point of view of the state these religious groups obtain their powers through state law, from the perspective of each of the religious communities their powers flow directly from Heaven and their law represents the divine will. As far as they are concerned (and this goes for the Jewish religious authorities as much as for any of the others), the state has only a minimal role to play in determining their existence, and certainly no legitimate role in determining their powers other than to which they are willing to acquiesce.* In sum, Israel is a republic compounded of different ethnoreligious groups, each recognized and supported by the state, yet claiming its own source of authority.

Each of the several communities represents a further compound within its ranks. Every Arab locality is a compound of extended families—really clans—so much so that voting and political officeholding, not to speak of decision making and the distribution of political rewards, are dependent upon the competition or cooperation among the extended families in each locality. Every so often, a group of young people emerges to challenge this arrangement, and there is talk in the land that the Arabs are modernizing and no longer will be found by this kind of familial loyalty; but every time, all but the most radical of the young end up following the lead of their families in these matters.

## THE COMPOUND OF IDEOLOGICAL PARTIES

As we have seen, the Jewish community in Israel is a compound of a different sort. Rather than being based upon the organic connections of extended families, it was based upon federal connections between different Zionist movements. This federation of movements became the basis of the present party system that organizes and informs Israel's political system. As a result of the transition from the settlement stage when ideological democracy was dominant to a stage of rootedness when territoriality asserts itself, it now may be weakening. Nevertheless, the state's institutional infrastructure continues to reflect these prestate federal arrangements through the party system and the Histadrut, so much so that the arrangements inform even the ostensibly neutral government, cooperative and private bodies shared in common.[18]

Since the late 1920s, the Jews of Israel have grouped themselves politically into three "camps": Labor, civil, and religious. Contrary to conventional wisdom, the three camps do not relate to each other on a left-right continuum but stand in something like a triangular relationship to one another, as portrayed in figure 4-2. For a long time, preoccupation with European modes of political thought prevented students of Israeli politics from seeing that, even though there never was a time when Israel did not operate on that basis. Thus, for certain purposes, each of the camps is more to the left or more to the right than any of the others. What each has staked out for itself is a particular vision of what the Zionist enterprise and its creation, the Jewish state, are all about. At times that vision has taken on ideological form, and at times it has been nonideological.

The camps themselves divide into parties, some of which are quite antagonistic to one another within the same camp (it is within the camps that left-right divisions can exist). The size of each camp is not fixed, either in

---

*It would not be incorrect to estimate that as many as one-third of all Israelis hold the religious law of their respective communities in higher regard than the law of the state, including a small group of Jews (perhaps several thousand) who reject state law altogether.

FIGURE 4-2

The Three Camps and the Parties in the 11th Knesset Elections

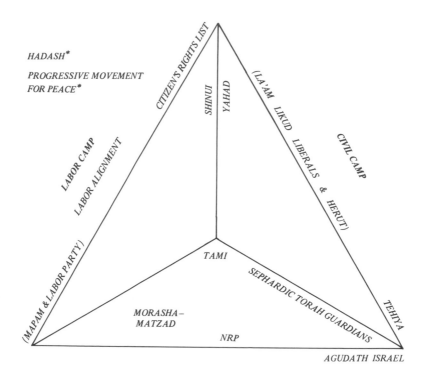

*These parties, although represented in the Knesset, are defined by Israelis to be outside the Zionist movement. Operationally, this means that under the rules of Israeli political games no governing coalition would rely upon them to attain a Knesset majority.

relation to the total Jewish population or in relation to one another, but whatever the fluctuations, the camps themselves persist. Their persistence is reflected in the Knesset elections in Israel and in the division of offices within the World Zionist Movement and the various other organizations and associations with Israel. The Israeli party system is presented in the following box.

Although the state was established only in 1948, Israel's electoral cycle spans two generations and is well into its third. The first elections in the

ISRAEL'S POLITICAL PARTIES

In the 1984 elections, fifteen different lists obtained seats in the Knesset. They are grouped as follows:

### The National Unity Government
The government coalition formed in September 1984 consisted of the following parties:

*The Maarach* (Labor Alignment), with 39 seats and 10 ministers.
* Avodah (the Labor party) was founded in 1968 as the successor to Mapai, Israel's dominant party since the late 1920s.
* Ometz, with 1 seat and 1 minister, was founded in 1984 by Yigal Hurvitz.
* Yahad, with 3 seats, was founded in 1984 by Ezer Weizman.
*The Likud* (Union), with 40 seats and 9 ministers.
* Herut (Freedom Movement) was founded in 1948 by veterans of the 'Irgun Tzvai Le'umi' and absorbed the Union of Zionist Revisionists (founded 1925).
* The Israel Liberal party is the successor of the General Zionists, founded in 1931.
* Tehiy-Tzomet holds 5 seats. It was formed in 1981 as the partisan manifestation of the Greater Israel Movement.

### Religious Parties
* Mafdal-Miflaga Datit Le'umit (National Religious party), with 4 seats and 1 minister. It was founded in 1956 by the union of Mizrahi (founded in 1901) and its Labor wing, HaPoel HaMizrahi (1921).
* Shas (Sephardic Torah Guardians), with 4 seats and 1 minister, was founded in 1984 as a breakaway from Agudath Israel.
* Agudath Israel (founded in 1912) obtained 2 seats in 1984.
* Morasha (founded in 1984), with 2 seats and 1 minister, broke away from Mafdal in 1984.
* Tami (founded in 1981 as a breakaway from Mafdal) obtained 1 seat.

### The Opposition
* Mapam (Mifleget HaPoalim HaMeuhedet-United Workers Party) fought the election as part of the Labor Alignment but broke away when the Labor party agreed to join in a coalition with the Likud.
* Ratz-Hatenu'ah Lezechuyot Ha'ezrach (Citizen's Rights Movement), founded in 1973, holds 4 seats.
* Progressive List for Peace, a radical Arab-Jewish party founded in 1984 to support the establishment of a Palestinian state alongside Israel, often viewed as having PLO sympathies, with 2 seats.
* Democratic Front for Peace and Equality (Rakah), front for the Communist Party, originally founded in 1919, with 4 seats.
* Shinui, with 3 seats, was founded in 1976.
* Kach, with 1 seat, was founded by Meir Kahane in 1981.

Jewish yishuv were held in 1921 under the auspices of the Zionist movement
and the British mandatory government. They were part of the founding of
the modern system of Israeli democratic republicanism at that time. It was
not until the 1931 elections that Mapai emerged as the dominant party. Its
domination continued to grow through the 1949 elections, the first after the
establishment of the state. In the 1951 elections, which began the second
generational cycle, Mapai's dominance was challenged by a swing toward the
General Zionists in the civil camp, which Ben-Gurion succeeded in fending
off during the 1950s through a series of activities designed to consolidate his
party's position. In many respects, what Ben-Gurion did after 1951 was
similar to what he did after 1931, when the Revisionists appeared to be
mounting a serious challenge to Mapai's hegemony in the World Zionist
Organization. At that time, he capitalized on the mysterious assassination of
Mapai leader Haim Arlozorov to beat the Revisionists into the ground, and
after 1951 he used the mechanisms of the state to pass out patronage and
benefits to the benefit of Mapai.

The Mapai coalition held together until 1965, when Ben-Gurion himself
took the lead in splitting Mapai by establishing Rafi. It took another twelve
years and three elections after that to break the Mapai hegemony, but Ben-
Gurion set the tide in motion. The second cycle came to an end in 1977 with
the Likud victory, the first time that Mapai had lost since the 1920s. The
1981 election started the next cycle by returning the Likud to power, making
it the coequal, if not the leading, party in the country.

An examination of the results of the elections to the Knesset since 1949
reveals that a governing coalition is formed when major shares of two of the
camps can be combined. Until the most recent elections, coalitions generally
consisted of some two-thirds of the Labor camp plus two-thirds of the
religious camp, plus a small crossover element from the civil camp. In the
Begin-led coalition, the same principle was observed, but in reverse. Virtually the entire civil camp, except for Independent Liberal Gideon
Hausner, linked with the entire religious camp. That, more than any mathe-
matical formula, explains the basis for coalition formation in Israeli politics.[19]

At one time, virtually all services for Jewish citizens were provided
through the parties, or, in the case of labor, through the Histadrut, the
General Labor Federation, which united several of the different labor parties
for certain purposes. Again, the analogy to a federal system is apt. Just as in a
federal territorial polity one has to be a resident of a state to avail oneself of
the services of the polity as a whole, so too in prestate Israel was it necessary
to be a member of a party. With the establishment of the state, the government took over more and more of the services. The camps or parties,
however, still retain control of health insurance and ordinary medical facilities, and, to some extent, banking. Sports (the football and basketball
leagues, for example) continue to be organized on the basis of party teams,
although the divisions have become meaningless since the players are re-

cruited on the basis of their talents. Moreover, government corporations, of which there are many in Israel, as well as the more formal institutions of government, remain major patronage vehicles, either for the party in control of each entity or through application of the party key.[20]

The importance of the compound of parties is such that even the most casual student of Israeli affairs is aware of it. In fact, however, many of the manifestations of the old divisions are disappearing. More and more services are provided neutrally by the state or local governments or, as is more often the case, through cooperative arrangements involving both. Party influence exists in the government structure and primarily touches those who pursue governmental careers rather than the public at large (although in a government-permeated society, that is by no means an insignificant bastion of party strength). The expectation is that, aside from the division between the strictly religious and the non- or not-so-religious, the divisions themselves will continue to grow weaker (but not necessarily disappear), unless there is a strong upsurge of secular ideology. The raison d'etre for many of the divisions has so weakened that only in the religious camp do the ideological justifications remain sufficiently strong to create demands of prestate intensity, and they are accommodated by allowing for parallel institutions in many fields.

THE COMPOUND OF SECTORS

A final means by which Israeli society is compounded is through what is known as the "sectors," whereby public activity is divided between distinctive governmental, cooperative, and private sectors along one plane and urban and settlement sectors along another.[21] While each of these sectors is distinct, all three are closely intertwined. That, too, is a result of Ben-Gurion's *mamlachtiut* (statism) policies of the 1950s. One dimension of mamlachtiut was to transfer services from the parties to the state. Another was to inject the state into every aspect of the country's public and economic life, to assist development but also to create dependency, which could be used for political purposes.

As a government-permeated society in an era in which government's role in development is great all over the world, it is not surprising to find that most enterprises in Israel exist by virtue of government assistance, through direct investment, loan guarantees, or simply sponsorship with appropriate tax benefits, favorable foreign exchange rates, and the like. While the Israeli government has veered heavily away from the strongly socialistic position it had at the beginning of statehood, that has not meant any movement toward laissez faire. Government's role remains as great as ever in promoting state-permeated social capitalism within a mixed economy. It even is enhanced by the fact that Israel's precarious security situation and narrow economic base give political decisions preference over economic ones in most cases.

If the government sector is invariably the strongest, the cooperative, or workers', sector is the oldest and most hallowed in the mythology of the state. It emerged in the 1920s when the various small collective efforts of the Jewish pioneers were brought together to create the Histadrut and the Hevrat Ovdim (Workers' Society), which was to be the means through which the Labor Federation could establish and maintain its own complex of economic activities. While the cooperative sector has diminished greatly in importance since the establishment of the state, as government has entered into activities formerly in the Histadrut domain, it remains the biggest nongovernmental owner and operator in the country, controlling 25 percent of Israel's economy. The largest industries, including the largest conglomerate in the country, are under its ownership. The internal public transportation companies, with the exception of the state railroads and the miniscule internal airline, which provide very limited service, are workers' cooperatives. The kibbutzim and moshavim are integral parts of the cooperative sector. The largest department store chain is Histadrut-owned. The Histadrut operates Kupat Holim (the Workers' Sick Fund), the largest prepaid medical service in the country, which serves over two-thirds of the population and, through it, a network of hospitals, old-age homes, and rest homes—in other words, the complete apparatus of a socialized health system. The local Kupat Holim clinic is one of the most vital service centers in the local community. All of that is in addition to being the great comprehensive union of the vast majority of the workers in the country.

The cooperative sector consists primarily of producer cooperatives, as exemplified by the bus companies, construction companies, kibbutzim, and moshavim. Even the nominal consumer cooperatives do not operate on the basis of Rochedale principles, since their profits are funneled back into the Histradrut and not to their patrons. Moreover, the Histadrut itself has become considerably bureaucratized over the years, so that, while it has sought to serve the Zionist mission of rebuilding the state and the public good as its leaders have interpreted that good, it has also become at least as distant from its own members as the government is from the man in the street in most of its operations. That needs to be emphasized, so as to gain proper perspective on the workings of that sector.

Finally, there is the private sector, which is growing after being the weakest of the sectors for many years. While there always has been private enterprise within the Zionist effort, since the overwhelming majority of the halutzim were socialists it was not a very acceptable form of pioneering activity. It was only in recent years that the importance of a healthy private sector both as a countervailing power to the other sectors and in its own right has come to be recognized, and even encouraged, by the government. It is typified by the range of private entrepreneurial activities characteristic of all modern Western societies.

By and large, these three sectors have not developed on a sharply competitive basis; rather, they tend to cooperate with each other, as could be expected in a small country with a relatively weak economy and a political culture that emphasizes partnership as does that of the Jewish majority.

Many enterprises are jointly developed by two or all three sectors. Efforts on the part of private investors—usually from overseas—to "buck" these arrangements generally have come to naught, since without favorable government treatment, it is very difficult to succeed in any economic enterprise in Israel. What is particularly important for our purposes, of course, is that the government, which generally is assumed to be primarily in the business of providing services, also has a strong economic stake in the society, while the general labor association, which in other countries would be an interest group, plays an even more important role as a provider of services on the "retail" as well as "wholesale" level and as an economic developer.

The division between urban and settlement sectors is perhaps even more important,[22] since it tied in with the original Zionist vision, which placed heavy emphasis on Jews' returning to the soil, where they would redeem themselves through cooperative toil in a natural setting. From the first, the Zionist enterprise allocated the largest share of its resources to rural pioneering. The disproportionate allocation grew from the time of the Third Aliyah, when *halutziut* (the pioneering spirit) became almost synonymous with *kibbutziut* (the building of kibbutzim). After the establishment of the state, the government shifted its emphasis from kibbutzim to moshavim because it had no choice. The new immigrants were reluctant to be settled on the land in the first place, and certainly refused to be collectivized, so the moshav olim (immigrants smallholders' village) became the favored form of rural development, with the government and the Jewish Agency providing heavy support for those moshavim, as well as continuing disproportionate support for the kibbutzim.

The first challenge to this system came with the Likud victory in 1977. The Likud as the preeminent instrument of the civil camp had always looked upon the kibbutzim as rivals and sources of Labor party strength. Hence, they set out to cut back on government assistance to the kibbutzim. On the other hand, the Likud government was much in favor of blanketing Judea, Samaria, and Gaza with Jewish settlements in order to establish firmer Israeli control over the territories in such a way as to prevent the possibility of returning any of them to Arab sovereignty. So it poured money into settlements of yet another type in the territories. These settlements, called *yishuvim kehilatiim* (community settlements), are essentially small towns, combining urban and rural economic activities in a free-enterprise framework.

The reader will notice that the counterpart of the urban sector in Israel is not a rural sector but a settlement sector. The actual Hebrew term is *hityashvut ha-ovedet* (working settlement), which is, of course, biased in favor of the original Zionist back-to-the-land vision. In fact, the kibbutzim and moshavim are not strictly farming settlements by any means. They are rurban (to use an American neologism), combining agriculture, industry, and services with a way of life that is not significantly different from that of Israeli city dwellers in its basic culture. In established kibbutzim today, less than 7 percent of the work force is engaged in agriculture, with the remainder equally divided between manufacturing and services. Hence, the settlement sector tends to be self-contained in many respects, because not only is almost all agricultural production in its hands, but it has a strong industrial base of its own, as well. Moreover, the kibbutzim and moshavim embody special ways of life, as well as a special status in the Zionist enterprise.

The kibbutzim are not only highly integrated political, social, and economic units, the exact antithesis of fragmented urban society, but in many respects they are even more modern than Israeli cities in their culture, behavior, and technological development. Every kibbutz is organized as a cooperative society, in which all except the most personal items of property is legally held in common (even today, when in many of the more prosperous kibbutzim members have television sets in their own apartments, the sets belong to the kibbutz, although the members fully control their use). Social life is necessarily intimate, with a common dining hall and other facilities to enhance the already great likelihood of high social integration that will exist in any community of a few hundred to a few thousand population.[23]

The kibbutz has municipal status as a *vaad makomi* (local committee) under state law. It actually is governed by two principal bodies, the general meeting (the equivalent of the American town meeting), which elects the local committee on a yearly basis and which meets monthly to consider major issues, and the local committee, which meets as frequently as necessary, sometimes daily, to deal with current business. Most of the day-to-day business of the kibbutz is carried on through a multitude of committees involving as many members as are capable of participating. Every kibbutz is also a member of a *moetza azorit* (regional council), a federation of usually contiguous settlements that provides secondary local government services, in which it is represented by a delegate chosen by its own general meeting (in some regional councils, the very largest settlements are given an additional delegate).

The moshav is slightly less integrated than the kibbutz, but not by a great deal. In the moshav every family has its own family farm and private life, with some work and all major purchasing and marketing done in common. That makes for a cooperative rather than a collectivized atmosphere, but since, like the kibbutz, the moshav is also small (in fact, moshavim are usually much smaller than kibbutzim), it tends to be a highly integrated social unit. Under the law, the moshav is both a cooperative society with shared economic functions and a municipal unit with its own general meeting and local committee. Moshavim are also federated into regional councils, usually separated from those of the kibbutzim.[24]

Because of the particular character of rural settlement in Israel, whereby even family farms are concentrated in villages with their own local institutions, the 913 rural settlements with their own local governmental autonomy have an average population of under 500. Moreover, in the Israeli situation, rather than being very limited-purpose local governments, such as those serving populations of that small a size would be in the United States, they are the most comprehensive local governments of all, providing economic and social services, as well as traditional municipal functions on a level that far exceeds almost anything to be found outside the Communist bloc.

In a self-selected population, which is what these settlements represent, it is possible to provide a very high level of services even in a community severely circumscribed in size. Even so, it is increasingly necessary to enlarge the scale through which certain specific services are provided. Hence the growing power of the regional councils, the federations of settlements, which have been called into existence to fill that gap. So, for example, many of the settlements are still able to maintain their own elementary schools, but the provision of an adequate high school requires a larger population base; hence, it is increasingly entrusted to the 53 regional councils. At the same time, it should be noted that the regional councils themselves are relatively small, ranging in population size from 200 to 23,000, with only eight over 10,000.[25] Regional councils play a particularly important role in economic affairs, as holding companies for larger-scale economic activities than the individual settlements can manage themselves. Some also maintain regional colleges for the benefit of their members.

Because these settlements can bring to bear a full range of options— political, economic, social, and cultural—to confront any problem, they are the most autonomous local governments in the country, and also the ones with the most effective cooperative arrangements with one another and with the state authorities. The greater internal diversity of the cities and their greatly limited corporate purposes prevent them from functioning nearly as well. Moreover, since cities are considered to be mere byproducts of the Zionist movement, which as a back-to-the-land movement was, in many respects, antiurban, they have no special claim on the resources or respect of the state, in the way the settlements do.[26]

The cities are open to greater permeation by the external society— including the institutions of the state and the cooperative sector—in every respect. While the kibbutzim and moshavim are actually part of the cooperative sector, as members and, indeed, as the elites of that sector in many respects, they hold a powerful position within it. The cities, on the other hand, are dependent upon decisions taken by the government and the Histadrut, over which they have very little control and minimal influence.

A clear sign of the separation between the urban and settlement sectors is to be found in the fact that there are no general local government structures that embrace both, no counties or federations of local governments that include both cities and settlements. The settlements have their regional frameworks, and the cities, through single or multipurpose city confederations, have theirs. In the last decade, formal cooperative relationships have developed between the two sectors in certain parts of the country around specific tasks, programs, or in some cases institutions, but they are still considered very bold steps that have not been widely replicated.

## THE COMPOUND POLITY AND "MAMLACHTIUT"

It has been suggested in this chapter that Israel shares the federal characteristics common to all new societies in a very special way. Of necessity, it is a compound republic rather than an organic state, in that it was built by the compounding of different elements, each of which claims its own identity and power base. The resultant system of diffused power in Israel is the result not of concession on the part of central authorities but of the construction of a general government out of highly autonomous elements, which have surrendered the absolute minimum of their power they felt was necessary to a comprehensive authority that appeared on the scene relatively late in the development of the polity it serves. Indeed, as we have seen, some of the elements out of which the polity is compounded have not yet fully recognized the supreme authority of those comprehensive bodies, even when they actively participate within them and accept their legitimacy within the specific sphere allocated to each.

Shortly after the establishment of the state, David Ben-Gurion attempted to change this pattern, to build a centralized state on the European model. Ben-Gurion, who in the thirties had argued for a consociational or federative pluralism, apparently could not resist the influence of the European political culture, which he shared, and saw statehood as bringing with it the necessity of creating a strong central government. He also was faced with an immediately practical problem of reducing the power of those prestate bodies that had dominated the Jewish yishuv and wished to continue to do so, in ways that he believed were divisive. The term he applied to this effort was *mamlachtiut*, roughly translated as "statism," but better understood in terms of its Hebrew etymology as the creation of a strong central authority. *Mamlacha* really means something more like dominion; it shares a common root with *melech,* or king. Given the force of Ben-Gurion's personality and his political power at the time, coupled with a general public sentiment on behalf of strengthening the institutions of the new state, *mamlachtiut* became a very popular political goal.[27]

Ben-Gurion's policy was most successful in regard to the Israel Defense Forces. Almost immediately after the state was declared, he forced the consolidation of the separate military and paramilitary organizations developed by the various political movements in the prestate period, into one national army, clearly under the full control of the state. Ben-Gurion himself served as defense minister for most of his career as prime minister, taking a direct hand in reshaping the army as an instrument of the state as a whole. As a result, the IDF became the symbol of mamlachtiut as a policy.[28]

The character of the new Tzvah Haganah LeYisrael (Tzahal), or Israel

Defense Force (the antimilitaristic dimension of Israeli socialism made it a matter of policy that the army be called not an army but a "defense force"), encapsulated Ben-Gurion's approach. The army was first and foremost to be an apolitical arm of the state; at the same time, it was to be a popular army, based upon universal military service and close links with the civilian world. The Israeli soldiers would be civilians in uniform, for varying lengths of time, whether for an initial period of service plus annual reserve duties or for twenty-year service as a career officer. Members of the standing army were expected to retire in their early forties, so that they still could pursue civilian careers. That was to prevent the development of an officer corps in the usual sense of the term.

The values of Tzahal were to be those of the Zionist movement, particularly as manifested in the kibbutzim.*

Relations between officers and men were to be comradely, and based as much as possible on consent. Orders were to be given sparingly; leaders were to lead by going in front of their men—the famous *Aharai* (after me) principle—and a premium was placed upon educating the soldiers to understand why they had to do what they were called upon to do. An elaborate educational program was developed for all ranks, involving such topics as Jewish and Zionist history, and contemporary political and military problems. In other words, Tzahal became a vehicle for political socialization and nation building, as well as a defense force.

At the same time, the army was glorified, even to the point of a certain vulgarity, as, for example, in slogans that took verses from the Bible regarding the Lord's role in protecting Israel and in place of the name of the Lord, put the name *Tzahal*. Moreover, within the framework of this popular, democratic, apolitical army tied directly to the civilian leadership of the state, the principle was covertly maintained that only a member of Mapai, or, later, the Labour party, could become chief of staff.

This latter point was in keeping with the general thrust of mamlachtiut. Ben-Gurion was successful in changing the structure, but he had to compromise when it came to the content of the state's new institutions. If the parties no longer could provide services directly through their own institutions, they insisted that control over the state institutions be shared on the basis of the party key. Strong as he was, Ben-Gurion was not strong enough to resist this demand—if, indeed, he opposed it—so the federation of parties was transformed into a consociational arrangement, whereby separate party-sponsored institutions gave way to common state institutions, whose control was shared by the parties more or less on the basis of the proportion of voters supporting each party. Funds, jobs, and other benefits were passed out according to the party key in institution after institution, preserving the

---

*Until recently, kibbutzniks excelled in the army; they came to it already socialized into its values and modus operandi. As the kibbutzim have changed, that has become less true, and the sons of the moshavim have taken the place of the kibbutzniks in most services.

diffusion of power, in one sense, but making cooperation more difficult, in another.

Mamlachtiut had the additional effect of reducing the spirit of volunteerism in Israeli society. In the prestate period, when the institutions of the Jewish community had a minimum of collective power, they depended heavily upon volunteerism to maintain both control and their activities. This period of volunteerism carried over into the early days of the state, especially in the period of the mass immigration, but statism by its very nature involved the substitution of bureaucratic institutions for voluntary work. In part, that was a necessary step toward the organization and regularization of governmental activities and public services, but, in part, it went beyond that.

Here, too, there was a subtle reinforcement of trends. On one hand, there was Ben-Gurion's desire to strengthen the state; on the other, there was desire on the part of the professional party leaders to retain as much control as possible, which they felt could be achieved by distribution of jobs that would make the party faithful dependent upon them for their very livelihood. Volunteerism was to be discouraged, because volunteers by their very nature were more likely to be independent. Finally, there was the need of individual Israelis to improve their economic lot, and their desire to get ahead, which led them, in a period of continual inflation, to confine their activities to those for which they could obtain appropriate compensation. These three factors, to name only the most pronounced, reinforced a view that once would have been abhorrent to the Zionist pioneers, namely, that services were to be rendered only for pay, and the politics in particular was for professionals.

The Six Day War strengthened the Israelis' commitment to mamlachtiut. The state extended its borders, and the army became its central symbol. Then came the Yom Kippur debacle, when Israel reaped the whirlwind of arrogance and overconfidence. Among the major casualties of the war was the uncritical acceptance of mamlachtiut. Israelis began to question whether the state was the be all and end all of the Zionist enterprise, an end in itself. Their questioning was intensified by the revived interest in Zionism that came out of the war. Zionism, as the "old-time religion" of most Israelis, had been more or less abandoned on behalf of a mamlachtiut ideology; then, in the manner of religious revivals in other crises in human history, the Yom Kippur War brought many to return to the old-time religion, precisely as the ideology that replaced it began to crumble.

Israelis today are grappling with the problem of their state in a new way. Not that there is any call to return to the prestate structure, but there is also little predisposition to continue the pattern of the first quarter-century of Israel's existence. Here, too, matters are in flux, and new forms are likely to emerge.

# FIVE

## The Local Dimension in Israeli Politics

Israel is well known as a state in which political power is concentrated heavily in its central institutions, both governmental and party. The small size of the country, its development as a result of ideologically motivated effort, the mamlachtiut of its first generation, and the conception of the state its founders brought with them from Europe coalesced to make that so. At the same time, it is a mistake to think of Israeli government as "centralized" in the usual sense of the word. Power is divided among several centers within the Israeli polity, but the centers are organized along cultural-ideological, rather than territorial lines. That means that local government in Israel, which necessarily is territorially based, operates at a handicap. It often is viewed as the weakest link in the state's political system. From a power perspective, local governments are indeed subordinate to governmental and party centers, not to speak of the religious communities, in many ways. Nevertheless, it is a mistake to underestimate either the role or the influence of local government in the state.

Local government plays an important role in Israeli society, particularly in connection with the following four tasks: 1) the provision and administration of governmental services; 2) the recruitment and advancement of political leadership; 3) the fostering of channels of political communication between the governors and the governed; and 4) the maintenance of necessary or desired diversity within a small country where there are heavy pressures toward homogeneity. All four of these tasks are of great importance in the integration of what is still a very new society of immigrants or the children of immigrants. The role played by local government in meeting the challenges they pose makes it a far more vital factor on the Israeli scene than it often is given credit for being.[1]

Prior to 1948, local government was fostered as an alternative to foreign government and was treated by the yishuv as an important element in the drive for a Jewish state. Local governments also served the cause of maintaining diversity within the framework of the Zionist movement. The General Zionists and other right and center parties that were excluded from positions of power in the Histadrut-dominated countrywide organs of the Jewish "state within a state" were able to establish power bases of their own in a number of the Jewish municipalities, which gave them a share and a stake in the upbuilding of the land. Moreover, many of the future leaders of the state took their first steps on the road to political careers in the local polities, especially in the kibbutzim. The full history of local government in prestate Israel is yet to be written, but when it is, there is no doubt that the record will show that it played an important role as a training ground for the state in the making.[2]

With the establishment of the state in 1948, local government passed off the center of the political stage. Not unexpectedly, the new state began to assume responsibility for many public functions that had rested in local governmental hands for lack of central institutions. Political leadership gravitated toward the offices of the new state, leaving only those members of the opposition parties for whom the limited responsibilities of service in the Knesset were not sufficient and those kibbutzniks who wished to stay home to seek local office actively. In the process of sorting out state and local functions, the party organizations and the Histadrut interposed themselves between the fledgling state and the local governments, further weakening the autonomy of the local leadership.

At the same time, the mass immigration to Israel in the years 1948–1953 shifted the patterns of settlement in the country in such a way that the kibbutzim and veteran moshavim, the local communities possessing the best access to the state and the most power to maintain their local autonomy, declined in importance relative to other local communities. On the other hand, the development towns and the immigrant settlements, potentially the least powerful local communities, became significant elements in the constellation of local governments. While new kibbutzim were established in this period, the kibbutz as such failed to attract many of the new immigrants, so that, although they preserved their own relatively autonomous position within Israeli civil society, they were unable to extend the benefits of their influential role to many of the new arrivals.[3]

The reduction in the power of local government was not necessarily the result of calculated policy but, rather, the result of a natural transfer of powers that could have only that effect. Indeed, the new state took it upon itself to foster local governmental institutions from the first. Reversing the pattern established in mandatory days, the central authorities themselves moved to establish new local authorities. The number of Jewish settlements enjoying municipal status rose from 36 in 1948 to 197 by 1968. The number of regional councils (federations of rural settlements) rose from 4 to 50. Moreover, all new rural settlements were encouraged to develop local committees of their own for their internal self-government. Finally, and perhaps most significant, the Arab and Druse villages also were encouraged to establish modern municipal governments of their own, and did so in substantial numbers, thereby opening the door to political participation for thousands of non-Jews who previously had been caught in the embrace of a traditional society that confined political power to the hands of a tiny elite. In addition to the establishment of new local governments, established local governments were upgraded and their structures and functions more or less regularized according to standard statewide patterns.[4]

The same standardization that was brought to governmental activities was extended to politics, as well. Regularization brought with it the patterns of voting on the local plane that were becoming fixed statewide. The opposition parties lost control of most of the local governments that had been in their hands in the prestate period, and were replaced by new coalitions dominated by Mapai, the Israel Labor party that was dominant in the country as a whole. If the establishment of the state strengthened the hands of central government institutions, the mass immigration strengthened the hands of the political party organizations. Whereas in the small yishuv before statehood the party members could play significant roles in party decision making, as the population grew and the elements which came in were for the most part politically unsophisticated, the professional party leaders took over direction of party affairs, relying upon the new voting masses, who turned out for them at the polls but were not yet prepared to participate actively in party government. That had the effect of increasing the role of the central organs of the political parties, enabling them to become the mediating institutions between state and local governing bodies with their respective versions of coalition politics, to the point of dictating who would be the candidates for local office.

Local government reached its lowest ebb in the political system sometime in the mid-1950s. At that point, the older local governments had lost many of their original functions and had been absorbed in the statewide party system along lines that harmonized with the patterns of rule established in Jerusalem. The most powerful local governments, those of the kibbutzim, and secondarily the older moshavim, were attracting a proportionately smaller share of the new immigrants and losing their importance in the local government constellation as a result. The new immigrant settlements that had been established after statehood were still too raw and immature to be self-governing. Even where they were given municipal status, their government offices were occupied or dominated by outsiders sent in by their respective political parties to manage local affairs until such time as "proper" (however defined) local leadership should emerge.[5]

In the late 1950s, the tide began to turn as the local governments began to find their place in the framework of a state in which power was divided on other than territorial bases, first and foremost, but which also wished to encourage local governmental activity in connection with most, if not all, of the aforementioned four tasks. The process of adjustment begun then is not yet completed.

Take the case of government services. After the period of mass transfer of functions from local government (and the Histadrut) to the state, the country entered into a period in which shared or cooperative activity began to be stressed. While the state took primary responsibility for program initiation, policy making, and finance, program administration—the actual delivery of services—increasingly was transferred to local government, or, in cases where the division was not so clear-cut, responsibility for the delivery of services was divided between the state and the localities. That became true over a wide range of functions, from welfare to education to civil defense to sewage disposal.

The nature of these sharing arrangements should be made clear. They were not conceived as a sharing among equal partners but rather as a sharing by superior and subordinate. But sharing did become the norm, which meant that, at the very least, the local governments were forced to develop cadres of civil servants with sufficient administrative skills to provide the services that the state promised all its citizens. In fact, it soon led to an increase in the real power of local governments, because once they possessed the authority to act, they simply took off. That, in turn, opened the doors to the recruitment and development of a new class of participants in the governmental process that has drawn in people from all segments of Israeli society out of necessity.[6]

Moreover, unlike local government in countries with very hetero- geneous populations, such as the United States, local governments in Israel undertake a range of social and cultural functions that extend beyond the ordinary local police functions. These range from the provision of religious services to the management of orchestras and drama groups, from the maintenance of day-care centers to the awarding of literary prizes. No small share of the importance of local government in Israel flows from its role in undertaking these functions as part of the task of fostering the social and cultural integration of the community.[7]

## FORMS OF LOCAL GOVERNMENT

Urban government in Israel takes two forms: cities and local councils, with the distinction between them minimal. The largest local communities are legally cities with full municipal powers, but, in the English tradition of *ultra vires*, they possess only those powers specifically granted to them, and in the case of conflict with the state, city powers are interpreted narrowly. Small urban places formally are termed local councils, a status which gives them almost as much power as, if not more than, the cities, but which makes them more dependent on the Ministry of Interior for hiring personnel.[8] Both kinds of municipalities are governed by mayors elected directly and by councils elected on the basis of proportional representation, in which the voter casts his vote for a party list rather than for individual candidates, and each party gets the number of seats reflecting the percentage of the total vote it garnered. Frequently, no party gains a majority in the council, and a coalition is formed to govern the city, much as is the case on the state plane. Usually, even parties winning a majority will form coalitions in order to strengthen the hands of the local government or to better distribute local political rewards as part of statewide coalition politics.[9]

Until the introduction of the direct election of mayors, these local governments were miniature parliamentary systems. However, in adapting the law to the constitutional change, a separation-of-powers system was introduced, indeed, one closer to the presidential system of France than to the checks-and-balances system of the United States. In this system, the mayor was given extensive executive powers, minimally dependent upon the council except with regard to budget approval, general legislation, and such oversight as the council might want to undertake (one difference was that the mayor is his own prime minister, since he still presides over the council). At the same time, provisions were introduced into the law making it possible to strengthen the councils as independent bodies. In fact, it is hard to say that the system has changed in more than one or two localities where there were already strong mayors. By and large, the local authorities have followed the country's political custom and maintained a parliamentary system in practice even when it is not required by law.

While cities and local councils are the basic urban municipal units, any two or more can federate with one another to create larger, special-purpose *iggudei 'arim* (confederations of cities) to undertake one or more specifically defined functions. They range from the Lod-Ramle joint high-school district to the confederation of cities of the Dan region, which encompasses the better part of the Tel Aviv metropolitan area and provides several services that seem to be handled best on a metropolitanwide basis.[10]

Israel has also utilized the equivalent of special districts for certain purposes. In Israel, these are called *reshuyot* (authorities). By and large, these authorities handle water drainage and sanitation problems, which require adaptation to watersheds that are less conveniently adapted to existing municipal boundaries. The local religious councils in the Jewish-dominated localities, the local planning committees, and the state-mandated, quasi-independent local agricultural committees established in most former agricultural colonies that have become urbanized are kinds of special districts also.[11]

The cooperative sector is represented locally by local workers' councils, which are elected by vote of all members of the Histadrut within each council's jurisdiction (which, in most cases, more or less conforms to the municipal boundaries). Many of the activities of these public nongovernmental bodies are of a quasi-governmental character, and, because of the power of the Histadrut, they usually wield great political influence. These workers' councils play a role somewhat equivalent to that played by chambers of commerce in small American cities. The fact that workers' councils play a role in Israel similar to that played by businessmen's associations in the United States is a significant indicator of Israel's unique political history and culture.[12]

There are today a total of 1,409 general and special-purpose local authorities functioning in Israel, or approximately one local government per 2,823 inhabitants. Table 5-1 summarizes the kinds of local authorities func-

TABLE 5-1
Local Authorities in Israel

| Type | Number |
| --- | --- |
| Cities | 37 |
| Local councils | 125 |
| Regional councils | 54 |
| Local committees | 825 |
| Confederations of cities | 32 |
| Religious councils | 204 |
| Agricultural committees | 26 |
| Planning committees | 84 |
| Drainage authorities | 22 |
| TOTAL | 1,409 |

tioning in Israel and the number of each. By any standard, that is a high figure. It is particularly high given the strong formal commitment in Israel the nonproliferation of local governments.

Most general-purpose local authorities serve relatively small populations. Tel Aviv, once the largest city in the country and still the central metropolis, has a population of approximately 329,500 and is already on the decline, having peaked at approximately 385,000 a decade ago. It now is undergoing the process of dedensification that has become common in central cities over much of the Western world, as the movement to better housing in newer parts of the metropolitan area, plus urban renewal with the construction of new housing at lower densities, has its impact. Jerusalem now has approximately 415,00 people, and Haifa approximately 227,400. There is a second cluster of five cities with populations between 100,000 and 140,000. The other 141 cities range in size from 80,000 down to 200. The average city size is under 18,000. Table 5-2 classifies Israel's cities by size. Nearly half of the population lives in villages or small cities of under 40,000 inhabitants, while approximately 25 percent live in cities of over 200,000.

Moreover, neighborhoods have real meaning in most cities. In part, they are associated with the very formation of the cities themselves, whose modern founding was the result not only of associations of pioneers established by compact for that specific purpose, but also of a compounding of different neighborhoods, each created independently by a pioneer association and then linked through a second set of compacts to form the present city. Both large and small cities have clearly identified neighborhoods. In fact, it is fair to say that such can be found in any city of over 10,000 population, and in some that are even smaller, because of the history of city building in Israel.[13]

Haifa, where formal neighborhood institutions are strongest and most widespread, reflects this process to the fullest. As each neighborhood merged with the growing city, it preserved a neighborhood committee with specific, if limited, responsibilities for the provision of services and for participation in the development of common citywide services insofar as they affected it. Finally, taking advantage of a provision in the law, the residents of Kiryat Haim, one of the city's neighborhoods, voted to establish a formal elected neighborhood council and to assume the powers to which it was entitled.

Jerusalem was unified by an external decision of the ruling power, but because most of the older neighborhoods represented clearly distinct sociore religious communities, Jewish or Arab, the city has refrained consistently from imposing itself upon them in those fields of particular concern to each. Today it, too, is trying to extend more formal devices for neighborhood participation throughout the city. At this writing, experiments in formally institutionalized self-government are under way in six neighborhoods, both old and new.

In Tel Aviv, the merger of neighborhoods was more thorough, and little, if anything, remains of the earlier framework other than names and recollections. In the past few years, however, the city has made some effort to revive consultative bodies in at least those neighborhoods that have preserved the most distinctive personalities.

Project Renewal has enhanced the already strong neighborhood orientation of Israel's cities. This massive program of urban redevelopment undertaken by the government of Israel, the Jewish Agency, and diaspora Jewry is based on targeting aid to specific neighborhoods through neighborhood steering committees, which bear major responsibility for determining what should be done to improve their neighborhoods. These steering committees determine projects, set priorities, and negotiate with state and diaspora counterparts.[14]

In Israel, as in other parts of the world, there has been occasional pressure to consolidate small local units. Despite the fact that the minister of the interior has full authority to abolish any local unit or consolidate two or more units, this authority has rarely been used, and then only when such a

TABLE 5-2
Israel's Cities by Population Size

| Population Size | Number of Cities |
| --- | --- |
| 200,000+ | 3 |
| 80,000–199,999 | 8 |
| 40,000–79,999 | 9 |
| 20,000–39,999 | 19 |
| 8,000–19,999 | 34 |
| 5,000–7,999 | 31 |
| Under 5,000 | 18 |

move has sufficient political backing from local elites. In the early days of the state, when political elites did not include representatives of the localities in question, more consolidations were effected. In the last two decades, however, even the weakest local governments have acquired political bases of their own, and any moves to consolidate would be strongly resisted. As a result, consolidation efforts essentially have ground to a halt, to be replaced by efforts to organize confederations of cities or interlocal service agreements to undertake those functions that the individual communities cannot undertake by themselves. [15]

The State Commission on Local Government (Sanbar Commission), which completed its work in 1980, rejected the notion of consolidation as a basic tool of local government reform, recommending that it be considered in one or two cases only. After extensive field work, the commission concluded that the civic virtues of the smaller local authorities compensated for most of the disadvantages of their small size and that, through interlocal arrangements based on federative principles, those disadvantages could be overcome.

To date, the confederation-of-cities device generally has been used to undertake functions of metropolitan concern and has been used little in the more rural parts of the country. That is partly because the device was developed to serve cities that adjoin one another, that is to say, those in metropolitan regions. The device has not been extended to free-standing cities within a region, which may be separated by no more than a few miles but which see themselves, and are treated as, totally separate entities. Thus, a certain amount of very real intergovernmental collaboration in planning and service delivery has been developed in the Dan region, which consists of some twenty cities whose boundaries are contiguous with one another. Yet in the Galilee, a region of several hundred thousand people with no single city of 40,000 population but with six cities of over 10,000, all within an area of less than 1,000 square miles, there are relatively few intermunicipal arrangements and little local concern with moving in that direction. That is true even though the region as a whole shares common state facilities (e.g., a large hospital in Safed, university extension courses in that city and near Kiryat Shmona, district offices in Nazareth, and rudimentary sewage treatment facilities near Tiberias) and has the potential for becoming a kind of multinodal metropolitan region of the kind that has developed elsewhere in the world. [16]

## STATE-LOCAL RELATIONS IN A
## GOVERNMENT-PERMEATED SOCIETY

The fact that Israel is a government-permeated society strongly affects state-local relations. One of the major consequences is that local government officials must spend as much time working with outside authorities either to provide or to fund services as they do in directing their own affairs. Another is that local governments have been quite restricted in their ability to finance municipal activities. Relatively few tax resources are at their disposal, and the local share of total governmental expenditures in Israel has been on the decline for nearly twenty years.

By and large, Israeli local governments manage to maintain their freedom of movement by managing deficits rather than through grantsmanship, with the former having become for them the functional equivalent of the latter. There are great restrictions on local government's taxing powers, but there are almost no restrictions on its borrowing powers, providing that any particular local authority can pay the high interest involved. Thus, local authorities borrow heavily from the banks in order to provide services and then turn to the state government to obtain the funds to cover the loans. As long as the services they wish to provide are in line with state policies (and there is almost universal consensus with regard to those services, so that that is not generally an issue) and there is some degree of unanimity within the local ruling coalition with regard to what is being done, the state will—sooner or later—provide the requested funds. Nevertheless, that does mean that the local authorities must spend a large share of their time in negotiations with their state counterparts.[17]

Local leaders are also able to turn, in some matters, to the Jewish Agency, and through it (or even directly, in some cases) to foreign donors, to gain additional resources, mostly for capital investment—e.g., the construction of a new high school, a community center, or a child-care center. Where services are provided directly by the state, local authorities will use their influence to try to negotiate more and better services or to influence those responsible for delivering those services locally, but in this area they are notably less successful than they are in mobilizing funds for their own programs, partly because the Israeli political culture encourages every officeholder to act as independently as possible.[18]

## LOCAL ELECTIONS: SHARPENING THE TREND TOWARD TERRITORIAL DEMOCRACY[19]

At least since 1969, the local elections have been major factors in Israel's transition from ideologically based politics to politics based on territorial subdivisions. Significantly, split-ticket voting—a phenomenon that emerged during the 1960s—continued its upward trend in the elections of the 1970s. It was widely recognized in Israel and hailed throughout the country as a sign of the growing maturity of the electorate. The increase of split-ticket voting should be understood as an indicator of greater political integration. The ability of voters to discriminate between parties and candidates on different governmental planes is a sign of the citizenry's increasing "at-homeness" as members of the body politic. Since political integration, particularly in a democratic society, necessarily must involve greater rootedness within the body politic on the part of the citizenry itself, this measure is important.

An unintegrated citizenry can be brought to the polls by party organizations to vote in overwhelming numbers. Such was the case in Israel in the 1950s and early 1960s, as it was in other countries of immigration during parallel periods in their development. It is clear that the link to politics for the average voter in such circumstances exists only through the mediating force of the organization that provides certain services—frequently apolitical in character—to the new immigrants in return for the right to manipulate their votes.[20] The shift away from this trend in Israel, at first confined to the local elections, led in 1977 to a radical shift in voting for the Knesset and the Likud electoral victory.

Beyond the vote itself, the characters of the candidates and of the campaigns reflect this growing political integration. Increasingly, the candidates represent not only local interests and issues but also a common statewide orientation and style. So, for example, while local lists have proliferated, they rarely present themselves as "ethnic" lists—even when their internal composition reflects a particular local balance between blocs of country-of-origin subcommunities, as in the past. The more successful ones present themselves as "good government" lists, designed to appeal to the voters on the basis of their ability to improve local programs and services (usually by taking a nonpartisan stance vis-à-vis the national parties). In this way, they emphasize what has become a common Israeli phenomenon and deny particularism as such.

The success of local lists in places such as Kfar Shmaryahu, Kiryat Tivon, and Ramat Hasharon, all typical upper-middle-class suburban communities, could well have been forecast by observers familiar with similar phenomena in similar suburban communities in other Western countries. The residents of these communities are oriented toward the separation of local government from the larger political arena, because they perceive local government as a means for providing appropriate services administered efficiently rather than as a vehicle for political activity per se. The emergence of such suburban communities in Israel over the past decade predictably has been accompanied by the emergence of local nonpartisan lists.

The triumph of local lists in cities such as Nahariya, Kiryat Bialik, and Rishon-le-Zion was less predictable but not necessarily surprising. Each is a full-fledged city in its own right, with a distinctive character of its own, even though the latter two have been engulfed by suburbanization in recent years. In all three cases, old elites (the children of older settlers) sought to preserve the character of their communities, and turned to local lists as a means of gaining political control. In 1973, for example, the Nahariya list was called, appropriately enough, Ichpat Lanu (We Care)—a slogan that has been spreading throughout Israel to symbolize a new or revived interest in civic responsibility. In Kiryat Bialik and Rishon-le-Zion, the lists were called

L'maan Kiryat Bialik (For Kiryat Bialik) and L'maan Rishon Le Zion (For Rishon Letzion); that is a more prosaic name, but one that also attempts to convey a sense of local concern. In the latter case, the incumbent mayor broke away from his party (Gahal-Likud) when the party's national headquarters attempted to dictate to him the other candidates on his list, and won a resounding victory.

Perhaps least expected were the triumphs of local lists in three development towns—Kiryat Ono, Kiryat Shmona, and Shderot. In all three cases, personalities who already had established themselves politically were the motivating forces behind the local lists. But in all three, the campaign was based on the same "good government" orientation that had become common countrywide. Again, the names of the lists are significant. In Kiryat Ono, the list was called Hakiryah Shelanu (Our City); in Kiryat Shmona, Hatnua lezechuyot haezrach (Movement for Civil Rights); and in Shderot, L'maan Shderot (For Shderot). In Shderot, for example, the Labor Alignment and its predecessors had been in power for close to twenty years, usually electing a clear majority on the local council. While they retained four of the council's nine seats, the local list also won four—a stunning achievement—and formed a coalition with the ninth man, from the NRP.

The extent of these localistic tendencies is even greater than the statistics reveal. In a number of local authorities, what were actually local lists won under the banner of the national parties. The local appeal of such lists is often revealed by the difference between the vote they received and the local vote for the Knesset. Take the case of Beit Shean, another development town. For several years prior to the 1973 elections, Beit Shean had been governed by a committee appointed by the minister of the interior under his power to dissolve a local council that radically fails to perform its duties. The previous local council had been controlled by the NRP, which normally has a local plurality. It had sunk to a level of inefficiency (and, it is said, corruption) that required this drastic step, one always taken very reluctantly by the state authorities. Local self-government was restored in the 1973 election, when the Labor Alignment, under the leadership of a very attractive local candidate running on a "good government" platform, won an absolute majority on the local council.

In general, where the local branches of the national parties adapted to the new style of politics, they were successful—even in defeating local lists. The Likud lists in Rehovot and Ramat Gan represented two clear examples, especially when contrasted with the situation in Petah Tikvah. In all three cities of roughly similar size and corresponding character, incumbent mayors won reelection—but under very different circumstances.

In Rehovot, the incumbent had proved himself to be a "new-style" mayor after his 1969 election. Hence he was able to gain control of his ticket and sweep to another victory. Advancing to the Knesset in 1977, he subsequently was convicted for accepting a bribe from a contractor.

In Ramat Gan, the incumbent was a relatively unassuming person who had inherited his position when the previous mayor, a legendary figure, died in office at an advanced age. He was not expected to do as well as his predecessor at the polls because of his ostensibly lackluster manner, but he, too, represented the new style and scored a smashing victory. He was reelected easily in 1978 but was defeated by a Sephardic candidate running on the Labor list in 1983, as Ramat Gan took another step down the road to political integration.

On the other hand, the veteran Labor party mayor of Petah Tikvah—perceived by the public to be a classic old-style politician—barely managed to form a coalition to keep himself in office after dropping in strength in the polls. By the end of the decade, he had retired from public life. His successor, also Labor, was at the forefront of the assault on the religious status quo that had prevailed in the city for decades.

The most visible example of this trend was Tel Aviv. There, the Likud headed their list with retired *aluf* (major general) Shlomo Lahat, widely known as "Chich"—a very attractive figure who had been a popular military commander. Lahat's good looks and informal manner make him an archetypical new-style civic leader of the sabra generation; he utilized these characteristics to the fullest in a campaign built almost entirely around him and his personality. In what could only be described as a campaign of innocent earnestness, he proceeded to rake the incumbent administration over the coals. His campaign was made doubly attractive by the fact that his opponent (who subsequently became finance minister in the Rabin government) was characteristically lackluster in the style of the politicians of the 1950s and 1960s, and almost a caricature of the old guard. In fact, the difference between victory and defeat lay in the incumbent's loss of support—because of his outmoded style—among upper-middle-class voters, whom his administration had helped the most.

Lahat's style, combined with the very visible problems of Tel Aviv (which is suffering from the ailments afflicting most contemporary Western central cities), gave the Likud a victory that was touted widely as reflecting the unbeatability of a handsome army officer on the contemporary Israeli political scene. However, the local circumstances that aided Lahat in Tel Aviv should not be taken as being universally applicable. In Rishon-le-Zion that same year, for example, the Labor Alignment, confronted by a popular local incumbent, utilized the same strategy—putting up a retired senior army officer to head its ticket. However, its candidate had only minimal connections with a town whose veteran population has always prided itself on its independence, and whose newcomers may well be seeking refuge from the Tel Aviv syndrome. In the alignment's advertising on his behalf, the best they could claim was that he had been commander of the local Palmach force in 1948. His effort was further complicated by family problems in the latter stages of the campaign, and he was defeated resoundingly.

The trend toward personalization of local elections has continued unabated since 1969, intensified by the introduction in 1978 of the direct election of mayors apart from their party lists. Across the country, outstanding mayoral candidates garner votes far in excess of those cast for their tickets. They have been able to carry lists of virtual unknowns into office on their coattails, while lists not headed by attractive personalities (however defined) have suffered as a result. In many respects, personal elections for mayor came to Israel, de facto, in the 1960s and the formal change in the law merely ratified and regularized what already had become the norm.

## THE LOCALIZATION OF POLITICAL ACTION

The rise of personalities as a factor in local elections is also a reflection of the growing localization of politics in Israel. By the 1973 elections, local party branches already were acting in an increasingly independent fashion. At their most extreme, they rejected all efforts by the party centers to determine who should appear on their local lists and what kind of campaign should be conducted—a posture that would have failed in earlier contests.

In fact, at least until the 1983 elections, there was a steady decline in attempts by party centers to interfere in local ticket making or campaigning. The party leaders apparently calculated that it did not pay to intervene in the case of the smaller localities; in the larger ones, they no longer had as much power to do so. Thus, in most cases, local branches could make their wishes felt on local matters without resorting to extreme measures. In those few cases where party leaders did actively try, they were challenged sharply and lost. After the elections, local branches have insisted on the right to undertake their own coalition negotiations—rather than allow themselves to be pawns in statewide deals by the central party leadership, as generally had been the case in the past. That, indeed, has led to a number of conflicts that became quite public; but these conflicts almost always have been resolved in favor of local autonomy. On the other hand, there are many cases where local party branches may not have undertaken initiatives—not because they were told not to do so, but because they expected the party centers to be opposed, and were unwilling to go against central authority.

In the 1983 municipal elections, there was an atavistic trend twoard national party intervention in several localities. In every case, strong local mayoral candidates succeeded in repelling the efforts, although in some cases the struggle cost them and their parties the elections. For example, the serious defeat of the Likud list in Ramat Gan and the narrow defeat of their incumbent mayor, the same man who had won so handily a decade earlier and was considered one of the most competent mayors in the country, had their origins in the efforts of his party to impose a list on him that went against his wishes. On the other hand, the efforts of the incumbent Labor party mayor of Herzlia to save his seat by bringing in the national party leadership to campaign for him and focus on state issues, failed against a populist challenger who made local issues the centerpiece of his campaign.

One of the decisive cases of central-local conflict in slatemating was that of Rishon-le-Zion in 1973. The incumbent mayor, a businessman and a member of a veteran family in the town, had entered politics in the 1969 elections after achieving public prominence as the head of the local Junior Chamber of Commerce. He had turned the JCs into an engine for civic improvement with considerable success; as a result, he had been elected mayor in 1969 on the Gahal ticket, upsetting the incumbent Labor list. At that time, he and Gahal had joined forces in order to dislodge the Labor party from control of the city. Just before the final filing date for the 1973 elections, the party center (then functioning as the Likud) attempted to force him to accept a ticket consisting of people chosen for internal party consid-erations. The mayor rejected the central body's efforts out of hand and bolted the party; with only a week to go before filing time, he organized his own list—which he then proceeded to lead to a landslide victory at the polls. The same person was subjected to similar pressures in 1978 and 1983, standing them off both times. He finally was defeated that last year by strictly local factors.

Rishon-le-Zion offers an excellent example of a proud, independent city responding to suburbanization by uniting new and old residents alike in an effort to preserve its independence through political means. Its victorious mayoral candidates have become the embodiment of that effort—through vociferous defense of the city's interests against the efforts of the metro-politan region to dump sewage within the municipality's boundaries, and against routing of the major international flight path to Lod Airport over Rishon's populated areas, and by actively resisting central party dictates on the political front.

The wide variety of electoral and political responses in the Tel Aviv metropolitan area is a very real indicator of the growing localization of Israeli politics. The usual statistical measures of socioeconomic and demographic variables tend to portray the region as being substantially homogeneous. Most of the governmental reforms that have been proposed for the region have been based on assumptions derived from that portrayal. The local election contests, on the other hand, demonstrate the great diversity within the region; it is being expressed more clearly and forcefully through the politics of the local authorities now than at any time since the establishment of the state.

## INCREASING LOCAL DIFFERENTIATION

What is true of the Tel Aviv region is true of the country as a whole. Hence, even more striking than the localization of local politics in Israel is the increasing differentiation in the character (political and otherwise) of the various cities, towns, and regions within the country. The two phenomena are, of course, closely linked. Indeed, a strong case can be made that it is the growth of local differentiation that has encouraged localization. Moreover, local differentiation has developed hand in hand with increased statewide political integration.

The paradox is more apparent than real. Based on evidence accumulated in recent years, it is reasonable to hypothesize that under the conditions that sustain pluralist democracy in its various forms, increasing political integration can stimulate internal differentiation on new planes. Thus, in polities benefiting from these conditions, integration and differentiation go hand in hand; with increased political integration bringing new forms of local and regional differentiation on new levels, Israel offers a fertile field for testing this hypothesis—particularly since the overwhelming majority of its cities, towns, and villages, emerged within the same two-generation period as did the state, pioneered by the same elements, under the same conditions. Despite the potentiality for sameness that this situation offers, they are acquiring quite distinct characteristics in the course of becoming rooted communities, even as the state is becoming better integrated politically.

In part, that is a reflection of the fact that different ideological, country-of-origin, and occupational groups were settled willy-nilly in different localities. These differences may be the result of a) ideological choices on the part of the original settlers themselves (particularly in the case of settlements founded before the state); b) the settlement of immigrant groups on the basis of when they arrived in the country (particularly in the case of those founded in the state's early years); or c) conscious planning on the part of the authorities (particularly in more recent years)—or some combination of the three. This process alone would have produced a certain amount of differentation, and has.

Even where the same kinds of people were settled in different places, the order of their arrival created its own patterns of differentiation. Moreover, the kinds of occupations in which the first arrivals were able to engage established local status systems that are, to some extent at least, specifically local in character. In general, economic circumstances have contributed to local differentiation. When combined with location, these circumstances have played a major role in determining whether a community would be relatively stable in its population or would have a great deal of population turnover. Migration itself is another factor promoting differentation. Either initially or subsequent to their initial settlement, most individuals and families have been free to make their own choices insofar as they have the means to do so; thus, population shifts have taken place to shape the character of local communities.

Finally, history—even the brief history of communities in Israel—brings about its own differentiation. Precedents are established; certain people acquire position and power and put their own stamp on local affairs; traditions emerge; and a local pattern of doing business is forged. Institutions—even ones mandated centrally for every settlement—develop differentially on the basis of local circumstances, thus solidifying certain patterns and preventing the development of others. The result is the emergence of what can only be described as separate "personalities" for each community. These differential characteristics, in turn, influence future developments, attracting or repelling both people from the outside and those born locally.

The local election results serve as indicators of this increasing local differentiation. The cases already cited are revealing, and there are many other examples. Take the country's three largest cities. In Tel Aviv and Haifa, men have been elected to the mayorality on the basis of radically contradictory appeals.

In 1973, Shlomo Lahat emerged as Tel Aviv's largest vote-getter by promising to focus City Hall on the problems of Tel Aviv. In his campaign, he argued against the kind of statewide party political involvement that had been characteristic of the politically powerful Labor Alignment administration that had preceded him. A great part of his appeal was that, although he represented the country's second-largest party bloc, it was apparent that his own interests would be oriented not toward the state's party politics but, rather, toward relatively nonpartisan involvement in Tel Aviv alone. The size and special diversity of Tel Aviv made him a most suitable candidate; in a smaller city, his particular background, lack of local connections, and inexperience in local affairs might well have worked against him. Lahat, as promised, turned his attention to the most local problems: parking, traffic, clean streets, and the like.

Lahat has had a rocky career as mayor but won reelection in 1978 and 1983 by continuing the initial thrust of his first campaign. He has fought for Tel Aviv against the government led by his own party hardly less than he fought against the Labor government prior to May 1977. He has championed the city's middle classes and their interests and has promoted Tel Aviv's distinctive role as the country's commercial, entertainment, and artistic center. He has gotten into trouble with the city's poor, the organized Sephardic population, and the religious community as a result of his policies, but in doing so he has established himself with the dominant elements in Tel Aviv.[21]

Haifa has had three mayors in as many terms, with none able to inherit the position of the legendary Abba Khushi, Labor mayor-boss of the city for most of the first generation of statehood. Each of the three has campaigned for mayor by arguing that he would put Haifa on the map, claiming that Haifa did not have its fair share of statewide political power and was not receiving the recognition and benefits due it as the country's third city—an approach exactly opposite to Lahat's neoisolationist campaign. In 1973, Yosef Almogi, labor minister in the outgoing government and long-time political power in the Haifa region, took over the leadership of the alignment list. From the moment of his election, Almogi struggled to build up Haifa's role as an innovative force for the state, but, as a veteran party figure, he was drafted to become chairman of the executive of the Jewish Agency and left the mayor's office before he could accomplish anything. His two successors have been local men with no visibility beyond Haifa. Both have pursued similar policies, but with little result. Haifa has remained in Labor hands, however, despite a 1983 challenge by colorful Likud figures. Lack of unity in Likud ranks and Haifa's still-strong Labor organization have made the difference.[22]

Jerusalem is the only one of the three major cities where aesthetic and environmental considerations figure significantly in local election campaigns, although grounds for raising such concerns are present in all three (as they are in every Israeli city). The specific character of the city is always a major factor in setting the focus of the campaign. While Jerusalem may not be more beautiful than Haifa, its historical position renders it more subject to aesthetic and environmental concern; it attracts people through a combination of historical, religious, and aesthetic attractions. Thus, a mayor cannot be committed to development above all—in the manner that has characterized Israel, as it has most developing countries. Teddy Kollek, mayor since 1965, found out in the late 1960s and early 1970s that he engendered a certain amount of very tenacious opposition when he applied that outlook to Jerusalem. Since then, he has been careful to balance development with aesthetic interests and, indeed, has become the agent for the beautification of Jerusalem.

Since those early experiences, Kollek has approached Jerusalem as a steward of a great treasure, and has been successful in return. His reelection to a fifth term in 1983 by an overwhelming majority is testimony to that fact. He had defined the mayor's role as conciliator of the diverse communities, Jewish and non-Jewish, living within the city and has encouraged both their separate development according to their own ways of life and their cooperation where necessary for the common good. In the process, he has become the world's number one mayor—a mayor's mayor, as it were.[23]

It could have been expected that the country's largest cities would develop distinctive political patterns, just as they have developed their own personalities in other respects. But the same phenomenon has made its appearance in smaller cities, as well—including those within the Tel Aviv metropolitan region, where conventional reformist wisdom has it that suburbanization had created a single metropolis of a million people. In fact, however, the region has relatively few suburbs in the currently accepted sense of the term. The overwhelming majority of the municipalities serve settlements that had been founded independently, even though subsequently they may have become engulfed by suburbanization. Even the commuting patterns in the area do not simply extend from Tel Aviv to peripheral dormitory settlements, but are becoming increasingly matrix-like—cutting across the metropolitan region in a variety of directions because the larger cities in the region are independent magnets in their own right. As a matter of fact, while Tel Aviv is the commerical and cultural center of the region and the country as a whole, it shares political and economic power with Jerusalem and Haifa in a manner more characteristic of large federal systems than of small unitary states.

Within the Tel Aviv region, Ramat Gan, Givatyim, and B'nei Brak—three adjoining cities—serve as major commercial and cultural foci with distinctive local characteristics. The first is a bourgeous city *par excellence*, and an alternative commercial center to Tel Aviv. The second is a workers' town, and the third is the seat of ultra-Orthodoxy in Israel, rivaled only by Jerusalem. Industry is scattered throughout the region; the largest single employer, Israel Aircraft Industries, is located at the region's eastern periphery, near Ben-Gurion Airport, and draws employees from the eastern ring of towns in an arc from north to south. Each municipality had developed a politics of its own to go with its particular location, economic base, and demographic composition.

For many years, the physical appearance of the development towns was one of bland sameness—differentiated only by the fact that in different years the central authorities used different architectural and town-planning styles. Of late, however, these towns also have acquired increasingly differentiated characteristics. Take, for example, Netivot, Ofakim, and Shderot—three development towns founded at approximately the same time along the road between Ashkelon and Beersheba, a few kilometers from one another. In Netivot, a progressive group attained power in 1973 by gaining control of the local NRP branch, in a manner particularly appropriate to a town whose population is overwhelmingly religious. They held on for a decade, until ruptured by the 1981 split in the NRP, and brought considerable new development to their town. In Shderot—which voted overwhelmingly for the Labor Alignment in Knesset and local elections until 1973—the same kind of local progressive movement achieved power through an independent local list but was unable to move the town forward to any great degree. Ofakim did not undergo the kind of political change that could make a difference in the quality of life until the introduction of Project Renewal from the outside after 1977. It remains the least politically advanced of the three towns. The differences among the three can be traced to a) differences in the composition of their respective populations, b) differences in their respective economic situations created by local and statewide considerations, and c) differences in the quality of their leadership. What is significant for our purposes here is that such real differences have emerged in so short a period of time.

The sum and substance of the foregoing is a strengthening of territorial democracy—both within the framework of the state's federated party system and, to some extent, beyond it. Localities increasingly are finding ways to express territorially rooted interests through political means; that is a matter of great necessity in a civil society dominated by politics, where even the economic sphere is subordinated to political concerns at almost every turn. In this respect, Israel is following a trend toward decentralization that seems to be worldwide.

The course of this pattern in Israel runs roughly as follows: From 1948 until the early 1960s, the trend was predominantly one of centralization. The state, animated by David Ben-Gurion's mamlachtiut philosophy, absorbed functions which in the prestate yishuv had been in the hands of local, voluntary, or party bodies. At the same time, the need for local administration even in a small centralized state, combined with the democratic values of Israel's leadership, led to the quiet creation of local self-government for both Jews and Arabs. Local government law was regularized, and new settlements acquired local governmental authority. From the mid-1960s onward, a trend toward decentralization has taken on greater intensity through the growth of local political power. Much of this trend is not visible in formal legislation, or even in the administrative orders upon which so much of the government of Israel is based. In characteristically Israeli fashion, there remains a wide gap between the formal framework, which is still pyramidlike in almost every respect, and the actual matrix of power relationships within the country.

Obviously, in neither case have all forces and factors led in the same direction. Contradictory developments abound, but overall, the pattern seems to be reasonably clear. In the earlier period of centralization, a basis was laid for local self-government; in the present period of increasing local power, new plateaus of statewide political integration are being attained.

The trend toward decentralization has been aided by two locally linked phenomena. First, the sheer growth in size of the individual municipalities has strengthened the ability of local authorities to accept serious responsibility and make decisions with greater independence. There are approximately 27 cities of over 30,000 population in the state today, and another five are approaching that figure; these have attained sufficient critical mass to undertake the responsibilities entrusted to them by the state or by their citizens. That, in itself, makes a big difference.

Beyond that, there is an emergent local leadership able to undertake the tasks that need to be undertaken, and eager to do so, if only as a result of natural ambitions. Thus, Israel's shift from the peak of centralization into a period of greater decentralization has been assisted by the new-style politics emerging in locality after locality across the country. By 1977, a few of these new leaders began to move into the Knesset, given new opportunities by the Likud victory. They soon demonstrated their competence in the state arena. The 1981 Knesset elections brought more of them to the fore in state politics. Some gave up their local posts, while others sought to combine state and local office. After 1981, twenty-two Knesset members also held local office, most as mayors of smaller cities. The localities may well be generating the most dynamic political leadership in Israel today. The question remains: Will all that lead to structural and institutional changes that will close the gap between the formal and the informal distribution of power in the state?

# SIX

## Serving the Public in an Emergent Society

### A GOVERNMENT-PERMEATED SOCIETY

As a general rule, Israel's public services are provided through complicated sharing arrangements involving national, state, local, cooperative, and private institutions. The fact that Israel is a government-permeated society has a major influence on those arrangements. Because it is a compound polity, the arrangements are additionally complex. A small country divided into a relatively large number of local jurisdictions, Israel reflects many of the advantages of small to moderate scale. Its history of development of multiple jurisdictions to handle specialized local governmental tasks, despite a formal tradition that denigrates that approach, suggests how natural that approach may be, regardless of other factors militating for or against it. At the same time, Israel's special political culture and a strong tendency toward bureaucratization in the country influence the impact of scale. Many services that in other countries are provided by municipal authorities are provided directly by the state in Israel. Still others are provided by the Histadrut and the cooperative sector (e.g., the bus system) but are linked closely to state services or policies.

Increasingly over the years, the situation of permanent crisis in which Israel finds itself has led to heavy strains on government budgeting. An inordinate share of the gross national product has to be devoted to defense, and there is great dependence upon externally generated funds, whether from the Jewish communities around the world or aid from foreign governments, particularly the United States.[1] As a result, the finance ministry has acquired extraordinary powers, not only in budgeting funds but in allocating and transferring funds already budgeted and appropriated. The finance ministry's power in this regard has been a feature of Israeli government since the early days of the state. It has become intensified since the mid-1970s, however, as a result of the country's high inflation rate, which makes budgeting virtually impossible and, in effect, gives the finance ministry a blank check as to how to pass our supplementary funds that are needed on an almost monthly basis, as the bills come off the government printing presses. As a consequence, every other ministry must come hat in hand to the finance ministry, while local governments have been quite restricted in their ability to finance their own activities. Relatively few tax resources are at their disposal. While the state provides remuneration for tax resources that it has taken from the localities over the years, the exact scope of the remuneration is a matter of continuing struggle.[2]

## THE SHAPING OF PUBLIC DEMANDS

The strongest single factor in shaping public demands in Israel until recently was the socialist ideology that predominated among the country's founders. So pervasive was this socialism that even the Israeli right wing was essentially committed to a government-permeated society. Only a small group of liberals in the center professed a different view, and it is hard to know whether their profession would have been echoed in reality, since they never really had a chance to try to implement their ideology. Israeli socialism always had a strong admixture of statism, although if there were differences between left and right, it was that the further left one went as a socialist within the Zionist camp, the more likely one was to favor small-scale collective or cooperative enterprises as the building blocks of the new society, while the further right one went into the nationalist camp, the more one found a purely statist ideology that expected the role of government to be very large indeed. In almost every case, Israelis assumed that if it was to be public in the first place, it should be governmental. Only the lack of a state prevented that from happening prior to 1948. That meant that public demands tended to be directed toward governmental action, at best in cooperation with public nongovernmental bodies that would be dependent upon governmental financial aid and political support, and otherwise activities that would be fully in the hands of the government. Thus, the understanding of public demand in Israel must begin with an understanding of how statist and government-permeated Israeli society is by design.

Even when the mass migration after 1948 brought in a population that was not socialized politically within the framework of the prevailing ideologies, there was little change in the character of public demands. It should be recalled that most of the Jews who came to the country came after the state was established, and not as pioneers. In general, they had very low expectations regarding government services, and even lower expectations regarding their ability to participate in or even influence the shape of those government services. The expectations of the Arabs, on both counts, were even lower. At the same time, many of the Jews, at least, were ambivalent, in that they saw the new state as a messianic achievement and hence expected its government to solve all personal problems of housing and employment in a very paternalistic way.

As the population acquired an understanding of modern democratic government, especially in its welfare state form, their demands intensified, passing, in some cases, from passivity to almost unrestrained insistence on having their way. With this escalation of demands came an escalation of complaints about the way in which services were delivered, albeit without a corresponding increase in the desire to participate on a general basis. Individuals would seek to influence those responsible for service delivery in specific cases affecting them, relying heavily on personal contacts to do so, but saw no general role for themselves as participants in the political process. That is changing slowly now, as more and more native-born Israelis reflect the socialization process of the school system and what we have come to associate generally with middle-class values in the political sphere.[3]

The network of interest groups in Israel not only is as complex as in any other Western state but is made additionally complicated by the role of government in connection with virtually all of them. Precisely because the prevailing ideology was that nothing should occur in the country without some government involvement, the government actually stimulated interest-group activity in the 1950s and 1960s, often subsidizing the organization and maintenance of such groups. On one hand, that gave the various ministries influence in their activities. On the other, it tied the government to them, as well, so that for most of them, and certainly for the more important ones, the government could not back away from their demands any more than they could back away from the government's policies.

Were that to have been a neat arrangement, it could have been considered to be a kind of Bolshevik or corporatist organization of society, but it is not at all neat and certainly not hierarchical. Instead, what one finds are groups making mutual demands on one another, and everyone locked into what variously has been described as a jigsaw puzzle or a house of cards, where, at the very least, the removal of any piece is immediately obvious and keeps the picture from being complete, and, at the worst, the removal of any card brings the house tumbling down. This situation developed very quietly, and it was only in the mid-1980s, when Israel entered a deep economic crisis, that the consequences of this high level of interdependence became painfully obvious. The government could not cut its budget sufficiently because it could not sufficiently cut any individual recipient of its largesse. It could not allow inefficient industries to close down, because the industries or their workers had claims on the government that the latter itself had fostered. In short, while there are rarely visible public demands, there are myriad private demands, to the degree that even the ministries and departments of the government are tied individually into the system of privatized demands more than they are articulators of public ones.

With that initial understanding, it is possible to identify three sources that do try to articulate and aggregate demands on a public basis. First of all, there are the mass protest groups. Perhaps foremost among them are those groups which protest a particular government's foreign or defense policies. They first became prominent in the 1950s, in the protest against the government's decision to accept German reparations. They surfaced again in 1974, in the aftermath of the Yom Kippur War, when they brought down the government responsible for Israel's lack of preparedness. They reemerged in

1982 in opposition to the Lebanon war. Clearly, only major events are likely to provoke mass organization and protest of this kind.

Somewhat less prominent but more frequent are the mass demonstrations surrounding ideological issues within Israeli society, principally having to do with the relation between religion and state and, since 1967, with the question of Jewish settlement in Judea, Samaria, and Gaza. These demonstrations rarely achieve the scale or the results of the first category, but they are a constant recurrence in Israeli society. Finally, there are the protest groups organized by the disadvantaged members of Israeli society, the immigrants from Africa and Asia and their children who have been left behind in the general upward mobility of the population. Periodically they put forward substantial claims on the state and local authorities, particularly in the areas of education and housing, on the grounds that they are suffering from discrimination and lack of equal opportunity. By and large, the form of those demands has followed traditional lines of protest rather than systematic efforts to transform the present situation.[4] Moreover, since the introduction in 1978 of Project Renewal, a massive statewide program of physical, social, and economic rehabilitation of disadvantaged neighborhoods, these protest efforts have been muted.

A second source consists of those with special interests in some service or service sector, who try to mobilize public support to secure better services in the realm of their interest. Those realms range from consumer protection to services for the mentally handicapped, from nature preservation to the provision of ritual baths for Orthodox Jews. Primarily middle-class in character, this source is a growing, albeit still small, segment of activists.[5] These groups represent an effort to deal with what is missing from the complex of services that have grown up to date and a response to the bureaucratization that has taken place in the administration and delivery of these services.

Israel hardly can be faulted for avoiding the delivery of social services. Quite to the contrary, it is a quintessential welfare state whose government and people almost invariably are willing to accept any reasonable justification to provide an additional service to some group in need. On the other hand, Israel has a mixed record in responding to certain interests, in part because of the uneven response generated by the uneven distribution of political power, as in any other political system; in part because of time lags between the development of new forms of service in other countries and their introduction in Israel; and in part because of bureaucratic inertia that does not look favorably on change in Israel any more than anywhere else.

Since Israelis tend to be very much involved in learning about the latest developments in every field, there are those within the system who are constantly pushing for change. They constitute the third source of demand articulation—those members of the academic and civil service communities who study Israel's social and economic problems and make recommendations for their resolution or improvement. By and large, these people have been tempted to follow conventional Western European and American thinking on those subjects, accepting the welfare, management-oriented, and statist reformism of the twentieth-century West. However, virtually all of those who have been in responsible positions have, whether for reasons of political prudence or intellectual skepticism, refrained from pursuing those ideas very far. Indeed, they more often than not end up endorsing the status quo because of their own links within the system.

More recently, there has emerged a small but significant group of academic dissenters who share many of the views of the "public choice" school, certainly with regard to public service delivery. They are impressed by the empirical evidence that the theses of the management and statist models regarding centralization, size, fragmentation, overlap, and the like are inadequate, if not just plain wrong. Some have done theoretical work to demonstrate that such things as "urban sprawl" are economically valuable aids rather than hindrances to metropolitan development.[6] Others have translated articles into Hebrew presenting the public-choice hypothesis. Still others are doing empirical research into problems of size and scale from a sociological perspective, whose results are strengthening the public-choice theses.[7] Finally, a group of free marketeers has emerged in recent years, albeit still without influence.[8]

Whether these forces are sufficient to overcome bureaucratic inertia and the natural preference of people who have grown accustomed to a hierarchical system of service organization to maintain that system is an open question. What is clear is that the political culture of Israel acts as a strong bulwark against changes in the present system. Perhaps as the Israeli political culture takes on a more consistent and harmonious character, the combination of a decentralized, hierarchical structure with a network of contractual agreements will prove to be dysfunctional, and one or the other aspect will undergo serious modification.

One of the factors that unquestionably has helped to limit demand pressures of a painful kind has been a relative avoidance of the problem of proportioning supply to demand on the part of the Israeli authorities, particularly, but not exclusively, the central authorities. By and large, until the end of the 1970s, state officials operated as if there were no need to limit their responses to what were otherwise legitimate demands. In general, Israel is a country in which political decisions are determinative even in economic situations, which means that requests are evaluated from the point of view of the social goals of the state and the political goals of the parties in power. Since the two can be made reinforcing and in both cases are likely to lead to more rather than less expenditure, the tendency has been to approve requests for funds and programs and then to worry about raising the money—outside Israel if it was otherwise unavailable inside (and Israelis consistently have been the highest-taxed population in the world). Of course, that meant that the authorities could respond to even modest citizen pressures in turn.[9]

The necessity for drastic belt tightening first became apparent after the Yom Kippur War but became imperative only in the 1980s. By 1984, new demands could not be met, and existing services even were cut back as the gap between the state's income and expenditures grew drastically and inflation got out of hand. That may lead to some greater effort to proportion supply to demand on the basis of economic criteria, but it is too early to suggest that an appropriate effort has been forthcoming. Needless to say, democratic pressure politics do not encourage any such effort, nor is there any clearly rational means for arriving at the requisite decisions.

Perhaps the one segment of the country in which this question has been addressed consistently is the kibbutzim, where the fact that all income is held in common has led to a regular consideration of the allocation of the surplus. Thus, in many kibbutzim there were for years running arguments as to whether the members' apartments should be enlarged so that they could house their young children at home instead of in the children's house, or whether amenities such as longer vacations and television sets should be distributed—a position favored by many of the older members, who did not stand to benefit from enlarged housing but did want to enjoy additional amenities after years of pioneering. In almost every case, the issue finally was resolved in favor of enlarging the apartments, as the older members perceived that the younger ones were beginning to leave the kibbutz because they wanted to have their children at home and could not under existing conditions. What is clear about the way in which such issues are disposed of in the kibbutz is not that kibbutz members turn out to be more enlightened human beings than their fellows, but that the face-to-face contact involved in kibbutz life makes possible more rational deliberation, in the classic meaning of the term, and a true shaping of opinion in such a way as to reach an intelligent result.[10]

## PROVIDING SPECIFIC SERVICES: PARADIGMATIC CASES

### Police

The police force in Israel is an instrumentality of the state, directly controlled by the Ministry of Police, as was the case under Ottoman and British rule. All police officers are part of the central government police force, although every community of significant size has its own police station attached to it, and in the course of time relations develop between the police officers stationed locally (many of whom are likely to live in the locality) and the local authorities. The quality of those relationships is determined principally by the personal chemistry between the mayor and the local police chief. Nevertheless, it is fair to say that, except in exceptional circumstances, the local authorities do not have any significant influence over the work of the police. The citizenry has even less, particularly since, while Israel generally has a tradition of maintaining the civil rights of individuals, there are fewer channels of citizen recourse for dealing with specific police violations of those rights than there are in the English-speaking countries.[11]

Perhaps the greatest force for enabling citizens to influence the police is the political culture, which makes it possible for any citizen to attempt to convince a policeman or policewoman to change his or her line of action in a matter of personal interest on grounds of justice or mercy, simply on the basis of bargaining and persuasion. This method tends to be most effective when showing mercy is involved, whether in the matter of not giving a traffic ticket or of not arresting someone who has been involved in a near-violent argument. The general tendency to mercifulness in the local culture tends to emerge at such times, and it is possible to play upon a police officer's sympathies. However, that is essentially a petitionary approach; citizens are far less successful when they base their claims on civil-rights grounds.[12]

While little has been done in the way of empirical study of the police, the force generally is considered both efficient and effective in ordinary matters and has suffered from a minimum of corruption over the years. In matters affecting security and the kind of personal considerations mentioned above, the police generally are considered responsive—in the former case because an awareness of a common problem of the utmost gravity leads them to spare no efforts to respond to citizen requests, no matter how far-fetched they might seem (one never knows whether a terrorist has really left a bomb or whether the sack of garbage out of place really is just that), and in the latter case because of the network of interpersonal relations that is characteristic of Israeli society and makes people wary of rejecting human overtures by failing to give a human response.

Police are considered less efficient, effective, or responsive in matters regarding burglary or the destruction of property—partly because this problem is on the increase and is much more difficult to deal with than most others, as policemen throughout the world have discovered, and partly because in general there seems to be an element in Jewish culture that views destruction of property as relatively unserious, particularly when compared to questions of life and health. Indeed, the fact that this value is shared allows the police even more latitude in this regard, since the victim of a robbery is likely to feel that as long as he or she has come through unscathed (and professional burglars in Israel—as distinct from drug addicts—are not given to physical violence), matters are tolerable.

Violent crime is on the rise in Israel, somewhat belatedly given worldwide trends. Here the police have not demonstrated sufficient capacity to deal with a kind of criminal behavior not known in the past. It is in this area where changes in police performance are needed.

In summarizing the relationship between structure and performance in service delivery with regard to the police, it would have to be said that since the force is organized on a countrywide basis and not locally, smallness of scale does not seem to be an immediate factor in stimulating effectiveness, efficiency, or responsiveness. However, a deeper look would show that the overall characteristics of Israel as a small society with strong interpersonal connections that cut across most social divisions, do function to prevent the impersonality that could arise—and seems to have arisen in many American local jurisdictions of similar size with regard to relations between police and public. On the other hand, because the police force is a state police, there is a lack of enforcement of local ordinances relating to health and safety, because they occupy a low place on the list of police priorities. To a limited extent, the municipalities have been empowered to appoint inspectors who can at least issue summonses for violations, but all local requests to establish local police forces have been turned down—despite the recommendation of the State Commission on Local Government in 1980 to permit the establishment of local police forces to supplement the state police.

## Education[13]

Elementary and secondary education is provided by a partnership between state and local authorities in Israel. The Ministry of Education funds all the operating costs of the regular elementary education program and the middle schools, and provides basic funding for the high schools. Teachers are certified and employed by the Ministry of Education but hired by the principals of each school. The principals, in turn, are appointed by the municipal education department from an approved list prepared by the ministry. Municipalities handle whatever tasks are devolved upon them in school matters, generally through a vice-mayor for education and an education committee of the council.

Despite this apparently highly centralized structure, education in Israel in fact is rather decentralized. The local authorities are responsible for providing and maintaining school buildings and equipment (including texts, based upon ministry lists), managing the schools, and registering and enrolling the students, and for virtually all ancillary and enrichment programs, beginning with prekindergarten education. Kindergartens, prekindergarten education, and high schools are the direct responsibility of the local authorities, albeit with financial and technical assistance from the Ministry of Education. In part, that is because the state has determined that it cannot yet afford to provide free pre-first-grade education and cannot cover all tuition costs of high-school education. Thus, tuition is charged for these programs—in the case of pre-first-grade education, a very nominal sum; in the case of high schools, a supplementary one. The Ministry of Education provides funds that enable this tuition to be waived in whole or in part in deserving cases. Thus, the local departments of education are in a key position to direct local educational affairs, and since the ancillary and enrichment services are becoming an ever larger part of every school's program, their influence is expanding.

Matters are additionally complicated, however, by two other factors. First is the division of the public or state schools into several distinctive units. Within the Jewish community, there are separate state and state-religious schools, the latter embracing approximately one-fourth of the total student population within the state system, each with its own department within the Ministry of Education and within each local office of education.[14] In addition, the state provides support almost equal to that given the state schools to an independent school system serving the ultra-Orthodox religious community, who are not prepared for what they conceive to be the compromises with Western secular civilization made by the state religious schools.[15] The state also maintains a network of Arabic schools for the Arabic-speaking minority.[16] Schools in the kibbutzim, while linked nominally to one of the two state systems, represent another subsystem, because of the particular orientations of the kibbutz movements.[17]

More recently, there have been several subtrends developed within the general state school system. The first was an experimental education trend, emphasizing more open classrooms and student-initiated studies. Then a state traditional trend was initiated, designed to provide non-Orthodox religious education within the state school system. Most recently, efforts have been made to revive a state Labor trend, to provide a socialist education for those families who want that emphasis. While all three are still minor elements in the state school system, they reflect Israel's commitment to educational diversity. These variations have been established within the framework of a state law that provides that parents can request variations in up to 25 percent of the curriculum of the school their children attend, which gives them a great deal of flexibility indeed. Each of these subsystems has its own set of educational goals, which reflect strong religious, ideological, or cultural predispositions and which make them somewhat less than amenable to outside interference. In a political system in which pluralism has become consociational in character, their claims to autonomy are recognized widely.

Furthermore, every school principal is almost sovereign when it comes to matters within his or her sphere of competence, which is quite a broad one. The law provides that every principal has a right to change up to 25 percent of the curriculum established by the Ministry of Education. Any educator knows that, given the extent to which certain subjects are commonly accepted as necessary in any school system, that percentage nearly encompasses whatever room for maneuver would be available even under an optimally flexible situation, and may well exceed it. When principal and parents are united in their commitment to a specific trend or direction for their school, they have great power to implement it.

An empirical confirmation of the principal's powers can be found in the fact that when a new school is opened, it rarely is opened as an independent institution, but rather as a branch of an existing school until it passes through a "colonial" period of development and is deemed by the local department of education to be entitled to autonomy. Were it to be established as an independent school in the first place, with its own principal, everyone knows that for all intents and purposes there would be almost no controlling it.

Some schools, indeed, never become independent but remain branches of others for one reason or another.

There are historical reasons for this situation, resting on the fact that the schools, like the rest of the state, were built from the bottom up, with parents and local branches of movements coming together to found individual schools before there was any central educational authority. The significance of this process was compounded by the fact that in a revolutionary situation, every educational institution was designed to foster the norms of the new society among the new generation, including whatever specific version of those norms a particular school represented. As a result, virtually every school became a bastion of ideological, as well as social and intellectual, development, as much a key element in the struggle for the creation of the new Jewish society as any army unit possibly could be. Principals and teachers were powerful figures—the colonels, captains, and lieutenants in the struggle for national revival. Given the Jewish cultural predisposition toward treating learning and teaching with the utmost seriousness, this condition was intensified even further. The end result was the coalescence of a number of individual schools into several independent "trends": A Labor trend, which emphasized socialist-Zionist education; a nonsocialist, General Zionist trend; a religious Zionist trend; and an ultra-Orthodox non-Zionist trend.

Once the state was established, it became inevitable that the schools would be welded together into a system, although the precise character of that system emerged only after a considerable political controversy in the early 1950s. While the schools formally had no choice in the matter, when they were compounded together to create the present system and sub-systems, the principals and teachers were able to preserve many of their erstwhile prerogatives, formally or informally. As is usually the case in democracies, compromises were reached in the process of reorganization that have become sanctified over time. The end result was a state system whose major component was a continuation of the Labor trend drastically denatured as the state general schools, and a separate religious Zionist trend as the state religious schools. The ultra-Orthodox trend was transformed into the independent school system with state support. Only the General Zionists, who had pressed for the reform in the first place, lost their separate school system.[18]

What of the parents in this situation? Education is one area in which there is a great deal of parental concern—if not a desire to participate in the educational process as such, certainly a desire to determine what process will involve their children and under what conditions the children will be learning. The parental role is manifested in several ways. In the first place, it is a matter of principle that parents must be involved in the education of their children. The school day in Israel is relatively short and the amount of homework great, on the assumption that the parents will undertake some of the responsibilities of teaching and will help their children with their homework. Thus, the parents are built into the system whether they like it or not. (That has led to some problems in the case of children of families from educationally deprived backgrounds whose parents cannot help them. Some efforts have been made to provide a corrective for this situation by providing study halls in community centers and local libraries, but the principle of parental involvement has been neither challenged nor limited in any way.)

By law, parents have the right to choose the school subsystem in which their children will be enrolled. The law mandates local authorities to provide appropriate school facilities, and the Ministry of Education must provide the funds for constructing the necessary buildings and providing the teachers once the local authority certifies that the requisite school population exists for one subsystem or another.

At one time, parents had completely free choice with regard to the specific school to which they would send their children, a relic of the prestate days. Today, districting and neighborhood schools exist in principle, but parents generally are able to choose the school for their children that they find desirable from their point of view (they like the principal and his or her approach, they like the environment, the potential classmates, or whatever). Moreover, the local authorities themselves are prone to circumvent their own districting if they believe that a school will be better balanced by mixing students from different neighborhoods, provided they can persuade the parents accordingly. Many parents of Ashkenazic background try to avoid sending their children to schools in which there are large numbers of Jews from the Arabic-speaking countries, on the grounds that the level of those schools is inferior. As a consequence, some local authorities aggressively pursue integration; others do so less. In every case, they must, in effect, negotiate with the parents involved, or else the parents will take energetic action to protest the decision, whatever it may be.

Parents additionally involve themselves in the schools on a regular basis through parent associations, parent-teacher conferences, and a sheer feeling of freedom to visit the school and speak to their child's principal or teacher at will. In fact, there is close contact between principals, teachers, and parents in most cases, because of the educational tradition that has been fostered in Israel. The parents' right to alter up to 25 percent of the curriculum of their school, in consultation with the principal, is limited by the reality that, outside the kibbutzim and examples mentioned above, there is not 25 percent of the curriculum that any but a handful of parents would want to alter, for good or for ill.

The same subsystems prevail on the high-school level as on the elementary. The major unifying force is the system of matriculation examinations required by the Ministry of Education and prepared, administered, and graded by Ministry of Education personnel on a uniform basis throughout the country. What is true of the elementary schools is even more true in the case of high schools. In the days before the spread of university education, the high schools possessed the status of colleges; their teachers were often great scholars, and the principals, lords. Every school had a very definite point of view, orientation, and even methodology. Many were sponsored by the national institutions of the Jewish people rather than by indigenous public institutions, a situation that continues to prevail. Thus, technical schools are mainly in the province of ORT (the Organization for Rehabilitation and Training, a worldwide Jewish body), and even today most high schools are built (though not administered) through special donations from diaspora Jews channeled through the Jewish Agency.

*Welfare*[19]

Welfare is a cooperative state-local service, in which recipients are funded through the National Insurance Institute, the Israeli equivalent of the Social Security Administration, out of its central office in Jerusalem, while the municipal welfare offices certify eligibility and provide social programs funded in all or in part by the Ministry of Welfare. The operation of the programs encompassed within this service is similar to that of grant-in-aid programs in other countries. The localities have essentially complete responsibility for determining who is eligible under general criteria promulgated by the National Insurance Institution. They create the packages of welfare benefits to be given to any individual or family on the basis of the various programs provided by law, and they furnish the social services needed to assist the family in rehabilitation or adjustment to its condition.

As in other countries, the effectiveness, efficiency, and responsiveness of welfare programs are attacked regularly, both in the press and in the studies. At the same time, it is quite clear that Israel does not suffer from problems of masses of permanent welfare cases of the kind that have come to exist in the United States, with all the attendant problems that that brings. Nevertheless, as the population in Israel sorts out, the lowest stratum is moving in that direction, and there are already cases on record of several generations of welfare clients from the same family. Israeli practice, on the other hand, has been to prevent the use of welfare to sustain the lower levels of the population, preferring instead to provide "made work" for people of marginal employment ability so that they can retain their self-respect and remain off the welfare rolls.

## LOCAL FUNCTIONS

There are a number of functions that are nominally purely local, among them garbage collection, libraries, and parks. With the exception of the first, which tends to be provided at uniformly high level by localities around the country, in part because there is no shortage of manpower to maintain services, these vary from locality to locality, depending upon the degree of interest on the part of the governing officials and relevant pressure groups in securing proper facilities. Outside Jerusalem and Tel Aviv, Israel's local park systems are relatively undeveloped, at least in part because that is the kind of amenity that requires a sophisticated population for its support. As is frequently the case, only where there are key people who are committed to the development of public parks is any progress made in that direction. Much the same is true for libraries. In both cases, capital expenditures and operating funds are mobilized to a very large extent from outside the community, the former from overseas contributors and the latter from the state government via the Ministry of Education, which is eager to encourage library services, more sports fields, and the like and which will provide appropriate subsidies when activated to do so.

Here the scale question seems to be one of minimum rather than maximum size; that is to say, there are local authorities that are too small to maintain effective libraries or to be concerned about developing parks. A population of 15–20,000 may be the cutoff point here, although there are striking examples of development towns of 5,000 population that are relatively poor to begin with, providing library services not substantially lower in quality that those in the biggest cities, because someone has made an effort to do so and has managed to mobilize internal and external support. In general, municipalities tend to set up wholly owned public corporations to provide services wherever possible, since such corporations are not subject to the restrictions that the state imposes on local government. Thus, they have been a device for strengthening local autonomy, as well as a more effective means for targeting particular kinds of services.

## THE ROLE OF PUBLIC NONGOVERNMENTAL BODIES

There is a whole range of services in Israel whose first providers are public nongovernmental bodies, some established within the framework of the state and others under the aegis of the Jewish people of the whole. One of the best examples of the former are the *matnasim*, an acronym for culture, youth, and sport centers. These supercommunity centers have been established in most localities around the country through a special Matnas Corporation, which is funded by the American Jewish Joint Distribution Committee, the Jewish Agency, the Israel government, and the local authority, as well as private contributions and dues. The bulk of the construction costs of each *matnas* building have been provided by private donors from abroad. Each matnas is a public corporation governed by a board on which all these elements, plus the consumers, are represented, and each corporation is a subsidiary of the statewide Matnas Corporation. Matnasim sometimes exist side by side with municipally sponsored community centers that are more modest institutions. The former may or may not be more effective than their more modest municipal counterparts.[20]

On another level, the Society for the Protection of Nature in Israel maintains field schools around the country, the bulk of whose support comes from the state budget. These field schools reflect the Zionist ideological commitment to reawakening the Jews' love of their land through bringing them into intimate familiarity with it. They are extremely popular and well-utilized instrumentalities.[21]

## CONCLUSION

Israel prides itself on its high level of public services and compares itself with the most developed Western countries in that respect. Indeed, Israelis expect nothing less. They have been assisted in obtaining facilities of the latest design by Jews the world over who want "their" state to have the best of everything. Unfortunately, neither the country's economy nor its society necessarily can sustain that level of services. The economy in particular is overburdened by the combination of an extraordinarily heavy defense and security burden, which cannot be reduced significantly as long as Israel is in a state of war or tension with most of its neighbors; an overdeveloped welfare state; and a high level of public demand for amenities.

The 1980s has proved to be a decade of reckoning in this regard, whose outcome is not by any means clear. On the other hand, in many cases expensive facilities and equipment are not utilized or maintained properly because they have been given to a population not yet prepared to handle them. Thus, there is a great deal of waste involved in the provision of amenities. The Israelis, who are soberly realistic about so many other things, have not yet developed such an approach to internal services.

# PART 3 *Cleavages*

# SEVEN

# Religion and the Polity

## THE SETTING

Formally, Israel is a secular democratic state, more so than any other state in the Middle East except Turkey. Israel has no established religion, nor any provisions in its laws requiring a particular religious affiliation, belief, or commitment—Jewish or other—as a requirement for holding office, (such a requirement is quite common in other Middle Eastern constitutions, most of which provide that only Muslims can hold certain offices.[1]) On the other hand, the place of religion in Israeli society very much follows the pattern of the Middle East, which means there is a close interconnection between religious communities and the state, and religions are held to have a claim upon the resources of the state to support their legitimate activities. Any religious community can apply for and receive official recognition in Israel and receive state support. Israel's Ministry of Religions is the ministry of *religions,* and not of one religion only. That is to say, it is a ministry that serves Jews, Muslims, Druse, various Christian denominations, and others. The government of Israel does not control or seek to control religion. Rather, the various religious communities and groups utilize state instrumentalities to further their own ends.

Informally, Israel's society and policy are permeated by Judaism and Jewishness, just as the other countries in the Middle East are permeated by Islam and Islamic sectarianism in one form or another. People from outside the region may not see or understand this characteristic element of the region, and even people living within it may not perceive just how much Israel's character as a "Jewish state" is closely parallel to similar phenomena among its neighbors.[2]

In addition, religion functions as a legitimizing device in Israel no less than in other Middle Eastern countries; that is what is meant when people talk about Israel as a Jewish state, and, of course, the majority of Israelis, as Jews, very much want Israel to be a Jewish state. Virtually all Israelis recognize this connection between Israel and Judaism, as well as Jewishness. It is well known that many of the original founders of Israel were secularists. They saw Israel as a Jewish state in the strictly or almost strictly national sense of the term *Jewish*—though one finds ambivalence in their thinking on

**119**

the subject. Their approach to Jewishness has failed to become dominant, however much it has served to loosen the bonds of religion with regard to the behavior of Israel's Jews.

## RELIGIOUS AND NATIONAL COMMITMENTS

The Jewish religious situation in Israel is one that defies conventional definition and is characterized by continued flux. The Jews in Israel reflect all the ambivalance of modern society with regard to the relationship between religion and society, if perhaps less with regard to religion and politics. In this respect, it is possible to discern a measure of modernization (in the sociological sense) that is taking place among Jews in Israel. That is partly because, for the majority of Jews in Israel or their parents who came from elsewhere, Israel itself has played only a partial role in the modernization process that started earlier. More significant, the Jewish religion is only partly rooted in premodern patterns. In many ways, the Jewish people was modern before modernity. Jewish religious tradition is associated with patterns that are also quite at home in modern society, so there has not been the kind of undiluted confrontation between traditional religion and modernization that has been true in some other cases. One sees that even in the way that the ultra-Orthodox Jews in Israel fit into modern economic and political life. There have been some elements of confrontation, but for the most part, there is not the same problem of confrontation and contradiction that there is in the Islamic world, for example.

To the outside observer, Israel often gives the impression of being divided into sharply separated camps—religious and nonreligious—whose lines are set. Actually, the situation is much looser, and more complex. Among the Israelis who call themselves religious, there is great diversity in attitudes toward the state and the modern world. Among the Israelis who call themselves nonreligious, there are large groups that are extremely close to the tradition, and there are groups which have espoused a secular humanist outlook and have minimal contact with the tradition. The word *dati*, meaning "religious," is used narrowly, referring to one who observes the religious law, but it by no means describes the extent of religious observance or commitment in the state. It is assumed that one who is observant also accepts the traditional Jewish world view and understands himself as bound by God's revelation as recorded in the Bible and developed by rabbinical authorities, whose word is authoritative. Thus, the word *religious*, as used in Israel, is not identical in meaning to the same word in the broader American sense, which suggests someone who is spiritual and might or might not believe in God. The difference in the use of the word is very important, since its opposite, *nonreligious*, also does not imply the same thing in Hebrew as it does in English. To be "nonreligious" in Israel does not necessarily mean that one does not believe in God or even that one does not observe any of the religious traditions; it means, rather, that one is not totally observant. Everyone who is not strictly *halachic* is included in the category "nonreligious," although many do accept numerous traditional views and preserve substantial elements of Jewish tradition in their own lives and in the lives of their families.[3]

Another usage has developed in Israel to distinguish between groups within the general "nonreligious" category. That usage is the word *masorati* (traditional), which refers to people who are selectively observant and who do not declare themselves to be atheists or agnostics. Only the latter, who are termed *hilonim* (secularists), are considered to be nonreligious, and many of them selectively maintain Jewish religious practices, particularly in their homes. The criterion accepted by the public for determining one's "religious" commitment is the traditional Jewish criterion of performing *mitzvot* (divine commandments). The presuppositions underlying such performance, that is, belief, are not defined. So, for example, while there are quite a few studies and polls of the former, very little research has been done on the latter.

Traditional Jewish acts and traditional responses to symbols of Judaism are common among vast numbers of the population who define themselves as "traditional" rather than "religious." Within this group, Judaism is a positive value, but it is not accepted as authoritative and obligatory in the traditional sense. Their Judaism is based on selective and sporadic acts of commitment.

The fact that these various types of religious commitment exist side by side in Israel must be remembered when considering the viability and strength of Jewish religion in the Jewish state. Moreover, the general social-cultural context is a supportive force in the survival of Jewish traditionalism. Thus, because the atmosphere of the Sabbath descends upon the entire country, observance seems appropriate, even when limited to certain aspects and not all. Because the entire country prepares for holidays and observes them in some ways continuous with the tradition, it is easy for some observance to take place in the home. Another factor strengthening the broad maintenance of tradition is the reality of a strong observing Orthodox community, which serves as a reminder for those inclining toward tradition in any case, and a justification of Israel as a Jewish state for many ostensible "secularists," as well.

Underlying all religious commitment in Israel is the inherent intertwining of the religious and national dimensions of Judaism. The two are inseparable. National historical consciousness does not exist without reference to the religious historical past. The sources to be confronted are religious sources. Thus, national holidays either are traditional Jewish holidays or incorporate traditional elements so that they become semireligious holidays.

Every people or nation has sanctified events and individuals and places that have critical associations in their history. In Israel, the power of Jewish symbols deepens this process of sanctification. Every society, traditional or modern, has certain rituals that increase group loyalty and integration.

Religion is obviously a source of group cohesion and solidarity. In Israel, Judaism or Jewish historical events fulfill this function in what from its founding has been the religion of the nation.

This religion of Israel, as a nation, is one that is linked to a force beyond the nation itself. That means that the events, people, and places sanctified by the State of Israel somehow become part of the ancient national-religious tradition. For some Israelis, the religious and traditional groups, Israel is a nation under God. For others, the reference to God has been dropped; however, the idea remains that the state must be directed toward a goal beyond itself.[4] Consequently, for Israeli Jews, Israeli and Jewish identity are difficult to distinguish.

## FUNDAMENTAL DIFFERENCES BETWEEN ISRAEL AND THE UNITED STATES

It should be obvious that the relationship between religion and state in Israel is radically different from that in the United States. The formal and sharp separation of church and state and the maintenance of neutrality toward religions in the public realm are the product of the specific experience of the United States, where free-church Protestants were influential in determining that there would be no established church and that all religions would be organized as voluntary denominations. Both Judaism and Catholicism had to accommodate to the Protestant definition of church-state relations.

The United States is a pluralistic society in which the individual, exercising free choice, is of central concern. The individual affiliates voluntarily with any number of groups, one of which may be a religious denomination. The religious denominations compete for members, as it were, with each other and with whatever causes or ideologies are popular in the general society. In this effort to attract members and hold them, religious organizations may place heavy emphasis upon the benefits which the individual will derive from his or her participation. Such participation is described as bringing a measure of personal happiness, moral improvement, and good for the family. Joining a religious institution, church or synagogue, is considered by most to be part of the American way of life. It is a positive value for the individual, the community, and the country. Religion is perceived in America as a beneficial force, and at the same time a force that does not demand too much in terms of obligations, moral or ideological.

Given the religious situation in America, it is not surprising that many Americans find it difficult to understand the religious situation in Israel and, indeed, the Middle East generally. If one attempts to transfer the American model of church-state relations to Israel, or if one attempts to understand Israeli Judaism through the eyes of the Reform or Conservative American Jewish models, one is likely to become confused. First, while there is no established church or religion in Israel, all major religious groups are state-supported. Second, Jews in Israel who are deemed "religious" are Orthodox and live according to the very demanding way of life of traditional Judaism. The synagogue is not central to Jewish religious life, since it does not serve as the center for nonritual functions. In Israel the entire country is considered Jewish space, and the synagogue is a place where one prays. Judaism is a very live force that drives and divides people, and in many ways legitimates the state. In both respects, it is closer to the traditional conception of Judaism than the American model. Moreover, the religious-national tradition of Judaism is in the classic Middle Eastern mold.

Jewish religion has become an increasingly important element in Israel's civic culture. The transition in this direction since 1948 is notable. When Israel's Declaration of Independence —a document that addresses itself to the secular democratic, as well as to the Jewish, character of the state—was issued, a strong secularist bloc opposed any mention of the Diety. The compromise was to use a traditional phrase, "Rock of Israel," which in religious circles is used as a synonym for God, but which also could be interpreted by atheists or agnostics in some other way. Contrast that with the scene that took place after the Entebbe raid in 1976, when the Knesset, in special commemorative session, was opened by the late Yisrael Yeshayahu, then its Speaker, who took out a skullcap from his pocket, ceremoniously placed it upon his head, and read from the Psalms.

## FIVE FORMS OF RELIGIOUS EXPRESSION

There are five forms of religious expression influential in Israel today.[5] First, there is Orthodox Judaism, as expressed through the established organs linked to the state. These include the chief rabbinate, the local religious councils, the rabbinical courts, and the state religious educational system. For the most part, it is the religion represented by the National Religious Party, which has been a coalition partner in every lasting government since the state was established, and even before. In that role, it has exercised a predominant, though by no means exclusive, influence over the public expression of religion in Israel.

Then there is the popular religion of the broad public, a combination of residual folk traditions, commonly accepted Jewish practices, and elements of the emerging civil religion. Popular religion is well rooted in Israel, in almost every quarter. It is presently changing, as many of the 55 percent or so of Israelis who come from Afro-Asian backgrounds pass through a process of detraditionalization, similar to that which reshaped the religious lives of Jews who came from European backgrounds a generation or two earlier.

The third element is Israel's rapidly developing civil religion.[6] In a sense, the civil religion represents the point of intersection between establishment and popular religion: it is grounded in traditional Judaism but is not traditional Judaism. It reflects the reemergence in new ways of Sadducean Judaism, the civil religion that existed in Israel prior to the destruction of the

Second Commonwealth and the great Jewish dispersion. In this respect, it is different from the Talmudic or Pharisaic Judaism embodied by Israel's establishment religion and which was the dominant mode of Jewish religious expression for at least 1,600 years.

This neo-Sadduceanism is based on the centrality of Jewish public life for the expression of Judaism. The evolving civil religion in Israel seeks to sacralize expressions of Jewish moralistic nationalism connected with the state and to infuse those expressions with traditional religious forms.[7] The origins of this civil religion are to be found in the original Zionist movement. Even the most secularist halutzim took Jewish festivals and reinterpreted them along lines that gave expression to the values of the Zionist revival.[8]

In recent years, celebrations that once were entirely secular have been infused with Jewish religious symbolism and modes of behavior. For example, Israeli Independence Day increasingly has taken on the elements of a religious holiday. It is expected that the president of the state and the prime minister will go to evening and morning religious services on that day. Those services, parts of the regular daily prayer cycle, now include recitation of traditional prayers of praise and thanksgiving for Israel's independence. In addition, the religious establishment is trying to develop some kind of appropriate recognition of Israeli Independence Day as a holiday that can be institutionalized in the Jewish calendar. Jerusalem Day, the anniversary of the liberation of the Western Wall and the Temple Mount in 1967 according to the Jewish calendar, is also acquiring the characteristics of a quasi-religious holiday.

After his electoral victory in 1977, Menachem Begin became the embodiment of the official expression of Israel's civil religion and the transformation of that civil religion into one that draws heavily upon Jewish religious expression in its traditional form. Following the approach developed by his mentor, Ze'ev (Vladimir) Jabotinsky, Begin actively cultivated the synthesis between nationalist politics and Jewish religion; hence his emphasis on Jewish ceremony and observance as part of the public life of the state. In doing so, he was ahead of his associates in the Likud, except for the Sephardim, but was very close to his constituency and his closest potential coalition partners from the religious camp, many of whom subsequently were drawn to vote for Likud. Begin—in so many respects the quintessential Polish Jew—managed to appeal to the Sephardim through his linkage of civil and popular religion, to which he gave expression in both his official and his private capacities. For them, he was an authentic Jew, even if one whose customs were different from theirs, unlike the Labor party leaders, who impressed them as being not very "Jewish" at all, since they seemed to have no links with Jewish religious tradition.

Fourth, there is ultra-Orthodox religion, so called because it is even more extreme in its expression of classical Talmudic Judaism than establishment religion. Included in this category are the people who make the headlines by throwing stones at autos that travel through or near their neighborhoods on the Sabbath, who protest the immodesty of women dressed in modern fashion, and the like. But it also includes the Agudath Israel and the various Hassidic sects who hold ultra-Orthodox views but express them moderately. The extremist activists are small in numbers, consisting of at most a few thousand by the broadest definition. The bulk of the ultra-Orthodox community, consisting of several hundred thousand people, live quietly within their own world. Nevertheless, both are constituents of a state within a state, and it is accepted that they will be. They maintain their own schools, institutions, rabbinical courts, and the like. There are points of intersection between them and the larger polity, but generally the policy of the latter is to try to leave them alone, to give them the same state support as every other group, in order to get them to leave the state alone. The result is an uneasy relationship punctuated by sporadic conflicts when the two communities clash over certain critical issues, but that should not obscure the degree of routine cooperation that exists between them at other times.[9]

Finally, there is an emergent nonestablishment Judaism in the form of the Masorti (Conservative) and Yahadut Mitkademet (Reform) movements, which remain tiny but, taken together, are approaching fifty congregations in strength.[10] With congregations now being formed in all parts of the country, two Reform kibbutzim and a M'sorati one on the land, small rabbinical seminaries for both, and the first Reform rabbi recently ordained in Israel, it is reasonable to conclude that these nonestablishment movements are in the country to stay. While they remain formally unrecognized, there are increasing contacts between them and the authorities in the course of their daily activities, and, in some respects, they have gained a certain tacit recognition. For example, the state traditional schools supported by the Ministry of Education cater to masorti Jews, although they are not linked formally to the movement. Various congregations have obtained land for buildings from the municipal authorities, and occasionally rabbis have been authorized to perform marriages.

Relations between the religious and nonreligious in Israel are both better and worse then ever. On one hand, there is widespread concern with maintaining elements of Jewish tradition in the Jewish state. On the other, the rise of a generation of nontraditional Jews whose links with Judaism as a religion are tenuous in the extreme has increased the gap between the religious quarter of the population and the other three-quarters.

## RELIGION AND PARTY: THE PRESENT ALIGNMENT

Four of the five forms of religious expression are represented in the political process by political parties, as indicated in table 7-1. Establishment religion has the Mafdal; popular religion, Tami; ultra-Orthodox religion, Agudath Israel; and civil religion, the Likud. The two new religious parties that emerged in 1984, on the other hand, represent combinations of types. Shas

TABLE 7.1

Religious Expression and Party Alignment

| Religious Expression | Political Party |
|---|---|
| Establishment Religion | Mafdal (National Religious Party) |
| Popular Religion | Tami |
| Civil Religion | Likud |
| Ultra-Orthodox Religion | Agudath Israel |
| Nonestablishment Religion | (Citizens' Rights Movement) |

combines elements of ultra-Orthodoxy and popular religion, while Morasha combines elements of establishment and civil religion. Only nonestablishment Judaism remains unrepresented in the political sphere, in great part because of its character as an expression of Western, particularly American, ideas about the relationship between religion and state and the need to maintain separation between them. Those views are reinforced by their own interests in Israel, which would require a separation between establishment religion and politics in order for nonestablishment Judaism to gain the full recognition that it seeks.

On the other hand, there is a growing minority among the nonestablishment leadership that has come to understand that the situation in Israel is inevitably different from that in the United States, and that for nonestablishment religion to get its share of the pie, it must have some representation in the political arena. This minority has worked in two directions. Some have tried to form an alliance with the Labor Alignment to get Labor to endorse the full recognition of the movements of nonestablishment Judaism. At one point in the 1981 campaign, this group seemed to be gaining a measure of success. When the Labor Alignment thought that it really was going to win an absolute majority of seats in the Knesset, it was willing to endorse such a stance following intensive lobbying by leaders of Reform Judaism in Israel. That was in the period when Labor was actively alienating its former coalition partners from the religious camp. However, once it became apparent that Labor would not win that majority and, indeed, was in a struggle for its very political life, its leaders tried to back away from that position—unsuccessfully, as it turned out, since they had become identified in the minds of Orthodox and non-Orthodox alike as essentially committed to secularism (see below).

The other element that has sought to link nonestablishment Judaism with Israeli politics consists of people who have become actively involved in the parties of the sabra reform movement, including the short-lived Democratic Movement for Change and Shinui, but most particularly Shulamit Aloni's Citizens' Rights Movement. The CRM, indeed, has offered them a certain hospitality, perhaps because of Aloni's intense hostility toward Orthodoxy coupled with her own search for a secular humanist Judaism. It would be premature to suggest that the CRM has become the political expression of nonestablishment Judaism. But it, more than any other party on the scene, has the potential for being that, if its leaders overcome their strong hostility toward religion in general and the movements of nonestablishment Judaism overcome their great reluctance to accept the linkages between religion and politics, which are part and parcel of the Israeli scene.

## THE RELIGIOUS CAMP, ZIONISM, AND THE STATE

The State of Israel was reestablished after a break of twenty centuries, during which Jewish law, although used in the governance of diaspora communities, was not applied to the operation of a state. Furthermore, the situation of a modern Jewish state is different from that of any earlier Jewish polity. Technological change and secularization have brought unprecedented changes in all spheres of life. Internal changes have occurred that have broken the religious unity of the Jewish people. Today there are various visions of national purpose, various interpretations of how one should live in Israel, and various views as to the cultural shape that the homeland should have. Finally, the state includes non-Jewish citizens, who are guaranteed equal rights as individuals, full religious liberty, and a measure of cultural autonomy.

A majority of the leaders of the modern Zionist movement were not traditional Jews. While they might have wanted to maintain certain continuities with Jewish tradition, they did not accept the authority of halachah and did not accept the values and goals of life as they were defined by the Orthodoxy they knew in Western and Eastern Europe. Rather, they wanted to construct a new Jewish society and a new Hebrew man, whose formation would be based upon general Western values and humanist ideas, which would include experiences and opportunities outside the purview and bounds of the Orthodox way of life. Nevertheless, the Zionist pioneers did not reject Judaism altogether. The situation and the relationship were much more complicated.

The Zionist movement, after all, arose out of the failures of Jewish assimilation in Europe. When it had become clear that emancipation and assimilation would not bring redemption to the Jews in Europe, the Zionist movement emerged to bring that redemption through a return to the homeland and the construction of an autonomous Jewish entity there. Many of the early leaders of Zionism were assimilated Jews who had little relationship to Jewish culture. Others, who were concerned about the continuity of the national culture, were opposed to its religious character. Therefore, the Zionist movement presented a revolutionary alternative to European Jewish life, whose ideals threatened the religious way of life and the religious establishment in Europe.

Among the socialist pioneers in particular were a group of militant secularists. People of enormous idealism and burning conviction, they came to Palestine to establish a Jewish homeland where they could realize their ideals and values while constructing a home for a reconstructed Jewish people. Part of the reconstruction for them involved a thoroughly secular Jewish state.

Religious Jews were inherently committed to ending the exile and returning to Zion as part of the process of redemption. Hence, Zionism was potentially appealing to them. However, the question was raised in Orthodox circles: Could one participate in the effort to end exile when the leaders of the effort were non-Orthodox Jews? And could one participate in the effort to end exile when it might be against the will of the nations of the world and against the will of God Himself? The tradition had warned Jews against rebelling against the foreign powers and against "forcing the end."

Even those religious Jews sympathetic toward the Zionist effort recognized that the Zionist movement was led by nontraditional Jews, and that the ideals of the movement were not those that Orthodox Judaism envisioned for a national homeland. For the latter, the establishment of a Jewish homeland necessarily implied the establishment of a Torah society and culture. Religious Zionists resolved the issue by accepting secular efforts to rebuild the land as part of the messianic process. All Jews, religious and nonreligious, who participated in the Zionist enterprise, even if unintentionally, were viewed as agents in God's scheme to initiate the redemptive process in Israel. Rabbi Abraham Isaac Kook, the first Ashkenazi chief rabbi of Eretz Israel provided the classic formulation. According to the Rav Kook, settling the land through an ingathering of the exiles was a commandment of such import, especially at this historical moment of the beginning of the redemption, that its fulfillment overrode hesitations regarding cooperation with secular Jews in the effort.

The theological grounding that existed, in addition to the particular historical situation of the Jews at the turn of the century, led a significant number of moderate Orthodox rabbis to support the Zionist movement and to form their own party within that movement. Accepting the Zionist principle of acting to achieve a political goal, the return to the land of Israel, they wanted to exercise pressure within the Zionist movement as religious Jews. Therefore, in 1902, under the leadership of Rabbi Isaac Joseph Reines, these rabbis formed the Mizrahi party. (Mizrahi is a play on words meaning "of the east," and also an abbreviation of merkaz ruhani, which means spiritual center.) From the beginning, the goal of the religious Zionists was twofold: to influence the Zionist organization in a religious direction, as they defined that direction, namely, in terms of the halachah; and to influence Orthodox Jews to support Zionism. That they could do only by legitimating the movement in the eyes of the Orthodox public, which then still included a majority of world Jewry. The manifest goal of Mizrahi, one that could draw such masses to its ranks, was "the land of Israel for the people of Israel according to the Torah of Israel," and could be accomplished only if Orthodox Jews joined in the Zionist enterprise and attempted to influence it.[11]

Turning to both the Zionist Congress and his Orthodox brothers, Rabbi Samuel Mohilever, a great supporter of Zionism, stated the Mizrahi position:

> It is essential that the Congress unite all "Sons of Zion" who are true to our cause to work in complete harmony and fraternity, even if there be among them differences of opinion regarding religion. Our attitude towards those among us who do not observe the religious precepts must be, as it were, as if fire had taken hold of our homes, imperiling our persons and our property. Under such circumstances would we not receive anyone gladly and with love who, though irreligious in our eyes, came to rescue us? Is this not our present plight, my brethren? A great fire, a great conflagration, is raging in our midst and we are all threatened. . . . If brethren put out their hands to us in aid, doing all in their power to deliver us from our dire straits, are there such among us who would spurn them? If all factions really understand this . . . this covenant of brothers will surely stand. All Sons of Zion must be completely convinced and must believe with a perfect faith that the resettlement of our country . . . i.e. the purchase of land and building of houses, the planting of orchards and the cultivation of the soil—is one of the fundamental commandments of our Torah. . . . Whoever assists us and does not hold faith is comparable to one who contributes to a cause in which he does not really believe. The basis of Hibbat Zion [love of Zion-ed.] is the Torah, as it has been handed down to us from generation to generation, with neither supplement nor subtraction. I do not intend this as an admonition to any individual. . . . I am nevertheless stating in a general way that the Torah, which is the Source of our life, must be the foundation of our generation in the land of our fathers. [12]

As long as the aim of the Zionist movement was almost exclusively political, the disagreements between religious and nonreligious Zionists over religious and cultural matters could be ignored. But when the Zionists focused upon the cultural program of the national renaissance, the issue could not be avoided, and ideological battles were fought out between segments within the movement. Despite the conflicts, the religious Zionists remained within the Zionist movement. Here, the unifying tendency embodied in the ideal of Love of Israel predominated over the centrifugal tendencies emerging from sharp ideological conflicts. As Rabbi T. J. Reiner stated:

> There is no greater sacrilege than to allege that Zionism is part and parcel of secularism for the truth is that it is precisely the holiness of the land that induces the secularists to participate in the movement . . . it is in this that we may see the greatest of Zionism, for it has succeeded in uniting people of diverse views, and directing them toward a noble aim—the saving of the people—and this is its glory. [13]

Many Orthodox Jews could not accept what they regarded as the illegitimate compromising postures of the Mizrahi organization. Following the Tenth Zionist Congress, in which a cultural program for the Zionist movement was approved, the anti-Zionists organized Agudath Israel (1912), a party whose explicit goal was to oppose all Zionist activities in Europe and Palestine and to deny the basic claim that the Zionist movement represented and embodied the will of the Jewish people. Agudath Israel claimed that it represented the Jewish people, and that those who deviated from the tradition (as they understood it) had left their people.

The theological grounding of Agudath Israel's position was old and firm. "Forcing the end" had long been a suspected effort in traditional circles. Flowing from this stance was the notion that Torah-true Jews ought to dedicate themselves to the traditional act of fulfilling the Torah in exile and waiting for redemption, which could come only at God's beckoning and in his own good time. There were Agudath Israel rabbis who favored and sanctioned settlement in the land of Israel, but only within the framework of ultra-Orthodoxy. There could be no possibility of cooperating with nonobservant Jews, and certainly not of living with them in the same community.

The Agudath Israel rabbis feared the inroads that the Zionists were making in Palestine. This fear increased following Great Britain's Balfour Declaration (1917), which brought Zionism the backing of a major power and made success of the Zionist enterprise imminent. The Askenazic Orthodox community in Palestine, often known as the old yishuv, which was centered mainly in Jerusalem, had in the interim become the Palestinian branch of Agudath Israel. Its members were determined to block Zionist efforts wherever possible and to separate themselves from all religious Jews who supported the Zionists.[14]

However, the separation could not be clear-cut, since the institutions of the old yishuv needed money to survive, and the control of such funds was delegated by the British to the Zionist-sponsored Vaad Leumi (National Council), composed of nonreligious and religious Zionists. Throughout the 1920s, great efforts were made by Chaim Weizmann, the president of the WZO, and others to bring the Orthodox anti-Zionists into the Vaad Leumi in order to bring unity to the Jews in Eretz Israel and increase the religious legitimation of the Zionist organization. These efforts led to a weak compromise: the Zionists agreed to fund Agudath Israel educational institutions in return for a truce between the two groups but no active cooperation.

It must be recognized that the battle between the Zionists and religious anti-Zionists was a principled one over the nature of the society to be constructed in the Jewish national home. Those Orthodox who took a radical anti-Zionist stance were those who had been fending off changes in their way of life and beliefs since the beginning of the enlightenment and emancipation. Ever since the modern period began, these people had felt they were witnessing the breakdown of traditional Jewish life. They were determined to resist the continuation of this process. In their view, Zionism was a secular movement and therefore a profanation. It was led by nonobservant men and women, usurpers of God's power, who were leading Jews astray. The use of Hebrew as a spoken language was an example of profanation; secular studies in the Zionist schools were another; granting women the right to vote in Zionist institutions another. The greater the influx of Zionists into Palestine, the greater the defensiveness of the Ashkenazic old yishuv. This defensiveness and opposition were expressed geographically in the determination to live in separate neighborhoods, which were to be as self-sufficient as possible.

Needless to say, the anti-Zionist Orthodox totally rejected the Mizrahi, seeing them as traitors to the Torah who were doubly dangerous because they purported to be otherwise. Although the position of Agudath Israel has undergone radical changes since the early 1920s, differences as to the meaning and valuation of the Zionist enterprise continue to be manifest today in the battle between the two party groupings in the religious camp: the National Religious Party (Mafdal), built around the Mizrahi, and the Agudath Israel.

Throughout the mandate period, the religious Zionists participated in Zionist activities and were integrated into the new yishuv. The Mizrahi brought to Israel many Orthodox settlers and developed the concept of the integration of Torah and labor, which projected the Zionist "back to the land" ideal as a religious one and encouraged the religious immigrants to engage in agricultural work, thereby becoming part of the major developing thrust of the new Jewish society.

Out of the Mizrahi there developed a new party, HaPoel HaMizrahi (Mizrahi Labor), for those who chose the way of life of agricultural pioneering and who had specific interests that could be furthered by this organization. HaPoel HaMizrahi joined the Histadrut (the Zionist Labor Federation and bastion of Labor Zionism). The religious Zionists succeeded in establishing a number of important kibbutzim and moshavim, based upon the concept that an integrated religious life included both labor and study.

In the 1930s, Agudath Israel's stance underwent great changes, although not without an internal struggle. The immediate cause of the change was the influx of ultra-Orthodox immigrants from Central Europe, who were more moderate in their approach to modernization and Zionism than were the old settlers. Second, the burning threat of Nazism forced Agudath Israel leaders to consider ways of cooperating with the Zionists in order to bring Jews out of Europe. Some of the old-time leaders remained firm in their position of negation of Zionism and continued to block all changes. Others, however, began to alter their position as the situation seemed to demand.

An example of the inner division and conflict within Agudath Israel may be seen in the battle over the establishment of the Horev school in Jerusalem. Agudath Israel members from Germany had immigrated in sufficient numbers in the early 1930s to wish to establish a school for their children that would follow their own educational principles. Influenced by the ideas of Samson Raphael Hirsch, the German Orthodox wanted to build a school that would include high-level general studies as well as Torah studies, would offer the same education to girls, and would conduct its program in Hebrew. The school was established in 1934 and immediately became a target of attack from the Old Jerusalem Orthodox, who objected to all the innovations. The German Jews did not yield. In fact, their position gained strength as more of their kind arrived in the country.

The conflicting approaches within Agudath Israel became more evident. They led to an agreement on the part of the world body to cooperate with the WZO in 1934. Agudath Israel was reorganized in Palestine under the leadership of Rabbi I. M. Levin. The reorganization recognized the various trends within the movement and, more important, effectively renounced the separatist policy of the old yishuv.

Agudath Israel began urging its members to abandon Europe and settle in Eretz Israel during the late 1930s. Following the war, when the need for an independent Jewish state was so painfully evident, it entered into an agreement with David Ben-Gurion, supporting the establishment of the state. This agreement succeeded in establishing unity among all elements of the Jewish population on the eve of the proclamation of the state. The nature of the agreement is very important, because it set out the basic guidelines that have been followed ever since and have enabled the religious parties to remain within the government. In a letter to Rabbi Levin, Ben-Gurion, as head of the Jewish Agency, guaranteed certain conditions demanded by the Orthodox with regard to public observance in the future Jewish state. Ben-Gurion pledged to continue practices embodied in legislation or that had become customary during the mandatory period. Thus, it was agreed that the Jewish Sabbath (Saturday) would be the official day of rest in the Jewish State, that *kashrut* (dietary) laws would be maintained in all public institutions in the state, that religious school systems would be maintained and funded by the state, that public transportation would not operate for the country as a whole on Sabbaths and holy days, and that matters of personal status, primarily marriage and divorce, would be controlled exclusively by religious law. On the other hand, the religious camp conceded that the state radio would continue to operate on Sabbaths and holidays and that local practices with regard to public transportation would be maintained.

These conditions constitute the famous "status quo" that the Israeli government and the religious parties have continued to support. Ben-Gurion, in agreeing to these conditions, sought to avoid conflicts within the Jewish population. He also sought to gain for himself the support of a sizeable and constant element of that population, namely, the religious community. Ben-Gurion felt that he had provided a national minimum in that area of religion, which would guarantee that observant traditional Jews and secular Jews could live as they desired without coercing each other or violating each others' principles in any intolerable way. At the same time, this minimum guaranteed the Jewish character of the Jewish state. Both religious parties accepted the arrangement and represented their constituencies in the provisional government formed by Ben-Gurion in 1948.

However, there is a great difference both in the mode of participation and in the ideology underlying the participation of the Agudath Israel-rooted and the Mizrahi-rooted parties in the life of the state. In the view of the ultra-Orthodox, a total halachic way of life can best be maintained by withdrawal from those areas contaminated by modern secular ideas, values, and sensibilities. These include most areas of life within a modern state. In the manifesto of Agudath Israel, written in 1912, it was stated that:

> The Jewish people stands outside the framework of the political peoples of the world, and differs essentially from them: the Sovereign of the Jewish people is the Almighty; the Torah is the Law that governs them; and the Holy Land has been at all times destined for the Jewish people. It is the Torah which governs all actions of Agudath Israel.

By entering the state framework, Agudath Israel effectively modified its manifesto. At the same time, because its participation remains partial and conditional, the movement remains loyal to the major aspects of its original position.

Given this reservation about the nature of a Jewish state that is not a halachic entity, it is not surprising that Agudath Israel has sought and received exemption from military service for its young people; that is to say, male yeshiva students and all women who choose exemption on religious grounds. In fact, it is not clear, according to the halachah, that males ought to be exempt. Agudath Israel persuaded Ben-Gurion to accept their demand with the claim that yeshiva students were needed desperately in the effort to rebuild the yeshivot that had been destroyed in Europe. Ben-Gurion, sympathetic to the overall goal and knowing that the total number of boys involved at that time was no more than 1,000, granted the military exemption. Today, that exemption extends to approximately 20,000 yeshiva students, generating resentment among all but ultras, yet is still respected by the Israeli government. What is important to recognize is that the very seeking of the military exemption reflects not only a fear of halachic violation that could be incurred during military service, but also suspicion of and withdrawal from the secular state and its political efforts.[15]

In contrast to the refusal of the ultra-Orthodox to permit military service, the Mizrahi and its successor, the National Religious Party, have regarded service in the armed forces as a mitzvah, a commanded act of devotion to the state and the land. While the state is religiously neutral or even negative in the view of Agudath Israel, in the view of the religious Zionists, the state is a positive religious value. The establishment of an independent Jewish polity in the land of Israel is a step in the messianic process, which cannot be reversed. It follows, obviously, that military service is of positive religious value, as is the army itself.

## RELIGION AND THE NONRELIGIOUS CAMPS

In understanding the status quo agreement and the entire position of Judaism in Israel, one must consider why the Zionist movement, and later the state, whose majority is far from Orthodox, have legitimated and established religious institutions in Israel and have sanctioned the presence and influence of the religious in Israeli society. Why has there not been a real kulturkampf, as is so often suggested will occur, against the powers of "religious coercion?"

Within the Zionist movement there were several approaches to religion and tradition. One was the negative approach that rejected religion and tradition totally. For these radical Zionists, Judaism represented a survival from more primitive times, and was now a brake upon the progress of the Jewish people. It was considered necessary, in the view of these radical Zionists, to break loose from the entire religious framework before the work of national and individual reconstruction could begin. This approach flourished for a generation or so in certain prominent circles and then began to decline. While spokesmen for it still can be found, it no longer is a significant force in the country.

Another approach was an ambivalent one, far more complicated than the abrogation of religious practices or the denial of religious concepts would seem to indicate. It remains characteristic of the leadership of Israel and prevalent among the secular population. The roots of the ambivalence of the secular Zionists toward religion and tradition lay first in their deep attachment to their immediate past, a sense of warmth and nostalgia for what had been received at home. These sentiments operated to moderate a staunchly negative ideological stance against Judaism. Far more significant than this rather passive, reflexive appreciation was an active sense that they, in some way, as pioneers in Eretz Israel, were actualizing selected but core elements of the Jewish tradition. They saw themselves as builders of a Jewish society and culture that would be freer, heartier, and within a more universal framework than had been possible within the fettered conditions of exile. Finally, they considered themselves, as a group, to be a vital link in the historical continuity of the Jewish people, identified themselves romantically with the ongoing historical spirit of Israel, and invoked history and destiny when speaking of the meaning of their Zionist activity.[16]

This sense of participation in a redemption process, the longing to establish a utopian society, and the sense of being actors in a drama that had world-historic significance linked even the secular halutzim with traditional religious ideals, ideas, and attitudes. Yet the religious equivalences must not disguise the secular grounding of the workers' movement and the secular approach of some of its leaders to the Jewish tradition. While there was a deeply felt need to maintain historical continuity, and even to receive legitimation from Jewish history, there was also a conscious attempt to dismiss the religious base of the Jewish tradition as meaningless or irrelevent.

The Jewish people thus became the carrier of sanctity, the representative of the sacred; and particular cultural values, previously religious values, also, now were sanctified because of their association with the nation. During the period of the Second Aliyah, a process of selection took place in which certain values from the religious tradition were sorted out to be retained in the new Hebrew culture. Those selected were chosen because they could be interpreted as meaningful to the national or socialist vision of the pioneers. Thus, the Bible retained its sacred quality but was interpreted in terms of its national value. The Bible was understood as a Jewish cultural monument, a link to Jewish history, the legitimator of Jewish claims to the land of Israel, and a source of universalist humanist ideals. It was emptied of its explicit meaning as the record of Israel's breakthrough to transcendence and became the treasure of Israel's national past.

An inescapable ambivalence toward Judaism derived from these developments is characteristic of Israeli society today. Within Israel, large groups of the population feel very positive toward the Jewish tradition and select elements from it that they observe within their own families. While not accepting the entire world view and structure of Judaism, they want to maintain ties to the tradition that once was identified with Jewish national religious culture; and they want to preserve elements and aspects of that tradition as part of Israeli culture and as values in Israeli society.

There is no clear consistency in the process of selection from the tradition on the part of either the Zionist pioneers or contemporary "non-religious" Israelis. Various customs, ideals, attitudes, and values are maintained, often for reasons that are not conscious and in ways that are not explicit. That is indeed the hold of living and dynamic tradition upon its descendants and the path through which it evolves in new situations. The result in Israel today is continuity despite rebellion. Both the pioneers of the early aliyot and the citizens of today feel the pull of ancient and submerged loyalties toward the Jewish tradition and consequently are more willing to compromise with those who are seen as most faithful to it.

## PROVIDING RELIGIOUS SERVICES

In order to provide regular services to all recognized religious groups, Jewish and non-Jewish, the State of Israel has established a Ministry of Religions, whose head is a cabinet minister. It is responsible for the government's role in the provision of religious services. All recognized non-Jewish communities maintain their own state-supported law courts for matters of religion and personal status; maintain their own places of worship, religious schools, and charitable institutions; and conduct their own marriages, divorces, and burials. The Israeli government guarantees their freedom in all these areas, and attempts to facilitate relations between all religious communities.

An extensive statewide and local structure provides services for the Jewish sector of the population. Its officials are appointed by the Ministry of Religions or elected by bodies outside the ministry but funded by it in all or in part. The highest Jewish religious body is the Supreme Rabbinical Council, which was established under the mandate. The council consists of seven Sephardic and seven Ashkenazic rabbis, including the chief rabbis of both groups. It is the high court of religious appeal, but its decisions are subject to review by the Israeli supreme court. Established by the Knesset, it is bound by state legislation. There have even been occasions when the decisions of the chief rabbis or the rabbinical council have not been accepted by the religious parties. The Sephardic chief rabbi, the Rishon-le-Zion, holds the oldest rabbinic office in the country, dating back to Ottoman times. It preceded the Ashkenazic position, which was established by the British, by several centuries.

Agudath Israel never has recognized either the rabbinical council or the chief rabbinate. It established its own independent Council of Torah Greats, which rules on problems that arise within its community. The other ultra-Orthodox groups also have separate courts.

Until 1984, the Supreme Rabbinical Council was authoritative for the Sephardic religious community, and for the Ashkenazim who did not identify themselves with the ultra-Orthodox. In that year, Rabbi Ovadia Yosef, the immediate past Rishon-le-Zion, who was bitter at being denied reelection to that post, united with a group of Orthodox Sephardim who organized a Sephardic religious party, the Sephardic Torah Guardians—*Shas* in Hebrew—to establish a parallel Council of Torah Sages under his leadership. Since Rabbi Yosef is the most highly respected Sephardic halachic decision maker (and perhaps the most highly respected halachic scholar in the country), his council instantly acquired substantial power, further weakening the establishment institutions. At this writing, it is fair to say that the formerly hierarchical structure of religious authority imposed by foreign powers (first the Ottomans, then the British) and reaffirmed by the state in its mamlachtiut period, appears to be breaking down.

On the local plane, there are two chief rabbis in every major city, as well as local rabbinic courts. Religious services in each locality are provided by local religious councils, essentially special districts, generally follow municipal boundaries. On the local as on the state plane, the ultra-Orthodox do not accept the authority of the religious councils and turn to their own councils and courts. The Conservative and Reform Jews, because they do not want to be recognized as separate religious bodies (that is to say, outside of the Jewish fold), do not have their own courts and utilize the institutions of the Orthodox establishment. Religious worship is organized privately in the country's 5,000 synagogues and prayer halls, many of which receive modest government subsidies.

## CONFLICTS BETWEEN RELIGIOUS AND NONRELIGIOUS

The existing arrangements belie certain real tensions between the religious and nonreligious sectors of the population over the place of religion in the state. These tensions emerge in several ways. There are often intellectual arguments over the place of Judaism generally, usually regarding a specific issue of public conflict but generalized to the entire relationship of Judaism to the State of Israel. These intellectual battles are waged in journals and newspapers, indicating a problem or reacting to one, but not in themselves leading to practical action.

There are numerous occasions, however, when the conflict between religious and nonreligious elements takes to the streets, even in violent ways. These seem to involve cases where a change in the strategic balance of power appears to be in the making or the status quo is upset (or seems to be). Thus, if there is an agreement as to which streets in Jerusalem should be closed on the Sabbath to preserve the rights of the ultra-Orthodox, and the Orthodox community attempts to expand the number of streets or enter a new area of the city and close it on the Sabbath, non-Orthodox elements may become incensed and resort to verbal arguments and more, all of which are returned in kind. The point is that people on both sides accept the status quo, grudgingly or willingly. When it appears that that staus quo is being altered, the principle of noncoercion arises, the fears of being pushed around by one group or another emerge, and violence may result.

Violent confrontations between ultra-Orthodox and non-Orthodox appear to be increasing, in part because the dynamic character of Israeli society since the Six Day War has created new opportunities for confrontation where the status quo hitherto has not been defined, or where one side or another has sought far-reaching changes. Thus, the development of new neighborhoods around the peripheries of Jerusalem has opened the door to a struggle as to who will control those neighborhoods, replete with stone throwing and other kinds of demonstrations. The substantial demographic increase in the ultra-Orthodox camp has exacerbated this problem, as young ultra-Orthodox couples need appropriate housing. On the other hand, the demographic changes among non-Orthodox Jews have produced a generation that is less constrained than even its secular fathers with regard to public violations of the Sabbath. They want entertainment on Friday night and Saturdays, and the city fathers, particularly in the Tel Aviv area, have sought to accommodate them, which leads to disruptions of the previously accepted status quo, which in turn have produced demonstrations and counter-demonstrations.

There also have been a number of issues debated in the Knesset or tried in the Israeli court system that shape the long-range policy of religion-state arrangement. The first was the question of a written constitution for the state, which was taken up in 1949. Proponents of a written constitution argued that the new state needed such a document to guarantee individual rights and democratic governmental arrangements, and that certain values of the Zionist revolution and halutzic realization should be recorded in this document to perpetuate the original vision. The Orthodox were among the strongest opponents of the constitution (although far from the only ones). They did not want the values of secular Zionism immortalized in a constitution for the Jewish state. As long as no explicit public document existed declaring the secular nature of the state, the religious could participate in its governance.

Moreover, it was not just the prospective secular character of the constitution that aroused opposition, but also the assumptions behind the writing of such a document. For the Orthodox, the Torah of Israel is the eternal constitution of the Jewish people, which eventually will be recognized as such by all. While the Jewish state could enact secular legislation—technically as an interim measure—a full-blown constitution was another matter.[17]

A compromise solution emerged, whereby the Knesset was empowered to enact "basic laws" of a constitutional character piecemeal which ultimately would form a complete constitution. Eight such laws have been acted to date, none touching on questions of religion. That leaves the issue of religious or secular authority unresolved, in a sense, but permits various factions to live together on a day-to-day basis in which the secular authority does make the decisions.

A perennial conflict surrounds the definition of "Who is a Jew?" As in many other countries, every Israeli is registered at birth with the Ministry of the Interior and is issued an identity card on which both religion and nationality are recorded. Jews normally are recorded as Jewish in both categories. The question is what defines a Jew as a Jew, and whether the category "Jew" can refer to nationality and not religion, or the reverse. These issues have been tested in several cases in the Israeli courts and have aroused intense interest and concern, not only in Israel but throughout the Jewish world. The matter is a weighty one, because it epitomizes the most basic question of who defines Judaism and being a Jew in the modern Jewish state. The religious leadership consistently has demanded that the only criteria admissible in these matters be halachic criteria, and that these halachic criteria be applied totally and without exceptions, although they have not always pressed the issue.

The most famous test case in this area resulted in a non-halachic decision, but one that the Orthodox accepted. This case, that of Brother Daniel, rests upon the meaning of the Law of Return, which recognizes anyone who is Jewish as an *oleh*, i.e., someone who has "returned" (literally, ascended) to Israel. That is a privileged status. The oleh is entitled to certain material benefits from the government or the Jewish Agency. A Jew can become a citizen automatically under the Law of Return, which implicitly recognizes Israel as the state of the Jewish people, whereas a non-Jew must pass through naturalization procedures. Thus, the law of Return guarantees all Jews (except those being sought as criminals by foreign countries) the right to enter and be citizens of Israel, and to receive national services from the moment of entry into the country as *olim*.

In 1962, a Polish monk, Brother Daniel, applied for recognition as an oleh, under the Law of Return, on the grounds that he was Jewish. Daniel had been born Oswald Rufeisen in Poland to Jewish parents and had been hidden by them in a monastery during the Holocaust, where he converted to Catholicism. Daniel claimed that because his mother had been a Jew, and he considered himself a Jew nationally, although he had become a Christian, he was entitled to be registered as a Jew on his identity card and was eligible for the privileges of an oleh. His application was rejected, and he took his case to court.

The court, in its ruling, recognized the halachic position claimed by Brother Daniel that under the halachah, one born of a Jewish mother remains Jewish for certain purposes, no matter what. The majority opinion then went on to distinguish between the halachah and the law of the state, in this case the Law of Return. The court stated that the law "has a secular meaning, that is as it is usually understood by the man in the street—I emphasize, as it is understood by the plain and simple Jew. . . . A Jew who has become a Christian is not a Jew." Thus, the majority opinion rejected the formalistic halachic view. In the eyes of the court, the national history of the Jewish people demonstrated that one cannot be a Jew in nationality and a Christian in religion. Religious conversion to Christianity implied, according to the judges, that Daniel indeed had rejected his Jewish national past. The decision was that he could become a citizen of the Jewish state only by going through the normal procedures of naturalization and citizenship (which he subsequently did).

Secular versus religious authority in matters of Jewish self-definition has been tested on other occasions, always causing complicated and emotional debate within the country. The cabinet crisis of 1958 is another example of such a test case, this time raised over the issue of how one registers children of mixed marriages in the national registry. It was asked whether the simple declaration of both parents that they consider the child Jewish and wanted him registered as such would be sufficient to have the government of Israel indeed recognize their child as Jewish. The interior minister declared that he would accept the subjective self-definition, and not insist on halachic standards. That meant that a person could intend or will his child Jewish if one parent was Jewish, and that the halachic criteria of either the mother's being Jewish or conversion to Judaism were overridden. The Mafdal resigned from the cabinet because of this decision, causing Ben-Gurion to revoke the decision temporarily and turn to the world's leading Jewish scholars for their opinion on the issue and the larger question of who is a Jew. After gathering the scholars' opinions, the government, in accordance with their views, ruled in favor of halachic criteria and against the minister of the interior, who subsequently revoked his directive. While the immediate crisis was settled, the basic problem was not solved but postponed.

Thus, the religious definition of who is a Jew has been accepted as the minimal one by the government. However, because some secularist Jews in the country feel "coerced," cases arise periodically that test the halachic definition. The Eitani case was in a sense the obverse of that of Brother

Daniel. Ruth Eitani was born of a Jewish father and non-Jewish mother. During the Holocaust, her mother identified herself with her Jewish husband and suffered the entire Holocaust period with the family. Ruth went through the war and immigrated to Israel, fought in the Haganah, raised a family, and became active in politics. It became known that her mother was not Jewish, had never converted herself or the child, and that, therefore, halachically, Ruth Eitani and her own children had to be converted: despite her self-identification as a Jew, the action she had taken on behalf of the Jewish people, and her having received Israeli citizenship as a Jew, on the basis of her honest self-representation as such. Again, the halachic position prevailed, and Ruth Eitani and her children did undergo formal conversion.

The Shalit case raised yet another set of questions. Benjamin Shalit, a naval officer, had married a non-Jewish woman. Shalit sought to have his children registered as Jews in nationality and nothing in religion, thus asserting a new conception: a Jew by nationality who rejects any religious profession. The government reaffirmed its 1960 decision in the "Who is a Jew?" case. Despite any subjective profession on the part of an individual, objective criteria determined one's status as Jew. One born a Jew was a Jew in both religious and national terms in the eyes of the state. And one born a non-Jew could become a Jew, even nationally, only through a religious conversion.

None of the legal cases or Knesset debates has altered the government commitment to the status quo, which supports the halachic interpretation in personal status, divorce, and marriage. It appears that the majority of the population either has agreed with this policy or has acquiesced to it. The reason behind the agreement or acquiescence has been suggested above: a sense that the religious definition protects the Jewish character of the state and a desire to maintain the unity of the Jewish people, religious or non-religious, diaspora Jews or Israeli.

Once the halachic basis of the definition of who is a Jew was established, the issue turned to who is entitled to perform conversions. The Law of Return merely specifies that conversion take place. It is silent as to what kind of conversion and by whom. That has led members of the Orthodox camp to press in the Knesset for an amendment to the Law of Return, to provide the conversions be halachic and recognized only if performed by Orthodox rabbis. That has transformed the issue into one affecting Israel-diaspora relations, since its main effect would be on diaspora Jewry.

As long as Orthodox Jews are in control of the religious courts in Israel, all Israeli Jews come within their jurisdiction, and any conversions are both halachic and by Orthodox rabbis. In the diaspora, however, where the vast majority of Jews are non-Orthodox, most conversions are performed by Conservative or Reform rabbis. The former follow halachic procedures as a matter of principle, while the latter may or may not. Thus, the amendment certainly would deny recognition to most Reform conversions. However, since one of its purposes is to maintain the Orthodox monopoly in such matters, and it is as much an intrareligious political issue as a halachic one, everyone assumes that its adoption would lead to the rejection of Conservative conversions, as well, no matter how halachically proper. Thus, it has become a major issue for the diaspora, one that has spilled over into Israeli politics, leading at this writing, to a stalemate and the retention of the status quo. Thus, the "Who is a Jew?" issue has become closely tied into another issue, that of religious pluralism within the Jewish people. In the diaspora, as a result of the vast increase in intermarriage, the number of such conversions has risen dramatically. Most of these are performed by non-Orthodox rabbis. If the Israeli government refuses to recognize such conversions, it refuses to recognize as Jews thousands of converts and their children who are recognized as Jews in the United States. That would spell a rift in the Jewish people. Thus far the government has held by a ruling that anyone who comes with a conversion certificate from a Jewish community, as long as he or she does not claim to be a member of another religion, will be recognized as a Jew. The Knesset has refused to get involved in questions of religious pluralism and legitimation in the diaspora, so that any conversion is a conversion. . . .

The matter goes further, because by accepting de facto the conversions of non-Orthodox diaspora rabbis, the Knesset also accepts the rabbis themselves as legitimate de facto. Conservative and Reform rabbis in Israel have requested and been denied the right to perform marriages in Israel. The religious parties in Israel are determined to avoid recognizing the non-Orthodox movements, claiming that they, the Orthodox alone, represent true Judaism, and further, that they alone are recognized as the legitimate bearers of Judaism by Israeli Jews.

It is hardly surprising that the Orthodox have a monopoly in Israel. Virtually all the religious Jews who came to Eretz Israel were Orthodox, and those among them who knew anything about non-Orthodox religious options opposed them firmly. The handful of Reform or Conservative Jews who came, even when they established congregations, were too few in numbers to have any impact upon the country. It is only in recent years, since centers of both movements have been built in Jerusalem and enough congregations have been founded throughout the country that their presence is beginning to be felt, making it possible for them to raise claims against the Orthodox monopoly.

In the diaspora, most Orthodox Jews tacitly recognize the marriages, divorces, and conversions of the Reform and Conservative rabbinate, out of necessity. No split within the Jewish people has occurred, because the Orthodox consider a marriage or divorce performed by a certain rabbi to be invalid halachically. Precisely in order to avoid such a rift, the Orthodox have ignored the issue. As Orthodox fundamentalism and militancy increase, however, there is less willingness to look the other way in these matters.

Moreover, extreme and unprecedented steps on the part of the Reform movement to ease the way for children of mixed marriages to be accepted as Jews had exacerbated the situation.

## CHANGING ATTITUDES TOWARD RELIGION AND STATE

The attitude of the nonreligious public toward Judaism have been changing since 1967. That is not to say that there has been a general return to Judaism, but rather, there has been a reawakening of interest in Judaism and Jewish sources among groups who in earlier periods displayed no such interest. That is at least partly a response to the inability of a nationalist ideology, Zionism in this case, to replace religion for either the individual or the community. Nationalism does not provide the answers for the ultimate questions of meaning that arise at critical moments, such as when a nation faces war or an individual faces death, birth, or other crises. Such moments occurred in Israel in 1967 and 1973. Both wars stimulated a heightened sense of self-examination and reconsideration of first principles among many sectors of the population. That was quite evident in the kibbutz movement, especially among some of the most articulate young members of the movement.[18] For a small but very visible group, it has meant a return to traditional forms and Orthodoxy.[19] For others, it has led to an effort to establish a movement for secular humanist Jews in an almost pathetic attempt to develop an a-theistic Judaism. For many more it has meant a searching for ways to express growing interest, openness, and positive sentiments.

Another aspect of these processes since the 1967 war is a growing acknowledgment among virtually all sectors of the Jewish population that the state cannot survive if it is not a Jewish state. Here a felt need to have God and the covenant as parts of the political order is reflected in the desire of many of the nonreligious to maintain contact with the traditional world as part of the complicated constellation of historically determined attitudes toward the substance of Jewish belonging and national meaning. Thus, the mutual needs of the religious and nonreligious, those of political power and those of spiritual ideas, lie beneath and undergird the existing interrelationships of religion and the polity in Israel today.

## NORMALCY IN A JEWISH STATE

Despite the expectations of some Zionists that the reestablishment of the Jewish commonwealth would lead to the kind of normalcy for the Jewish people in which they would be no different from the French or Italians, in the sense of taking their nationality and homeland for granted, Jews remain more like the Americans and people from other new societies, who must be moved by a shared vision in order to feel comfortable in their national identity. For Jews, it seems that this vision must come from Judaism and, indeed, must have a religious component, since every effort to secularize Judaism to date has failed to move more than small groups of Jews.

What, then, has continued in the relationship between religion and politics in comtemporary Israel, and what has changed? The major point of continuity has been the continuing division of the political parties in Israel into three camps and the necessity for the governing coalition to embrace majorities in at least two of the three. On the other hand, there is a clear weakening of the camps qua camps. This weakening was first apparent in the Labor and civil camps, but since the emergence of Tami it has affected the religious camp as well. Both ideologically and politically, the camps are less hermetically sealed from one another than ever before and are more likely to overlap at the fringes and to attract at least a small segment of the electorate that will swing from camp to camp, something that did not occur before 1969 and occurred for the first time with regard to the religious camp in 1981.

The obverse of this situation is the spread of elements of religious expression into the civil camp. If the religious camp is no longer hermetically sealed, and it was perhaps the most hermetically sealed in the past, the civil camp has committed itself to express some combination of civil and popular religion. This development bears watching closely. Many American political scientists have posited a "modernization" model with regard to the future of Israeli politics—namely, that as Israel's population becomes "modernized," Israeli politics will move toward the American model of separation of church and state, or at least greater secularization. In fact, however, as Israel becomes further removed from its founding generation, its Jewish majority is even more concerned about the state's Jewish authenticity and is looking for ways to link the state to appropriate forms of Jewish religious expression that will reaffirm and strengthen that authenticity.

At the time of the second Jewish commonwealth, over 2,000 years ago, the Jewish people also were divided into three camps; Sadducees, Pharisees, and Essenes. The former were the party of Jewish statehood, in the sense that their Jewishness was expressed principally through the political institutions of the state and those religious institutions, such as the temple and its priesthood, that were bound up with statehood. The Pharisees, on the other hand, emphasized individual internalization of Jewish norms and a system of religious behavior designed to give those norms expression independently of the formal institutions of statehood. For them, the state was an important convenience but not the central focus of Judaism. The Essenes sought their salvation in the religious life of the commune. It seems that, for Jews, normalization is the restoration of these three camps as modes of Jewish expression. Pharisaic Judaism, solely dominant for 1,800 years or more, is continued through the Orthodox minority in Israel. The so-called secular Zionists are neo-Sadducees, while the kibbutzim have revived the Essene vision in semisecular form.[20]

The growth in the number of Jews who are "traditional"—who mix secular and religious norms—is bringing the neo-Sadducean camp more into line with its earlier counterpart. The civil religion that is emerging in Israel is essentially Sadducean in character. That is to say, the religious forms are designed to bolster ties with the state and its institutions rather than treat the state and its institutions as handmaidens of the Jewish religious vision. That, indeed, is what separates the civil camp from the religious camp. But since the religious camp itself places a high value on the state and its institutions as instruments to achieve the religious vision, in practice the difference often becomes irrelevant. Menachem Begin was the fullest expression to date of neo-Sadduceanism handled in such a way as to be a bridging rather than a divisive force. The Labor leaders are also neo-Sadducees, but their expression of that tendency emphasizes its divisive side.

Just as it is very difficult to define or delimit Judaism in Israel, it is difficult to predict its future. The shift toward greater concern for Jewish tradition on the part of pace-setting elements of Israeli society is a reflection of at least two factors: the perennial search for meaning (the "wrestling with God" that is embedded in the very meaning of the Hebrew word *Israel*) characteristic of Jews, including Israeli Jews, and the concern for the Jewish future of Israel.

# EIGHT

# Ashkenazim and Sephardim

The Jewish settlers of contemporary Israel come from 103 different countries, speaking 70 different languages—in other words, from wherever Jews found themselves at the end of the modern epoch. Thus, a central issue in Israeli politics has been the ingathering of the exiles and their fusion into a new Israeli Jewish people. Initially, Israel's founding fathers had a romantic view of what was possible in this regard, seeing Zionism, especially socialist Zionism, as a device with unlimited transformatory powers that within a generation would produce this integrated new Jewish type no matter what people brought with them. In fact, as we all know today, that was an impossible dream, which, even in a country that has witnessed the triumph of impossible dreams, did not come to pass.

That is not to say that a great deal of fusion did not take place. During the first half-generation after 1948, Hebrew became the common language of Israel, in fact as well as in theory; a common set of external forms emerged in dress, in public behavior, in civic participation, and in a dozen other areas. Yet, beneath all of that, not surprisingly, differences remained to a greater or lesser extent, depending on the group involved and where they had been settled upon their arrival in the country. Those located in the main centers were more likely to have moved along the path of fusion, while those in the country's peripheries, in the development towns and the moshavei olim, were less likely to have done so.[1]

On one level, then, integration is a reality, and no one doubts the Israeliness of all Israelis. On another level, the major country and region-of-origin groups have maintained their separate identities through social networks, subcultural, albeit in ways that are weakening and declining. Thus, the distinctions between Moroccan and Iraqi Jews, Polish and Rumanian Jews, Jews from Kurdistan and Iran, and Litvaks and Galicianers are still detectable for anyone who looks closely. More important, however, is the coalescence of these country-of-origin groups into two major subsections of Israeli society: Ashkenazim and Sephardim.

The emergence of these two groupings in Israeli society is not surprising, since, despite the differences among Jews from different countries and regions, they represent the two great subdivisions that have dominated

145

Jewish life over the past thousand years. Until the tenth century, virtually all Jews were located in the Islamic lands of Western Asia and the Mediterranean basin. A separate Ashkenazi world emerged in the Franco-German border lands at the end of the tenth and the beginning of the eleventh centuries, at about the same time that the center of Jewish life was shifting from Babylonia to the Iberian Peninsula. From the twelfth century onward, Ashkenazi Jewry grew continuously in absolute and relative terms, coming to equal the Sephardim by 1700 and to exceed them in the eighteenth century. By 1931, 93 percent of world Jewry was Ashkenazic, in contrast to 97 percent Sephardic at the end of the eleventh century. As long as these European, Asian, and North African regions contained the great majority of world Jewry, these divisions remained critical in Jewish life.

## WHO IS WHO?

While the term *Sephardi* is often restricted to the Jews from Spain, in fact it describes the entire Jewish world of Western Asia and the Mediterranean basin, with their eastern and western extensions in the modern epoch—from Hong Kong to Seattle. Historically, the Jews in that part of the world shared for a thousand years the same patterns of halachic expression, a common cultural base, and certain patterns of communal organization, tied together by a closely knit communications network. This network took shape initially in Eretz Israel and Babylonia, gained its full form on the Iberian Peninsula, and then was developed and preserved in the Ottoman Empire, from Morocco to the Persian Gulf, where the exiles from Iberia found refuge—all over one thousand years of Jewish history.

Conversely, the term *Ashkenazi* originally was applied to the Jews of northern France and the Rhineland, and later became the universal term for the Jewries of Europe north of the Alps, with their eastern and western extensions in the modern epoch—from China to Hawaii. Their shared *halachic* patterns, common cultural base, and forms of communal organization and governance differed from those of their Sephardic brethren within the context of their common Jewishness, linked by their own parallel communications network, which they developed over the same thousand years. In essence, Sephardic Jewry is the Jewry of the south, as distinct from Ashkenazic Jewry, which is the Jewry of the north.

That is not to suggest that two Jewries developed out of that thousand-year separation. Quite to the contrary, what is amazing is the degree to which the two groupings remained interconnected, to some extent by inter-regional migrations, although in fact mass migrations between the two spheres occurred only at certain crucial timing points in Jewish history, and most migrations were from east to west to east within each sphere. What kept them bound together was a common constitutional and legal framework, which preserved their shared halachic and religious grounding despite regional variations, and which kept the Jewish people intact within the bounds of a common Torah and halacha. This common framework was maintained by a continuous flow of constitutional, legal, cultural, and intellectual communications between virtually all parts of the Jewish world.

Nevertheless, differences did develop, perhaps because Ashkenazic Jewry lived in a predominantly Christian environment, while Sephardic Jewry lived in a predominantly Moslem environment (except for the Jews of Italy and, for a brief period, most of the Jews of Spain). Nor should we overlook the general cultural differences between the Mediterranean world and northern Europe, which have been noted by historians since the days of the Roman Empire.[2]

## THE NEW DEMOGRAPHICS AND THEIR POLITICAL IMPLICATIONS

At about the time of the Six Day War (1967), the number of Sephardic Jews in Israel came to exceed the number of Ashkenazim for the first time since the demographic balance had shifted from Sephardim to Ashkenazim a century earlier (table 8-1). This shift reflects the considerably higher birth rate among Sephardim. Since then, the percentage of Sephardim has increased steadily. The trend is most visible in the elementary schools, where some two-thirds of the students are Sephardic.

The demographics tell the story: the age cohorts in which first- or second-generation Israelis of Ashkenazic background are strongest are 55-74, while those in which the Sephardim are strongest are 5-29. Under the age of 5, the statistics as collected by Israel's Central Bureau of Statistics do not reveal the original country of origin of the person's family, but it is safe to assume that by now, most third-generation Israelis under the age of 5 are also of Sephardic background (table 8-2).[3] Although the Sephardic birth rate is dropping to closer to that of the Ashkenazim, it will remain higher for at least another generation.

Among other things, that means that a real and growing majority of Israel's Jews not only are native to the geocultural region conventionally known as the Middle East or the Islamic world, but are from families that have been in that region from time immemorial and have as much right to be there as any other of the region's inhabitants. By any measure, Israel cannot be considered a "settler state" in Third-World terminology, if it ever was. Rather, it is a product of an intraregional exchange of population.

It is equally indisputable that over two-thirds of the Sephardim vote for the Likud or other parties in coalition with it. The Ashkenazim voted in something like the reverse percentages. Moreover, despite the Labor myth that it is only the less-educated, lower-SES Sephardim who vote Likud, the evidence is overwhelming that the Likud and its coalition partners draw almost as well from all strata of the Sephardic population, albeit a bit less from white-collar workers and professionals, including the growing number

TABLE 8-1

Population,* by Population Group, Origin, Continent of
Birth and Period of Immigration

| | 31 XII 1983 | 31 XII 1982 | 31 XII 1981 | 31 XII 1980 | 19 V 1972 | 22 V 1961 | 8 XI 1948 |
|---|---|---|---|---|---|---|---|
| | *Thousands* | | | | | | |
| GRAND TOTAL | 4,148.5 | 4,063.6 | 3,977.9 | 3,921.7 | 3,147.7 | 2,179.5 | 872.7 |
| JEWS—TOTAL | 3,436.1 | 3,373.2 | 3,320.3 | 3,282.7 | 2,686.7 | 1,932.4 | 716.7 |
| Origin: Israel | 574.2 | 532.8 | 494.6 | 459.6 | 225.8 | 106.9 | . . |
| Asia | 745.2 | 742.3 | 739.7 | 738.3 | 655.9 | 818.3 | |
| Africa | 766.3 | 754.3 | 744.4 | 736.7 | 617.9 | | |
| Europe-America | 1,350.4 | 1,343.6 | 1,341.7 | 1.348.1 | 1,187.0 | 1,007.1 | . . |
| *Israel born—total* | 2,029.4 | 1,959.8 | 1,894.0 | 1,835.3 | 1,272.3 | 730.4 | 253.7 |
| Father born in: Israel | 574.2 | 532.8 | 494.6 | 459.6 | 225.8 | 106.9 | . . |
| Asia | 451.8 | 445.9 | 440.0 | 434.9 | 339.8 | 288.5 | . . |
| Africa | 434.2 | 422.6 | 411.1 | 400.2 | 269.1 | | . |
| Europe-America | 569.2 | 558.3 | 548.3 | 540.6 | 437.6 | 335.0 | . . |
| *Born abroad—total* | *1,406.7* | *1,413.4* | *1,426.1* | *1,447.4* | *1,414.4* | *1,201.9* | *463.0* |
| Asia | 293.4 | 296.4 | 299.7 | 303.4 | 316.1 | 300.1 | 57.8 |
| Thereof: Immigrated 1972 + | 23.1 | 22.4 | 14.1 | 13.4 | — | — | — |
| Africa | 332.1 | 331.7 | 333.4 | 336.5 | 348.9 | 229.7 | 12.2 |
| Thereof: Immigrated 1972 + | 24.8 | 21.1 | 15.6 | 14.1 | — | — | — |
| Europe-America | 781.2 | 785.2 | 793.0 | 807.6 | 749.7 | 672.1 | 393.0 |
| Thereof: Immigrated 1972 + | 234.8 | 224.9 | 197.1 | 195.2 | — | — | — |
| NON-JEWS—TOTAL | 712.5 | 690.4 | 657.5 | 639.0 | 461.0 | 247.1 | 156.0 |
| Moslems | 548.6 | 530.8 | 513.7 | 498.3 | 352.0 | 170.8 | . . |
| Christians | 96.2 | 94.0 | 91.5 | 89.9 | 72.1 | 50.5 | . . |
| Druse and others | 67.7 | 65.6 | 52.3 | 50.7 | 36.9 | 25.8 | . . |
| | *Percentages* | | | | | | |
| GRAND TOTAL | 100.0 | 100.0 | 100.0 | 100.0 | 100.0 | 100.0 | 100.0 |
| Jews | 82.9 | 83.0 | 83.5 | 83.7 | 85.4 | 88.7 | 82.1 |
| Moslems | 13.2 | 13.1 | 12.9 | 12.7 | 11.2 | 7.8 | |
| Christians | 2.3 | 2.3 | 2.3 | 2.3 | 2.3 | 2.3 | 17.9 |
| Druse and others | 1.6 | 1.6 | 1.3 | 1.3 | 1.2 | 1.2 | |
| JEWS—TOTAL | 100.0 | 100.0 | 100.0 | 100.0 | 100.0 | 100.0 | 100.0 |
| Origin: Israel | 16.7 | 15.8 | 14.9 | 14.0 | 8.4 | 5.5 | . . |
| Asia | 21.7 | 22.0 | 22.3 | 22.5 | 24.4 | 42.3 | |
| Africa | 22.3 | 22.4 | 22.4 | 22.4 | 23.0 | | |
| Europe-America | 39.3 | 39.8 | 40.4 | 41.1 | 44.2 | 52.1 | |
| *Israel born—total* | 59.1 | 58.1 | 57.1 | 55.9 | 47.3 | 37.8 | 35.4 |
| Father born in: Israel | 16.7 | 15.8 | 14.9 | 14.0 | 8.4 | 5.5 | . . |
| Asia | 13.2 | 13.2 | 13.3 | 13.2 | 12.6 | 14.9 | |
| Africa | 12.6 | 12.5 | 12.4 | 12.2 | 10.0 | | |
| Europe-America | 16.6 | 16.6 | 16.5 | 16.5 | 16.3 | 17.4 | . . |
| *Born abroad—total* | *40.9* | *41.9* | *42.9* | *44.1* | *52.7* | *62.2* | *64.6* |
| Asia | 8.5 | 8.8 | 9.0 | 9.2 | 11.8 | 15.5 | 8.1 |
| Africa | 9.7 | 9.8 | 10.0 | 10.3 | 13.0 | 11.9 | 1.7 |
| Europe-America | 22.7 | 23.3 | 23.9 | 24.6 | 27.9 | 34.8 | 54.8 |

*Incl. potential immigrants as of 1972.

of Sephardim teaching in the universities. Since 70 percent of all Sephardim are in the middle or upper SES categories, that is highly significant.[4]

Since the Sephardic population is growing faster than the Ashkenazic, and is likely to become even more of a majority in the future, demographic

TABLE 8-2
## Jewish Population, by Continent of Birth, Sex, and Age
### Average 1983

Thousands

| Age group | Born in Europe-America | Born in Africa | Born in Asia | Israel born / Father born in Europe-American | Africa | Asia | Israel | Total | Grand Total | |
|---|---|---|---|---|---|---|---|---|---|---|
| GRAND TOTAL | 783.2 | 331.9 | 294.9 | 563.6 | 428.5 | 448.9 | 553.5 | 1,994.7 | 3,404.6 | |
| 0 | 0.4 | 0.0 | 0.0 | 12.4 | 12.4 | 7.2 | 41.2 | 73.3 | 74.0 | 0 |
| 1–4 | 5.2 | 0.6 | 0.3 | 50.8 | 52.9 | 34.0 | 141.2 | 278.9 | 285.0 | 1–4 |
| 5–9 | 12.4 | 1.2 | 1.2 | 70.7 | 81.5 | 63.9 | 133.1 | 349.2 | 364.0 | 5–9 |
| 10–14 | 19.0 | 2.2 | 2.3 | 63.1 | 82.1 | 72.3 | 80.4 | 298.0 | 321.4 | 10–14 |
| 15–19 | 21.4 | 6.2 | 4.9 | 50.5 | 74.8 | 66.6 | 49.1 | 240.9 | 273.4 | 15–19 |
| 20–24 | 29.2 | 22.6 | 8.3 | 54.7 | 58.9 | 63.2 | 30.8 | 207.6 | 267.8 | 20–24 |
| 25–29 | 39.3 | 37.4 | 11.3 | 67.1 | 41.9 | 63.8 | 20.6 | 193.5 | 281.5 | 25–29 |
| 30–34 | 50.2 | 46.0 | 26.6 | 78.4 | 19.3 | 42.7 | 15.7 | 156.2 | 279.0 | 30–34 |
| 35–39 | 66.6 | 44.3 | 40.4 | 43.0 | 1.6 | 11.4 | 10.2 | 66.2 | 217.6 | 35–39 |
| 40–44 | 34.8 | 33.9 | 35.2 | 25.5 | 0.8 | 7.4 | 7.0 | 40.8 | 144.6 | 40–44 |
| 45–49 | 46.7 | 32.8 | 34.5 | 22.2 | 0.7 | 6.7 | 7.1 | 36.6 | 150.5 | 45–49 |
| 50–54 | 61.0 | 29.5 | 34.3 | 10.4 | 0.4 | 4.0 | 5.5 | 20.4 | 145.3 | 50–54 |
| 55–59 | 78.5 | 23.8 | 27.2 | 7.8 | 0.4 | 2.5 | 4.3 | 15.0 | 144.4 | 55–59 |
| 60–64 | 84.8 | 19.3 | 22.3 | 2.7 | 0.3 | 1.4 | 2.8 | 7.2 | 133.6 | 60–64 |
| 65–69 | 72.9 | 13.4 | 15.0 | 1.4 | 0.2 | 0.6 | 1.5 | 3.8 | 105.1 | 65–69 |
| 70–74 | 77.0 | 9.7 | 14.1 | 1.4 | 0.2 | 0.6 | 1.5 | 3.7 | 104.5 | 70–74 |
| 75–79 | 48.6 | 5.2 | 8.4 | 0.8 | 0.1 | 0.3 | 0.8 | 2.1 | 64.4 | 75–79 |
| 80 + | 35.2 | 3.8 | 8.5 | 0.5 | 0.1 | 0.2 | 0.5 | 1.3 | 48.5 | 80 + |
| | | | Thereof: females | | | | | | | |
| Total | 414.0 | 169.4 | 149.7 | 276.2 | 209.2 | 221.0 | 269.2 | 975.7 | 1,708.7 | |
| 0 | 0.2 | 0.0 | 0.0 | 6.0 | 6.0 | 3.6 | 20.0 | 35.6 | 35.8 | 0 |
| 1–4 | 2.5 | 0.3 | 0.2 | 24.7 | 25.7 | 16.7 | 68.4 | 135.6 | 138.5 | 1–4 |
| 5–9 | 6.0 | 0.6 | 0.5 | 24.4 | 39.9 | 31.3 | 64.6 | 170.2 | 177.3 | 5–9 |
| 10–14 | 9.3 | 1.0 | 1.1 | 30.6 | 40.2 | 35.4 | 39.1 | 145.2 | 156.7 | 10–14 |
| 15–19 | 10.6 | 3.0 | 2.3 | 24.4 | 36.4 | 32.7 | 23.9 | 117.4 | 133.3 | 15–19 |
| 20–24 | 15.0 | 11.3 | 4.0 | 26.5 | 28.7 | 31.0 | 15.0 | 101.2 | 131.6 | 20–24 |
| 25–29 | 20.7 | 18.5 | 5.7 | 32.3 | 20.5 | 31.5 | 10.1 | 94.4 | 139.2 | 25–29 |
| 30–34 | 26.1 | 23.0 | 13.2 | 38.3 | 9.5 | 21.1 | 7.8 | 76.7 | 138.9 | 30–34 |
| 35–39 | 33.8 | 22.5 | 20.1 | 21.5 | 0.8 | 5.7 | 4.9 | 32.9 | 109.2 | 35–39 |
| 40–44 | 18.3 | 17.6 | 17.6 | 12.8 | 0.4 | 3.8 | 3.4 | 20.3 | 73.8 | 40–44 |
| 45–49 | 24.3 | 16.9 | 17.7 | 11.2 | 0.3 | 3.4 | 3.5 | 18.3 | 77.2 | 45–49 |
| 50–54 | 33.0 | 15.2 | 17.5 | 5.5 | 0.2 | 2.1 | 2.8 | 10.5 | 76.3 | 50–54 |
| 55–59 | 44.8 | 12.2 | 14.2 | 4.2 | 0.2 | 1.3 | 2.2 | 7.8 | 79.1 | 55–59 |
| 60–64 | 44.5 | 9.9 | 11.1 | 1.4 | 0.1 | 0.7 | 1.3 | 3.6 | 69.1 | 60–64 |
| 65–69 | 39.9 | 7.0 | 8.0 | 0.8 | 0.1 | 0.3 | 0.8 | 2.1 | 56.8 | 65–69 |
| 70–74 | 40.5 | 5.3 | 7.7 | 0.8 | 0.1 | 0.3 | 0.8 | 2.0 | 55.6 | 70–74 |
| 75–79 | 25.0 | 2.9 | 4.3 | 0.5 | 0.1 | 0.1 | 0.4 | 1.1 | 33.4 | 75–79 |
| 80 + | 19.5 | 2.2 | 4.5 | 0.3 | 0.1 | 0.1 | 0.3 | 0.8 | 26.9 | 80 + |

*Incl. potential immigrants.

inertia alone will lead the Labor Alignment to lose an additional 1 percent of the electorate from election to election, with a corresponding Likud gain, which translates into a 2 percent shift (two or three Knesset seats) in the latter's favor every four years. The trend toward the Likud is enhanced further by the fact that since the 1965 elections, a majority of new voters, Ashkenazim as well as Sephardim, have supported its parties in clear preference to Labor. By now, those successive waves of new voters constitute the majority of the electorate.

The seeming increase in the Labor Alignment seats between 1977 and 1981 was illusory, consisting of the return to the fold of traditional Labor voters who supported Yigael Yadin's Democratic Movement for Change, and Arab voters who decided to vote for a mainstream party rather than separate ethnic lists. In reality, Labor probably reached a peak strength, which it will be unable to duplicate for the rest of this political generation, except under unusual and idiosyncratic circumstances. That was demonstrated in the 1984 elections, when the alignment actually lost four seats even while coming in ahead of the Likud.

## ASHKENAZIM AND SEPHARDIM—MYTH AND REALITY

In the 1980s, Israel-watchers discovered Israel's Sephardic majority. Initially prompted by the recognition that Menachem Begin's 1977 electoral victory was not a fluke but possibly the beginning of a new political era in Israel dominated by the Likud as a new majority party, this discovery has been accompanied by a myth that the Jewish people are deeply divided into "two cultures,": the first—and best—the "Western" culture of the Ashkenazim, the Jews of Europe and the Americas, and the other the inferior culture of the Sephardim, the Afro-Asian Jews. The "two cultures" idea began as part of the attempt to mobilize support both within and outside Israel for the better integration of the masses of new immigrants into Israeli life. It originally was presented in terms such as the following (written in the 1950s by a leading Ashkenazi Israeli social scientist and government spokesman in a brochure designed for wide distribution to Jews and non-Jews in the United States):

> During recent years, we have had a large influx of Jews from the Near East and Africa . . . most of the people who come to Israel from these countries have darker skin . . . many of the countries from which they come are underdeveloped. Some of these darker-skinned Jews lived in the Casbah in Casablanca in ghettoes under the most miserable conditions, deprived of all opportunities for education or a decent life. And if you think their lot was bad, put yourself for a moment in the place of some of our Jewish brethren who come from the Atlas Mountains, N. Africa, where they lived in caves! . . . the lighter-skinned Jews who came from Eastern Europe include professionals, tradesmen, and those who have been exposed to the sciences, the arts, and the professions. I would say that the average Jew who comes from these countries has a minimum of a high school education. So, when you put these relatively cultured, advantaged Jews

into the melting pot with the Jews from Africa, some of whom have no primary education, you get a great discrepancy. This is a socially unhealthy situation.

This "two cultures" thesis rests upon three misleading but generally unquestioned assumptions made by the Ashkenazim and apparently accepted implicitly by many Sephardim. The Ashkenazim believe that they are the sole representatives of Western culture in Israel, that they have a monopoly on prestatehood Zionist pioneering, and that the Sephardic cultural heritage is basically unsuited for Westernization. More recently, it has been revised to suggest that military aggressiveness, "hard line" with regard to the territories captured as a result of the Six Day War, internal violence, antidemocratic thinking, and religious fundamentalism in Israel are of Sephardic origin and are becoming more widespread as a result of the growing role of the Sephardim.[5]

The prevalent myths are presented through an appropriate semantics.[6] In conventional usage, the Ashkenazim are labeled "Western" and the Sephardim "Oriental," terms clearly loaded to reflect the prevailing assumptions with regard to culture and modernity. Unfortunately, these terms are more self-serving to the former than accurate. For example, former president Itzhak Navon is acknowledged by one and all to be a man of broad culture. Formerly active in Labor party politics, he has been hailed by all Israelis, most especially by those of the Labor camp, for his moral leadership. In every respect he is the quintessential representative of what propagators of the anti-Sephardic myths seem to mean by "European middle-class and liberal." The only problem is that he is a Sephardi, born in Jerusalem into a family both sides of which have lived in the country for many generations and who came to Eretz Israel in the seventeenth and nineteenth centuries from Turkey and Morocco respectively. In other words, President Navon is not only Sephardic but a quintessential member of the "Afro-Asian" group by any definition.

Navon is only the most visible exemplar of a large population like him, including the thousands of descendants of other old Jerusalemite families, plus Jews whose families were part of the civic elite in Iraq, sophisticated products of French culture in North Africa, heirs of the young Turk revolution in Turkey, or what have you. Indeed, before the establishment of the state, Sephardim in Israel tended to look down upon the Ashkenazim, including the Zionist pioneers, as uncouth and lacking all cultural refinement—for reasons that Amos Oz puts positively, namely, their rejection of bourgeois refinements.

On the other hand, the so-called Western Jews did indeed come from Europe, in a geographic sense, but principally from Eastern Europe. As a class, they no more are to be considered "Western" than Jews from the Islamic East. Indeed, within Ashkenazic Jewry, the Jews of Germany looked down upon those of Eastern Europe, terming them "Ostjuden" (Eastern Jews)—in other words, making the same stereotyped generalizations about them as these former "Ostjuden," now the self-proclaimed bearers of Western culture in the Middle East, make about the Sephardim.

What is truly characteristic of the Jews of Israel is how alike they are on the basis of every significant measure, especially when compared to non-Jews anywhere. Their similarity begins with genetics. Studies that have been conducted to date show that Jews are more alike genetically than anyone hitherto had believed, a result of centuries of endogamy. Those similarities and differences that, combined with constant intermarriage and migration, do exist within the Jewish people do not particularly divide along Ashkenazi/Sephardi lines.[7]

At the other end of the spectrum from genetics, Jews continue to be the same in their moral standards and sensibilities. Again, one dramatic illustration tells us much. The shocked and horrified Israeli response to the Lebanese Christian massacre of Palestinians in the Beirut refugee camps was spread through the entire population of Israel to an equal degree. While undoubtedly there were people who took it more seriously and people who took it less so, this difference was not a matter of Sephardim and Ashkenazim.[8]

All of that is not to imply that there are no differences between Ashkenazim and Sephardim. There are subcultural differences that are real enough, derived from different realities of the Mediterranean world and Islamic civilization, the host environment of the vast majority of the Sephardim, and Northern Europe and Russian Orthodox or Catholic civilizations, the host environment of the vast majority of the Ashkenazim. The Jews from the Arab lands are no more like Arabs than the Jews from Poland or Russia are like Polish Catholics or Russian Orthodox Christians.

So, for example, Ashkenazic food tends to partake of a certain plain heaviness (often erroneously termed "Jewish cooking") charactristic of Eastern and parts of Central Europe, while Sephardic cuisine is light and sophisticated, in the manner of the fine cuisines of Spain, Italy, and Greece. While all Jewish music has been traced back to a common root, Ashkenazic music developed under the influence of the Russian Orthodox Church, while Sephardic music mixes Iberian and Arabic elements. What is little noted is that classical Sephardic music is much closer to the Western music of Bach, Haydn, and Mozart, which drew from late medieval Spanish influences, while Ashkenazic music, which developed exclusively out of Eastern influences, stayed Eastern.

Even more important for Israel's future, the Sephardic attitude toward religion tends to be open and tolerant, with both the religious and non-religious sharing a common respect for Jewish religious tradition, despite varying degrees of formal observance, with each willing to respect the level of observance of the other. The Ashkenazic attitude, on the other hand, tends to be ideological and uncompromising, with so many Israeli Ashkenazim, especially those that set the tone, either unbendingly religious or unbendingly secular. The militant, black-garbed Jews who throw stones at vehicles on the Sabbath and refuse to serve in the army are not Sephardim. Sephardim pride themselves on the fact that there was no religious reformation in the Sephardic world, and hence no counter reformation establishing orthodoxy—that however individual Jews chose to practice their Judaism, they stayed within a common fold, because they were not ideologically bound to make clear-cut divisions.

Sephardim see themselves as less dominating, aggressive, and "pushy" than Ashkenazim, rightly or wrongly, and attribute their own perceived lack of advancement in Israeli society to that cultural difference. On the other hand, some Sephardim give the impression of being more violent, probably because, as they learned that they did not have to be submissive to authority as they were under Arab rule, they reacted in the other direction, until they learned how to function in a moderate way, in a democratic society. By now that difference has almost disappeared.

Part of the myth is that Sephardim are particularly chauvinistic, militaristic, or xenophobic. There is no evidence of that whatsoever. Meir Kahane's tiny band of followers—the only group in Israel fitting that description—is dominated by immigrants from the United States, with not a Sephardi among them. The few Sephardim who have been attracted to him were among the last to respond to his appeal.

The cultural differences between the two groups are not those that divide east and west—there are easterners and westerners in both groups. In fact, most Israelis come from cultures that people from Western Europe and America would label as "Eastern." Some are from Eastern Europe, the north's east, and some are from the Islamic world, which is really the south's east. Hence, the differences between them reflect the differences between the eastern cultures and societies of the north and south.[9]

## SEPHARDIM, ASHKENAZIM, AND MODERNIZATION

Another set of differences relates to modernization. While the matter is by no means unilinear, it is generally true that the majority of Israeli Jews from the north's east began the process of modernization a generation or so before the majority of those from the south's east. That is true even though the Jews of North Africa were emancipated by the French before the Jews of the Russian Empire were emancipated by the Russians. Moreover, conveniently overlooked are the many eastern Sephardim—of Palestine, of Iraq, of Egypt, of Turkey, of the Balkans, and even of North Africa—whose families encountered Western civilization at least at the same time as their Ashkenazi brethren in Russia. In many cases, Sephardim were being educated in the modern schools of the Alliance Israelite Universelle, while Ashkenazim seeking secular knowledge still had to hide "Western" books in their Gemarot in the yeshiva.

It must be recalled that the Sephardic world underwent its great migrational upheaval only in the post-World War II generation, some two generations after Ashkenazic Jewry underwent the same experience. What 1880 was for Eastern European Jewish masses, 1948 was for the masses of Sephardim in Africa and Asia. It is true that the Jews of the Balkans and Asia Minor began their migrations some two generations earlier, just as the Jews of Germany and Central Europe began their migration two generations before their Eastern European brethren. In fact, the ratio of German Jewry to the total Ashkenazi population was much the same as the ratio of Balkan Jewry to the total Sephardi population.

It is entirely possible that most of the Jews of Europe acquired such things as indoor plumbing and toothbrushes somewhat earlier than most of their Afro-Asian brethren, but while many in the Labor establishment have made much of this difference over the years, in fact everyone in Israel has learned to use or misuse such devices and others like them. Hence, the whole issue is already a matter of history. Establishment commentators on the Israeli scene often have pointed to just those differences as basic, indicating that all Israel's Jews have in common is a shared Jewish tradition. Those who see such differences as overriding that shared Jewish tradition reveal more about themselves as products of Israel's "Bolshevik Revolution" than about the Israeli reality.

If any serious differences remain with regard to modernization, they are mostly differences having to do with equality of opportunity. Thus, the Ashkenazim, either because they came to Israel before the Sephardim or because they could turn to relatives who came before and thereby get preferred treatment, managed as a group to advance more rapidly up the economic ladder than did the Sephardim, most of whom came a little later and had virtually no personal links to the then-existing establishment. The official justification for such preferment is invariably based on the Ashkenazi "two cultures" argument, that the Sephardi immigrants were inferior in skills and talent and thus could not be given responsible positions. While that was undoubtedly true in the case of the cave dwellers of the Atlas Mountains (approximately 20,000 of the 650,000 Sephardic olim of that period were from primitive backgrounds), the plain truth is that no effort was made to utilize the talents and skills of those who did have them. Ex-judges from Iraq, college graduates from Egypt, and technically skilled members of old Jerusalem families were ignored or forced to accept lower-status occupations because they did not have the "old-school tie" from Eastern Europe.

Even so, it is a mistake to think of the Ashkenazim as an upper group and the Sephardim as a lower one. While it is true that 90 percent of those living in neighborhoods considered disadvantaged are Sephardim, only 30 percent of the Sephardim live in such neighborhoods.[10] In other words, the other 70 percent are well integrated into the society at every level, including former president Navon and the Recanati family, who are the principal owners of the Israel Discount Bank, one of the country's three largest; storekeepers and professionals, who make a comfortable living in their chosen fields of endeavor; university professors, taxi drivers, or whatever.

It is true that the statistics show that most Sephardic children are in need of special educational assistance, but that is, in great part, a self-fulfilling prophecy, since the definition of who needs special educational assistance includes as one of its elements the mere fact of Sephardic background.[11] Studies of Sephardic families repeatedly have shown that they have motivations for achievement similar to those of the Ashkenazim. They want their children to acquire an education, and they are interested in "getting ahead" in the same ways.

To the extent that Sephardim are undereducated, it is as a result of their position in Israeli society in the early years after the mass migration. There are studies that show that among families who separated, including twins, some going to France or North America and others coming to Israel, the ones who came to Israel suffered educational deprivation, while the ones who went to the West became doctors, lawyers, and academics in the same proportions as other diaspora Jews.[12]

One of the causes of Sephardic resentment toward the Labor party goes back to those days when the majority of the Sephardim were still in immigrant camps, and social workers sent by Mapai or the government pressed them to leave school after the seventh grade so that they could work in the fields and orchards. The social workers often did so for the best of motives; they sincerely believed in the Labor Zionist ideology, which held that the Jews had to become normal by becoming agriculturists. The fact that they were sending their own children to high school and college at the same time may reflect some of the absurdity of the human condition, but it was no laughing matter to the Sephardim, who were being doomed by good intentions to the bottom of the pyramid and who had to fight their way up from there. It should be emphasized that whatever the pressures on the Sephardim, they were pressures based upon good intentions on the part of idealists. Still, their consequences were, for all intents and purposes, demeaning and discriminatory.

That indeed led to the real intergroup problem in Israel today. Many of the Sephardim have accepted the low Ashkenazi evaluation of their way of life and consequently are going through a major crisis of identity, casting aside their "inferior" Sephardic heritage as quickly as possible. An objective observer would have to conclude that this very drive to succeed in the new Israeli society is itself a refutation of the "two cultures" thesis. Again, there are independent measures that confirm the assessment that there are no basic differences in educational ability between Sephardim and Ashkenazim. Those Sephardim native to Israel whose families lived in Israel before World War I (and the Sephardim formed the Jewish majority in the country until the 1880s, with some families going back hundreds of years—at least to the fifteenth century) occupy the same socioeconomic positions as their Ashkenazic brethren, whether as industrialists or academics, and even to some extent in public life—witness ex-president Navon—although for the most part, after the Russian Zionists came, they abandoned public life, precisely because of what even the Ashkenazi apologists call the quasi-Bolshevik tactics of the socialist Zionists after World War I.

The Sephardim suffered from one other disadvantage that could not have been foreseen. Some ten years after the mass migration that followed the establishment of the state, German reparations to Holocaust victims began to flow into Israel. Most of the Ashkenazic Jews in the country benefited directly from those reparations as individuals because of their Holocaust experiences, while most of the Sephardim did not. The reparations came at a crucial point in the emergence of the then still relatively new immigrants, at precisely the moment when they had become sufficiently rooted to take a great leap forward economically. Thus, the Ashkenazim acquired the resources to do so, while the Sephardim did not, creating an economic gap that now is having social and political consequences. No one was to blame for that, but, nevertheless, it became a fact to be reckoned with.

Finally, there are differences between the secular Jews of Israel and the Sephardim in the way in which they relate to Jewish tradition—secular Jews, not Ashkenazim per se. That minority in Israel who have, to all intents and purposes, rejected Jewish religious tradition and have sought to express their Jewishness through a highly secularized Zionism, are indeed far removed from the Sephardim. It is these secularists, particularly the intellectuals among them, who have given voice to the whole "two cultures" issue, who have created the existing myths, who are furthest removed from the world of the Sephardim, and, indeed, who are unhappy if Israel moves in directions comfortable for the latter.

For those intellectuals, the question of familiarity with the ideological fads and accepted behavior of the Western intellectual world is the touchstone of whether one is modern or not. Ironically, they have taken this stance at a time when precisely the kind of secularist left-liberalism that they have embraced is in so much trouble in the West that these secularists are so desirous of imitating. But they represent a small minority in the Country, even if they are the most vocal. To the extent that the Labor party has accepted their vision of an ideal Israel, it has alienated itself from the larger number of voters, Ashkenazim as well as Sephardim, who are turning in increasing numbers to the Likud.

Even those who are not bound by the aforementioned myths often rely on yet another one, namely, that only the Ashkenazim were Zionists and that they were solely responsible for building the third Jewish commonwealth—that the Sephardim came along only after the state was declared, motivated by the necessity to seek refuge from Arab persecution in the wake of the Israel-Arab war of 1948 and, to some extent, by traditional messianic longings. According to this myth, the Sephardim were the passive beneficiaries of the work of the (Ashkenazic) halutzim but the active corruptors of the society built by those halutzim.

In fact, not only were most Ashkenazim in the world non- or anti-Zionists until the Holocaust and the struggle for the establishment of the state, but most still have not come to Israel, which is why the Sephardim, who constitute only 18 percent of the world Jewry, are now the majority in Israel. Perhaps more to the point, as has been noted in chapters 1 and 2, Sephardim were among the first founders of the new yishuv. They continued to be pioneers throughout the prestate period, albeit in different spheres from those of the Ashkenazic halutzim.

In the period between 1919 and 1948, Sephardim accounted for about one-tenth of the world Jewish population, yet they provided about one-sixth of the migrants to Palestine. The Third Aliyah brought a large mixture of Sephardim from every part of the Sephardic diaspora, while the aliyot of the 1930s brought the fruits of Zionist education work, particularly from the Balkans and North Africa. Salonikan Jewish stevedores manned the ports of Haifa at Tel Aviv in the 1930s.

Nor were the Sephardic migrations any less motivated by Zionism than the Ashkenazic. Sephardim were active in the Zionist movement from the first, not only as individuals—Theodore Herzl and Max Nordau both affirmed their Sephardic descent—but in their communities, as well. Sephardic Bulgaria was the first Jewish community to be "captured" by the Zionist movement. Salonika, the "capital" of the Sephardic diaspora, had Zionist clubs and newspapers from the time of Herzl, and the Zionist organization of Yugoslavia represented an important force in the Jewish life of that country. True, the North Africans, Iraqis, Iranians, and Yemenites had less in the way of formal Zionist organization becasue of the more traditional nature of their societies, and the existence of powerful Arab nationalist elements that actively repressed open Zionist activity. Even so, Zionist groups existed in the first three in the interwar period. If we tend to exaggerate the strength of the Zionist movement in Eastern Europe, there is no reason to minimize its strength in the Sephardic world.[13]

One of the reasons it has been minimized is that most of the Jews who came to Israel after 1948 did not come out of any organized Zionist framework. Still, there is no particular reason to believe that there was proportionately less Zionist interest among the Moroccan Jews than among the Rumanian Jews who came at that time.

In the last analysis, there are no real differences among Sephardim and Ashkenazim in their commitment to Zionism and the State of Israel. Sephardim and Ashkenazim alike responded to the beckoning call of Zion during the century or more of resettlement prior to the establishment of the state, and since then have stood together to support Israel wherever they themselves might happen to reside. In the Zionists' struggle for recognition and support, Sephardim divided just as Ashkenazim did, just as today they divide over what state's policies should be. Any analysis that fails to recognize this basic fact of Jewish unity misses the essence of the Jewish experience, which is one of unity with diversity, a shared sense of kinship uniting all the tribes of Israel, and a consensus with regard to the importance of a shared Jewish destiny, as well as in recognition of the common Jewish fate.

Within this common framework, it is still possible to identify and examine a Sephardic role and set of attitudes, which, while not radically different from that of their Ashkenazic brothers, do add another dimension to the contemporary Jewish response to Zionism and renewed statehood. That is more a matter of emphasis than of kind; nevertheless, it is an important emphasis, one that becomes especially important at this particular stage in the history of the Zionist revolution.

What is special about Sephardic Zionism is its merger of religious and political aspirations. Never having undergone reformation and secularization, on one hand, or embraced otherworldly pietism, on the other, both of which have characterized the Ashkenazic world in the modern epoch, the Sephardic world earlier was attuned to seeking political solutions to the Jewish condition, while at the same time never divorcing those political solutions from a deep religious commitment.

In a very real sense, the Sephardic world was never outside the political arena. Even in the aftermath of the Spanish exile, at the darkest period of their history, the Sephardic leaders sought remedies to the Jewish condition in the political realm, through an alliance with the Ottoman Turks against their Christian persecutors and in efforts to restore at least a measure of Jewish self-rule in Eretz Israel. While these efforts failed, the very fact that they were made is a reflection of the kind of practical messianism that is characteristically the mainstream orientation of the Jewish people and that for a long time was given a particular emphasis in the Sephardic world.

Sephardic political efforts—from the sixteenth-century Ancona boycott, to Don Joseph Nasi's abortive effort to resettle Tiberias, to Rabbi Manasseh Ben Israel's mission to Cromwell, to Mordechai Emanuel Noah's dream of Ararat—persisted down through the centuries and represented the principal political involvement of Jews until the emergence of the Zionist movement in Christian Europe. If they failed in their efforts, it was only because the time was not yet ripe for them to succeed.

Sephardim have persisted in this synthesis of religious and political impulses as part of their integral Jewishness. The Sephardic world has not produced a Neturei Karta, politically paralyzed (except for an adeptness at promoting civil strife) while waiting for the Messiah, or an antireligious social revolutionary camp. With a bare minimum of exceptions, no matter how far any Sephardi has drifted from religious observance, his respect for Jewish traditions remains intact, and no matter how extreme he may have become in observance (and by and large Sephardim do not tend to extremism), it never has been at the price of a commitment to political redemption. If there is any contrast between the Zionism of the Ashkenazim and that of the Sephardim, it is that the former was a Zionism that demanded internal revolution as much as a transformation of the Jewish condition, while the latter was a

Zionism of redemption, which sought continuity with a tradition that was not perceived as requiring revolution.

## CULTURAL AND MORAL IMPLICATIONS FOR ISRAEL'S FUTURE

It should be clear that, intellectually and socially, the demographic shift in Israel is not going to bring any loss of what is perceived in the West as the Jewish character of the state. Jews, both Ashkenazim and Sephardim, still will flock to the universities in great numbers. They will support cultural institutions of all kinds. They will continue to share the same moral sensibilities and the same willingness to be realistic in defense of Israel, with the same strategic and tactical disagreements falling, as they do now, along lines far removed from the Sephardic-Ashkenazic issue.

There may be some changes in the offing in the style of Israeli culture. Right now, for example, there is a struggle going on between new Sephardi theater groups growing out of the Sephardic experience in Israel, and the Israeli theatrical establishment, which has been open only to Sephardim who have accepted their particular dramatic and political approaches. Sephardic influences on music may become more pronounced. If the Ashkenazic-dominated religious establishment and the Ashkenazi secularists do not succeed in squelching Sephardic self-expression in that sphere (which seems to be what is happening), the Sephardic religious approach may become more influential.

In general, Israeli society has become more polite and refined as the Sephardim have become more influential. It was the early socialist pioneers who rejected decent dress, social graces, and manners as "bourgeois," all of which were reintroduced by Sephardim as much as by the bourgeois elements from Central Europe. In general, the keen observer would forecast a society that would be less abrasive, but no less keen, as it loses the Eastern European mannerisms of the former Ashkenazic majority and replaces them with the Mediterranean ways of the Sephardim.

That leads to the question of "Levantinization"—the earliest of the canards hurled against the Sephardim by the same Ashkenazi establishment. Shortly after the establishment of the state, it became fashionable to blame every deviation from the socialist ideal on "Levantinization" brought by the immigrants from the Arab world. The fact that during this entire period these immigrants were essentially powerless did not keep them from being used as scapegoats in this way.

The truth is that the deviations from the ideal patterns of socialist Zionism and the occasional corruption that accompanied them were indigenous to the pioneers and the sons of the pioneers, the members of the Ashkenazic socialist elite. One need not be surprised that such things occurred in Israel, human nature being what it is and men being far from angels. It is to Israel's credit that whenever and wherever discovered, corruption has been attacked head on and, if not entirely eliminated, certainly has been kept to a minimum.

Beyond that, lesser deviations from the norm are a reflection as much of the culture of Eastern Europe as of that of the Middle East. That may be small comfort to those who would like an ideal Israel, but at least it puts matters in the proper perspective. Perhaps there will be a Levantinization of Israel when the Sephardim become dominant, but as yet they have not had the chance to introduce any such thing. Whatever there is that deserves that label is fully the property of the Ashkenazim. In short, the moral implications of the demographic shift are not more likely to be drastic than the intellectual and social ones. There are indeed differences throughout Israeli society with regard to moral issues, but they do not align themselves along any Ashkenazic-Sephardic division.

Ashkenazi intellectuals are fond of accusing Sephardim of being antidemocratic, or at least not prodemocratic, citing such "evidence" as the chant "Begin, King of Israel" during Begin's election campaigns. Aside from the fact that the chant, derived from a folk expression, was generally the work of teenagers at Begin rallies, probably organized by the local Herut party branch, and hardly represents a considered political ideology, the leading antidemocrats in Israel (and every polity has some) are people such as Dr. Israel Eldad, a native of Poland, and Meir Kahane, who want strongman rule, and certain members of the extreme Orthodox camp, all Ashkenazim, who look forward to the restoration of the Davidic monarchy when the Messiah comes.

The truth is that the overwhelming majority of Ashkenazim and Sephardim alike share the same attitudes toward and expectations of democratic government. The Jews who gathered in Israel from various parts of the world brought with them the political cultural influences of their respective environments. Those from Eastern Europe and the Arab world, with few exceptions, came from subject political cultures where the whole idea of citizenship did not exist, while those who had been exposed to continental European politics came with Jacobin views of what a state should be.

What is most important, however, is that all shared a common Jewish political culture, to a greater or lesser degree, which has been republican since the earliest beginnings of the Jewish people, and often democratic at that. Jewish communities in the diaspora, no less than Jewish states in the Land of Israel, functioned along republican lines throughout the ages. With the exception of Attalia, who usurped the Judean throne during the First Commonwealth, and one Second Commonwealth ruler, Herod, who reached the throne legitimately and then usurped power, the Jewish people never have known autocratic rule, except, perhaps, sporadically on a local basis.[14]

Jewish political culture cannot be other than republican. Even its corruptions tend to be oligarchic within a republican framework and resting on a democratic base. That, indeed, is the secret of Israel's success as a democracy, and it is a secret that is shared by all Jews, whatever their country of origin. The political culture of Israel has not taken full shape yet, but it can be taken for granted that it will be republican and democratic. So far, Israel has done nothing to disappoint in that respect.

There may be differences in attitude between Sephardim and Ashkenazim with regard to Arabs. The Sephardim from Islamic lands are both more at home with Arabic culture and more realistic about Arab intentions— no more prone to hate Arabs than to love them. Ashkenazim, on the other hand, tend to be further removed from understanding either Arabic culture or the Arabs themselves, for lack of experience and background.

## POLITICAL IMPLICATIONS

During the first generation of statehood, Sephardim failed to make progress commensurate with their strength in Israeli society in most spheres. That has begun to change in the second generation, and nowhere more so than in the political sphere.

A bit of historical recapitulation: As indicated earlier, it was only after the British conquest during World War I and the establishment of mandatory Palestine that power passed into the hands of the Zionist movement, and within the Zionist movement, after a brief struggle, into the hands of the socialist Zionists, the Labor camp. With the victory of the Labor camp in the late 1920s, most Sephardim withdrew from politics, seeing little point in competing with what was essentially a Labor monopoly. Thus, among the old Sephardic families who were rooted in the country, relatively few continued to engage in public affairs.

When the new Sephardic immigrants came after the establishment of the state, they had to undergo a period of settling in before they could even aspire to compete in a highly organized, centrally dominated political arena. Even so, by the late 1950s, a mere decade or less after their immigration, they began to assume leading positions in local government in the development towns and rural settlements, where they formed the majority, often after contests with Mapai "carpetbaggers" who had been sent in by the party headquarters to run things.

In addition to the advantages for political and social integration gained through local governmental responsibility for the delivery of services or local governmental assistance in the perpetuation of legitimate diversity, it was the role of local government in enlarging the arena of political recruitment and fostering channels of political communication that had the most impact toward bridging the cleavages within Israeli society. Between 1955 and 1965, the proportion of Sephardim in the total population grew to 47 percent, and the proportion of local elective or appointive offices held by them rose from 23 percent to 43 percent. By 1968, it was estimated that they were represented roughly in proportion to their share in the total population. Moreover, in the development towns, where they are the dominant elements in the population, they were overwhelmingly in control of the elective and administrative offices of loval government. Although Sephardic officeholders principally were confined to the development towns and rural settlements rather than the older, established communities, within less than a generation they had achieved a political base and a jumping-off point for what, in the last few years, has become a major move into state politics.[15]

The existence of opportunity on the local plane functioned to encourage those with native talent among the Sephardim to pursue satisfying political careers within the system rather than agitate against the system. Even though the outside observer may well note that they received proportionately less for their efforts than those of Ashkenazi background, with few exceptions, their expectations were lower to begin with; hence, they initially were satisfied with less. Nor is that surprising. Comparisons between them and the present generation of American "ethnics" are misleading. They are to be more appropriately compared to the new immigrants to the United States at the turn of the century, to whom any recognition in the political sphere was considered a great sign of acceptance and advancement, while equality or parity at the highest level was not even within the range of expectations of the immigrants. As in the American case, a generation later, the opening up of local government was paralleled by a similar opening up on the state plane, as well, as political socialization, general acculturation, and expectation levels rose.

The rapid infiltration of members of the disadvantaged immigrant groups into political life on the local plane was due to the efforts of the political parties, however distorted. The "bosses" of the political parties were among the first to recognize the persistence of what elsewhere is referred to as ethnicity among Israelis of all kinds, even while the more "statesmanlike" leaders of the country and its more idealistic elements still were hoping for rapid and complete amalgamation of populations. The former recognized that country- and region-of-origin patterns would influence voting and that either they would assimilate those patterns into their own party organization or local "ethnic" tickets would develop and perhaps siphon votes away from their tickets, statewise as well as locally. They moved in to align themselves with specific immigrant communities and to recruit their more talented members for political office. By doing so, they not only succeeded in binding the new immigrants to the existing parties, but also bound them to the political system itself. As a result of their efforts, combined with the widely shared ideology of the integration of the new immigrants, separate tickets have had a dismal record on the Israeli political scene, even though communal voting patterns are very noticeable in the party alignments in locality after locality.

It was during this period that Mapai and its Labor party successor made their fatal mistake. While they sooner or later began to encourage Sephardic officeholders in the local arena, they discouraged any effort on the part of Sephardim to advance beyond that within their ranks, except when chosen by the established power holders for symbolic purposes. It is true that more Sephardim appeared on the Labor lists in the beginning of the 1960s, but these were essentially people without independent political power, dependent upon the party hierarchy for their office. As younger people approached the Labor party organization seeking places within it, they were told in effect, sometimes directly and sometimes obliquely, that there was no room for them. Most of the bright young Sephardic Knesset members within Herut today had the experience of being rejected personally by the Labor party, to which they turned first because it was the majority party and they were interested in pursuing political careers. Herut, on the other hand, being an opposition party, with a weak local base and nothing much to lose, welcomed these Sephardim and gave them the opportunity to embark on political careers, thereby forming a cadre that now is coming into its own and is beginning to play a major role in the government of Israel.

In the meantime, the Labor establishment was getting tired, as all establishments do, and even a bit corrupted by power, in the way of the world. Moreover, it was making enemies, as every ruling establishment must in due course. Beginning with the 1965 elections, there began to be defections from Labor's ranks, both in the form of unsuccessful splinter parties within the Labor camp and, more important in the long run, in a trend by younger voters, new to the political process, to begin voting Herut (then Gahal—the original Herut-Liberal alignment) and then Likud. This trend has continued, so that today voters under forty-five, Ashkenazim as well as Sephardim, are more likely to vote Likud than Labor.[16]

At the same time, the Sephardim began to gravitate to Likud for their own reasons, as well as a result of this intergenerational shift. In part, it was the opportunity for the younger politicians to get ahead, which was denied them in the Labor party. For the rank-and-file voters, it was the accumulation of resentments that could come to the fore once they became affluent enough to consider their situation.

Once the struggle of the Sephardim to achieve a solid economic base was completed, social and political issues could come into play, two of which were particularly important, one negative and one positive. The negative was the recollection of the way in which they had been treated by Labor— whether it was the way in which the people who received them in Israel had tried to secularize them in the name of modernization, to remake a people with traditional leanings in the mold of socialist Zionism; whether it was the way they tried to convince them to go to work in the fields instead of continuing their education or sent them off to become agricultural workers on the peripheries of the country; or whether it was the way their culture and habits were misunderstood by people from a different background and therefore were subject to absorption pains that went beyond the mere fact of dislocation.

The Sephardim in the 1950s were incapable of resisting Labor pressures or even understanding them sufficiently to distinguish between what was real, such as the necessity to settle the country's open spaces, and what was not, such as that socialist Zionist ways represented the right way to express Jewish ideals and achieve "modernization." Two decades later, once it became clear that Labor had lost its idealism and was simply a party like others, pursuing political office and the rewards thereof, and that the Ashkenazim were not really all that Western, Labor's hold on the Sephardim collapsed. That was especially true for the younger generation, which had not been habituated to thinking of Labor as the only legitimate rulers of the state. Thus, even younger Sephardim with leftist views voted Likud in protest against the Ashkenazi establishment.

In a more positive vein, Menachem Begin appealed to the Sephardim as one outsider to others. (It is immaterial whether he really was an outsider, about which there are conflicting views in Israel.) He could empathize with their need for self-respect and embody their sense of Jewishness and the necessity for that Jewishness to find expression in the Jewish state. So, as the Sephardim were alienated from Labor, they were attracted to the Likud as an alternative.

Labor's response at first was to ignore Sephardic grievances, assuming that the Sephardim could be kept in line. Then, after Begin's upset victory in 1977, they reacted with a politics of nostalgia that insulted the Sephardim. Both approaches denigrated the Sephardim as a group. It is not surprising, then, that Sephardic alienation turned to intense dislike of a camp whose members acted as if they were the only legitimate governors of the country, and as if anyone who did not recognize that was somehow deficient. The more the Labor party talked about the good old socialist days, the more it repudiated any religious expression of Judaism for a secular one, and the more its extreme elements gave vent to their feelings about Sephardim as punks and bums, the angrier the by now politically sophisticated Sephardic population grew.

In 1981 elections reflected the results. By then it was not so much a love for Begin, who was recognized for the Ashkenazi that he is, but a sense that he could be counted on to offer opportunities to Sephardim, because it was in his political interest to do so. Moreover, in the interim Sephardim had come to constitute some two-thirds of the Herut party membership and were in positions of real power in that party.[17] There is every likelihood that the Sephardim will stay with the Likud, because they are likely to inherit that party in the future and to use it as a vehicle to move from their second-level positions to first-level ones in short order.

## THE REALITY—AND THE FUTURE

Whatever the myths that abound, Israel as a democratic society has given the Sephardim great opportunities to advance, and advance they have. Beginning with the 1977 Knesset elections, the bright young local officials who emerged in the late 1960s or early 1970s surfaced in state politics, up to and including cabinet positions. By 1983, David Levy, of Moroccan birth, who began as a labor leader in Bet Shean, one of the most dismal of the development towns, was deputy prime minister and a contestant for the prime minister's office after Begin's resignation. Moshe Levy, of Iraqi background, was chief of staff of the Israel Defense Forces. Even Ramat Gan, a bastion of the old Ashkenazi establishment, elected an Iraqi-born mayor in that year, perhaps ironically, as the Labor Alignment candidate. These examples represent only the tip of the iceberg. The present struggle between Sephardim and Ashkenazim over political power, including the myths associated with that struggle, is a transitional phenomenon, which may disappear within the next decade and almost certainly is not likely to last longer than the end of this generation. That is testimony to the vitality of Israeli democracy.

What it does mean is that the Likud is likely to become and remain the majority party in the country, at least for this generation. That does not preclude an occasional Labor victory, in response to some immediate set of events. Israel now has become a political system in which two major parties compete for control of the government, but the difference in the backing of the two is much more than the present distribution of seats in the Knesset would indicate. Both parties can govern only in coalition with each other or with the smaller parties. Here Labor is at a disadvantage. Most of the smaller parties cannot really transfer their ties from Likud to a Labor-led coalition, each for its own reasons: the religious parties because Labor has become so demonstratively secular; the Sephardic-dominated parties because Labor is so demonstratively anti-Sephardic; and Tehiya, and Greater Land of Israel party, because Labor is for "territorial compromise." Since the Likud synthesizes all these elements within its coalition, its "normal" strength is something like three-fifths to two-thirds of the Jewish vote—a very strong base indeed. That is why, despite the 1981 Likud government's failures, Labor could not win the 1984 elections. Unless the latter modifies its positions, it will come to be in that position.

What, then, are the aspirations of the new Sephardic majority? Put simply, their aspirations are to have an equal voice in Israeli society, whether in the form of political power roughly equal to their share of the population (and that is a matter not of mathematics or affirmative action but simply of more openness in party politics) or in the matter of equal expression for Sephardic culture as part of the evolving culture of Israel.

The present struggle between Ashkenazim and Sephardim is simply a normal struggle for power among "ins" and "outs." It should not be read as more than that. On the other hand, it will be the dominant struggle for this generation of Israeli politics. Those who would understand Israel and who want to communicate with the Israelis who will be in power should understand that and should begin to build their bridges to the new Sephardic leadership now emerging.

Beyond that, we even may see the emerging Israeli culture acquire more Sephardic elements—not only in the street, where Sephardic folk culture already is felt, but in the realms of high culture and religion, as well. We even are likely to see the coming of age of a "Sephardic" understanding of Zionism, which will reflect a more traditionally Jewish outlook regarding the necessity and purposes of a Jewish state than did the revolutionary socialist Zionism brought from Russia three generations ago.

Revolutionary Zionism not only emphasized the Jews' revolt against their surroundings, it also sought an internal revolution designed to overthrow old Jewish forms and ways and replace them with a new, predominantly secularized Jewishness, to make the Jewish people a nation like all others in its own land, doing away with Jewish distinctiveness, particularly in the twin realms of belief and behavior. Sephardic Zionism, on the other hand, as the Zionism of redemption, saw the Zionist effort as one of fulfilling the old ways, not overturning them, of redeeming Jews without requiring them to abandon Judaism in the process. Ashkenazic Zionism triumphed in the founding of the state, so much so that Israel has raised at least two generations, and perhaps a third, of Jews who are detached from authentic Jewish roots—a matter that has led to no little hand-wringing and other expressions of concern on the part of the heirs to the selfsame Zionist establishment that brought this situation about, and who now are seeking ways to remedy it. Indeed, one of the few aspects of the Sephardic aliyah to Israel that possibly can be labeled as tragic is the way in which young Sephardim were brought into the order of revolutionary Zionism and lost the Jewish dimensions of their old heritage in the process.

But revolutionary Zionism has run its course. However great its successes in the past, and they were indeed great, it has little, if anything, to say to the present and the future. Like the other revolutions of the time of its origin, it has played itself out. Most Israelis, however, believe that there is a definite need for a Zionism of redemption, a vision of a renewed Jewish people rather than a set of more or less dogmatic ideologies regarding the character of that renewal. Needless too say, Sephardim will not have a monopoly in the effort to renew that vision or in the ability to do something about it. Nevertheless, the Sephardic version of Zionism is more in tune with the kind of Zionist expression that is needed now than with its predecessor. That renewed understanding of Zionism will reflect more closely the aspirations of the first founders of modern Israel, principally Sephardim, who began their work in the 1840s and were joined by Ashkenazim in the 1880s, before the rise of socialist Zionism—whose history and contributions are beginning to be rediscovered. That, in turn, could lead to a new vision for Israel.

# NINE

## Israel, the Arabs, and the Territories

### JEWS AND ARABS

The views of Israeli Jews regarding the Arabs in their midst are hardly monolithic, but whatever their character, all flow out a common wish and a general ambivalence. The common wish of virtually all Jews is that the Arabs simply would go away (and vice versa, it may be added). It is possible to get many Israelis to articulate this wish when they are pushed to do so, but needless to say, its very unreality means that it is rarely articulated, and, if articulated by a few extremists, such as Meir Kahane, it is rapidly dismissed from consideration by the vast majority. Yet it should be noted at the outset, because for Israeli Jews, every other option, no matter which they choose, is clearly a poor second.

If that wish existed without the fundamental ambivalence, then one might even conclude that there is a certain symmetry between it and the Arabs' fervent desire to be rid of the Jews. But it is the ambivalence that makes the difference. Most Israelis can sympathize with the Arabs as human beings, and do—even if they cannot take the steps that even moderate Palestinian Arabs view as necessary to solve their national problem.

It often has been remarked that there is a notable lack of hatred toward the Arabs on the part of the Israeli population as a whole. That remains true, although this assessment, too, is laced with certain ambivalences. Most expressions of hatred come from teenagers, a group not generally noted for its sensitivity and, in Israel, one for whom Arab hostility is a matter of life and death.

It has been claimed that the Jews who originally came from Arab countries harbor greater hostility toward the Arabs than those who did not. In fact, there, too, feelings are ambivalent. On the one hand, there are those who bitterly recall—or have learned about from their parents—the hostile attitudes and behavior of Arabs toward the Jews in their midst. At the same time, however, there is a certain cultural kinship on some level that moderates antagonistic feelings. Similarly, it has been suggested that Israeli Jews of European or American background have fewer negative feelings toward the Arabs. That seems to be true on the political level, but they also seem to have a distaste for Arab culture, considering it foreign and unappealing, that influences their views of Arabs as people.

There is no problem in the Israeli Jews' recognition of the Arabs' humanity—that is taken as a given. The problem lies in how the Jews perceive the Arabs' sense of being Palestinians and the legitimacy of the Palestinian Arabs' search for a place in the sun. The Israeli Jews correctly perceive that the Palestinian Arabs as a group are uncompromising, not prepared to recognize reality and to share in a land that now contains two peoples, whatever the historic situation may have been in the immediate past, and hence are sworn to the elimination of Israel and its Jewish population, however much they may sugarcoat the issue for political purposes.

Most Israelis are also ambivalent about the fact that, as Jews, they do not like the role of conqueror, occupier, suppressor of a national movement, or whatever, but as Israelis they must be concerned with their security vis-à-vis an apparently implacable foe. This view is shared widely in Israel; it is as much a part of the outlook of those most committed to making maximum concessions to the Arabs as of that of the "hardliners." Only their efforts to deal with the problem are different.

Hence, if Israeli policy vis-à-vis the Palestinian Arabs and the territories in which they reside has not always been clear cut—and indeed it has not— that is a reflection of the depth of the ambivalences among Israeli Jews, which affect the highest governmental circles as well as the person in the street. Often these ambivalences have served as a paralyzing factor in Israeli policy-making, a factor that has been brought no nearer to resolution by the actions of the Palestinians themselves.

Beyond these shared ambivalences, there are the three historic approaches to the problem of the Arabs in Eretz Israel that, while no longer tenable in view of developments since 1967, have strongly influenced the thinking of policy makers in the past and continue to do so today.

## THE ZIONIST VISION: THREE INTERPRETATIONS

It often has been suggested that the original Zionists utterly ignored the Arabs in their eager pursuit of Jewish national revival in the ancient homeland. At the very least, that is a great oversimplification, and in most respects it is simply not true. With a few exceptions, all the early Zionist leaders make clear reference to the indigenous population, and many even suggest directly or obliquely what the relations between the returning Jews and the indigenously settled Arabs should be.[1] What the Zionist movement failed to note— again with few exceptions—was Arab nationalism, developing parallel to Jewish nationalism.[2] As nineteenth-century Europeans, the Zionists saw the indigenous population as essentially passive. Indeed, beginning with Herzl, if not before, they saw the Zionist enterprise as taking the Arabs as individuals out of backwardness and passivity, and elevating them to an active role in the new Jewish society. Herzl provides the classic model of this view in his utopian novel *Altneuland*.[3]

It was not until the 1920s, when the facts of Arab nationalism were brought home brutally to the Jews in Palestine and to the Zionist movement, that any effort was made to revise Zionist thinking.[4] Indeed, it is one of the tragedies of the history of the Zionist enterprise that the leaders who negotiated the beginnings of the Jewish national home in Palestine after the Balfour Declaration and the British conquest of the land during World War I were so utterly unaware of the national aspirations of the indigenous Arabs that they preferred to leave dealing with them to the British. They did so against the advice of the indigenous Jewish notables, mostly of Sephardic background, who had governed the Jewish community for centuries under the Turks, who knew their Arab neighbors and understood what was happening.[5] For obvious reasons, the Zionists were quite willing to recognize Arab nationalism in other parts of the Middle East, simply hoping that an undivided Arab nationalism would be willing to compromise with Jewish aspirations in Palestine, at least west of the Jordan River.

By the time the local expressions of the national spirit began to have an impact, the Palestinian Arabs already had adopted intractable positions, from which they never have receded. The Jewish response at that point was reasonable enough, suggesting that, since the Palestinian Arabs were espousing Arab nationalism and not a separate Palestinian nationalism, they should find their satisfaction in the vast territories of the Arab world, leaving the mere 10,000 square miles of western Palestine for Jews. (By that time, eastern Palestine had been detached from the Jewish national home, renamed Transjordan, and launched on the road to becoming Jordan.) The indigenous Arab inhabitants would remain as a cultural community rather than as a national collectivity.[6]

What is notable about the early Zionist consideration of the Arabs is that, while it may have been tainted with colonialist ideas of what native expectations were, it was not colonialist in character. Rather, it looked upon the Arabs as potential citizens, not as hewers of wood and drawers of water. The various ideas advanced by Zionist leaders and thinkers, and even by ordinary settlers (if such a distinction can be made, given the strong intellectual and ideological equipment that individual settlers brought with them), addressed the issue of how to bring the Arabs into the new Jewish society on an appropriately humane and egalitarian basis. Three general positions were developed in response to this question, one by the Labor, or socialist, camp, one by the Revisionists and Liberals (or what in Israel became known as the civil camp), and one by the religious camp.

## LABOR PREPARES THE WAY FOR PARTITION

By and large, it can be said that the Labor camp's position was separationist or partitionist in character, for reasons originally having nothing to do with Arab counterclaims to the land.[7] Labor sought the development of a separate Jewish society in the land. Its interest was in transforming what its members saw as the unnatural character of diaspora Jewry into a more natural socioeconomic order in which Jews attained self-fulfillment through their own agricultural and manual labor, rather than by exploiting (in the socialist sense) the labor of others. This classic socialist position led its original exponents, members of the second and third aliyot, to engage in bitter battles with the Jewish settlers who had preceded them in the country over the employment of Arab labor on their farms in place of Jewish labor. Ultimately, Labor was impelled to develop its own institutions, from agricultural settlements to industrial and commercial enterprises, within the framework of what later became the Histadrut.[8]

In their effort to build a society of Jewish workers, the Labor Zionists simply excluded the Arabs without any intended malice. They had no design to diminish the Arabs' economic opportunities; the Arabs simply did not fit into their scheme. Thus, the Labor parties and their members became separationists and partitionists long before partition became a political option. While there was a very serious struggle among the Labor Zionists as to whether or not to accept the partition of western Palestine, in fact it was relatively easy for them to do so when the time came, because their major goals was building a separate Jewish society on socialist principles.[9] For most Labor Zionists, this goal was more important than the territorial integrity of the country, especially in light of other considerations, such as the desire for a politically sovereign Jewish state of any reasonable size, in control of its own immigration policy in order to save the Jews of Europe.

Since Labor became dominant in the late 1920s and early 1930s, it led the way to partition in 1947–48. In the late stages of Israel's war of independence, when its generals urged Ben-Gurion to utilize the by-then-superior Israeli military power to extend the borders of the new state into what is now known as the West Bank and the Gaza Strip, Ben-Gurion held back, principally because he feared the opposition of the Western powers, but also because he did not want to absorb the Arabs in those territories (by that time Arabs were no longer fleeing from the Jews). A secure Jewish majority was apparently more important to him than territory.

This position continued to be held by veteran Labor figures all the way through the post-1967 period, but it encountered two major problems. First, while a Jewish majority materialized after 1948 and indeed became very substantial in Israel, the Labor commonwealth collapsed as both an idea and a reality. The mass influx of Jews did not bring committed socialist pioneers; quite to the contrary. Moreover, socialism in Israel showed the same deficiencies it has elsewhere, and even the socialist leadership of the country had to modify its policies drastically to cope with new realities.

As Israel moved from socialism to social democracy with an increasingly state-capitalist base, a major portion of the underpinnings of the old Labor argument for Jewish-Arab separation diminished. Thus, after the Six Day War changed the map of Israel, the second-generation leaders in the Labor Zionist camp, dominated by Moshe Dayan and Shimon Peres, were not moved by the old partitionist considerations. While they shared the general

Jewish ambivalence about accepting a large Arab minority with a high birth rate, they also saw the necessity (and had the desire) to maintain a Jewish presence in the occupied territories. Looking for a compromise between outright annexation and repartition, they supported what they termed a "functional solution"—a form of shared rule, whereby Israel and Jordan would jointly exercise sovereignty over the territories; divide responsibility for local government, citizenship, and most municipal services; and share control over such functions as land, water, currency, and security. Thus, they turned a major segment of the Labor group away from partitionist thinking as simply no longer practical.[10] Only Yigal Allon tried to find a new basis for a repartition that would solve Israel's security needs, but even he, in his last years, came to the conclusion that simple partition was no longer possible.[11]

What characterized men such as Allon and Dayan, natives of Israel, was that they personally had developed serious relations with their Arab neighbors. Thus, their attitude toward the Palestinians was one of openness, a readiness for friendship on an individual basis. Yet they showed the same ambivalence as their fellow Jews with regard to the precise relationship that should develop between the two groups.

The collapse of Labor's solid partitionist position in the face of internal dissension and the abandonment of that position by the post-1967 Labor governments did not, to all intents and purposes, lead to the creation of a new policy; it led, rather, to political paralysis. The party was too divided to take a firm stand in any direction. Its diffidence was reinforced by Arab intransigence, which led to the Palestinians' rejection of even the tentative solutions the Labor government frequently put forward.

Only after the Likud assumed power did a majority of Labor coalesce around a repartition scheme of some kind, the so-called Jordanian option, but without much conviction, particularly since there has been no acceptable response from Jordan. And even Labor would like to define that option in such a way that Israel retains military control of the territories, and Jordan gains only civilian rule. Peres by then the party's leader, adopted this position, probably for tactical purposes.

In the interim, changes in military technology have transformed the security situation, so that repartition of the territory west of the Jordan becomes increasingly difficult for Israel. In October 1984, within a month after Shimon Peres assumed the office of prime minister as the head of the national unity government, he reaffirmed his support for a functional solution, disregarding the current Labor party position, for which he received no significant criticism from any of his Labor compatriots. Under the changed circumstances brought about by the Likud during the previous seven years, relatively few Labor party leaders still see partition as an option.

### THE CIVIL CAMP CHAMPIONS INTEGRATION AND EQUAL RIGHT
If the Labor camp had its reasons for falling into a partitionist position, the Revisionists and the Liberals had theirs for adopting an integrationist stance.

For them, too, it was a matter of combining idealism and self-interest. The original farmers of the First Aliyah and their heirs, as well as many Jews in the urban areas, employed Arab labor as a matter of course, to gain economic advantages. They opposed the demands of the socialist Zionists to employ Jewish labor exclusively and hence became economic integrationists willy-nilly, although, like all other Jews and Arabs, they saw the two peoples as otherwise maintaining national and cultural separation.

On the other hand, the Revisionists envisioned a unified country with equal civil rights for Arabs and Jews as the basis for maintaining the unity of Eretz Israel. As nineteenth-century nationalists, they were committed to a Jewish state in all of historic Eretz Israel, and as nineteenth-century liberal democrats, they could not justify such a state even in their own minds unless all its citizens had equal rights. That is why they emphasized the rapid creation of a Jewish majority in the country through mass immigration, so that the extension of civil rights to Jews and Arabs alike would not interfere with the building of a Jewish national home. This principle was so important to them that it became part of their party anthem, whose central theme is a Jewish state on both banks of the Jordan, a state in which Arabs and Jews, Muslims and Christians are all equal citizens.[12]

The Herut party, the heirs of the Revisionists and the dominant element in the Likud, has remained thoroughly consistent in its commitment to this position. It is expressed in Menachem Begin's proposal of autonomy as a prelude to full Israeli absorption of the West Bank on the basis of civil equality for its Arab inhabitants. Begin said as much in his original proposal of December 1977, a month after Anwar Sadat's visit to Jerusalem, and he and his supporters have reiterated this position regularly, whenever they deem it appropriate.[13]

The integrationist position foundered on the rock of Arab nationalism. The Arabs wanted no part of equal rights in a state with a Jewish majority; they wanted to maintain their Arab majority and keep the Jews out. They did not accept the Revisionist position in the past, and they do not accept it today. The Likud government presses on with its absorption policies and finds no takers among the Palestinian Arabs who live beyond the 1949 armistice lines.

## THE RELIGIOUS CAMP IGNORES THE ARABS

By and large, the characteristic position of the religious camp was to ignore the Palestinian Arabs as an issue. Preoccupied as its members were with forging a place for themselves within the Zionist movement or with bringing Zionism into the sphere of religiously sanctioned behavior, they found little to say about the Arabs, except when circumstances brought them into contact with them and improvised responses prevailed. Otherwise, the religious socialists followed the general position of the Labor camp, and the nonsocialist religious Zionists went along with the civil camp.

Inattention was a feasible stance as long as the religious community did not have to deal with the Arab problem in other than an ad hoc way; nor did it until after 1967. The arguments over partition in the 1930s and 1940s centered around the question of whether to insist on all of historic Palestine or to compromise in order to get at least some kind of Jewish state. The Arab question barely figured. Between 1948 and 1967, the religious camp, like the other political camps, rarely had any relations with the Arab minority in the country, except in preelection negotiations between political leaders.[14]

A radical transformation occurred after 1967, with the members of the religious community coming into what was perhaps more contact with the Palestinian Arabs in the administered territories than any other Jewish population. This contact has assumed many forms. Members of the religious camp led settlement efforts on the West Bank. First they reestablished the former religious Zionist settlements in the Etzion Bloc that had been destroyed by Jordan in 1948. Then there was the resettlement of Hebron and the establishment of Jewish right of access to the shared religious shrines there. Finally, there were the efforts of Gush Emunim (a predominantly— but not exclusively—religious faction) to extend Jewish settlement into every part of the administered territories. Day-to-day contact of an intense kind takes place in Jerusalem, where religious Jews, even more than others, are attracted to the Western Wall and to other places of historical and religious association in the Old City, on a continuing basis.

Through the participation of members of the religious community in these activities, by way of actual implantation of settlements or the establishment of yeshivot on the West Bank, or marches and demonstrations in favor of settlement, their contact with the Arabs grew and intensified. By and large, it was an antagonistic contact, based on the fact that the Jewish vanguard came into conflict with Arab claims and rejected them.

The religious camp as such is divided on the issue of the future of the territories. Most of its adherents share Likud's view of finding some way to hold onto them, but many of the ultra-Orthodox—Agudath Israel, for example—are quite willing to withdraw even from historic sites for the sake of real peace. A very small handful of extremists, by no means all religious, would like to see the Arabs expelled from the land. At the same time, the religious mainstream has a hard time accepting the absorption of the mass of Palestinian Arabs as equal citizens, not because these Jews reject civil equality for Arabs—they do not—but because they are concerned about the Jewish character of the state. A small but vocal segment of the religious camp, particularly from the religious socialist parties, shares the view that since the Palestinian Arabs also have legitimate claims, partition in some form leading to the separation of the two communities is the best way to enable both to maintain their respective national characteristics and personalities. In any case, the original position of the religious camp has collapsed, because its members no longer find it possible to ignore the Arabs and still achieve their goals as Jews and Zionists.[15]

## BEFORE THE SIX DAY WAR AND AFTER

After Israel's independence was achieved, not only did Labor maintain control of the government of the new Jewish state, but its position became the official Israeli position vis-à-vis the Palestinian Arabs. The self-induced mass exodus of Arabs from the territory of the infant state strengthened this policy as a natural one. Had there been a very large Arab minority scattered throughout the country, Israeli Jews might have had to confront the existence of the Palestinian Arabs in a different way. In fact, almost all of the new state was left free of Arabs after 1948, while those Arabs who did not flee were concentrated in the Galilee, particularly in its central and western portions, where there were few Jews. Hence, a natural geographic separation reinforced other factors, making for a separationist solution. Moreover, as the remaining Arabs tended to be rural peasants, there was little economic contact between the two groups.

The Labor-dominated Israeli government pursued a policy of securing group cultural rights for the Arabs by encouraging them to organize municipalities under their own leaders, by providing them with schools in which Arabic was the principal language of instruction, and by extending state support for their religious institutions insofar as they wished to avail themselves of this assistance. Thus, over nearly two decades, a separate Arab society developed within Israel, one that had little contact with the Jews, permitting the latter virtually to ignore the former except in matters of formal government.[16]

At the same time, the Arabs did become citizens of Israel with equal civil rights, including the right to vote in Israeli elections. Indeed, they were entitled to elect a proportionate share of members of the Knesset, a fact guaranteed by the existence of an electoral system based on proportional representation. Even here, the separationist position was maintained through the organization of separate Arab parties, most of which were sponsored by or came under the protection of the mainstream Zionist parties of the Labor camp, in which the Arabs could pursue their own political advantage by linking with the government coalition.

The only integrated political parties were Mapam, which, until the ninth Knesset, always had an Arab Knesset member and does again today, and the Communist party. The latter stood outside the Zionist movement and for that reason won the largest share of the Arab vote. It had few Jewish members, a handful of dedicated Communists who, in fact, dominated the party leadership.

Although the Arabs probably had more in common ideologically with the parties of the civil camp, they saw no advantage in affiliating with what were obviously minority parties unlikely to become part of the governing coalition, much less lead a government. Perhaps surprising to those unacquainted with the Israeli scene, the National Religious Party also developed a modest but significant base of support in the Arab sector, in part because of

NRP control of the Ministry of the Interior, which is responsible for funding and overseeing local government.

Israelis viewed those Palestinian Arabs outside the boundaries of the state as refugees held hostage by the Arab states in which they found themselves, or as terrorists seeking the destruction of Israel. In the former capacity, Israelis pited them but saw their condition as being perpetuated by an Arab world seeking to foster hatred of Israel. In the latter case, they were simply enemies to be fought with every possible means.

All of that must be perceived in a context in which the Jews, like the rest of the world, for that matter, never considered the Palestinians as a separate people, certainly not within the Arab world. For them, Palestinians were just like all other Arabs who happened to have lived in Palestine. While the most sophisticated Israeli Jews did understand that there were cultural and even linguistic differences between Palestinians, Egyptians, Syrians, Iraqis, and others, and students of the field were aware of the religious sectarianism within Islam, it was an accepted axiom that Arabs were Arabs.

This view was as characteristic of the Arabs as of non-Arabs. Indeed, the only argument one heard in the Arab world was whether the national spirit should be developed in the direction of Pan-Arabism or Pan-Islam. Christian Arabs, including the Palestinians among them, advocated Pan-Arabism and resisted Pan-Islam for obvious reasons.

As long as the Arabs of Palestine were struggling against the Zionists alone, they did not particularly foster a separate Palestinian identity. That identity, to the extent that it exists, was forged in the aftermath of the creation of Israel; it was a response of the Palestinian Arabs to their confrontation with their Arab brethren in the Arab states of the Middle East as much as, if not more than, a result of their confrontation with Israel.[17]

## WHO ARE THE PALESTINIAN ARABS?

The Palestinians' sense of being outsiders, supported with lip service but rejected in reality by their fellow Arabs, has created a Palestinian Arab "public," that is to say, a body of people tied together by common inter-generational interests based upon shared externalities and a common vital issue. The final impetus for the emergence of this public came in the aftermath of the Six Day War. The Palestinians, who up to that time had been moving to integrate themselves within Jordan (which, after all, was and is a Palestinian state geographically, historically, and demographically, except for its ruling family), suddenly found themselves divided territorially between an East Bank that remained under Hussein's rule and a West Bank occupied by Israel as a result of a disastrous war. They also confronted an Arab world that, at the very least, was ambivalent toward them.

Given the relatively late emergence of a shared identity among the Palestinian Arabs, it is no wonder that Israeli Jews have taken even longer to acknowledge the reality of their separate identity. For example, throughout her term as prime minister, Golda Meir refused to recognize any Palestinian Arab public, much less a Palestinian people, arguing openly and forcefully against the existence of such a thing. During those years, her view was shared by a majority of Israelis. It was not easy to disabuse them of such a view, given the fact that the refugee camps swarmed with non-Palestinians who had acquired refugee identity cards in order to gain the benefits of United Nations relief efforts, while the terrorist organizations actively recruited non-Palestinians for their missions as readily as they recruited Palestinians.

Many Israelis today are at least grudgingly willing to recognize some sense of "Palestinian-ness" among the Arabs in the territories or those who trace their roots to western Palestine. But most remain quite skeptical of the long-range survival of such an identity. Many view the claim made by the Palestinians and other Arabs as a tactical maneuver to evoke world sympathy for yet another Arab state in historic Eretz Israel (there already is Jordan) without any basis in national realities. On the other hand, Palestinian Arab persistence in proclaiming a collective identity has had its effect on Israeli opinion to the point where even Prime Minister Begin spoke of "Palestinian Arabs." If Israeli Jews do not have a firm "fix" on who is a Palestinian or whether being one is more than a temporary expedient, they are not that different from the Palestinian Arabs themselves, only the Israelis have a greater interest in moving cautiously toward any recognition of Palestinian identity, as well as a greater skepticism with regard to it.

## GEOGRAPHIC AND ECONOMIC INTEGRATION

The aftermath of the Six Day War brought an influx of Palestinian Arabs into the Israeli economy and an influx of Israelis, visitors or settlers, into Arab territory. Contacts were established where none had existed before. For Israelis, these contacts were seen as basically noncommittal. The Palestinian Arabs were there; they had to live. Therefore, it was reasonable to do business with them and to employ them so that they would have jobs. The territories were there, and since they had strategic, historical and religious value, it was good to settle parts of them where strategic, historical, or religious considerations were involved. By and large, however, the two populations continued to go in their own separate directions.[18]

Since the Israelis did not face up to a final disposition of the territories, they paid relatively little attention to the ultimate relationship that would have to develop between Israeli Jews and Palestinian Arabs, except for those who persisted in their old positions. Thus, the Likud, emphasizing that Israel was in the territories to stay, also stressed the necessity of bringing the Palestinian Arabs into the polity as individual citizens. (It should be noted that Gahal did not insist upon any particular course of action in this regard while they were in the government between 1967 and 1970.) The old-line Labor activists opposed the retention of the densely populated parts of the territories on the grounds that the natural increase of the Arab population would drastically dilute, and perhaps even end, the Jewish majority. They also feared that the transfer of most of the less attractive jobs from Jewish to Arab hands would be demoralizing to the Jewish population and a violation of the principles upon which socialist Zionism was built.

For many years, neither of these groups dominated the government. It remained in the hands of "pragmatists," who avoided making strategic decisions, although they pursued practical goals that led to the integration of the territories into the Israeli economic and security systems. The principal Israeli leaders, like those of so much of the rest of the world in the 1960s and 1970s, were ultrapragmatic in the sense of avoiding actions deliberately directed to the advancement of ideological goals. The result was ad hoc decisions without ever reaching a defined long-range policy, in the hope that such decisions ultimately would lead to conditions in which an appropriate policy could be framed.

## THE CHANGED RESPONSES OF THE 1970S

Between 1967 and 1973, while Israel had the upper hand in the region, the inhabitants of the administered territories were relatively quiescent. Hence, the pragmatists' policy continued unchallenged and even seemed to be working. After the Yom Kippur War, it had to change, as did Israeli attitudes toward the Palestinian Arabs. The latter gained new-found confidence in resisting any extension of the Israeli presence. Moreover, the world began to press Israel to recognize the Palestinians as a people with legitimate national rights.

With its victory in the 1977 elections, the Likud undertook to fulfill its vision that the territories be absorbed within Israel as a matter of historical, military, and religious necessity. As world pressure and local resistance grew, supporters of Likud policy became more active in implanting a Jewish presence in these territories. At the same time, the Israeli government became more anxious to seek a way out of the impasse, as American pressure for an agreement increased. Out of this situation came the first Israeli recognition that the Palestinian Arabs did have some kind of an identity, though there emerged no clear-cut understanding, or willingness to reach an understanding, as to precisely what that identity was. As suggested above, there was no reason to expect the Israelis to have a clearer sense of Palestinian identity than did the Palestinians themselves. On the other hand, Israel's unwillingness to absorb a population whose hostility was becoming increasingly overt also made it impossible simply to reject a separate Palestinian identity in favor of the old Revisionist approach. The end result is a continued murkiness, coupled with a desire not only to have one's cake and eat it too, but to avoid defining the cake. The Labor camp remains officially partitionist but assumes that whatever the solution, Israel will retain military control and economic integration will continue. That certainly does not square with Palestinian Arab demands for self-determination. The Likud remains firmly integrationist, but few within its ranks can have many delusions that the Palestinian Arabs are content simply to be individual citizens of a Jewish Israel without expressing any national identity of their own other than their Arabness.

The religious community is divided between those who see the preservation of the Jewishness of the state as requiring repartition and those who see the achievement of the Jewish national-religious vision as requiring continued Jewish control of the territories. As a result, its views are spread over the spectrum of perceptions. They range from the position that the Palestinian Arabs, whoever they are, represent a non-Jewish threat to the Jewishness of the state, and therefore their areas should be separated from it; to those who support the notion of civil equality for all, as long as the Jews can settle wherever they wish in Eretz Israel; all the way to those few who see the Palestinians as implacable enemies who must be controlled or expelled.

For all of the above, and for those who do not have clear positions on the issue, an Israeli national consensus remains—no separate Palestinian Arab state west of the Jordan, no recognition of the Palestinian Liberation Organization as the spokesman for the Palestinians, whoever they may be, no Israeli withdrawal to the pre-1967 borders, no redivision of Jerusalem, and no substantial return of Arab refugees to Israeli territories.

## A CHANGING TERRITORIAL PERSPECTIVE

While Israeli Jews were beginning to reckon with the new collective consciousness of the Palestinian Arabs in the aftermath of the Six Day War, other changes were taking place with regard to the territory in dispute between them. Those changes had to do with the arrival of new technologies in the world as a whole, which opened up new frontier stages in Eretz Israel.

As an extension of the great frontier of the Western world, the original Zionist settlements were principally rural in character. With the establishment of the state, Israel moved into a second frontier stage, which also had its parallel in other Western countries, that of industrialization and urbanization. In the latter years of the 1960s, approximately coincident with but not a result of the Six Day War, Israel began to move into the next stage of development, namely, metropolitanization. Its industrial base was transferred through the application of sophisticated new technologies while its patterns of settlement were being transformed by new modes of transportation and communication. The earlier unity of place of residence and place of work began to disappear as the possibility of moving quickly across substantial distances on a daily basis became real. So, for example, during the days of the urban frontier, Israeli Arabs living in the Galilee had to forego involvement in the industrialization process because their villages did not attract industry, or move to Jewish cities away from their own cultural frameworks and live lonely lives in order to achieve greater economic advantage. With the coming of metropolitanization, the same Arabs could remain residents of their villages and take a bus to some destination in the Haifa Bay metropolitan region to work in the morning and then back again at night, without being unduly burdened as a result.

Israel's urbanization and metropolitanization began along the coast in the Tel Aviv and Haifa Bay regions. Jerusalem, whose urban development always had taken a very different turn, never really entered the urban-industrial frontier, because at the time it was cut off at the end of the Jerusalem corridor, surrounded by territory under Arab rule. Then came the Six Day War, and suddenly Jerusalem was reunited with its potential hinterland, precisely at the time that metropolitanization was beginning to engulf the country.

In the ensuing decade, Jerusalem not only gained strength as a focus for Jewish developmental activities related to servicing the metropolitan frontier, such as high education, government, and other public sector activities, but also was reintegrated with a hinterland in Judea and Samaria that increasingly was drawn toward it. From an agricultural point of view, the region from Hebron in the south to Nablus in the north, Jericho in the east, and Bet Shemesh in the west became a single market, with produce flowing into Jerusalem daily from every part of it. Jerusalem, in turn, became a magnet for employing the residents of the mountain ridge along the same axes, particularly as development of its Jewish sections required more hands for building, a need met principally by the Arab population. Some of these new workers moved to the city; others remained in their native towns and villages and commuted. Thus, the country's metropolitan region united both Jewish and Arab nodes within a single economic framework, whose prosperity rested upon their mutual interaction.[19]

This new development, as much as any security or other considerations, makes a return to partition an atavistic step. History has shown that politics can overrule economics even in such circumstances. Jerusalem probably could be cut off at the end of a corridor again and returned to the peripheries of Israel. The Arab areas around the city could be cut off from their natural focal point if political decisions are made to that effect. But in such a case everybody would suffer; not only as individuals, who would lose their only significant oportunities for employment, but the two peoples as peoples would lose a major opportunity for economic and social development to enhance their prosperity, which has been the result of the reconnection since 1967. Thus, there should be a major interest on the part of both parties to work out a political arrangement that will recognize the unity of the country even as it provides for maximum self-government for its peoples, combined with shared rule where necessary.

Jerusalem by its very nature does not lend itself to becoming a major industrial center. Indeed, there are many reasons why the city and its environs have escaped the impact of industrialization so as to preserve

Jerusalem's special character. Prior to the metropolitan frontier, that, in effect, doomed Jerusalem to being a backwater and its region to suffering from lack of development. One of the characteristics of the metropolitan frontier, however, is that other nodes in the metropolitan region can industrialize to everyone's benefit without damaging Jerusalem's special character.

On the metropolitan frontier, education itself becomes a major industry, a means of developing a population that is equipped to participate in the sophisticated socioeconomic systems of the metropolitan era. Jerusalem is ideally suited to be a major educational center. Indeed, education is one of the functions that is most appropriate to the city, given its historic role.

Jewish Jerusalem already has become the educational center of the Jewish people, through the Hebrew University, its many yeshivot, and, increasingly, the technical colleges sponsored by the Orthodox community and social and humanistic research institutes of various kinds. There are, in addition, many renowned Christian-sponsored institutions for Bible and theological study. While no similar development has taken place in Arab Jerusalem, the beginnings of serious institutions of higher education serving the Arab population are to be found in neighboring Birzeit and Bethlehem. Only peace will enable those institutions to develop further. United within a common metropolitan region, they will add an additional dimension to Jerusalem's position on the world's educational map. Together, these institutional complexes can put Jerusalem in the forefront as a world educational center. But it is precisely the ability to concentrate a number of separate institutions, each maintaining its separate identity in every respect but within close proximity to one another so that synergism can play its role, that will make the difference. That, indeed, is the essence of the metropolitan frontier—separate but synergistic—and is the way in which other great educational centers in the world have become what they have become.

For the foreseeable future, there will be clearly separate Arab and Jewish cities and villages. Thus, it will be not only possible but probably necessary to build links between the two peoples via particular local jurisdictions, either Arab or Jewish. That, indeed, is the direction in which things have developed informally since 1967.[20] In local governmental matters, Arab municipalities and villages already have substantial self-rule in local matters, while Israeli settlements began with internal self-rule and recently have been organized into regional councils or given more clear-cut municipal status under Israeli law so that they can exercise those selfsame powers formally.

The importance of these local organs should not be minimized. In an age and region where the focus tends to be on national governments and international relations, it is far too easy to minimize the importance of local self-government. Jews with good historical memories will recall how the local Jewish community became the focal point for Jewish self-government and the maintenance of a Jewish corporate identity throughout the long years of the exile in very meaningful ways. Similarly, it truthfully can be said that the Palestinian Arabs never have had so much self-government as they have had since 1967 under the Israeli policy of maximizing local self-rule through Arab municipalities.[21]

That is not to suggest that the Palestinian Arabs would be satisfied with a simple continuation of the present arrangement. There are certain areas of self-government that are closed to them, some of which are substantively important and others symbolically necessary. Be that as it may, the possibilities of building an appropriate combination for governing people with some local territorial base is a real one that offers many advantages.

Whatever the final arrangements for Judea, Samaria, and Gaza, there is enough experience around the world, and, for that matter, in the territories themselves, with regard to the mechanisms for combining self-rule and shared rule upon which to draw. For example, all the tools are available, and much already has been done to establish a legal basis for an arrangement in which persons take precedence over territory in determining who belongs where legally. There are nearly one hundred models of diversity of jurisdiction arrangements, mixed governments, power sharing, and the like presently in operation around the world. The problems that often are presented as the most difficult in fact can be overcome technically without any particular inventiveness.[22] More important by far are the political barriers to implementing any solution. For in the last analysis, it is a political problem, not a legal or technical one. As a political problem, it can be solved only when the parties perceive a political advantage in solving it.

Israel, the Palestinian Arabs, and Jordan must come to grips with a situation in which two energetic peoples and two states with certain fundamental interests that are diametrically opposed are fated to share the same land. Somehow they must find sufficient common interest upon which to build a basis for a settlement. Over sixty years of conflict, including three full-scale wars, have shown the improvidence of continuing on a collision course. In human history, peoples often continue to be improvident, but it is not necessary for them to be so.

In the language of contemporary international relations, there are symmetrical elements in the relationship between Israel and the Palestinian Arabs. Increasingly, the latter are becoming the Jews of the Arab world. Their diaspora is spread throughout that world and increasingly plays the kind of role within each of the Arab states that the Jewish diaspora communities traditionally have played in the Christian and Muslim worlds. In both cases, the peoples, wherever they live, look to their original homeland as a focal point in their lives, even if they do not intend to live there, and are willing to supply it with resources and to exert political and other forms of influence as necessary to protect or secure what they perceive to be their homeland's interests.

These symmetries have become widely recognized. At the same time, they should not obscure the asymmetrical aspects of the relationship. The Palestinian Arabs remain Arabs; that is to say, their relationship to the Arab world is one of kinship, even if it is a kinship that sometimes is less recognized in practical policy matters than the Palestinians would like. Whatever their difficulties outside Palestine, they have a score of other Arab states that share the same language, religion, and culture. They even have a state—Jordan—which always has been considered a part of their claimed homeland and in which they form a substantial demographic majority.

The Jews, on the other hand, may have a more widespread diaspora, which feels at home in other parts of the world, but as Jews they have only one possibility for a homeland in which their own language, religion, culture, and ways form the basis of its society and polity. Moreover, no one has tried to exterminate the Palestinians. The Jews not only have undergone centuries of persecution, at times bordering on extermination, but they came close to being exterminated in our own time and have been subject to further extermination efforts on the part of their immediate neighbors.

Finally, the Palestinian Arabs may indeed be on the way to becoming a separate people, as well as a separate "public," within the Arab world. It is too early to determine whether that is indeed the case. The Jews, on the other hand, are the most ancient of peoples, a nation whose history stretches back to the early eons of civilization and that has tenaciously preserved its peoplehood and its national identity under the most adverse conditions for thousands of years.[23] Both the symmetries and the asymmetries must be taken into consideration as a relationship is developed and the peace process advanced.

# PART 4 *Futures*

# TEN

# An Emergent Political Culture

## THE CONFLICT OF CULTURAL INHERITANCES

The shape of Israeli politics in years to come is heavily dependent upon two factors that flow out of Israel's character as a new society and its movement from ideological to territorial democracy. The first of these is the conflict between the three political cultural inheritances of the Jewish population, and the second is the continuing frontier of development in Israel. The resolution of the former and the political consequences of the latter will be major aspects of Israeli political life over the next generation and will provide the basic tests for Israeli political leadership.

As a new society, Israel has had to forge a political culture of its own out of the political cultural inheritances which the Jewish population has brought with it in the ingathering of exiles.[1] For the student of politics, the very fact that Israel must create a political culture of its own by weaving together disparate strands offers a fascinating opportunity for the study of the emergence of a new civil society. For those concerned with Israel first and foremost, as a society that promises much for the Jewish people, the problem of its emerging political cultures takes on a direct and immediate significance that transcends the analytical.

Three major political cultural strands were brought to contemporary Israel. Most of the Jews who came to Eretz Israel and all of the indigenous Arabs had lived as subjects in premodern polities where the idea of citizenship was unknown. Hence, in part, they shared a common subject political culture that perceived of the governing authority in very personal terms as a ruler with whims, a powerful force existing outside of and independent of the people. Government of this kind often is seen as malevolent although relatively limited in its interests. At most the ruler exploits the people and their resources but is not interested in extending services or intervening in the people's daily lives more than necessary to achieve those limited goals. Rulers can tolerate religious and cultural pluralism among their subjects as long as the rulers' power is not challenged in any way.

Products of the subject political culture have no concept of political participation, properly perceiving themselves to be subjects, not citizens. Indeed, they perceive their task as avoiding contact with government officials as much as possible. If they must approach their rulers, they generally take a petitionary approach that recognizes the superior *power* of the official without necessarily endorsing his *authority*, and that humbly requests a consideration of their needs. The state definitely is not looked upon as a vehicle for the provision of services or for social improvement; rather, the hope is that its role will be as limited as possible so that it will interfere in the life of its subjects as little as possible.[2] While in the mind of the Israeli public this subject political culture is associated primarily with Jewish immigrants from the Afro-Asian countries, in fact it is found equally among most Eastern European Jews who came to Israel directly from the *shtetl* (the Yiddish term for the Eastern European townlet where the average Jew lived at the turn of the century) or a shtetl-like anvironment, and had not undergone modernization, and equally among the Arab population.

Those Jews who had undergone modernization, whether from Europe or from the African and Asian countries, brought with them to Israel a statist political culture. Because they had undergone modernization within the context of European statism, which provided them with their only knowledge of modern statehood, their expectations were that a proper state must be a reified one, that is, one standing outside of and above its citizens and existing independently of them. Such a state, influenced by the French Revolution, socialism, and then the Russian Revolution, was viewed as a major instrument for social change and, accordingly, was expected to be comprehensive in its approach to its citizens, prepared to intervene in every aspect of life in order to bring about the necessary changes. The officials of the reified state necessarily were perceived as standing in a superior relationship to the general public by virtue of their role, either as servants of the state itself, as in conservative Germany, or as servants of the revolution, as in France and the USSR. It further was expected that the reified state would be a centralized one, since it required centralization of power to achieve its comprehensive economic, social, and political ends.[3] It was this conception of the state that lay behind the "Bolshevik Revolution" of the Third Aliyah and Ben-Gurion's mamlachtiut after 1948.

At the same time, the Jews brought with them a third political cultural strand, one that grew out of the indigenous political experience of the Jewish people in their own communities. Traditional Jewish political culture is civic and republican. Since God is the only sovereign, there can be no reified, sovereign state. Equally repellent is the notion of a ruler ruling by whim, since all rulers are bound by God's Torah and by popular consent, which are the joint sources of their empowerment. Politically, the Jewish people constitute an *edah*, a popular assembly, under God, constitutionally bound by the Torah; and each unit within the edah is perceived as a partnership constituted by its citizens within that constitutional framework, though, once constituted, perhaps more than the sum of its parts.

Jewish political culture starts with the basic equality of all Jews combined with a basic responsibility to participate in the life of the community.

Individual responsibility to the community is perceived to be of prime importance, and members of the community are held to have civic obligations to fulfill by virtue of their association with it. At the same time, the leaders of the community are perceived to be responsible in three ways: to the constitution, to God and Torah, and to the people. Moreover, both authority and power are constitutionally allocated among three domains, referred to as *ketarim*, or crowns, in traditional sources: that of Torah, including prophets and rabbis who communicate God's message to the people and act as interpreters of that message through the Torah; *kehunah* (priesthood), through which members of the priestly families and their successor religious functionaries in the synagogue serve as channels for communication from the people to God (a domain that has been de-politicized over the centuries); and *malkhut* (civil rule), with its kings, judges, *nesi'im* (chief magistrates), and *parnassim* (magistrates) charged with the civil governance of the Jewish people. Thus, a separation of powers system functions to strengthen republicanism.[4]

In the Jewish political culture, the role of the community in dealing with human needs is perceived to be substantial, but never all-embracing. That is to say, politics is not conceived to be the be all and end all of life, or its architectonic principle. Rather, politics is perceived to be an important means for creating the good society necessary for living the good life, both of which are defined through other (traditionally, religious) means. Whereas the first two political cultures see authority and power as hierarchical, Jewish political culture sees it as federal—that is to say, as the product of a series of covenants (or partnership agreements) derived from the great covenant that created the Jewish people, and reaching down to the immediate compacts that create specific communities within the Jewish body civic or politic that affirm the essential equality of the partners, as well as the authority of the institutions they create.[5]

The origins of this political culture are as old as the Jewish people itself, but circumstances of Jewish political life in the modern epoch, which witnessed the demise of autonomous Jewish communities in the diaspora, submerged the Jewish political culture so that the Jewish strand was more latent than manifest. At the same time, every Jewish community has maintained an internal political organization of its own to a greater of lesser extent, which, even when not conceived to be political by its members, has served to socialize them into certain specific patterns of political behavior vis-à-vis one another and the community as a whole, which sustain the elements of Jewish political culture. This strand is spread across the entire Jewish population of Israel to a greater or lesser extent, which means that, more than any of the others, it provides common points of reference and possibilities for communication among Jews from widely varying diaspora environments.

While the understanding of the influence of political culture in shaping political affairs is relatively new, Israeli concern with the struggle between

Jewish and alien cultures is as old as Jewish settlement in the country, a continuation of one of the original tensions introduced at the first founding of th Jewish people. Here, too, David Ben-Gurion elucidated the theme for the Zionist enterprise. In a 1950 address appropriately entitled "Mission and Dedication," Ben-Gurion traced out the course of Jewish history in terms of the Jewish confrontation with opposing ideologies in order to show the continuity of the Jewish people and of its spiritual and cultural struggle.[6] In the process, he outlined much of the content of Jewish political culture as it is manifested in modern Israel. The themes he emphasized are worth noting: 1) the continuing struggle between Judaism and authoritarian or totalitarian systems and the sense that the struggle continues in all generations, including today's; 2) the Jewish people as personified "moral will and historic vision"; 3) the ability of the Jewish people to survive as a small group (the "saving remnant" in traditional terminology), even though many individual Jews have fallen away; 4) the ability of Jews to adopt elements from surrounding civilizations without giving up their own integrity, and their parallel ability to contribute to the flourishing of world civilization beyond their numbers; 5) the periodic problem of Jewish renegades; 6) the Jewish emphasis on both the physical and the spiritual dimensions, with the latter the most important but not separate from the physical; 7) the belief of the Jews in the dignity of man; 8) Jewish messianism and commitment to a messianic age; 9) the character of Jewish chosenness, especially in its modern interpretation; 10) the problem of diaspora; 11) the democratic and populist character of Israeli society; and 12) halutziut, or pioneering, which gives meaning to Israel, and, indeed, the Jewish people, as a new society.

## MOVING TOWARD A COMMON CULTURE

The three political cultural strands that have come together in Israel obviously have points at which they overlap, and even more points where they conflict. To some extent, Israeli civil society is already an amalgam of the three strands, with different institutions reflecting one strand more than others. Thus, the Israeli bureaucracy is very European and statist in its organization, while the Israeli Defense Force—the most fully Israeli institution in the whole country—comes far closer to the covenantal model of authoritative relationships noted in Jewish political culture.[7]

Ben-Gurion, in "Mission and Dedication," emphasized the role of the army as an integrating factor in Israeli society. Indeed, much emphasis was placed on the army's role in this regard, at least from the very early 1950s, and many myths were developed about the army's successes, which, like all such myths, had some basis in truth but were carried beyond reality. In many respects, the army is the major embodiment of Jewish political culture, at least in its formal expectations with regard to popular participation, underlying democratic values, and the achievement of discipline through understanding, utilizing a minimum of coercion and a maximum of consent. At the same time, the subliminal cultural content of the army tends to be European statist in character and Eastern European-Israeli in thrust, so that the experience of Oriental Jews within it does represent some kind of a cultural confrontation.[8]

On the other hand, Israel's administrative culture embodies statism in its most intensive form. One of the major themes of the emergent Israeli political culture is the way in which institutions with such a statist orientation are linked to very different, even antistatist, patterns. As Gerald Caiden explains in his study of Israel's administrative culture, "Israelis are not yet a bureaucratic people."[9]

Thus, the first results of this mix of political cultures could be found in the development of a strong, centralized state apparatus, paternalistic in approach to the population and involved in virtually every aspect of public life, including and especially the economy, but informed throughout with a system of negotiation and bargaining that affected every operational detail. In the process of synthesis, the statist strand already has been modified by the Jewish rejection of the reified state. Those reflecting that strand have had to transfer their tendency to reify institutions to the nation (in this case, meaning some ambiguous combination of the Jewish people as the whole and most particularly its Israeli segment), of which the state is a vital instrument, but still an instrument. This transference is consistent with Jewish political tradition, up to a point, and hence acceptable at least on an interim basis.

It is the subject political culture that has undergone the most change, however. Since it never really was recognized as legitimate among the Jews of Israel, almost all efforts at political socialization of those shaped by that political culture have been toward teaching them the norms, responsibilities, and rights of citizenship, and with great success at that, as the near-universal participation in elections demonstrates. Thus, former subjects have come to accept the fact that they can function as citizens. Nevertheless, a residue of the subject political culture remains in the form of an understanding of the state as paternalistic—a nursing father, to use a term from Jewish tradition. This paternalistic view of the state coincides nicely with the statist approach of comprehensive government intervention in the society, and the two have been mutually reinforcing throughout virtually every segment of the Israeli public.

To the extent that it survives at all, the subject political culture still may be found in Arab villages, where ordinary people vote as instructed by their *hamula* (clan or extended family) leaders, who are deemed to be the only ones entitled to exercise political judgment for the hamula. While a similar phenomenon was visible, particularly among Jews from the Afro-Asian countries in the development towns, in the early years of statehood, it essentially has disappeared among Jews.

In all of these ways, the upward thrust of the previously latent Jewish political culture is becoming increasingly evident. In some cases, there are direct institutional manifestations of this phenomenon. Take the role of the

Supreme Court in relation to the Knesset. The Israeli political system was designed on the basis of European models from the first, following the model of the statist political culture. According to those models, the parliament is the highest repository of authority or sovereignty in the state, with its supremacy both specified and taken for granted. European political systems do not give their supreme courts power to declare acts of parliament unconstitutional. Even in the Federal Republic of Germany and in Italy, where (under the strong influence of American precedents) the highest courts were given powers of oversight in their postwar constitutions, there has been little exercise of those powers. Accordingly, Israel makes no formal provision for judicial review of legislative acts of the Knesset. [10]

At the same time, courts always have held very authoritative positions within the framework of Jewish political life, and Jewish political culture has emphasized judicial decision making as being of the highest importance. The Supreme Court of Israel has taken its obligations very seriously and in 1969 did, in effect, assert a power of judicial review, effectively declaring an act of Knesset to be unconstitutional by holding that it was unenforceable. 98/69 *Berman* v. *Minister of Finance and State Comptroller,* Israel's *Marbury* v. *Madison*, came about by the action of an individual citizen who filed suit against the implementation of a Knesset act to finance election campaigns out of public funds, on the grounds that the act was discriminatory on behalf of existing parties and against new seekers of Knesset seats. The court held that even though Israel's written constitution is not complete, the article dealing with elections had been adopted properly and could be held to be of constituional validity, and that under its terms the act was indeed discriminatory and hence unconstitutional. It enjoined the minister of finance from paying out any funds under the act's provisions. The Knesset, in response, accepted the court's ruling and passed a revised act designed to accommodate its constitutional objections, thereby effectively affirming at least a limited power of judicial review as part of the country's constitutional mechanism. [11] Since then, the court has not hesitated to pursue an activist course in setting and maintaining constitutional standards. It is now accepted in Israel that the Supreme Court will play that role, and few controversial decisions of public bodies escape constitutional challenge as a result.

Though Israel's overall political culture is still in its formative stages, certain common elements within it already can be identified. First, there is the strong sense of national unity—one might say embattled national unity—that pervades the country. This sense of national unity is a synthesis of the effects of Israel's immediate security position, surrounded as it is by hostile Arab nations, and the whole history of Jewish isolation in the larger world. Since the former is simply a continuation of the latter in a different context, this aspect of Israel's political culture is no doubt rooted very deeply in the Israeli psyche.

Along with it is a common sense of vocation inherited from the larger Jewish political culture. Until the 1950s, this sense of vocation was manifested clearly through the Zionist vision of rebuilding Israel to redeem the Jewish people. Since then its precise character has become somewhat less explicit as it has become ideologically simplified and intellectually broadened. The revival of elements of the Zionist mystique after 1967 briefly gave it new life and even new directions. It was most fully exemplified in the "Complete Land of Israel" movement, whose members viewed the utterly unexpected liberation of the ancient Jewish heartland of Judea and Samaria in the Six Day War as providential and hence deserving of a whole-hearted human response. Gush Emunim was the product of that response and, at least in its first period, was acknowledged even by those who opposed its political aims as the fullest expression of halutziut (the Zionist pioneering spirit) of the times. Subsequently, the discouraging events of the 1970s, beginning with the Yom Kippur War in 1973, led to widespread questioning of whether Israel had lost its vocation. This questioning grew among the old Labor "establishment" after the Likud victory of 1977, which they saw as a disaster, and spread to the rest of the population after the financial crisis of 1983. The jeremiads which accompanied this questioning were, in themselves, testimony to Israelis' need to feel that their polity was pursuing its proper vocation properly.

Loss of their sense of vocation has profoundly affected Israelis' collective self-confidence. Hence, while not described in precisely these terms, its recovery is a major item on the current Israeli agenda. The great appeal of fundamentalist religion to previously a-religious Israelis is one response to this malaise. Jewish religion is, of course, highly vocational and offers a vocationally fulfilling path to righteousness for those who enter its precincts.

For a decade or so prior to 1967, Israelis viewed the major effort that they were making to provide technical assistance to the developing nations of Asia, Africa, and Latin America as an extension of Israel's vocation. While Israeli technical assistance efforts usually were justified in terms of the country's foreign policy, there is abundant evidence that this particular vehicle of foreign policy had its roots in the sense of national vocation.

Thus, Third World rejection of Israel after the 1967 war came as a great blow. Israelis have come to view subsequent technical assistance efforts in a more sober, even cynical, light as a result, but the sense of vocation still lurks beneath the surface and easily could be revived if the recipient countries were to become less cynical themselves.[12]

What is clear is that the original mystique of Zionism remains the faith of the fathers that undergirds the constitution of the Jewish state. It is expressed through an encompassing national-civic political cultural synthesis in which the Jewish nation (as Israelis understand the Jewish people) anchored in the State of Israel stands at the heart of Israel's political concern in place of a reified state. The nation is the focus of popular loyalty and commitment which properly is expressed through proper civic behavior—voting, military service, paying taxes, cooperating in the rebuilding of Zion—in short, what may be termed a national-civic political culture. Granted, these are idealized norms, as all norms must be in a political community with a sense of vocation.[13] Through them, Zionism has been internalized in the emergent political culture of the state. This reaffirmation of the sense of vocation that gave birth to Israel, even when presented in negative terms, is likely to have important constitutional consequences, both internally and externally.

A national-civic culture of this type is inevitably moralistic, in the sence that it generates popular expectations of the polity as a commonwealth, functioning for the good of all of its citizens, in which public office is a public trust and citizens have high expectations of office holders. Indeed, the original Zionist vision of the Jewish commonwealth in Eretz Israel, especially in its socialist form, made no allowance for human weakness, which is one of the reasons why there is such great disillusionment at present. Two generations were educated in the notion that the Zionist movement was producing a new Israeli man, so when normal human nature reasserted itself, as it inevitably will, the generations so educated were crushed. That was especially hard for people who were born into the socialist camp and nurtured by it, who discovered those impulses in themselves. In many cases they have projected their disillusionment with themselves onto the society as a whole. Yet, in fact, that disillusionment is a result of excessive expectations rather than real failure.

Still, the end result is a political culture with moralistic expectations and individualistic behavior, whereby individual members of the body politic not only pursue their own personal goals but seek to benefit from access to state-controlled goods to do so. Again, that is an unanticipated consequence of the kind of state that the socialist Zionist founders built. In their desire to eliminate the evils of capitalism, they emphasized collective institutions, culminating in the Histadrut and in the state itself, with extensive power over the economy as well as the polity, and thereby able to influence every aspect of the society. Their success was their undoing, since what emerged was a state-permeated society and economy dominated by bureaucratic institutions in which political access became a necessary vehicle for economic advancement, replacing the marketplace.

Jews in the diaspora long had been used to pursuing their individualistic goals vis-à-vis the outer society, using whatever channels were open to them. Hence, it is not surprising that they adapted to the political conditions of Israel, introducing a strong measure of individualistic behavior into the Israeli polity that often ran against their own moralistic expectations, creating a dilemma that has yet to be resolved and, indeed, has been aggravated since the Yom Kippur War. The resolution of that dilemma is one of the major items on the Israeli agenda for this generation.

In the meantime, the remnants of the subject political culture among Jews have been transformed into a traditionalistic subculture within the larger political culture, which looks upon the state as a nursing father, as indicated above. Here, too, rather than the kind of traditional culture that

FIGURE 10-1
The Matrix of Political Cultural Types

| ORIENTATION | Moralistic | Individualistic | Traditionalistic (Traditional) |
|---|---|---|---|
| Civic | | | |
| Statist | | | |
| Subject | | | |

linked patrons and clients in premodern societies, or even a modern traditionalistic culture in which particular populations respond to power elites who presumably take care of their own needs, in Israel the state is central for the traditionalistic subculture, as well, coming in place of private patrons. Unlike the case with the individualistic subculture, which stands apart from—even in opposition to—the ideals of Zionism, those who view the state in this way are able to identify their traditionalistic demands with the Zionist, especially socialist Zionist, moralistic norm that it is the state's obligation to look after its citizens.

Moralistic, individualistic, and traditionalistic subcultures are present in other polities as well as Israel. [14] In each, they take on the characteristics of the other political cultural dimension, which they modify appropriately (figure 10-1). Thus, both Israel and the United States have civic cultures, but the civic culture of the United States is individualist-oriented, while that of Israel is group-oriented. The collectivity, in this case the Jewish people, is at the center of civic concern rather than the individual. Hence, the three subcultures have a far more communal tinge in Israel than their American counterparts, but with that caveat they still can be defined in the same terms.

In most countries, the three subcultures are far more geographically rooted than in Israel. While it is hard to find geocultural clusters in Israel, there are identifiable reference-group clusters, some of which are acquiring a geographic base. Thus, there is evidence that Mapam, Kibbutz HaMeuhad, and Hapoel Hamizrahi kibbutzniks share a moralistic political subculture, along with members of Gush Emunim and Oz VeShalom (a religious peace movement, the obverse of Gush Emunim). Similarly, Jerusalem as a city seems to be dominated by a synthesis of the moralistic and individualsitic political subcultures, while Tel Aviv as a city is highly individualistic in its political culture. Unskilled and semiskilled factory workers and members of the *moshvei olim* seem to have synthesized the moralistic and traditionalistic political cultures, while a purer form of the traditionalistic political subculture is to be found in the development towns on the geographic and social peripheries of the country.

The very fact that these subcultural patterns are becoming identified with particular spatial entities is part of the general transition from ideological to territorial democracy. People from different countries and regions of origin bring with them cultural baggage that is further modified by their experiences in the new land. Particular localities attract people with different cultural orientations, who then establish their patterns as dominant locally. Moreover, the first founders willy-nilly impose their cultural predispositions on the polity they have founded, which then are transmitted to subsequent generations and to no little extent to new arrivals, unless they are so inundated by later migrations that the original culture is overwhelmed or forced into a new synthesis with that of the latecomers. All of these patterns can be found in the Israeli experience, which is so new that the cultural synthesis is still under way.

In the last analysis, Israel, like every other modern democracy, has had to develop its own synthesis between commonwealth and marketplace aspirations, the two faces of democratic politics. Having been founded with a heavy emphasis on the commonwealth dimension, Israel initially provided no legitimate space for the marketplace, but the latter was not to be denied, there or anywhere else, so it has carved its own space within the very heart of the commonwealth, often transforming the latter in unanticipated ways.

The federal, or contractual, element (in the social even more than the political sense) is an important component of Israel's emergent political culture. The party system, the affiliated federations of agricultural settlements, and Histadrut itself perpetuate Israeli society's original structuring along lines that provided for the autonomous action of separate ideologically based movements within a common framework—a classic case of federalism in both the political and the socioeconomic realms. Substantial traces of millet federalism are preserved in the institutionalized relationships between the state and the country's several ethnoreligious groups (including the Jews). The regional councils and federations of cities—the two forms of local government developed by the Israelis themselves—are federal in character, as well. These institutional arrangements are simply the most visible manifestations of the federal principles that permeate Israeli society and its political culture, from its congregational religious organization to its system of condominium housing, even though the state has no acknowledged federal structure. Contractual government, the constitutional diffusion of power, and negotiated collaboration are all elements of the Jewish political culture that are finding expression, albeit imperfectly, in the restored Jewish state.[15]

The federal dimension in Israeli society is manifested especially in the interpersonal relationships that shape the conduct of business, particularly public business within the state. The pattern of those relationships is clearly in tune with Jewish political culture. Jews as a people are bound to each other by kinship and consent, by descent from common ancestors that make all Jews feel as if they are members of one family, and by virtue of the ancient covenant that transformed that family into a nation, linking its members together through a shared vision. This book is not the place to trace the history of the Jews or the dimensions of the relationship between the constitutional act of covenanting and its behavioral consequences, but it should be clear to any observer of the Israeli scene that there are behavioral consequences that flow from this particular amalgam of kinship and consent. Because every Jew feels related to every other one in a family way, yet at the same time is a consenting individual in a covenantal way, the Jews of Israel have developed what can only be called a federal relationship to one another.

Anyone who ever has tried to accomplish any task in Israel can reflect on the way that this sense of federative kinship informs the behavior of Israelis. No Israeli feels compelled to do anything; rather, he or she exercises freedom of choice in responding to requests for action. Certainly position in a putative organizational hierarchy is not sufficient to determine one's obligations; at most it is a starting point, useful in gaining the attention of the one whose cooperation is sought. To take a homely example, it is nearly impossible for a boss to relate to an Israeli secretary on the grounds that, as a secretary, she *must* do this or that. Instead, the fact that a person has accepted a secretarial position creates a certain framework for negotiation between her and her boss. Thus, it is possible for the boss to turn to the secretary on the grounds that he would like her to undertake a particular task, which he sees as falling within the scope of her responsibility in the position she has accepted. At that point there ensues an explicit or implicit negotiation, based upon the structural framework binding the requester and the secretary involved. The subtlety of this negotiation should not obscure its reality. Moreover, it is a negotiation that is most successful when it is conducted within a cooperative framework, when the people involved feel that they are acting on the basis of their own free will and according to their own values and expectations.

Some have interpreted that as a kind of an individualism, but it is not that at all, since it is based upon the assumption of cooperation. In fact, the more the parties feel that what they are doing is done on a cooperative basis, the more likely they are to engage in mutually satisfying behavior. Conversely, the more the coercive element is emphasized, the more resistance there is likely to be on the part of one or both of the parties.

All of that leads to the paradox that, in Israel, at least, hierarchical organizations are by far the least efficient and least responsive. The same Israeli who on the street will go out of his way to be helpful to someone in need of assistance, in his official capacity in an office may become officious and unresponsive. I would suggest that the difference lies in this dichotomy between the highly centralized and overregulated character of the formal structure of the state and Jewish notions of equality and independence. For Israelis, it would be a surrender to authority simply to obey regulations, a surrender that could affect one's autonomy, given the hierarchical character of the structure. On the other hand, where free consent is involved, a sympathetic response would be in keeping with another dimension of the culture. Thus, rigid centralization becomes dysfunctional because of the culturally rooted conflict it provokes within the institutions themselves.

One result is that Israeli society, even more than most, lives on two dimensions: the visible dimension of the formal institutional structure, and the invisible network of kinship and consensual ties that not only animate the formal institutions but in many cases bypass or replace them. Successful functioning within Israeli society is based most immediately upon an understanding of and, more important, an involvement in this implicitly federal cultural dimension. Beyond that, however, the transformation of Israeli society into one that functions more successfully very well may depend upon a restructuring of the formal institutional framework to take that federal political culture into account.

In this connection, institutionalization of bargaining has to be considered another aspect of Israel's political culture. As befits a society whose origins lie so heavily in covenantal arrangements, bargaining and negotiation are, and always have been, important features of Israel's political process, though, as befits a society torn between institutions representing one particular political culture and tendencies reflecting another, much of the bargaining is conducted within frameworks that, by themselves, would not suggest that they were open to it. While public patterns of political communication remain ideologically declamatory and uncompromising in the Eastern European manner more often than not, bargaining (traditional in Jewish political life) has come to be of immense importance and is growing in scope. The Knesset committee system is simply one way in which it has been institutionalized without formal constitutional changes.

The character of bargaining in Israeli society is unequivocally Israeli. In the first place, where more parties are involved, it tends to be collegial; that is to say, people sit around a table, whether as individuals or representatives, and conduct a fairly stylized discussion, with the convener of the meeting either presenting an opening statement setting forth the direction of the negotiations as he sees it or designating someone to do that, if he is designated as a neutral or seeks to be. Each person around the table then speaks his or her piece, with as many round robins as the chairman deems necessary or time will allow. The chairman then makes a summary based upon what he or she has heard, which, if unchallenged, becomes the decision and then is presented as such in the minutes. The minutes, referred to as protocols, are, in effect, contracts deemed more or less binding on all the participants, which is why participants read all minutes carefully and register any dissent which they feel necessary before the protocols are finalized. If there are those in the group who do not want any decision at all, they will act in a verbally disruptive manner during the course of the meeting, which will be a sharp signal that no consensus can be reached. That, in turn, may lead to more private negotiations between the convener and the objecting party or parties, and/or another meeting.

There is another side to the federal element on the Israeli scene that must be noted, particularly since its implications seem to be growing. It has to do with the perceived relationships between Israel and the world Jewish community.

We already have noted that, according to its own political doctrines, Israel sees itself as a state within the Jewish nation, which includes other corporate units (the Jewish communities of the diaspora) that are, in the Israeli view, willy-nilly federated with it. Israel enjoys a superior status—not only because it is a comprehensive, politically sovereign state, and the diaspora communities are voluntary and partial in scope, but because it is the only Jewish state, is located in Eretz Israel, and functions as the center of Jewish life. This theoretical framework not only provides the basis for conceptualizing Israel as part of a worldwide body politic, but it also sharpens the federal character of Israel itself.

If the Law of Return provides that any Jew coming to Israel automatically is entitled to citizenship, it is not by virtue of his being born somehow an Israeli, wherever he may have come from, but because of his kinship ties with the Jewish people. He must, as it were, contract with Israel to be part of that particular subdivision of his people, but he is considered to have an inalienable right to do so.

In this regard it is important to recall the premises underlying formal political discussion of this proposition in Israel and the terminology used by the Israelis themselves. There is no Israeli nationality in a legal sense, only an Israeli citizenship, which is not confined to Jews. Moreover, a clear distinction is made between *state* and *nation* as they apply to Israel. The State of Israel is the Jewish *state*, but it is not the Jewish *nation*. The national institutions formally belong to the Jewish people as a whole; they operate within the state but are not legally subordinate to it. Constitutionally, they are linked with the state by special contracts affirming this unique relationship.[16] The fact that, in reality, the state's political leadership plays a dominant role in the governance of the national institutions when they care to is very important, but does not change the theoretical basis upon which they are structured and which does influence their operations.

In the decade more immediately prior to the Six Day War, most Israelis were happy to ignore these little points of political theory. Indeed, many tried actively to do so. Nor were they alone. Diaspora Jewry, for the most part, was equally happy to ignore them, if not more so. After 1967, however, they took on a new reality and a new concreteness and are now clearly significant factors in determining the direction of Israeli political development. The most important operational manifestations of this change are to be found in the reconstituted Jewish Agency and its growing independence from Israeli governmental direction, and in Project Renewal, the largest single social development effort undertaken in the country since the Six Day War, whose whole character is that of a partnership between the diaspora communities, the Jewish Agency, and the government of Israel, organized and implemented in a fully federal manner. [17]

Just as there is a certain contradiction between the hierarchical structure of the state and the federal political culture that animates those who make it work, so, too, is there a contradictory dysfunctionality and ambivalence in the matter of Israel-diaspora relations. The latter are federal in structure, but Israelis view them from a monistic ideology, that is to say, they expect those relations to be hierarchical, or at the very least based on a center-periphery model, with Israel either dominating the hierarchy or at the center of the circle. As in the first case, reality is quite different from the expectation, but the issue is a matter of perennial contention in discussions between Israeli and diaspora Jewish leaders and intellectuals. [18]

*Cooperation* is yet another great influence on Israel's political culture. In a sense, it is closely related to the federal element, but in a way that informs contractual relationships, shaping them in its way as individualism does those selfsame elements in the United States. Cooperative activity has characterized the development of Israeli society from the first. Its most dramatic manifestations were in the pioneering agricultural communities, where the cooperative ideal in both its collectivist and noncollectivist forms permeated the very erection of the communities themselves and every aspect of their functioning. Moreover, each settlement is part of a chain of cooperative societies, each designed to provide some service or set of services that embraces the whole settlement movement in a series of ever-widening arenas of cooperative activity.

This cooperative activity was a manifestation of an effort to create a certain kind of highly integrated community and was based upon a much higher level of consensus than that demanded in most contemporary Western societies. It reached its most intense form in the kibbutzim, whose experience seems to indicate that a shared response to the fundamental life questions of religion and politics is utterly necessary in cooperative communities of this character, or the community will be faced with intolerable factionalism. In the early 1950s, many kibbutzim actually split into two over questions of political ideology.

Cooperative ties in the cities, where over 90 percent of the population is located, are far less intense. At the same time, even the cities can be understood as networks of cooperatives in at least one sense. Most people in Israel live in what Americans call condominiums, and what in Israel are termed cooperative houses. The cooperative house represents an interesting merger of the exigencies of urban living with the cooperative orientation of Israeli society. For reasons that will not be elaborated here, it was determined early that urban Israelis would be encouraged to own their own homes. Today some 70 percent do. At the same time, urban areas in Israel have been developed primarily through the construction of apartments. Indeed, there is a conscious governmental policy to encourage relatively high-density settlement, and since land is controlled either by the government or by the Jewish National Fund, which works closely with the government, it has been able to make this policy stick. Thus, most Israelis, except for those in the rural areas, the Arab villages, and a few bedroom suburbs, live in apartments.

The solution to the potential contradiction was to create a situation in which Israelis essentially were required to buy their apartments. There are almost no rental units available; the cost of rental is so prohibitive that virtually no one rents for other than a temporary period, and the return on capital is so small that few investors are prepared to provide rental apartments. Under the prevailing arrangement, every family upon purchasing its apartment also acquires an undivided share in the commons of the building (the roof, the garden, the parking area, if there is one, and the stairwells) and must cooperate with his neighbors in the maintenance of those common areas and in the provision of common services for the exclusive areas (for example, central heating, the common water supply, electricity, gas). In some cases that is required by law where the building is legally a cooperative house, but even where it is not, it is required by necessity.

Thus, for the overwhelming majority of Israelis, the simple act of living requires cooperative links to control externalities. In the case of small buildings (up to eight families), it is likely that the building committee will consist of all adults, with one or more persons taking on specific responsibilities on a rotating basis, usually for one-year terms. In larger buildings, a committee is elected at an annual meeting of all tenants, and its responsibility is then to handle all but exceptional problems during its tenure, which is also usually a year.

This arrangement follows the pattern of self-governing institutions in Israel and, indeed, in the Jewish political tradition—the general meeting and the operating committee. It is taken as a matter of course and in general is not utilized consciously for public purposes, but, rather, is considered a private arrangement among each building's residents. On the other hand, it is securely anchored in law and local custom.

Also linked to the federal and cooperative dimensions of Israel's emerging political culture is a commitment to comity in the legal arena derived from the Jewish political tradition as well. For example, the Contracts Law adopted by the Knesset in 1973 introduces the principle of "duty imposed upon the contracting parties to act in customary manner and in good faith," a radical innovation in English law but a matter of great importance in Jewish law and, indeed, in Jewish political culture. As part of its covenantal foundations, the latter developed the concept of covenant obligation (*hesed* in

Hebrew) very early on as absolutely necessary to prevent covenantal relationships from declining into mere contractualism, whereby each party seeks to interpret contracts on the basis of self-interest alone.[19]

Once again, these legal changes are locked in a web of ambivalence. On one hand they reflect the continuing effort to detach Israeli law from dependence on foreign forms—Ottoman and British—introduced prior to statehood, and to base them insofar as possible on traditional Jewish legal sources. At the same time, the secular elements of Israeli society are fearful of carrying that too far, lest the door be opened to subordinating Israeli law to halachah. Their fears are intensified by the inflexible posture of Orthodox rabbinical authorities, who are the custodians of halachah under Israeli law and who have shown a minimum of understanding of the needs of non-Orthodox Jews on virtually every front.

The response of the Knesset has been to reaffirm that Israel is a state of secular law (*medinat hok* in Hebrew), rather than a state based on halachah, but, at the same time, to write in somewhat vague and ambiguous formulas providing that the secular law of the state will be based upon the eternal principles of Jewish jurisprudence. At the same time, the Ministry of Justice has a department headed and staffed by observant Jews whose task it is to find practical ways to translate those ambiguous formulas into concrete practical applications, which they have done successfully in a wide variety of fields without introducing theocratic elements into the law of the state. That is possible because Jewish civil jurisprudence is as well developed as its religious law, and as much a part of the halachah. Indeed, ancient Jewish civil jurisprudence is considered among the enlightened legal systems of the world, even by modern standards.[20]

The struggle over the character of the legal system is a reflection of a larger dimension of Israel's general and political cultures, namely, the Israeli Jews' search for roots in their ancient past while at the same time being firmly committed to modernity. In the general culture, this dimension manifests itself in Israelis' interests in archeology and the Bible—which, in fact, was considerably stronger in the 1950s and 1960s, when the Jews in the country still constituted a nation of immigrants, than it is today, as a new generation that feels personally at home in the land has grown to adulthood. Indeed, the decline of Biblical studies in the elementary and secondary schools is a matter of some concern to Jewish educators and leaders in the state, as young Israelis relate to Bible study much as young people relate to the study of their national histories elsewhere, respectful more in the breach than willing to apply themselves to learning the subject.

Democratic republicanism and constitutionalism also are rooted deeply in the emergent political culture of Israel. Whatever the problems faced by the country, threats to constitutional legitimacy, democracy, or the republican form of government are not among them. Indeed, it is precisely because such threats are virtually unthinkable that we know that cultural rather than simply strategic or expediential supports for constitutionalism and republicanism are involved.

Since 1977, various voices on the left end of the Israeli political spectrum have suggested that antidemocratic tendencies are on the rise in Israel. In chapter 8 it was noted how the Sephardim have been improperly accused by those voices of such tendencies and of lacking a democratic political culture. Those same voices accuse the Likud and its supporters more generally of falling into that category, a somewhat toned-down charge when compared to the days when Labor camp spokesmen regularly charged the Herut with being fascist. Most recently, the emergence of a genuinely antidemocratic figure on the Israeli political scene, Meir Kahane with his Kach party, has led to new hysteria on the subject.

While eternal vigilance is as much the price of liberty in Israel as elsewhere, any possible threats to democratic republicanism in the Jewish state are political, not cultural, in character. That is to say, there may be political circumstances that could bring about antidemocratic actions in Israel as in any other polity, but the political culture of the vast majority of Israelis does not lend itself to such developments, and indeed can be expected to serve as a basis for mounting strong resistance to them, should they occur. Jewish political history has been characterized by a variety of regimes, which have included some that were quite oligarchical, but even the kings of ancient Israel were constitutional monarchs, required to share power with other authorities: prophets, priests, and popular assemblies, and, later, halachic sages and notables. With the exception of Herod's rule in Judea, imposed on the Jews by the Romans, there never has been a case of an authoritarian regime in Jewish political history, excepting only the smallest local arenas. Where an occasional exception is found, Jews simply do not take to authoritarianism, no matter what their backgrounds.

That is not to suggest that republicanism in Israel has not been influenced by the environments from which the Jews who settled in the country came. In fact, very few of the Jewish settlers of modern Israel came from democratic societies. As noted earlier, they came as subjects from some of the worst examples of premodern autocracy or modern totalitarianism available. The very fact that democratic republicanism is rooted so strongly in Israel is testimony to the importance of the latent Jewish political culture that they share.

This democratic republicanism extends to a sense of constitutionalism even in the absence of a written constitution. Again, centuries of commitment to the Torah as constitution have left their mark. The Knesset is already chary of interfering with established constitutional traditions, even in the absence of a written document, and virtually every effort to tamper with those traditions advanced in the last fifteen years has failed to gain sufficient support in the Knesset to be adopted, with the argument against accepting such proposals explicitly constitutional.

In many respects, the Israeli constitution resembles that of the British, that is to say, an ancient constitutional tradition concretized periodically in specific legislation that, while enacted on a basis hardly different from ordinary legislation, is recognized as having constitutional import. The difference is that the British explicitly define their constitution in these terms and have had a thousand years, more or less, in which to develop it, while Israelis, wary of recognizing their ancient constitution as such because of the conflict between religion and secularization in Israeli society, have been less willing to be explicit in the matter, and have had to develop the concrete documents within the space of hardly more than a generation. But the model is still the same, as witnessed by the fact that these instant constitutional documents, which in theory can be changed by sixty-one votes of the Knesset, have been accorded the respect they have. Moreover, while none of them has been framed as explicitly relating to the Torah as constitution, none of them has explicitly negated the traditional constitution, either.

In other matters, the shape of the emergent Israeli political culture is more equivocal. Systematic observation seems to reveal that there is a change taking place in the relationship of the bureaucracy to the public. While the bureaucrats may or may not be becoming more efficient, they are becoming less officious, as a new generation of Israelis shed some of their resigned acceptance of overbearing bureaucratic behavior, which their immigrant parents accepted as a matter of course.

The same equivocal situation prevails in regard to the role of the citizen. It seems to be generally assumed that citizens should be concerned with political affairs in principle, and citizen participation as voters in elections is particularly high. At the same time, attempts to develop a widespread "participatory" outlook run into difficulties because of the nature of the political, particularly the party, system, where centralized control and adherence to the ideological symbols and forms of an earlier generation act to discourage participation by those who are not "political" in Israeli parlance (that is to say, those who do not make politics the overriding concern in their lives).

In this connection, it is important to note the first signs of the emergence of the "citizen" or "amateur" participant in political affairs. Still occasional and tentative, the two principal efforts to enter state politics in this way, the Rafi effort in 1969 and the Democratic Movement for Change in 1977, both failed. Local efforts in municipal elections have been considerably more successful (see chapter 5). The rise of consumer and environmental protection movements among cosmopolitans since 1970 and the participatory aspects of Project Renewal are other manifestations that augur well for the future development of a participatory political culture.

Here, too, it is on the local plane that the most innovative developments have taken place. Local governments are far more advanced than the government of the state in institutionalizing citizen participation in Israel. The kibbutzim and, to a slightly lesser extent, the moshavim are the best examples of citizen give-and-take in the governmental sphere, because of the possibilities inherent in them for the highest degree of participation, namely, direct democracy. Not unexpectedly, the reality is somewhat less than the potentiality, but Israel's agricultural settlements still remain among the last places in the world where direct democracy is practiced to the extent that local citizens wish to do so as individuals. The formalization of the "local committees" (the governing bodies of these settlements) as a fourth form of local government in Israel and the extension of that form to unincorporated urban settlements within the more densely populated regional councils, have extended the Israeli version of the town-meeting principle in new directions.

The problem of public expectations from politicians is more complex. On one hand, formal public expectations are high. The people believe that very high standards of behavior should be demanded on the part of those they entrust with power. At the same time, they have not been seriously concerned with devising ways to impose sanctions if their leaders do not live up to that standard. Here, especially, there has been no crystallization of political cultural patterns. The Eastern European and Oriental ideas of the privileges of "rank" still are locked in conflict with classical Jewish standards of responsibility.

## Mamlachtiut and Halutziut: Cultural Tension and Cultural Synthesis

For Israelis, as for all others, the political culture reflects the deep structural synthesis between the two faces of politics, the organization and management of power and the pursuit of justice. The former has to do with "who gets what, when, and how" and the latter has to do with the development of the good society. It is the major continuing task of every polity to deal with the tensions between these two faces, to bring them to complement one another in pursuit of the polity's larger political ends and in light of the realities of political power within it.

Modern democratic polities are torn between two conceptions of the proper or just political order. The first sees the polity as a marketplace, in which the primary public relationships are products of bargaining among individuals and groups acting out of self-interest, but held together through agreement to common rules of the game. The second conceives of the political order as a commonwealth, in which the whole people have an undivided interest, and in which citizens cooperate in an effort to maintain the best government in order to implement shared moral principles. In the polity-as-marketplace, the role of the government is defined as insuring compliance with the rules of the game and equitable access to the political marketplace for all citizens. In the polity-as-commonwealth, the role of government is to mobilize the polity's resources in pursuit of its moral ends.

Most arguments over what constitutes democracy have their roots in one or another of these two conceptions of the political order. Thus, individualists and pluralists tend to see the political order as a marketplace first and foremost, while moralists, collectivists, and nationalists tend to view it as a commonwealth first and foremost. In fact, modern democratic polities somehow must synthesize aspects of both, first in their political culture and then in their institutions. They do so by linking the two through conceptions of efficiency (the use of power) and legitimacy (the pursuit of justice), rooted in their own political cultures as a result of their respective experiences.

The conceptions of efficiency and legitimacy rooted in Israel's political culture are based upon deep-rooted commitments to mamlachtiut and halutziut respectively. The Zionist enterprise in Eretz Israel was initiated to pursue the commonwealth model in the fullest sense of the term. Therein lay the Zionist conception of justice. But the realities of power, first in the Jewish people and then in the land itself, meant that the Zionist movement from the first had to accommodate itself to a politics of the marketplace, as well. The fact that different Zionist parties had different visions of the commonwealth to be established, in itself assured that unity in the movement could be preserved only through accepting some dimension of the marketplace approach. It already has been noted that the introduction of the proportional representation system as the foundation stone of Zionist and later Israeli politics was a consequence of this reality and, indeed, marks an institutional manifestation of the effort to reconcile these two dimensions of political order for the sake of national unity.

The pursuit of the commonwealth model led to the utilization of voluntary cooperative and collective enterprises to build the yishuv. The extent and success of these enterprises led to the entrenchment of the principle of pioneering, or halutziut, within the emerging political culture. At the same time, the collectivist orientation of the founders was transformed easily into mamlachtiut, or a heavy reliance on the state, after 1948. Ben-Gurion tried to link halutziut and mamlachtiut, repeatedly suggesting that once the state was established, the real field for halutziut was within the domains of the state institutions, the army, for example.

While his synthesis carried a great deal of weight, in fact, there remained tensions between halutziut and mamlachtiut. The former by its very nature emphasizes voluntary and covenantal relationships, while the latter by its very nature emphasizes coercive and hierarchical ones. It already has been noted that after an initial love affair with mamlachtiut, Israelis have moved away from it. Still, it has entered their political culture as much as halutziut, so that even Israelis who are not enamored of the state have a hard time conceiving of a society less state-permeated, or of the state's not playing a leading role in the pursuit of national goals.

At the same time, the very fact that the state was so active meant that it not only pursued commonwealth goals but became the principal marketplace for personal achievement and advancement, thereby encouraging the introduction of marketplace behavior within the framework of a commonwealth

FIGURE 10-2

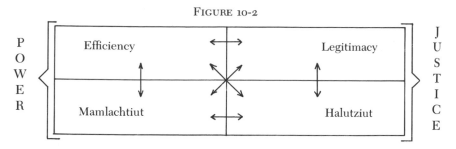

orientation not always to the advantage of the latter, and in ways that ultimately produced disillusionment and cynicism among many Israelis. Today, mamlachtiut and halutziut stand in uneasy tension in Israeli political culture, with the former assumed to be necessary for the organization and management of power, and the latter assumed to be necessary for the pursuit of justice, Israeli style.

Figure 10-2 presents the value concepts that provide the framework within which the value orientations of Israelis are shaped. In the figure, power and justice represent the two faces or poles of politics. In every polity, efficiency has to do with the achievement of common goals in a manner that involves the least wasteful or minimum necessary expenditure of resources and relates particularly to the organization and management of power, while legitimacy embodying the definition of justice, refers to those aspects of the polity that are supported by the underlying values of its citizenry, particularly as embodied in its constitutional system. In Israel efficiency is measured predominantly in terms of mobilization of state power (mamlachtiut), while legitimacy is defined fundamentally by the complex of voluntary initiatives within a cooperative and covenantal context, as embodied in the value concept of halutziut. Emphasizing the role of the state does not necessarily mean statism, even though for a brief period it seemed to come close to that. The elements of mamlachtiut can change over time, although the history of the state is too short for them to have changed very much. The complex of ideas and aspirations surrounding halutziut is somewhat better developed, since it has a longer history, going back to the beginnings of the Zionist enterprise, and hence it has undergone greater change from the days when it simply involved being in the forefront of redeeming and rebuilding Eretz Israel.

Each of the four elements of the matrix is pulled in the direction of power or justice, and also is modified by every other element. Thus, in every form that it has taken, halutziut has had a strong collectivist, or mamlachti, aspect, while at the same time mamlachtiut has not become statism because it has been modified by the ideals of halutziut, which limit legitimate state activity even at the expense of what otherwise would be deemed as efficiency. Each of these elements has its own subtleties, and the changes that are taking place in their cultural definition are often very subtle indeed.

Political culture is not easily visible as a factor shaping politics. As in the case of culture generally, it does not spring out in front of the casual observer. Its impact is more often latent than manifest, subtle rather than direct. Nevertheless, cultural, political, and social institutions become what they are to a very great extent as a result of the cultural matrix in which they are imbedded. Israel is no exception. Hence, the political cultural synthesis now being developed there will shape the character of the Jewish state for generations to come.

# ELEVEN

## The Impact of the Frontier

The emergence of an Israeli political culture is intimately tied to the course of development in Israel, which, as we already have suggested, is tied to a continuing frontier experience. Building upon the classic frontier model of Frederick Jackson Turner, this writer elsewhere has delineated the frontier phenomenon in its complexity.[1] Here the thesis can only be summarized briefly.

### THE GREAT FRONTIER AND ITS STAGES

Since the opening of the great frontier on the eve of the modern epoch, frontier societies have passed through or into three to four stages of frontier development, each of which has, in turn, affected every aspect of its society's civilization. The first stage, at the very beginning of their settlement, was the rural-land frontier, during which the pioneers founded rural settlements of various kinds to conquer and directly exploit new lands through agriculture and the extraction of natural resources. That was the classic frontier delineated by the frontier theorists, especially Frederick Jackson Turner.[2]

In the manner of a chain reaction, the rural-land frontier gave birth to a second frontier stage, the urban-industrial frontier, based on the conquest of nature through industrialization, which radically transformed the heretofore rural society and reorganized its basic pattern of settlement by moving the major portion of the population into cities (urban places) to man and manage the new industrial system. After the onset of industrialization, the new cities of the urban-industrial frontier became sufficiently strong from an economic point of view to generate their own continued development, in contrast to preindustrial cities, which existed to serve their rural hinterlands and depended upon those hinterlands for survival. After the opening of the urban-industrial frontier, the rural hinterlands came to serve the industrial cities.

The urban-industrial frontier continued the chain reaction and led to the opening of the metropolitan-technological frontier. Simple industrialization gave way to the development of sophisticated technologies, which not only transformed the nature of industrial activity but, through the development of synthetics, changed the relationship between industrial activity and the natural world, opening a whole new universe to conquer. At the same time, new transportation and communications technologies were developed that offered radically new possibilities for organizing space. Just as cities were the most efficient form of settlement for the urban-industrial frontier, so, too, did metropolitan settlements (cities and suburbs) emerge to form a new basis for the spatial organization of society.

Beginning in the late 1970s, the most advanced frontier societies passed into yet another fourth frontier stage, the citybelt, or rurban-cybernetic frontier, a step beyond the metropolitan-technological frontier that generated it. The spread of cybernetics, from information storage and retrieval, to communication, to production, has led to another quantum jump forward in economic enterprise and its inevitable social and political consequences, which only now are beginning to be felt. Spatially, the newest technologies have made it possible for populations to deconcentrate, either by transforming existing metropolitan areas into chains or belts of cities, or by settling in hitherto rural countrysides, establishing bands of rurban settlements tied together through computers and telecommunications. This fourth frontier stage is still in its earliest phase, where it has appeared at all.

Each new frontier stage has generated a new economic basis for society, which, in turn, has created new patterns of settlement. Taken together, the two have regularly transformed the society's dominant patterns of social organization, causing great and substantial political responses and adjustments. The changes wrought out of each new frontier experience have served to renew the "new societies" periodically and thereby reinforce their "newness."

The United States is the paradigmatic example of the frontier experience, passing in its history through the entire frontier process to date.[3] The American rural-land frontier opened in the early seventeenth century and persisted until World War I, during which time the continental expanse of the United States was settled and its natural environment tamed for agricultural or extractive pursuits. Beginning early in the nineteenth century, the rural-land frontier gave birth to the urban-industrial frontier, whose expansion accelerated after 1848. Cities that originally developed to market agricultural surpluses began to transform natural resources through the manufacturing process, thereby acquiring an existence independent of the rural environment around them. By the late nineteenth century, the urban-industrial frontier was dominant in the United States, with the rural areas becoming increasingly tributary to it and industrial production becoming its own reward.

The urban-industrial frontier persisted until the mid-twentieth century. Even before its passing, however, it had generated the metropolitan-technological frontier. Metropolitanization of the large industrial centers of the United States was noticeable as early as the turn of the century, and began to develop a life of its own even before World War II. It was not until after 1945, however, that it became the dominant pattern, capitalizing on the new transportation and communications systems invented in the preceding frontier stage plus the new technologies of synthetics to reorder American society.

By the late 1960s, the energy of the metropolitan frontier was played out. Metropolitanization had become routine rather than frontierlike. For a brief period, Americans were concerned about the "limits to growth," some even going so far as to adopt an antigrowth and antifrontier outlook. In the meantime, however, technological change was in the process of laying the foundations for the fourth frontier stage, which began to have its impact a decade later. By the early 1980s, the United States was well into the citybelt-cybernetic frontier, which was manifested by new political issues such as competition between the Sunbelt and the Frostbelt, and such phenomena as the revival of the small industrial towns in eastern Massachusetts as production sites for the latest cybernetic technologies.

The phenomenon of the great frontier is often mistaken for a form of modernization. While it is true that there are modernization dimensions to the frontier process, there is a real difference between the two. The frontier process is one of extending human dominion over the natural environment, and the frontier zone is that region where humanity and the natural environment meet in a dynamic way as that process unfolds. The essence of modernization is the transformation of people and peoples "in place," that is to say, the transformation of established societies, traditional or feudal, into modern ones without having them change geographic location. The frontier process involves a complete locational change, not only temporal but also spatial, which offers the opportunity for a wider variety of transformations precisely because people have moved away from the locus of earlier vested interests. The transformation of Jews in Old World diasporas was indeed modernization, even if the Jews already were born modern to a great extent. The transformation of the Jews who came to Eretz Israel is more a product of their encounter with the frontier of Jewish resettlement in the land.

Each of the new societies has gone through its own frontier patterns in ways generally similar to that of the United States. Israel is no exception. In its case, however, the process has been condensed radically, because its development did not begin until the closing generations of the modern epoch.[4] Thus, the first three frontier stages have been compressed into a single century.

The compression of the three frontier stages into one century of development in Israel has created a highly diverse society and economy in which the three stages are closely intertwined. Agricultural pioneering continues on the country's peripheries, less than an hour's drive away from examples of typical Western suburbia. Israel has made its own small contribution to the lore of the great frontier of the Western world in its opening of new lands through collective and urban settlement. The country's kibbutzim and development towns are of particular interest for those reasons alone.

David Ben-Gurion defined the character of Israel's frontier and set its agenda in "The Key to Immigration," a 1932 address. Even then, he suggested that the agricultural frontier must be supplemented by an urban one. Fourteen years later, in his speech "Unity and Independence," he issued a challenge to pioneer on the metropolitan and technological frontier, as well.[5] In that speech, Ben-Gurion also emphasized the way that halutziut, or pioneering, had to remain a continuing value in Israeli society if the Zionist enterprise was to succeed. The very fact that today Israelis bemoan the demise of halutziut is indicative of its continuing importance in Israeli society. Indeed, the greatest claim that Gush Emunim and its supporters have on the Israeli public in their efforts to settle Judea and Samaria flows from their perceived role as continuers of the classic tradition of halutziut.

## ISRAEL'S RURAL-LAND FRONTIER

As in the case of the other new societies, the building of modern Israel began with the opening of a rural-land frontier. The Zionist pioneering effort began in the late 1870s and early 1880s. It was a true land frontier, in that the Zionist settlements invariably were located on empty lands, which abounded in the country despite its ostensibly settled character. Until the mid-1970s, over half of the territory of Israel in its pre-1967 boundaries had less than six people per square mile. When the territories occupied after 1967 are added, perhaps 40 percent of the West Bank fell into that category. These lands consisted of either swamps, coastal sand dunes, eroded mountains, or deserts, which had to be reclaimed prior to their settlement. As already indicated, the ideology of the first Zionist pioneers was "back to the land"-oriented, based upon the idea that productive agricultural labor would reclaim the Jewish character from the ravages of ghetto life, while reclaiming the land, as well.

At the same time, the character of settlement in the Middle East meant that the Zionist frontier advanced by forming nuclei or settlement nodes and spreading out around them rather than on a linear basis, as was the case in the United States. The oasis geography of that region has made nodal rather than linear development a more realistic option, so much so that the former has become part of the culture of the region's inhabitants.

Three original nodes of settlement were established by the First Aliyah, all of which emerged at roughly the same time in the early 1880s. The first was to the south and east of Jaffa, particularly on a line from Rishon-le-Zion to Gedera. Most of these settlements now have become cities within the Tel Aviv metropolitan area. In the process they have passed through the first three frontier stages.

The second node was in the "finger" of the Upper Galilee in the far northeast of the country, on a line from Rosh Pina to Metulla. These settlements have remained small and peripheral but of great strategic importance, and, as settlements, never passed on to subsequent frontier stages.

The region in which they are located subsequently was settled by kibbutzim, which did, and which now are moving on to the fourth frontier stage. In between, two development towns were established in the region in an effort to bring it into the urban-industrial frontier, neither of which has been particularly successful in that respect.

The third node was on the lower reaches of the Carmel range, near the Mediterranean coast, south of Haifa from Hadera to Zikhron Ya'akov. After languishing for a long time, Hadera became prominent on the urban-industrial frontier, while Zikhron Ya'akov and Binyamina were absorbed slowly into the Haifa metropolitan region as a result of the spread of the metropolitan technological frontier.

The Second Aliyah established two new nodes, one in the hills just to the west of the Sea of Galilee, and the other in the Jordan Valley, just to the south of that lake. Both were extensions of the northernmost node of the First Aliyah, creating a multinodal belt from the Hermon to the Yarmuk. It was in that belt that, in the latter years of the mandatory regime, the first regional councils were later formed as little republics, quasi-autonomous Jewish territories.

The Third Aliyah reclaimed the Jezreel Valley and the Sharon Plain, establishing them as their major nodes. The first was contiguous with the northern settlement area, and the second with the southern. By the 1930s there was a contiguous belt of Jewish settlements roughly in the form of a lopsided Z, running along the Mediterranean coast from Gedera to Haifa, then down the Jezreel Valley to the Jordan River at Afikim and northward to the Lebanese border at Metulla, consisting of some nine nodal or linear regions, nine separate concentrations of settlements. It was this "lopsided Z" that was to form the basis of the territory allocated to the Jews under the various partition proposals, beginning with the Peel Commission in 1937 and culminating in the United Nations partition a decade later.

Not every one of the early efforts at settlement was successful. For example, efforts to build concentrations of settlements in the Golan Heights, east of the Jordan River north of Amman, and around Jerusalem did not succeed, in great part because they were too far removed from existing Jewish centers and in part because the attempts were made with isolated settlements rather than in settlements clusters.

The successes and failures reveal one anomaly in this frontier process. Under the poor agricultural and economic conditions of Eretz Israel at the time, agricultural settlements could sustain themselves only where they had the support of preexisting Jewish communities in the country's cities. Thus, the first successful nodes drew upon the Jewish communities of Jerusalem, Jaffa, and Safad, and the second group upon that of Tiberias. While this assistance sometimes was given grudgingly, it was crucially important. While these urban Jewish communities were part of the first founding of modern Israel, they hardly can be called frontier phenomena in the classic sense.

Rather, they are a kind of prefrontier manifestation that, given the lack of a strong rear echelon support system outside the country, of the kind that sustained other New World frontiers, served in its stead.

Like all of the other modern rural-land frontiers, Israel offered those who pioneered on it the opportunity to try new ways of social and economic organization. On the other hand, it was utterly unique in that its pioneers emphasized collectivist approaches to land settlement as the norm. In every one of the other modern land frontiers, there were some collectivist experiments in the initial stages, but all were abandoned in very short order, usually within the first year of their initiation. In Eretz Israel, on the other hand, the kibbutz was viewed as the epitome of land settlement, and even more individualistic settlement systems such as the moshav required a high degree of institutionalized cooperation. The reasons were partly ideological—a product of the socialism that the halutzim brought with them from Russia and surrounding territories—and partly practical. Under the conditions of settlement of Eretz Israel, where capital was lacking and halutzim had no state to back them, even from outside the country, the collectivist approach offered a way to combine meager resources so as to focus them on the problems at hand. Even in the prefrontier stage of urban settlement in the mid-nineteenth century, the construction of new neighborhoods was undertaken collectively through cooperative societies, which not only husbanded capital but imposed a way of life reflecting one or another dimension of traditional Judaism on its members with their consent. It remained for later frontiers to change this situation.

In the meantime, the rural-land frontier itself persisted as the dominant frontier until statehood in 1948. It reached the heyday of its influence between 1920 and 1948 and the peak of its activity in the 1950s, and since has declined drastically in importance, though it persists as a minor factor on the country's peripheries.

As in the case of the United States, the rural-land frontier shaped Israel's basic values, even though it had less time in which to do that job and involved only a minority of the Jewish pioneering population. It was on the rural-land frontier that the basic settlement forms and social patterns that have determined the character of the most "Israeli" of Israel's institutions were forged, just as it was the work of the pioneers on the rural-land frontier that created the environmental setting for modern Israel.

## THE LIMITED URBAN-INDUSTRIAL FRONTIER

While the first sprouts of modern urbanization emerged in the same generation as the opening of the rural-land frontier, the movement toward urbanization in the modern sense did not begin to get under way until the second pioneering generation—between World War I and the establishment of the state. The first serious signs of industrialization in the country appeared in the 1930s, primarily in the Haifa area, which became known as the country's "industrial center" and was the first node of the urban-industrial frontier.

The latter can be said to have opened in the 1930s, but it was not until after 1948 that it emerged as a major element on the Israeli scene. Until that time, city development was oriented primarily toward the provision of commercial and other services for the agricultural hinterland or, because of the unique character of the settlement experience, to house groups committed to religious study or the relatively large number of public employees for both the governmental and cooperative sectors that emerged early in the settlement process.

The urban-industrial frontier began to reach a position of dominance in the 1950s, and remained the dominant frontier stage in Israel through the first generation of statehood. Spectacular growth of the country's cities and the development of new towns for industrial rather than agricultural pursuits both reflected this trend. As was the case in other urban-industrial frontier situations, industrial development was primarily in basic industries rather than in advanced expressions of new technologies, and the working population tended to reside within the same local political jurisdiction as its place of work.

After 1948, a major effort was made to industrialize the country in at least two ways. First of all, agriculture was industrialized; that is to say, it was transformed by new technologies from old-style farming into an agricultural industry. The kibbutzim, and to a lesser extent the moshavim, were excellent vehicles for this effort, offering concentrations of labor, land, and resources necessary to achieve this goal, which remains Israel's greatest success in the economic sphere. At the same time, more conventional forms of industrialization also were initiated, both in the established urban areas—particularly along the coast, and most particularly in the Haifa Bay area—and in the new development towns that were established in the country's land frontier regions.

The development towns were established primarily to house the mass of new immigrants coming into the country in such a way as to maximize population dispersal. At the end of the first Arab-Israeli war, the Israelis found themselves with relatively large unsettled tracts of land on the state's peripheries. For security reasons, they desired to settle these lands as rapidly as possible, and with as large a number of Jews as feasible. They accomplished this task in part through the extension of agricultural settlement and in part through the planting of over twenty development towns during the half-generation between 1949 and 1963. While efforts were made to give these towns at least a modest industrial base, in fact most of their settlers ended up working in the nearby farming communities as agricultural laborers. (That is a unique reversal of the usual pattern, whereby agricultural areas are tributary to cities. In Israel, the cities have been tributary to the agricultural communities more often than not.) Moreover, the industries established in these development towns generally ran into difficulties sustaining themselves.

Nor did the towns acquire regional commercial functions. The small size of the country, coupled with the sectorial and political infrastructure—the federation of parties—meant that every kibbutz and moshav belonged to one or another of the kibbutz and moshav movements, which provided, among other things, for common marketing and purchasing services. Thus, the bulk of their commercial activity was conducted through Tel Aviv, the country's commercial center, where the various movements had their headquarters and did their business, bypassing the local towns. Even individual members of the settlements preferred to travel to the major cities, where the selection of goods was larger and service facilities better, to avail themselves of urban services.[6]

As a result, the advance of the urban-industrial frontier tended to be confined to the coastal areas. Even Jerusalem remained minimally affected by it, because of its geopolitical situation. The 1948 war had left the western part of the city in Israeli hands, but at the eastern end of a narrow corridor of Israeli territory stretching in from the coast. It was surrounded on three sides by Arab territory absorbed by Jordan, and was cut off from its natural hinterland. Its exposed position and lack of local markets acted as strong barriers to manufacturers interested in locating new industries. Even government efforts to encourage the growth of Jerusalem, again for security reasons, came to little.

One of the impacts of the urban-industrial frontier was to begin to break down the collectivist orientation that set the pace on the rural-land frontier. At their peak, in the days just prior to the establishment of the state, the kibbutzim comprised over 7 percent of the country's Jewish population and over a third of the Jewish agricultural population. However, few of the new immigrants who were settled on the land after 1948 chose kibbutzim. Instead they preferred the moshav, with its family farming element.

While agriculture flourished as an industry in post-1948 Israel, it declined as a percentage of the total population. Most of the new immigrants settled in the cities and became industrial workers. Ben-Gurion and his finance minister, Eliezer Kaplan, recognizing the need for substantial infusions of capital, were the first to indicate a willingness to downplay the socialist and collectivist dimensions of the prestate yishuv in order to attract foreign investors. The greatest of the collectivist creations of the interwar period, the Histadrut, with its Hevrat Ovdim holding company, opposed any such change. The compromise reached provided for the encouragement of foreign investment, but in such a way that the Histadrut would acquire or retain a controlling interest in every major enterprise not government-owned. That had the effect of discouraging significant foreign capital from flowing into the country, but enough did flow in or was earned by the

Histadrut through its own expansion to transform that body into a capitalistic instrumentality under the guise of socialism.

The Histadrut grew mightily for the first decade and a half after the establishment of the state. Its enterprises expanded not only within Israel but overseas, as well, as such companies as Solel Boneh, the Histadrut construction company, undertook contract work throughout the Third World. But this new Histadrut was socialist only in that it technically was not owned by private capitalists. The workers had no share in the management of the Histadrut enterprises, or even in setting policy for the managers. Even its consumer cooperatives, which initially had avoided the distribution of surplus revenues to their member customers on the grounds that the money should be reinvested in the development of the Zionist enterprise, continued the practice, thereby adding to the capital available to the Histadrut leadership to expand its operations but further removing those enterprises from the workers. Actually, what emerged was the equivalent of state capitalism without government ownership, with the Histadrut controlling approximately half of the country's industrial base during most of this period.

In fact, the urban-industrial frontier stage was aborted somewhat in Israel by the fact that it came at the time when the Western world was moving on to the metropolitan frontier, and Israel, as a small country but one interested in keeping up with the West, began to adopt the new technologies of that frontier. Thus, for example, from the first the country's internal communications have relied very heavily on automotive vehicles and the internal combustion engine. The land of Israel has no navigable waterways. A minimum number of rail lines were built in the country in the last generation of the nineteenth century (Jerusalem was connected to the Mediterranean coast by rail in 1890), but it would be an exaggeration to call them a network. Moreover, they never have been utilized properly for internal transportation. The country is too small for the development of an internal air network. Hence, roads became the principal means of transportation, and the internal combustion engine the principal vehicle. Similarly, in a country with a great shortage of timber, the plastics industry offered a chance to reduce the requirements for paper that are part and parcel of a modern society. Israel expanded its plastics production rapidly to achieve that goal. In general, the new synthetics offered Israel a way to overcome its great natural-resource deficiencies.

The kind of heavy industry upon which the urban-industrial frontier is based in the West was for the most part beyond Israel's capabilities. A country poor in raw materials and lacking large indigenous or adjacent markets, Israel simply was not suited for heavy industrial development. While it has made many efforts in that direction, none of them outside of the military sphere has been successful. Most have failed, and a few survive as marginal enterprises maintained for reasons of national interest. Thus, with the exception of Haifa and the small cities adjacent to it, one would be hard put to find an Israeli city whose growth was due to the urban-industrial frontier per se. (It may be that in retrospect Beersheba will prove to have been another city that developed on this basis, but the observer would suggest that it is the industries of the metropolitan-technological frontier that are giving that city its industrial base.) One or two other smaller cities may have been transformed by it. So, for example, Hadera, with the Alliance Tire plant and the local paper products industry, was transformed from an agricultural settlement established at the very first stages of the rural-land frontier into an industrial town.

## PIONEERING ON THE METROPOLITAN-TECHNOLOGICAL FRONTIER

The metropolitan-technological frontier began to emerge as a factor in Israeli life by the 1960s. Since then, it has become the dominant factor in national development, particularly since it has reshaped the country's most populated areas, containing over half of its total population. The emergence of the metropolitan frontier involved much more than the development of metropolitan regions; it brought about the economic and technological transformation of Israeli society.

The spread of the metropolitan-technological frontier has followed that of the rural-land frontier, without extending as far. It began in the Dan region, which remains its focal point. While outsiders tend to view the Dan region as Tel Aviv and its environs, in fact, every town in the region is quite distinct as a city in its municipal organization, in its social composition, and in the minds of its residents.

Even people who live in a bedroom suburb will identify themselves as being from their municipality rather than from Tel Aviv. Since Israel has no county government or its equivalent and no other mediating government between the state and the municipalities (cities are not members of regional councils), there is an added structural incentive to local self-identification. The municipality is the provider of all local services, either directly or through some confederation of municipalities in which its own identity is clearly maintained.

Within this context, the region has three principal nodes: Tel Aviv proper, which is the commercial and administrative headquarters for the enterprises of the new technology; the Lod district, which is the site of Israel Aircraft Industries, Israel's largest single enterprise, with 18,000 workers and the principal manifestation in size of an industry based upon the new technology; and Rehovot, the site of the Weizmann Institute, which has attracted a number of small science-based industries. Each of these three nodes represents a classic pattern on the metropolitan-technological frontier.

Tel Aviv, the commercial center, is diminishing as a place of residence for the inhabitants of its metropolitan region, even as its position as a headquarters city is being strengthened. Those who work in the city's offices

increasingly live in a chain of suburbs to the north, south, and northeast of
the city that have many of the characteristics of American bedroom suburbs.
As more and more of these people acquire automobiles of their own, they can
commute from relatively outlying areas, where they develop their own
municipal institutions with most of the middle-class, reform-oriented politics
characteristics of such suburban communities. That is a radical transformation in a country where political parties have dominated almost every aspect
of life. As noted in chapter 5, politics within these municipalities are dominated or strongly influenced by local lists, whose goal is service-oriented, to
provide relatively inexpensive, efficient administration in which partisan or
career-oriented political considerations play a minimal role.[7]

The Lod node focuses on Ben-Gurion Airport, the country's major
international airport, and not on any particular municipality. Israel Aircraft
Industries is not even associated with a particular city. Seemingly it is located
out in the fields, though in fact it is within a local jurisdiction. Its workers
come from all parts of the metropolitan region, and there are no particular
concentrations of them. The most that can be said is that it and the other
airport-related, science-based industries in the vicinity have stimulated the
creation of two or three bedroom suburbs similar to those generated by Tel
Aviv. In one, for example, the city government is dominated by El Al flying
personnel, who have acquired houses next to the airport and have been
attracted into local politics in order to develop and maintain a community to
their taste. There, too, suburban-style politics is the norm.[8]

The Rehovot node is focused on one of the original settlements of the
first generation of the rural-land frontier, which now has reached a population of over 50,000. Rehovot is perhaps the most successful town in its size
range in the whole country. In many respects, it is a classic example of a city
that has capitalized on every aspect of the metropolitan-technological frontier. The Weizmann Institute gives it a major institution of higher learning,
oriented toward science, both theoretical and applied. The institute not only
has attracted a resident population of high caliber, but it has served to attract
a large number of industries and other institutions that seek an academic-
cum-scientific atmosphere. That, in turn, makes Rehovot a prestige address
within the Dan region, attracting other people to come settle there so as to
be able to say that they live in Rehovot.

At the same time, the city has capitalized on its old agricultural connections to acquire a role in the new industrialized agriculture, both as a
shipping point for agricultural produce and as the locus of the Faculty of
Agriculture of the Hebrews University, the principal agricultural experimental unit in the country. Finally, Rehovot has captured the commerce of much
of the southern part of the country, almost as far as Beersheba, despite the
objectives of the state's planners, who sought to develop other regional
nodes. The aforementioned combination of factors has led to the development of a substantial retail trading base, plus many professional services that
offer a full range of possibilities to people living in the south without their

having to go into Tel Aviv proper. Thus, despite extensive governmental efforts to encourage the development of other centers, Rehovot has captured the market in almost every retail and service field.

All of that has been reflected politically in two ways: the emergence of strong local candidates with something of a reform orientation, and minor problems of corruption connected with the rapid development of the city in the 1970s. Since Rehovot is not a new city, the state parties are well entrenched on one level, and separate local parties have not emerged. On the other hand, recent incumbents in the mayor's office rose to power on the kind of reform platforms associated with the metropolitan frontier and have been able substantially to eliminate state party influence. Moreover, Rehovot's city administration is known as a progressive one, on the forefront of governmental innovation in the country and highly service-oriented.[9] On the other hand, the leading mayor of the period was tried, convicted, and jailed for taking bribes from building contractors in return for building permits.

The overall structure of the Dan region reflects the special pattern of the metropolitan-technological frontier in Israel. From the beginning, Tel Aviv was unable to become the kind of central city that emerged in the United States and Western Europe as a result of the urban-industrial frontier, since cities that were sufficiently independent in their own social and economic character developed simultaneously adjacent to it. Today Tel Aviv represents approximately one-fourth of the total population of the metropolitan region. Three other cities of over 100,000 share borders with it, and a fourth lies just beyond. The four together have nearly 100,000 more people than Tel Aviv proper. Another 400,000 people live in cities of between 30,000 and 100,000 population in the region, while some 200,000 more live in smaller places. Moreover, because commercial and residential development is mixed in Israel in the European manner, Tel Aviv cannot even maintain its dominance through a concentrated central business district and must share its commercial role with other cities in the inner circle of the region, especially adjacent Ramat Gan (population 135,000).

The commuting patterns in the region reflect the impact of these three nodes, crisscrossing the region in every direction, with many Tel Avivans traveling outward, people from Rehovot commuting to Ashdod, and vice versa, and commuting to the Lod node from all directions. Thus the model for the region is more that of a matrix than that of a center with periphery, the pattern characteristic of early metropolitanization in other Western countries. In that respect, from the first it followed the model of more advanced metropolitan regions in the West, a jigsaw puzzle of separate municipalities, each contributing its own share to the overall region.

For a long time, Israel's planners, still thinking in terms of the urban-industrial frontier, looked for a way to consolidate the Dan region under one municipal government, or at the very least to create a two-tier structure in which the major powers would be vested in a new municipal entity embracing the entire region. These efforts met with such strong resistance from the existing municipalities, and either resistance or apathy on the part of the region's residents, that they were abandoned after several attempts, including a major study by a state commission in the early 1970s. Instead, the most problematic matters of local coordination were handled through interlocal agreements, among the cities involved, whether with regard to the maintenance of shared streets or the consolidation of the Tel Aviv Zoo with the Ramat Gan Safari wild animal park. As a result, the Dan region has done much to foster the use of market mechanisms, rather than bureaucratic solutions, to achieve political and social adjustments, further moving the country away from the collectivist approach of its early days.

As the region metropolitanized, it developed institutions of higher education of its own. The oldest is the Weizmann Institute in Rehovot, which serves the state as a whole but which makes an important contribution to regional economic development because of its presence within it. Its neighbor, the Hebrew University Faculty of Agriculture, also in Rehovot, makes less of a contribution to the region in that sense, but still remains an important element in maintaining the region's economic centrality in the country.

The third university to be developed in the region was Bar Ilan in Ramat Gan. Founded in 1955 to serve the religious Zionist community, it has developed into a regional university of considerable importance, one that is particularly attractive to groups such as career military officers because of its easy access from their base in the Dan region, which include the Ministry of Defense and the headquarters of the general staff. The fourth institution is Tel Aviv University, initially developed by the municipality and now the largest university in the country. While it serves a primarily regional constituency, like the others it has become an institution of international stature. Finally, Beit Berl College on the northeastern periphery of the region was developed by the Labor movement into a degree-granting institution that offers yet another option for advanced education. These major institutions are supplemented by several teachers' colleges and the principal adult education center of the kibbutz movement.

Thus, the region follows the standard metropolitan pattern of offering a marketplace of higher educational opportunities. Here, too, the region pioneered in reversing the policy of the state, which was to develop only a single institution each in humanities, sciences, and technology and to prevent other institutions from emerging. The struggle was waged first in the early 1950s over the establishment of Bar Ilan University, which was justified more easily because of its religious character. In the 1960s, it was waged over the transformation of the Tel Aviv branch of the Hebrew University into a full-scale independent institution, which succeeded as a result of the strenuous efforts of the Tel Aviv establishment. In the 1970s, the struggle revolved around the issue of extending to Beit Berl and the teachers' colleges the right to grant degrees, again, coming to a successful conclusion by the end of the decade. These changes were direct products of the changed frontier situation, in which higher education is a vital gateway to the new frontier.

The Haifa Bay area became a second metropolitan region, developing almost simultaneously with that of the Dan region. It now has about a third of the population of the Dan region. The growth of population is spread more or less evenly among the cities in the regional metropolitan matrix, with the usual commuting patterns tying them together.

While this transformation has opened up new possibilities for the region, in fact, because of its ties to the urban-industrial frontier, it really has not made the transition to the metropolitan-technological frontier and is suffering economically as a result. Unlike the industries in the Tel Aviv area, most of the Haifa Bay industries entered into a crisis in the early 1980s because of changing economic circumstances. They have survived because of heavy government subsidies that have become even more glaringly uneconomic than they were in the past. In short, the Haifa Bay is suffering from the kind of readjustment common to older industrial regions in other Western countries that have moved from being at the cutting edge of one frontier to backwaters of another as a result of the change in their geohistorical location.

The hope of the Haifa Bay region lies in its universities. The Technion is the country's oldest university, founded during the Second Aliyah as a technical school, and since expanded into Israel's "MIT." The University of Haifa was developed by the municipality in the wake of the establishment of Tel Aviv University and pushed forward on the same terms as a regional institution. But Haifa does not have the variety of higher educational institutions available to the Dan region. A kibbutz teacher-training and adult education center at Oranim, on the peripheries of the metropolitan region, is the only other significant institution of higher education, and it confines its services to the kibbutz movement.

The impact of the Technion is countrywide. The University of Haifa remains a relatively small regional institution, whose major function is to provide higher education for the inhabitants of the region including the Arabs of the Galilee, and which has served a secondary function of stimulating the settlement of an academic community in a working-class town, something that the Technion could do only partly because of its engineering orientation. These are important but still limited contributions in the region's effort to make the transition from the urban-industrial to full participation in the metropolitan-technological frontier.

After the Six Day War, both the rural and metropolitan frontiers were extended into Judea, Samaria, the Gaza District, and the Golan Heights. For a decade between 1967 and 1977, these ventures gave new life to the land frontier, particularly in the Golan and the Jordan Valley. After 1977, however, with the Likud election victory and the consequent expansion of the effort to settle the territories, the thrust of new settlement became part of the metropolitan-technological frontier.

As noted above, Israel's urbanization and metropolitanization began along the coast in the Dan and Haifa Bay regions. Jerusalem, whose urban development always had taken a very different turn, never really entered the urban-industrial frontier, because at the time it was cut off at the end of the Jerusalem corridor, surrounded by territory under Jordanian rule. Then came the Six Day War, and suddenly Jerusalem was reunited with its potential hinterland, precisely at the time that metropolitanization was beginning to reshape the country.[10]

The impact of Jerusalem's reunification with its natural hinterland and the possibilities of peace between Israel, the Palestinians, and Jordan, described in Chapter 9, is indicative of a major frontier impact on the political future of Eretz Israel. It was the metropolitan frontier that transformed the city from a regional center for marketing agricultural produce into an independent source of livelihood for those in the city and its hinterland. In this way Jerusalem became the first truly ethnically mixed metropolitan region in the country, bringing together Jews and Arabs on approximately a three-to-one ratio. The city was strengthened as the capital of Israel and the Jewish people, on one hand, and also emerged as the only Arab metropolis west of the Jordan River, so much so that Israeli Arabs who wanted an urban environment have begun to settle in Jerusalem, something that did not happen between 1948 and the mid-1970s.

By jumping over the urban-industrial frontier, Jerusalem was able to capitalize on the basically nonindustrial orientation of its population, and to focus on those aspects of the metropolitan frontier that are particularly suitable to it, namely, higher education, government, and other public-sector activities. Such industrialization as has taken place has been on the peripheries of the metropolitan region rather than at the core.

As Jerusalem's place on the metropolitan-technological frontier became more secure, it influenced the Jewish resettlement of Judea and Samaria. Gush Emunim and its Likud ally, after it ascended to power in 1977, instinctively realized that new settlements in the Judea and Samaria hill country, even along the western edges of Samaria, could not rely on agriculture for their principal sustenance. In most cases the land was not suitable for extensive agricultural production. In any case, the country did not need more agricultural land in production, and the people who wanted to settle in those communities were beyond the land phase of Zionism. They wished to help resettle Judea and Samaria but also to pursue their careers, which were tied closely to the metropolitan-technological frontier in most cases. Hence, the settlements developed in those regions were based on the latest technologies and provided sites for what could be described as high-tech cottage industries. Consequently, they were tied in closely with the adjacent metropolitan centers, whether Jerusalem or the Dan region, often through computer networks that presaged the fourth frontier stage, which already had emerged in the United States but which just now is beginning to show signs of emergence in Israel. In western Samaria, and to a lesser extent north and

east of Jerusalem, the new settlements were actually bedroom suburb extensions of the metropolitan region across the old Green Line, where daily
commuting to work to the Lod and Kfar Saba industrial nodes or to Jerusalem itself provided employment for most of the settlers. Thus, the latest
frontier stage functions to reinforce the political goals of Zionism much as did
the first.

The metropolitan-technological frontier has generated the greatest challenge to both collectivism and state capitalism to date, although not necessarily in the direction of a free market. The new trend was toward private
enterprise closely tied to state assistance and government participation in
economic decision making. In a sense, that is inevitable, because Israel is too
small a country and too dependent on world markets for it to generate the
kind of market economy that a very large country such as the United States
could, at least until recently, because it provided an almost complete market
for its own production. There will always have to be greater state intervention
in the Israeli economy for that reason alone.

On the other hand, the role of private venture capital has increased on
the metropolitan frontier and could increase further. As the metropolitan
frontier developed, the role of the Histadrut in Israel's economy receded. By
the mid-1980s the Histadrut controlled slightly under one-third of the
country's economy, and while it was still the largest single force, it no longer
could insist on acquiring the dominant share or even any share at all in new
enterprises.

Moreover, with the expansion of Israel's banking system, Israeli companies could generate enough capital to begin to invest abroad, so that Israel
became a headquarters for far-flung industrial empires, still modest by world
standards, but far greater than anything that Israel had ever seen. At least
outside of Israel, these empires could not rely on government support in the
same way that they could inside, especially when they tried to penetrate the
United States, establishing subsidiary corporations in North America and
raising money to do so on the various American stock exchanges. This leap
forward in space is transforming the location of Israel from a small self-
contained country on the periphery on the Western world, isolated within its
region as if it were an island, to a strategically located state involved in
developing markets in every direction, using economic mechanisms to try to
reduce Israel's political isolation.

Finally, the kibbutzim, which served as the cutting edge of the first
frontier and which had a minimal relationship to the second, even suffering
some decline during the emphasis on urban development, have demonstrated an affinity for the third frontier, with its emphasis on smaller units of
settlement fitting into a matrix of specialized units linked by a highly
advanced technology. That may seem paradoxical at first glance, but one of
the most pronounced phenomena in Israel today is the degree to which the
kibbutzim have diversified and moved from reliance upon agriculture to a
mixed economy. Approximately one-third of the output of the kibbutzim

today is derived from industrial production, and the strongest kibbutzim are those that have done the most to industrialize, first spreading the urban-industrial frontier into the hinterland in the process, and creating a surplus that has enriched the kibbutzim and enabled them to expand their range of services and amenities.

At the same time, the kibbutzim have suffered from the increased privatization and anticollectivist spirit in the remolded Israeli society of the metropolitan-technological frontier. Few new kibbutzim are being established, and most of them remain marginal. Established kibbutzim attract few new members and even have reached the point of accepting needed professionals—doctors, dentists, teachers, engineers—as permanent nonmember residents in order to obtain their services. Most serious of all, the attrition rate among youth born and raised in the kibbutzim is approximately 50 per cent, as the young go off to seek their fortunes in the cities (or abroad) after military service.[11]

## TOWARD THE FOURTH FRONTIER

During the 1970s, a fourth concentration of industries based upon the new technology emerged adjacent to the Dan region north of Petah Tikvah, centered on Kfar Saba and Ra'anana. This fourth concentration initiated the transformation of the coastal plain into a minimegalapolis or citybelt combining urban and rural uses in what soon will be an unbroken line of human settlement at metropolitan densities approximately 150 miles long from the Egyptian to the Lebanese borders. Within this rurban belt there are industrial cities, resort towns, nature preserves, and ports—municipalities of all sizes and shapes, and the full range of population types to be found in Israel. In other words, it is a true megalopolis. At its southern and eastern fringes it crosses the former Green Line, offering a primary means to integrate the territories acquired after 1967 into the original state.

At present this minimegalopolis still is divided into three segments: The principal one stretches from Netanya to Ashdod, with developments filling in north, south, and east from Gedera to Hadera. The second in importance reaches from Nahariya to Atlit, and the third from Ashkelon to Rafiah. These three segments are being tied together by the development of new high-tech industries in both the heartlands and the interstices of each.

In true frontier style, Israel has made a strong commitment to high tech as its economic future. At the present time the country is undergoing the adjustments necessary to move in that direction. These include the dislocations accompanying the decline of the industries and communities of the urban-industrial frontier, whether in the Haifa Bay area or the development towns; the necessity to transform the structure of governmental intervention in the economy from a system of subsidization of ineffcient enterprises to technical assistance for the development of new, more efficient ones; and the forging of new links between the universities and industry in order to link science and technology in the way that exploration and pioneering always have been linked in earlier frontiers.

All of this development is still in its earliest stages, but it suggests that Israel may indeed be a true frontier society, able through the chain reaction to move from frontier to frontier, even in a small, relatively densely populated space. Thus, the kibbutz today is a true rurban settlement. Even in an outlying kibbutz such as Kfar Blum, located in the Upper Galilee, far removed from the nation's industrial centers, manufacturing and services employ over 90 percent of the labor force, while agriculture occupies less than 7 percent, a ratio not dissimilar to that of the countries of Western Europe. [12] As such the kibbutz is in an ideal position to continue its pioneering role on the fourth frontier.

## THE IMPACT OF THE FRONTIER

The impact of the frontier in Israel followed the classic pattern, with each stage bringing about greater flexibility and opportunity in what otherwise would have been unlikely in a polity such as Israel, where centralized authority tends to act to choke both. On the rural-land frontier, the kibbutzim and moshavim were governed by the *asefah kellalit* general meeting, the Israeli version of the kind of direct democracy found in the New England town meeting and the Swiss *gemeinde*. This system of the general meeting was institutionalized and remains in existence to this day. Participation in the asefah kellalit has declined as governance has become routinized. Still, when critical issues arise, people do participate, and the general meeting comes into its own.

This type of participation was, of course, denied to larger urban municipalities established on the urban-industrial frontier. While that frontier did not produce much of anything in the way of innovation in citizen participation, it did provide vehicles for political participation to large populations which never had possessed rights of citizenship before. Development towns are a case in point. Most of them were founded by the direct action of the central authorities of the state, in some cases overriding immigrant-initiated attempts at founding their own towns. State officials and representatives of the national parties together undertook the organization of the development towns and became their leaders. While they often attempted to hold onto power locally, within a decade an autonomous local leadership had developed from among the immigrant settlers, and the outsiders were forced to leave. While state and outside party power-holders continued to intervene consistently in local affairs and tried hard to maintain the development towns' dependency upon them, the latter now had their own local leadership able to bargain with those outsiders on behalf of local interests.

Thus, within half a generation, the development towns, settled by people who presumably had no notions of democratic self-government, who had been denied their natural leadership as a result of the upheavals of their aliyah (some of the latter stayed behind, others went to other countries, and the more traditional ones simply were excluded from leadership positions as inappropriate to a modern society), demonstrated in town after town that they could take control over their own lives to the extent that they could force the authorities to let go. Powerful new figures appeared on the Israeli political scene in Dimona and Kiryat Gat, Ashkelon and Migdal HaEmek, Beersheba and Kiryat Malakhi.

The new spirit spilled over into development towns dominated by the sabra generation, the sons of the founders. Arad, a development town founded in 1962 to be the most Israeli city in Israel, is an atypical but fascinating example of this process. Located in the southern reaches of the Judean wilderness, overlooking the Dead Sea, as residential center for workers in the Dead Sea potash works and the Zohar gas fields, it was established deliberately as a development town for native Israelis, drawn primarily from prestate pioneering stock at that. Since its beginning, Arad has been governed by a local list that is deliberately nonpartisan and citizen-dominated. The triumph of that list reflected a conscious effort on the part of the majority of the local citizenry to govern their community outside of the partisan politics that embrace the state as a whole. Significantly enough, one of the city fathers and the present mayor is the son-in-law of Israel's late prime minister Levi Eshkol, an engineer who apparently has embraced these citizen values like most of his compatriots, most of whom are also technically trained professionals.

Political power in the city of Arad seems to be diffused widely among a variety of local institutions, all of which appear to be dominated by the local citizenry. The handful of professional politicians to be found in Arad serve the minority parties and have little influence. Indeed, Arad's citizens have had a relatively high level of success in transforming the state agencies functioning within its boundaries into institutions that serve local ends to a very substantial degree (a pattern that is classic in the United States but that can exist only under very selective conditions).[13]

By the third decade of their existence, the development towns were producing figures able to enter state politics and achieve commanding positions, including people such as David Levy, deputy prime minister and minister of housing, who began his career in the Beit Shean Labor Council; Moshe Katzav, minister of social development, who at a very early age became mayor of Kiryat Malakhi; and Knesset members such as Meir Shitrit, the mayor who turned Yavne from a depressed semislum to one of the most attractive communities of the southern coastal plain, and David Magen, the influential mayor of Kiryat Gat. Today there is no doubt that key positions in the development towns are means for political advancement for those outside the old political establishments. Indeed, just as the kibbutzim provided the country with leadership when they represented the cutting edge of the frontier and for a generation afterwards, the development towns are providing more than their share of the leadership and great opportunity for advancement into the countrywide arena, a generation after their founding.

It is too soon to determine what will be the full impact of the metropolitan-technological frontier on citizen participation. It already has been noted that the changes it has brought have catalyzed the emergence of local lists in municipal elections. These first emerged in the dormitory suburbs of the metropolitan frontier and then spread broadly and widely throughout the country, albeit with a preponderance in those towns caught up in the metropolitan frontier process. At the same time, the first efforts to bring that movement into state politics, through the reconstitution of Rafi and then the Democratic Movement for Change, failed.

Now there seems to be some new concern on the part of the new managers in the enterprises that dominate the metropolitan frontier to begin to think about political reform in serious ways, which ultimately may bring them into political involvement. Since there is generally a generation's lag between the emergence of a frontier stage and its political impact countrywide, it is not surprising that that has not developed successfully up to now. If the past is any predictor of the future, we should see it happening in the 1990s. If that turns out to be the case, then once again the frontier process will demonstrate how vital it is for the maintenance of an open society.

All in all, after the initial ideological impetus that led to the opening of the Zionist rural land frontier, each frontier, including the first, has led to the gradual increase in importance of territorial democracy. The territorial organization of the clusters of settlements on the first frontier was always subordinate to ideological considerations, and the individual nodes were even developed by clustering settlements of the same ideological orientation. That ceased to be possible on the urban-industrial frontier, where the territorial principle gained the upper hand while with a strong ideological component, so that the Haifa Bay area became not only the heartland of the urban-industrial frontier but also the greatest bastion of the Histadrut. With the coming of the metropolitan-technological frontier, even the secondary role for ideological considerations broke down, as every territory combined something of everything, maintaining only the separation between urban and nonurban elements. The fourth frontier stage promises to break down even that separation, as is evidenced by the emerging shape of the coastal megalopolis.

## THE DIMENSIONS OF ISRAEL'S FRONTIER EXPERIENCE

As Europe's last frontier, Israel has found itself caught in the clash between the forces of decolonization and national self-determination in the Third World and the principles of the European frontier movement. The first emphasized that territories belong to the people who live in or adjacent to them, regardless of the people's stage of development, while the latter has emphasized that territories, if previously empty, rightly belong to those people who develop them. In the world as whole, after four hundred years of the great frontier of Europe, these issues were resolved in favor of the latter principle where those territories were sufficiently empty or at least had been emptied when settled by European frontiersman and pioneers, and in favor of the former where local populations continued to clearly outnumber the European arrivals. In only a handful of places, including Eretz Israel, was the balance such that the issue was not resolved easily. These are areas of conflict in the world today.

Israel's frontier experience has two principal dimensions. On one hand, modern Israel is an extension of the great frontier of Eruope, perhaps the last such extension to take hold. It is one of only two frontier efforts initiated by people from Eastern Europe (the other is the Siberian frontier) with collectivist rather than individualistic beginnings. While the first Zionist pioneers were indeed from Europe, they did not see themselves as Europeans performing a civilizing mission but as Jews returning to their ancient homeland. At the same time, they did see themselves as frontiersmen, since they understood the land to be empty and accepted the thesis that to the developer belongs the property, provided that it was acquired legally through formal purchase.

More than that, Israel is the latest manifestation of the Jewish people's continuing frontier experience. Since its emergence on the stage of history, the Jewish people have been a pioneering people, a people found on the frontiers of every generation. Thus, the Zionist experience of the past century must be viewed in that light, as well.

Israel as frontier is closely linked with Israel as "West." Every continent has its "West," which functions with respect to its larger environment as Frederick Jackson Turner portrayed the American West, namely, as the place where the frontier ethos is dominant, freedom is the expectation, and the society is organized on a covenantal basis. Moreover, every continent has its westward movement that is related to the creation of that West, each within its own context and on its own terms.

The Jewish people were involved in the first great westward movement of historical record, the movement to Western Asia four millennia ago, which made the fertile crescent the first center of civilization. Their return to Western Asia in our time coincides with the revival of the Asian role in the world scene. The European-centered civilization of recent centuries has obscured this fact by defining the map of the world in such a way as to locate Israel in the "Middle East," a term that is quite correct from a European perspective but not from the perspective of the continent of which Israel is a part. From an Asian perspective, "Western Asia" is far more appropriate. I would suggest that it is also more appropriate historically, in the sense that Israel is Asia's West in the way that the region bordering on the Atlantic Ocean and particularly the North Sea, what might be called the Celtic-Calvinistic borderlands, represents the West of Europe, and the area from the Great Plains westward represents the West of North America. Each of these Wests is the region where the culture of its respective continent reached its greatest fulfillment, at least from a moral perspective—in terms of social opportunity, human freedom, and moral development. In each case, this fulfillment took place within the context and according to the terms of the continental culture of which the particular West is a part.

The Jewish people defined "Westernness" for Asia by combining the sophisticated tribalism characteristic of the peoples of that continent with the kind of venturesome change associated with the frontier. In this connection, it is ironic that so many Asians view the Jews of Israel as European inter-lopers, when, in fact, the Jewish people represents a continuing expression of the Asian pattern of sophisticated tribalism, not to speak of the fact that the majority of the Jews who have settled in Israel came from African and Asian homelands and from families that never had left those continents.

A century ago, Zionism got its start, in part because of the charge of the European antisemites that the Jews were Orientals to their roots and never could be assimilated properly into a European society, certainly not without subverting that society by introducing Oriental ways within it. Today Jews are accused by the Africans and Asians of just the reverse. Perhaps the problem lies in the fact that as frontiersmen and perennial Westerners in that sense, the Jews challenge the societies they touch to become more than what they would like to be, and that their challenge to Asia, whence they spring, is even greater than it is for anyone else.

Thus, Eretz Israel was home to both the first frontier and the first West. The moral breakthrough of the Jewish people that emerged in the process of migration to that first West and the taming of that first frontier is also paradigmatic of every subsequent West and frontier associated with it.

# TWELVE

## The Future of Israeli Politics

### POLITICAL RESPONSES

As of yet, the Israeli political system has made little conscious effort to respond to the problems generated by the factors discussed in the foregoing chapters. The political cultural factor apparently is not even recognized for what it is, while the frontier is treated by the powers that be as a development problem, pure and simple, whereby the central authorities have responsibility for advancing the country's development in various ways. It has not been possible for the country's leadership to ignore the problems arising from the decline of ideological democracy, but their responses have been reluctant and minimal.

However, to say that the problems are not getting a conscious response does not mean that the political system is not responding to them at all. The importance of the compound of parties is such that even the most casual student of Israeli affairs is aware of it. In fact, however, these manifestations of the old divisions are disappearing. More and more services are provided neutrally by the state or local governments or, as is more often the case, through cooperative arrangements involving both. Party influence in the government structure primarily touches those who pursue public careers rather than the ordinary citizens, although in a government-permeated society, that is by no means an insignificant number. The expectation is that, aside from the division between the strictly religious and the non- or not-so-religious, the divisions themselves will continue to grow weaker (but not necessarily disappear), unless there is a strong upsurge of secular ideology. The raison d'etre for many of the divisions has so weakened that only in the religious camp do the ideological justifications remain sufficiently strong to create demands of prestate intensity, and they are accommodated by allowing for parallel institutions in many fields.

Similarly, those communities that have acquired a primariliy territorial identity are becoming increasingly important as the country makes the transition from the days of its ideologically rooted founding to a more settled character. Whatever the criticism sometimes raised against territorially based communities, it generally is recognized that the expression of interest on a territorial basis is natural enough to any society, and certainly not foreign to Israel. While the political parties may seem to oppose the shift to territorially based representation on ideological grounds, in fact they do so primarily because their own self-interest demands that they protect their present bases. At best they can argue that such interest supports parochialism, an argument that is countered by the strong desire on the part of Israelis to achieve greater rootedness in the country—rootedness that includes local patriotism.

It is possible to recognize the impact of these factors in at least three arenas: the developing structure of Israel's constitution, in the character of republican government in Israel, and in the quality of Israeli democracy.

*Constitutionalism*

The political institutions of all new societies are built upon the premises of constitutional legitimacy which flow from the basic covenantal consensus that forms each. Though it does not have a written constitution in the sense of a single complete constitutional document, Israel is no exception. The constitutional character of a polity is not based on the existence of a written constitution alone. We already have noted how the covenant idea, with its underlying premise that the body politic is really a partnership among the contracting individuals who form it, is basic to Israel both as a new society in the modern sense and as the heir to Jewish political principles. The line from the Israelite tribal federation through the kehillot of the diaspora to the kibbutzim of modern Israel is tied to the idea of constitutional legitimacy flowing from covenantal consensus.

By and large, modern political science has made the distinction between written and unwritten constitutions basic to the understanding of constitutionalism, citing the American constitution as the prime example of the former and the British constitution as the prime example of the latter. That distinction has come under increasing attack in recent years. The American Constitution cannot be understood on the basis of the plain text of the United States Constitution alone, but only as it has been interpreted by the Supreme Court of the United States and in light of various conventions and usages that have grown up in the course of nearly two hundred years of political life. Similarly, the "unwritten" British constitution is built around a series of fundamental documents as hallowed as their American counterparts.[1]

The proper distinction to be made is not between written and unwritten constitutions but between constitutions-as-positive-law and constitutions-as-convention or -custom. This understanding can encompass the fact that every constitution in the larger sense possesses written and unwritten elements, the difference being whether the basic constitution whole is embodied in positive law or simply a reflection of the underlying conventions and customs of the polity it serves. Thus, in the American constitutional system, the conventions surrounding the Electoral College that bind presidential electors to follow the decision of the majority of the voters in their respective states are considered by Americans to be a matter of fundamental law, even though, on reflection, they are recognized as merely customary. The periodic efforts to reform or abolish the Electoral College rest on the fact that Americans are somehow uncomfortable with "mere" convention, or customs. For the British, on the other hand, convention or custom is considered to be much stronger than "mere" law, since law can be changed by Parliament, while a sitting Parliament would have to be very bold indeed to change a basic convention or custom. This difference is well embodied in the difference between Edmund Burke and John Adams, both associated by contemporaries with modern conservatism. The conservatism of the first was based upon the appreciation for ancient usage, while the conservatism of the second was based upon a belief in fundamental law and the neccessity to build a constitution in harmony with it.[2]

New societies, in general, are committed to writing down their fundamental laws rather than relying principally on custom or usage, precisely because they are too new as societies to have had time to develop customs that are sufficiently rooted in the psyches of their people. Since customary usage is not available to them, they have to create laws and legitimize them by linking them to the fundamental law. More important, new societies reject customary usage as inconsistent with their efforts to build something new. At most they are willing to incorporate elements of the customs that they brought with them into their positive constitutional laws.

Israel has been unable to adopt a constitution full-blown, not because it does not share the view of constitution as fundamental law but because of a conflict over what constitutes fundamental law within Israeli society. Those Jews loyal to Jewish tradition in the Orthodox sense hold that the only real constitution for a Jewish state is the Torah and the Jewish law that flows from it. They not only see no need for a modern secular constitution but even see in such a document a threat to the supremacy of the Torah and the constitutional tradition that flows from it and that has developed over thousands of years to serve the Jewish people in their land and in diaspora communities.[3]

Their opposition sometimes is interpreted as the opposition of traditionalists to modernists, in a way that could be understood as a struggle between supporters of convention and custom versus supporters of a written constitution as law. That would be a serious misreading of the situation. Orthodox Jews are as convinced that their constitution, the Torah, is law, and not custom or convention, as the most ardent supporters of a modern written constitution. Jewish political culture does not recognize constitutions derived from convention; conventions and customs are important and, indeed, may attain the status of law for some purposes, but they are derived from a constitutional base and are not replacements for law. Quite to the contrary, the Jewish people as the first new society is strongly committed to the principle of fundamental law, and the sense of constitutionalism was derived from it.

## FIVE BASIC CONSTITUTIONAL MODELS

The world's modern constitutions can be classified according to: 1) the constitution-as-frame-of-government; 2) the constitution-as-code; 3) the constitution-as-revolutionary-manifesto; 4) the constitution-as-political-ideal; and 5) the constitution as a modern adaptation of an ancient traditional constitution.[4] Israel should be considered an example of the last. Polities utilizing this model have a deeply rooted commitment to what can only be characterized as an ancient and continuing constitutional tradition, rooted in their history or religion, or both. This commitment usually finds expression in a collection of documents of constitutional import, each of which marks (or purports to mark) an adaptation of the great tradition to changed circumstances.

The United Kingdom is the most widely recognized example of this model. The British constitution is celebrated for being just what I have described above. Except for the brief interregnum of the English civil war, its piecemeal constitutional development has been uninterrupted at least since the Norman Conquest, and perhaps even before, if William the Conqueror's claims to the throne are recognized. The only time there has been constitution writing in the United Kingdom or any of its constituent countries has been in connection with some strong necessity to clarify or adapt what are viewed as ancient principles, as in the case of the Magna Carta (1215), the 1689 Bill of Rights connected with the Glorious Revolution, and the 1832 Reform Act; and to establish new relationships among its constituent countries, as in the case of the Act of Union between England and Scotland (1707) or the reconstitution of Ireland in the 1920s. Indeed, when this element has been lacking, efforts to change the British constitution in so formal a way generally have failed. That was true most recently in the attempted devolution of legislative powers to Scotland and Wales. At all times, constitutional change is achieved through ordinary legislative procedures, which are endowed by convention with constitutional status.

Israel is a somewhat different example of the same model. Formally committed to the adoption of a written constitution its Declaration of Independence explicitly provided for one. The first Knesset was elected as a constituent assembly and spent the better part of a year debating whether or not to write a constitution. The body was deadlocked as the traditional religious parties opposed the idea of a constitution other than the Torah (Five Books of Moses-as-interpreted), while the left-wing socialists were equally opposed, because they knew that the constitution that would emerge would not embrace their Marxian vision of what the new state should be.[5]

In a classic speech delivered in 1950, David Ben-Gurion, Israel's first prime minister, moved that the idea of writing a comprehensive constitution at a single sitting be set aside in favor of a system of enacting basic laws piecemeal as consensus was achieved with regard to each subject, which ultimately would form a constitution. His argument was presented in the spirit of federal prudence that has animated the Zionist enterprise at crucial moments; hence, it offered good reasons for doing so (if not the real ones). He suggested that polities need written constitutions for one of two reasons—either to link constituent units in a federal system or to republicanize absolutism. Since Israel was not a federal state, and the Jewish people always has been republican, Israel did not need a written constitution on the spot.[6]

The proposal for piecemeal writing of the constitution was accepted, since it did not contradict anyone's basic constitutional commitments. Hence, every Knesset is a constituent assembly when it wants to be, and can enact a basic law by a modest special majority, namely, half plus one of its total membership (61 votes). The Knesset deals with basic laws and other constitutional matters through a standing Constitutional, Legislative, and Judicial Committee. It is charged with the responsibility of drafting basic laws on a chapter-by-chapter basis for submission to the plenum.

Basic laws constitutionalizing Israel's legislative, executive, and judicial organs, the presidency, the state lands, civil-military relations, and the status of Jerusalem have been enacted since the early 1950s. Israel's Declaration of Independence has been given quasi-constitutional status by the courts in lieu of a formal bill of rights, since it specifies the basic principles of the regime. Known in Hebrew as *Megillat Ha-Atzmaut*, the "Scroll of Independence," its name and content serve as a bridge between this idea of an ancient traditional constitution still possessing a certain validity, and a modern frame of government. The Law of Return also has been accepted on the same terms, while unsettled issues such as local government and its status and powers vis-á-vis the state, and controversial ones such as a bill of rights, have been left in abeyance. The relationship between Israel and the Jewish people also has been constitutionalized, through covenants negotiated with the World Zionist Organization and the Jewish Agency, and enacted as legislation by the Knesset (table 12-1).

In the Israeli case, direct consideration of the ancient Jewish constitution is disguised through presumably neutral rhetoric because of the ideological disagreements surrounding it, namely, the whole conflict between those who seek a traditional grounding for the Jewish state and those who want the state to have a strictly secular grounding. Most Israelis view their state as a regime based on civil rather than religious law but believe it only proper that the Knesset has specified in law that the state's legal system should be based on traditional Jewish legal-constitutional principles, which include a full civil code, to the extent possible. To the extent that the Torah, however understood and interpreted, is perceived to have constitutional import, it provides a larger constitutional grounding for the frame of government that is emerging out of the Israeli constitutional process. For the truly religious, since the Torah does not specify any particular regime, it is relatively easy for them to accept Israel's freedom in constitutional design on that level. At best, however, this model is implicit only to the Israeli situation, since there are still strong voices in Israel who would reject such an interpretation, albeit with ambivalences of their own.

One of the characteristics of this model is the inclusion among its

TABLE 12-1
The Constitution of the State of Israel

*I. Basic Constitutional Texts*

| | |
|---|---|
| The Declaration of Independence | 1948 |
| The Law of Return | 1950 |
| World Zionist Organization— Jewish Agency (Status) Law | 1952 |

*II. Basic Laws*

| | |
|---|---|
| The Knesset | 1958 |
| Israel Lands | 1960 |
| The President of the State | 1964 |
| The Government | 1968 |
| The State Economy | 1975 |
| Israel Defense Forces | 1976 |
| Jerusalem, Capital of Israel | 1980 |
| The Judicature | 1984 |

constitutional documents of basic laws that relate to specific ancient traditions. Almost all the documents of the British constitution do just that, as to do two of the basic laws of Israel, those relating to state lands and to Jerusalem, plus the Declaration of Independence itself, the Law of Return, and the covenant with the institutions linking Israel and the diaspora. Thus, five of the nine constitutional texts of the contemporary Jewish state speak directly to the issues of the ancient traditional constitution.

It already has been noted that the role of the courts, particularly Israel's Supreme Court, in the development of the state's constitutional law is expanding. The courts' role is further enhanced by the range of constitutional issues confronting Israel because of its unique character as a Jewish state. Table 12-2 summarizes the major concerns of Israel's constitutional law. The Supreme Court of Israel has led in the movement in that direction, not only with regard to those sections of the Basic Law already enacted by the Knesset, but also by transforming (or affirming) Israel's Declaration of Independence into a constitutional document.[7]

The Declaration of the Establishment of the State of Israel, as it is officially known, represents the consensual basis upon which the state rests. In essence, it is Israel's founding covenant.[8] As indicated by the range of signatures appended to it, it was proclaimed as the expression of a wall-to-wall consensus that extended beyond the Zionist movement to include Communists and ultra-Orthodox non-Zionists. As a synthesizing document, its phrasing reflects the problems of reaching consensus. For example, there was the well-known controversy over whether or not the name of God should be mentioned in its text. For the secularist, antireligious left, which in 1948 was still very powerful, any such mention of divine providence was anath-

TABLE 12-2
## The Concerns of Israeli Constitutional Law

### I. The Foundations of the State
  A. The constitutional force of the Declaration of Independence
  B. Continuity of prestate legislation
  C. The territorial integrity and boundaries of the state
  D. Official languages and their use

### II. Basic Constitutional Principles
  A. Israel as a Jewish state
  B. Religion and the state
    1. Personal status
    2. Organization and constitutional position of religious communities
    3. Religious freedom
  C. Citizenship, nationality, and immigration
  D. The rule of law
    1. Law enforcement and observance
    2. Equality before the law
    3. Equality of the sexes
    4. Rights of individuals in dealing with public authorities
  E. Separation of powers
    1. Independent judiciary
    2. Delegation of rule-making powers to the administration
    3. Jurisdiction of the administration
    4. Administrative immunities
  F. Basic Laws
    1. Enactment
    2. Constitutional status

### III. Basic Political Institutions
  A. Elections
    1. Knesset
    2. Local authorities
  B. The Knesset (*Basic Law: The Knesset*, enacted 1958)
    1. Organization
    2. Rights and obligations of members
    3. As a legislative body
    4. As overseer of the activities of the government
  C. The government
    1. Formation and dissolution
    2. Responsibilities
    3. Authority
    4. Prerogative
    5. Powers

    D. The presidency (*Basic Law: State President's Law*, enacted 1964)
       1. Election
       2. Authority and powers
    E. Local government

IV. **Other State Institutions**
    A. Israel Defense Forces (*Basic Law: Israel Defense Forces*, enacted 1976)
    B. Lands (*Basic Law: Israeli Lands*, enacted 1960)
       1. State lands
       2. National lands
       3. Private lands

V. **The State and the National Institutions**
    A. The Jewish Agency and the World Zionist Organization
    B. Specialized national institutions
       1. Keren Hayesod
       2. Israel lands and the Jewish National Fund (*Basic Law: Israel Lands*, enacted 1960)
       3. The Universities

Source: Adapted, with modifcations and additions, from Amnen Rubenstein, *HaMishpat Hakonstitutzioni Shel Medinat Yisrael*, and Yehoshua Freudenheim, *Government in Israel*.

ema. For religious Jews, and those perhaps not so personally observant but still within the framework of Jewish religious ideas, the proclamation of the reestablishment of the state could not appear without such a reference. The compromise that was worked out was built around the inclusion of a traditional phrase, used as a euphemism for the Almighty, *Tzur Israel* (Rock of Israel), one that was vague enough to allow for various interpretations.[9]

In line with the political theory under which the state operates, what emerges in legislation will continue to be called a "basic law" and not a "constitution" (the latter term apparently is reserved for use by the Jewish people as a whole, whether one takes a religiously orthodox or a secularist approach to the constitutional problem of Jewish peoplehood). Beyond the basic laws, other legislation has constitutional implications and is so treated. So, for example, the Knesset has constitutionalized the definition of who is a Jew for registration purposes through the Law of Return. Its resolution of that issue periodically is called into question and has been given strong constitutional status through court interpretation and through the reluctance of the Knesset itself to change what it has done, even when pressed hard to do so.[10]

No discussion of constitutionalism in contemporary Israel can be concluded properly without reference to the evolving constitutional relationship between national and state institutions. In 1954, the Knesset enacted into legislation the covenant concluded two years earlier between the government of Israel and the World Zionist Executive in its role as the directorate of the Jewish Agency, allocating functions between the two bodies and making it clear that the agency was not a state institution but a national one. That legislation was supplemented by a joint declaration in 1960 that specified that "the State of Israel sees itself as the creation of the Jewish People in total, and expects efforts from the ZWF's [Zionist World Federation—sic] side to reach the unity of the nation for the state. . . ."[11] Subsequent agreements have transferred other functions to the state and have altered the structure of the agency to make it more representative of the Jewish people as a whole, but the basic constitutional framework remains the foundation of the federal pattern that Israel and its diaspora partners are fostering as a means of unifying world Jewry.

## BUILDING A DEMOCRATIC REPUBLIC

Republican institutions are the mainstays of all of the new societies and their constituent parts. Indeed, the demand for republican institutions—which was linked inextricably with the demand for constitutional government—was one of the great political reasons for the founding of most of the new societies in the first place. The principle of republicanism, of government as a public affair rather than the private domain of a single person or group, has meant government through institutions somehow representative of the governed.

Republicanism in Israel has been democratic republicanism from the first, which has meant that the governed are to participate in their own governance. In Israel, as we have seen, representative government originally was conceived to be government through representative institutions (i.e., parties and movements) rather than representative individuals. And, as we also have seen, this approach is now under attack in a developing struggle over the means of representation and the constitution of the institutions themselves.

The character of republicanism and the quality of democracy in Israel have been outlined in general terms in the previous chapters. There it has been suggested that institutionally, a growing tendency toward enhancing the role of the judiciary and the expansion of the principle of the separation of powers can be detected on the Israeli scene. These two themes need some elaboration.

Israel's courts are perhaps the most politically inviolable institutions in the country. The emphasis on judicial independence throughout the court system is pronounced. That contributes directly to the enhancement of the courts' power and prestige, since the citizenry, tired of partisan "politics-as-usual," have tended to look increasingly to the courts as the best way to obtain authoritative decisions in a nonpartisan spirit on a statewide basis.

Republicanism as originally introduced in Israel rested on European models, which meant that its parliamentary institutions were structured as if the ideal were undivided responsibility of the governors to the governed through the legislature. What has emerged, in fact, is a growing concern with and a continuing trend toward separation of governmental powers. The government (i.e., the cabinet) has taken on an existence increasingly independent of the Knesset and vice versa, even though most, if not all, of the members of the government continue to sit in the Knesset and, in the last analysis, dominate it.

The ability of the government to achieve independence is not difficult to fathom. Indeed, the central problem in parliamentary systems all over the world is how to make cabinets responsible to their parliaments rather than simply converting the parliaments into routine ratifiers of cabinet decisions. While Israel has not solved this problem, it has developed and institutionalized certain techniques that aid the Knesset in preserving some independence of its own—within the limits indicated by the parliamentary system—and also give it real opportunity to help shape government proposals into better legislation.

The Knesset has achieved that by using a very unparliamentary device: standing committees with functional areas of responsibility akin to the American model and strikingly opposed to the classical parliamentary one. These standing functional committees include representatives of all the party factions sitting in the Knesset. By meeting regularly, often behind closed doors, they allow members from the opposition parties or the minority parties in the government to influence and shape legislation by use of their talents as individuals and their role in representing various interest groups in the polity, in a way that would be impossible if they had to act openly on the floor of the Knesset and have their suggestions judged on a partisan basis. Thus, for many years the Likud and its predecessors, Gahal, Herut, and the Liberal party, the perennial opposition parties until the eve of the Six Day War, were able to make substantial contributions to the legislative process through the committee system, where their more able members could participate as individuals rather than be treated simply as spokesmen for their parties and be opposed publicly by the Mapai or Labor majority at every turn.[12] After 1977, Labor party figures acquired similar influence through the same committee structure. Certain key committees actually are chaired by opposition members to ensure that they will function independently of the government.

Classic separation of powers has been institutionalized even more fully in the local arena. The introduction of the direct election of mayors, implemented in the 1978 local elections, led to legislation that year defining the separate powers of mayors and municipal councils. Under the new system, mayors are responsible for conducting the affairs of the executive branch, while the councils are repositories of local legislative and oversight powers. Mayors still seek to gain council majorities, through election or coalition, to secure legislative support for their programs, but their executive powers are no longer dependent on those legislative coalitions, unless the mayors themselves choose to make them so.[13]

All told, power is far more diffused locally than it may appear at first glance. In addition to the municipal council and administrative departments, every locality has at least two local bodies that are essentially independent of the local council.[14] One is the religious council, a governing body appointed through a formula that involves both local and state organs and responsible for the provision of local religious services.[15] The other is the labor council, which, as the local agency of the Histadrut, actually functions as the equivalent of a local chamber of commerce in the United States, a quasi-governmental body that plays a major political role locally.[16] In addition, many of the small local councils elect an agricultural committee under the terms of a state law that provides for such an elected body when a sufficient percentage of the local population is engaged in agriculture. Finally, in the larger cities there are neighborhood committees, one of which, in Kiryat Haim (Haifa), is elected formally by the local residents as a kind of borough council.[17]

All of these bodies, taken together, widen the scope of local political participation considerably. More than that, they also alter the shape of Israel's republican institutions and the quality of its democratic life. On one hand, the development of a multiplicity of local decision-making bodies clearly alters the structure of bargaining in the local arena, and perhaps beyond it, as well, expanding the arena in which negotiation is both necessary and possible. More than that, the dispersal of bargaining power substantially weakens the strong tendency toward centralization or monolithic control in the country, acting to diffuse power among citizens or spokesmen for groups of citizens.

At the same time, the necessary interaction among these power nodes within the local community expands the role of local government by transforming localities into "civil communities" (that is to say, communities organized primarily for civic or political purposes, able to utilize a wide variety of mechanisms to shape actions affecting them as localities so as to better serve their local value system). A civil community consists of six kinds of elements:

1. The local governments that give the civil community its basic shape (the local council, the religious council).

2. The agencies of the state or the offices of the national institutions located in the community that function to serve local as well as supralocal ends (e.g., the labor exchange, the police detachment, the local office of the Jewish Agency).

3. The public nongovernmental institutions that function in the locality to supplement the governmental ones (e.g., the labor council, the various public welfare institutions, the local schools sponsored by overseas Jewish groups).

4. The political parties or factions that compete within the locality to organize political power.

5. The local interest groups (or powerful individuals) that affect decision making in the community.

6. The local value system as crystallized in the constitutional documents and traditions of the various local governments within the community.

When the institutions representing these elements work together, they provide a powerful means for widespread citizen involvement, for the sharing of decisions, and for bargaining and negotiation to set policy; in addition, they offer the local community greater leverage over decisions made outside its boundaries that affect it.[18]

The range and level of civic activity required to transform a municipality into a civil community just now are beginning to emerge in Israel, as the population settles in, develops roots, and generates the economic base necessary for an active civic life. Since voluntary effort is required to sustain so many of the components of a civil community, one can only flourish under such circumstances. Moreover, even when the objective conditions are present, civil communities are fostered only in the appropriate cultural settings. Israel's latent political culture happens to be an appropriate one, but it confronts two others that are far less so, if not actually inappropriate in many ways. Thus, the transformation of simple municipalities into civil communities (a trend still in its early stages in Israel) represents a major change in the political character of the country, one that is likely to have great repercussions for the country as a whole in terms of increasing its stability (since more people will have a stake in that stability), expanding the range of political recruitment, and changing the bargaining process through which countrywide decisions are made.

## ADJUSTING TO NEW CIRCUMSTANCES

To sum up, circumstances have led to the emergence of a state that is more or less organized to accommodate certain of the complexities of its population, but within a formal structure borrowed whole from another context altogether. In fact, that structure goes against the grain of most of the realities of Israeli society and politics and has had to be accommodated to those realities by a heavy reliance on extralegal methods. The mismatch between the two has led to an increasing dysfunctionality in the governance of the state. This dysfunctionality has been evidenced in a number of ways in recent years, not the least of which were the series of scandals resulting from people carrying extralegal methods to extremes beyond moral limits, as well, which have occurred since the mid-1970s and led to the fall of the ruling Labor camp and then to the weakening of the Likud.

While there is something to be said for having allowed the system to just evolve on a pragmatic basis, as it has, focusing on the relationships desired in each case rather than on the formalities of structure, there does come a point where structure itself is crucial, if only because of the way it influences relationships. Israel has now reached that point, as evidenced by the demands for structural reform that abound as many Israelis have begun to perceive, even dimly, that the structure of their governing institutions does not square with their expectations as citizens. The character of the die-hard resistance to those structural changes on the part of those in power only adds weight to the evidence.

The present structure also goes against the grain of the Jewish political tradition. That is not perceived readily by a population that remains unaware of that tradition, even though it is the impact of the behavioral aspects of that tradition on a structure derived from nineteenth-century European models that has led to the mismatch. In the past few years, much has begun to be said about the problematics of the Jewishness of the Jewish state. That is but another reflection of every new society's need for justification. It has not yet led to a recognition of the institutional and behavioral mismatch.

Nor are Israelis particularly aware of the compound character of their polity. Even those who would be, for the most part look at the system through glasses colored by nonindigenous ideologies or methodologies that lead them away from a proper perception of the reality in which they live. Thus, the religious camp has not come to grips with the pluralistic compound in the state, the Labor camp has not come to grips with the nonideological character of the emerging territorial democracy, the civil camp has not come to grips with the large Arab population west of the Jordan River, and none of the camps are prepared to come to grips with the structural problem.

## THE FUTURE OF ARAB-JEWISH RELATIONS

Finally, Israel's situation as a compound of Jewish and non-Jewish element is likely to be a permanent one. Even within the pre-1967 borders, the percentage of non-Jews is growing, because of the higher (if now declining) Arab birth rate. If Israel keeps Judea, Samaria, and Gaza, as is also likely, the situation will only intensify, and the majority will have to take serious cognizance of it.

The 1981 elections were notable because of the shift in the Arab vote away from the Communist-dominated popular front party and the various separate lists that have paralleled the several Zionist parties in the Arab community, particularly the Labor Alignment, to the alignment itself. At a time when there were all sorts of reports about how the Israeli Arabs are deserting the state, this trend represented very important evidence to the contrary. In 1981, for the first time, the major parties included Arabs as integral members and put Arab candidates on their lists, appealing directly to the Arab voters rather than working through their "front" Arab lists, as has been the case in the past.

During the first generation of statehood, even those Arabs most committed to developing a modus vivendi within Israel maintained separate party lists. It generally was agreed that they would not be at home within any of the Zionist parties (that is, all the major parties in Israel, except for the Communists), nor were the Zionist parties eager possibly to dilute their Zionist character by accepting Arabs as members. Thus, each of the Zionist parties either established a parallel Arab list or made arrangements to support a separate party established by the Arabs themselves.

The Labor parties were past masters at that, since they had funds and patronage to distribute, and Arab politicians understood that they could benefit themselves and their constituents by supporting what was then obviously the majority camp. Even the NRP acquired supporters in the Arab sector in this way. Those Arabs who wished to demonstrate their anti-Zionism or their rejection of accommodation with Israel voted Communist, even though the Communist party also was led by Jews.

This system began to break down along with the breakdown of the rest of the party alignment in the course of the 1970s. Arabs began to vote for Zionist parties, and Zionist parties, beginning with Mapam, began to include Arabs as members and even to give them at least symbolic places on their party lists. Integration at this level was more or less completed in 1981. Indeed, one of the additional problems that the Labor party brought on itself was that, after promising to slate an Arab in a safe position on the list (that is to say, one assured of being included in the Knesset, barring some debacle), it was forced by the changing electoral situation and the overcommitment on the part of Shimon Peres to many of the party faithful that they, too, would have safe seats, to initially place the leading Arab candidate lower down on the list. That led to a considerable reaction on the part of the party's Arab adherents, and a subsequent adjustment of his place.

Perhaps the Arabs overcame their previous reluctance to vote for avowedly Zionist parties because of their integration into the mainstream of the political process. However, an even more likely reason was that they believed that a Labor Alignment victory would advance Arab interests (which include Palestinian ones, of course), while a Likud victory would inhibit those interests. They came close to succeeding in putting the Labor Alignment over the top in number of seats.

In fact, the Arab vote camouflaged a growing Palestinian consciousness among certain sectors of the Israeli Arab population, as much as it reflected a greater willingness to participate in mainstream Israeli politics. That became apparent in the 1984 elections when the Progressive List for Peace, a mixed Jewish-Arab party of the non-Communist left that supports the establishment of a Palestinian state alongside Israel, succeeded in winning two seats, drawn from voters who three years earlier had supported one or another of the Zionist parties. While extremist in its platform, in fact the PLP reflected both dimensions of the new Arab vote.

In the aftermath of the 1984 elections, the rise of Palestinian consciousness among Israeli Arabs, coupled with the electoral victory of Meir Kahane, led to issues of Jewish-Arab relations surfacing on the Israeli public agenda. The extremist, even racist statements of Kahane led to a new concern on the part of other Jews for greater tolerance and consideration for the Arab minority, and even the provision of greater opportunities for them.

Building bridges between Jews and Arabs, particularly among the young, became an issue of some importance, which gained governmental support. In essence, the second generation of statehood has brought with it an end to the separation and near-isolation of the two populations. From now on, it is clear that Jews and Arabs will have to learn to live together, in contact with one another, and not just occupy separate spaces under the same flag. This new situation will undoubtedly bring with it a new set of problems, but it is both right and inevitable in an increasingly interdependent world.

## INTO THE SECOND GENERATION OF STATEHOOD

The first signs of response to these issues emerged after the 1977 Likud victory, and even more so after 1981. The most important aspect of the 1981 elections is that they offered clear confirmation that Israel now has entered its second generation of statehood, and that its political system has turned away from the alignment of forces that was formed in the generation before the rebirth of the Jewish state and that prevailed during the whole first generation. Israel may not have a two-party system, but it does have two parties capable of contesting for control of the government.

When the Labor Alignment was defeated in 1977, it had enjoyed two generations of political hegemony, having come to power in the prestate Jewish yishuv in the late 1920s and having consolidated its political hold in the early 1950s. From the mid-1930s until its defeat, it had no effective rival, so much so that political scientists writing about Israel classified Israeli party politics as a multiple-party system with a single dominant party.[19] Thus, the shock to Labor was even greater than it might have been had it been involved all along in a competitive situation.

The changeover took place precisely because of generationally induced changes in the voting population. Beginning with the 1965 election, the trend to the Likud among new voters entering the lists was clearly visible. In the intervening years, those have become the majority. In that respect, as well as in others, the 1977 and 1981 elections can be viewed as critical elections in Israeli history.

That is not to say that the Likud vote consisted only of Begin's faithful. The 1984 elections proved that support for the Likud was deeper than that. Perhaps half of its seats were gained from those who happily voted Likud. The other half, I would suggest, were gained through the votes of those who held their noses and decided whom they disliked least. That is a slender reed upon which to build a new majority, but, in Likud's favor, one of the reasons that most of those voters disliked Likud least was their antipathy to the socialist camp. Hence, they are more likely to become Likud voters over time than to shift to Labor. By and large, their opposition to the Labor camp had to be balanced against their dislike for the Likud leadership and lack of confidence in Likud policies.

Too many of Labor's leaders still persist in acting as if Labor is the only legitimate governor of the state, and that it is the height of effrontery for Likud or anyone else to challenge its control of the government. If there was anything that turned moderate voters who were not among the strong pro-Likud, pro-Begin forces away from Labor in the last three elections, it was that arrogant attitude on the part of the Labor Alignment which came through in its campaign at every turn. However much electioneering may involve efforts at dissimulation, in Israel, at least, the truth will out.

A major manifestation of Labor arrogance was in the camp's callow attitude toward the Sephardic Jewish majority, whose support is increasingly necessary for victory. Most visible in this regard were the numerous uncomplimentary expressions directed against Sephardim as a group, associating them with undesirable lower-class behavior. These were, presumably, individual slips of the tongue, but as video tapes shown after the 1981 elections revealed, the overall tone of the Labor leadership toward the Sephardic population was patronizing at best, and often downright hostile.

Part of this arrogance was associated with a strong tendency towards nostalgia in the Labor camp, manifested quite clearly at the Labor party convention and even reflected in some of the popular songs written by products of the Labor camp during 1981. The essence of this nostalgia was that Israel somehow had lost its way, presumably as a result of the changes that had taken place during the thirty years of statehood, and implictly because of the introduction of a population that did not share the pioneering and socialist ideals of the prestate yishuv (implicitly the Sephardim, although that could be said of the Ashkenazim who came after the state was established—and many of both communities resident in Eretz Israel even before 1948—as well), and that it was necessary for Israelis to find their way back to the socialist Zionist ideals that had dominated the pioneering yishuv in the interwar generation. This nostalgia for the socialist idealism of that period of course could not be separated from the nostalgia for the days in which an overwhelming Ashkenazi Labor establishment ruled.

Perceptive observers of the scene, watching the conflicts and bickering among the Labor leadership and mindful of the scandals that had brought down the Labor Alignment in 1977, could only consider the irony of this nostalgia, in the sense that the failures of Labor were the responsibility of that generation that had been born in Israel in those years (e.g., Moshe Dayan and Yitzhak Rabin) or had emigrated to the country as children then (e.g, Peres and Bar Lev) and were, therefore, the products of socialist Zionism. In other words, they are presumably the best and brightest children of what was presumed by them to be the best generation of the Zionist enterprise.[20]

This kind of attitude made it easy for Begin and the Likud to capitalize on their greatest strength, namely, their role as spokesmen for the outsiders. Thus, the government in power was able to win the substantial vote of those citizens who felt themselves excluded by Labor's attitude. Labor did somewhat better in controlling itself in 1984, although it started with some of the same prejudicial attitudes that were reflected in its television campaign. It was only toward the end of the campaign that its public relations people dropped presentations offensive to Sephardim. Unlike in 1981, however, Labor did back away from overtly antagonizing the religious camp throughout the election. Still, it is a measure of how deeply Labor is disliked that after all the disasters that the Likud carried into the election, Labor could barely eke out a three-seat margin over Likud, and both parties actually lost seats.

## THE FUTURE OF SEPHARDIC-ASHKENAZIC RELATIONS

Contrary to the lurid newspaper accounts, Jewish Israel is not divided into "two nations," not into two cultures, and not even into two societies. The degree to which Jews from all parts of the world have integrated into one society goes far beyond the kind of divisions that get headlines at election time. If there is a division, it essentially consists of those who believe that the country is theirs by right, and would be if they could only go back to the old ways of the socialist aliyot, and those who believe that the country belongs to all Israelis, with nobody having special claims by virtue of seniority. It is a division between those who patronize and those who are patronized, those whose particular culture is considered normative, regardless of how good or bad it may be, and those whose particular culture is considered quaint and picturesque or "ethnic," no matter how good or bad it might be.

The fact that this division cuts across parties and camps does not prevent the patronized from seizing upon one party in particular as coinciding more closely with their present interests. In any case, this situation is likely to get worse before it gets better, but bad as it is likely to get, it does not represent what it suddenly has been seen to be by outsiders—namely, a fundamental split in the nation. The Sephardim already have developed too many legitimate channels through which to express themselves and advance in public life, including the Likud, not to expect to come into their own in the near future. What the recent elections have highlighted is the true character of Sephardic grievances—not economic, but cultural and political—and the ability of Sephardim and Ashkenazim to forge alliances to gain political power.

Beyond the headlines, one can see the new synthesis developing. Politically, it is built around a group of outstanding young Sephardic leaders in the Likud, all of whom have emerged from the development towns and are now Knesset members, representing a new and immensely capable power bloc. Each has a story to tell about how he tried to break into the Labor party (or its predecessor, Mapai) at the outset of his political career and was rejected with prejudice by a short-sighted establishment.

That is a sign of the times. Having achieved economic stability and even success in having gained power roughly proportionate to their share of the population in local communities in which they represent majorities or substantial minorities, the Sephardim are ready for a great leap forward in public life. In the months following the 1981 elections, there were a number of gatherings of Sephardim in their thirties and forties, mayors and vice-mayors of cities and towns, local councilmen, school principals and vice-principals and deputy directors general of various governmental departments and public corporations—in other words, the equivalent of upper-middle-level management in the business world, all of whom see the time as right to begin to claim what they believe to be their due, namely, the opportunity to advance into the upper echelons of public life in Israel.

With the exception of Tami and Shas, these groups have been making their demands within the present party political framework and either are succeeding, as in the case of the Likud, or are likely to succeed in due course, perhaps even in the Labor Alignment, in due time, although there they are at least one step further removed from success than in the Likud. These are the people to watch as the politics of the second generation of Israeli statehood unfolds. Since the best opportunities for these people lie with the Likud, their advancement is likely to strengthen that party's majority.

## THE FUTURE OF RELIGIOUS POLITICS

Culturally, like most such syntheses in democratic societies, the Ashkenazic-Sephardic synthesis is likely to emphasize not the highest elements of the various cultures that have been brought to Israel but, at best, their respective middlebrow elements. That is both the glory and the dilemma of contemporary society. Israel, at least, still has standards, and Israelis can tell the difference between better and inferior forms of cultural expression, no matter what their origin.

The year 1981 was a decisive turning point for the religious camp in the way that 1977 was decisive for Labor. The camp as a whole dropped from a maximum strength of seventeen to thirteen, a loss of four seats for what generally was considered the most stable bloc in Israeli politics. The NRP absorbed the entire loss—its strength was cut in half, losing seats to the Likud and to its offshoot, Tami, the breakaway party of Religious Affairs Minister Aharon Abuhatzeira, who tried to capitalize on North African resentment over his trial to build a communal list and, to a degree, succeeded. Agudath Israel, on the other hand, held its own and, because of the virtual tie between the two large parties plus the skills of its leaders, much enhanced its bargaining power. The former presumably are undergoing a reassessment of who and what they are, in the way that Labor should have done four years ago.

The NRP has a particularly difficult row to hoe. After winning twelve seats in 1977 under the effective dominance of the Young Guard (now its strongest faction), its new leadership was filled with thoughts of expanding its base to become the Israeli equivalent of the European Christian Democratic parties, in other words, a broadly based, religiously oriented political alignment capable of contesting for governmental power and not simply continuing as a balance wheel between the two large parties as in the past.[21] Those hopes were dashed severely in 1981 and destroyed in 1984, when the NRP, torn by internal dissension and secession, dropped to four seats.

The advance of Agudath Israel in strength and, briefly, in stature, as well, is one of the most interesting phenomena of the new generation.[22] After 1977, its leaders gained the respect of many who are utterly opposed to the kind of Orthodoxy they advocate, because of their skill in utilizing their position and their essential moderation in the application of that skill. For them, the "Who is a Jew?" issue, however significant, can be sacrificed in return for additional financial support for their institutions. They are building for the long pull and need funds now, far more than they need to win what is, for the most part, a symbolic issue in its effects. Moreover, at a time when the NRP looked as if it was dominated by nationalist fanatics, the political moderation of Agudath Israel in matters of national policy was apparent to one and all.

The emergence of Shas out of the breakdown of the Agudath Israel consensus and the shattering of the NRP has introduced a new institutional dimension in the religious camp: the breakdown of the monopoly (or at least near-monopoly) of the official chief rabbinate. As long as 80 percent of all Orthodox Jews and 95 percent of the total Jewish population in the country recognized the chief rabbinate as the sole source of rabbinical authority—which was the case from the introduction of the institution in 1921 until 1984—the existence of a separate Moetzet Gedolai HaTorah and smaller rabbinical courts for the ultra-Orthodox to the right of Agudath Israel did not present a serious challenge to what was, for all intents and purposes, a monolithic structure. With the emergence of Shas, however, and their establishment of the Moetzet Hakhmei HaTorah, that monopoly has been broken. Today, approximately half of Israeli Jews, Orthodox and non-Orthodox, are more likely to follow the halachic leadership of that body, because they are Sephardim and have greater respect for its head, Rabbi Ovadia Yosef, the former Rishon-le-Zion, as a halachic authority than for the present incumbent of that office.

With the religious camp now split between five parties, and threatened on the right by Meir Kahane's Kach and the ultra-Orthodox, its political future is clouded, to say the least. Even Agudath Israel has lost influence as it has tried to accommodate ultra-Orthodox demands, and hence has become greedier for funds and more intransigent on religion and state issues. The religious parties often give the impression of digging in for the last stand, but, as was the case in the United States early in the twentieth century, they are doing so by making one last assault on the polity to try to secure legislation to enforce public norms that used to be maintained by consensus. These include laws restricting the availability of abortions, preventing the sale of pork, keeping places of entertainment closed on the Sabbath, and changing the definition of who is a Jew to ensure complete Orthodox hegemony in such matters in Israel and abroad. These campaigns should remind Americans of the campaigns for prohibition and against the teaching of evolution of sixty to eighty years ago, when die-hard proponents of what had been the dominant religious consensus of the nineteenth century tried to save the products of that consensus from the secularization affecting American society in the twentieth.

That means that, at least in the short run, the religious issue will be a major one in Israeli politics, one likely to exacerbate conflict between the religious and nonreligious. While most of the latter are apathetic in religious matters and are not interested in interfering with the religious observance of others, they will become militant if those others try to impose religious observance on them that interferes with their convenience and pleasure. On the other hand, Jews are a people with a basic religious impulse, so it would not be unexpected if there was a resurgence of religious concern on a different level, after this initial controversy. Again, there is some precedent in the American situation. Although it took half a century between the collapse of the first fundamentalist drive for power and the emergence of a new drive in the late 1970s, today Americans, who also have a religious impulse, are very much involved in just that kind of militant, fundamentalist reassertion that has attracted a certain sympathy even from people who would not be found within the evangelical movement themselves but who have come to recognize the limits and, indeed, the deficiencies of secularism.

In the interim, the emergence of an articulated and well-formed civil religion in Israel, which draws heavily on traditional Jewish sources and gives them expression in a traditional manner, is one of the striking aspects of the Israel of the past decade. This civil religion differs significantly from that fostered under Labor hegemony earlier in the Zionist enterprise, when the socialist Zionists sought to take traditional Jewish forms and infuse them with clearly secular content.[23] The emergent civil religion in Israel takes traditional forms with their traditional content selectively and attaches them to the civil society. This trend reflects the demise of the old ideologies that flourished during the modern epoch and that have become increasingly irrelevant throughout the world in the postmodern years, coupled with the revival of concern for traditional religion also characteristic of our times.[24] In that respect, the contemporary Israeli experience is simply a Jewish variant of a worldwide phenomenon.

## THE ECONOMIC CHALLENGE

This situation has been compounded by the serious economic difficulties into which Israel has gotten herself. The false prosperity of the late 1970s and early 1980s led to the disturbance of an already delicate economic balance and brought about a virtual collapse of the major institutions of the Israeli economy, which were kept from going under only by government action, which in turn fueled an already high inflation, bringing it to astronomical proportions.

The proximate cause was the economic policy of the Likud, especially after Yoram Aridor became finance minister just before the 1981 elections. But the problem is a deeper one. From the 1950s onwards, Israel's economy was managed like a house of cards, with successive finance ministers personally keeping the cards in balance. Whenever one card became shaky, he would shore it up with another. That led to great economic growth for several decades and record growth between the Six Day and Yom Kippur wars as a series of brilliant finance ministers, Eliezer Kaplan, Levi Eshkol, and Pinhas Sapir, kept things moving through their personal genius and perspicacity. Israel's great economic growth after the 1967 war created a more complex economy, more heavily tied in to the world economic system and thus less manageable at home.[25]

The coming of the Yom Kippur War ended the great boom, not only because it imposed huge new defense costs on the Israeli economy and brought Israel into the same problem of increasing its expenditures for oil tenfold, but also because it marked the transition to an economy too complex to be juggled by one man, no matter how brilliant. Israel's military successes led to a response on the part of the Arabs and their Soviet allies that brought the latest in weapons technology into the Middle East. Rather than fighting Middle Eastern wars with last generation's weapons, the contestants first acquired this generation's and then the next generation's weapons, with the battlefields becoming testing grounds for great power and, in Israel's case, local innovations in military technology. All of that cost far greater amounts of money than had the pre-1967 weapons. After the Yom Kippur War, Israel's economic growth came to a halt. Military expenditures increased further, and fuel expenditures soared out of sight.[26]

As long as Israel occupied the Sinai Peninsula, it had a ready source of oil, which provided up to 40 percent of its local needs. Abandonment of the Sinai oil fields as part of the general evacuation of the peninsula once again brought Israel to nearly full dependency on outside fuel sources, most of which were purchased on the spot market for full market price. In a real sense, these changes were not dependent upon a change in government, but the Likud introduced new problems, including a half-baked liberalization of the economy that increased foreign currency expenditures without leading to compensatory economic growth. Then, the agreement negotiated with the Egyptians and negotiated at Camp David with regard to the evacuation in Sinai, did not provide for sufficient compensation to Israel for the infrastructure it built in the peninsula and the costs it had to incur in the evacuation, further stimulating economic difficulties, especially inflation.[27] Aridor's policy of borrowing dollars from overseas to enable Israelis to increase their consumption of consumer goods proved to be as disastrous as could be expected.

To add to all of that, the banks, with government support, connived to artifically raise the price of their shares in the stock market until the bubble burst in October 1983, setting off a chain reaction that brought down the whole structure. Inflation soared to the vicinity of 1,000 percent annually, growth actually declined, and even with government efforts to maintain full employment, unemployment increased as large and small enterprises went bankrupt. The new Israeli entrepreneurs had discovered that they could invest in subsidiary companies offshore, and move their money around outside of Israel, so that they were relatively immune to all of the problems, provided that they did not repatriate their funds and invest them in Israeli enterprises. Thus, even the prosperity that a new class of Israelis was generating for itself personally added only marginally, if at all, to the Israeli economy as a whole.

These economic disasters were what kept the Likud from winning the 1984 elections and enabled Labor to capture the prime ministership in the national unity government on the basis of essentially tied results. The new government returned to Labor's pattern of raising taxes, especially on consumer goods and services, and placing new restrictions on private spending. It was only when that proved to be insufficient that the government instituted a serious economic reform package designed to get at some of the basic problems. This package, which went into effect at the beginning of July 1985, brought some initially positive results, but its end result has yet to be seen.

These, then are the items on Israel's agenda in its second generation of statehood, the fifth generation since the beginning of the modern Zionist enterprise. The passage of generations is significant. In each new generation, a new set of issues has come into play, growing out of older ones that in their time exercise people mightily but either were resolved or became passé. While the rhetoric of Israeli politics has continued to concentrate on the old issues, at least until the elections of 1984, in reality, after 1977 the business of Israeli politics was turned increasingly toward new issues, or at least the effort to identify and define them in political terms. It is not to be expected that governments would be responsible for doing so. In Israel, as elsewhere, they are preoccupied with day-to-day chores and crisis management, which in the Jewish state is an everyday occurrence. To some extent, the mainstream politicians were involved in doing so through the electoral campaigns of 1981 and 1984, but all too frequently it was left to the peripheral politicians of the small parties and to others outside of electoral politics to attempt to do so.

In the mid-1980s, this process is in full swing. By now the outlines of several of the new issues are clearly visible, and will be more so by the 1990s, if not sooner. Those will be the issues that will determine the future of Israeli politics for the rest of this century and into the next.

# A Final Word

Israel's polity and society are still raw, still emergent in a certain sense. There is much about it that appears shrill and ugly, aggressive and uncouth. Its drivers are reckless, its mass housing unattractive. Casual interpersonal contacts can be abrasive. Knesset debates often give the appearance that there is no culture of public discourse. Strikes and demonstrations are commonplace. The country has an unfinished look at every turn.

Yet paradoxically Israel is one of the most conservative of states. Israelis behave in ways that make them appear quite wedded to existing forms and practices. They show little inclination to change or experiment. Someone who presents a new idea in Israel expects to be given an immediate "no." Only if he persuasively persists is it possible to even gain a hearing. Nor is this situation of recent vintage. This observer recalls being struck by it at his first encounter with Israel, in 1953, at a time when the country's external image and self-image both were of a pioneer society in the making.

To be both raw and conservative is perhaps the worst possible combination, but, in fact, the superficial view is at least partially misleading. Change does take place, usually without being announced. In this respect, Israelis are very different from Americans, who wear change on their sleeve, who pursue the new with a vengeance. But there is every reason to believe that Israelis are like old-time Americans, many of whom at least also gave the external appearance of being reluctant to change, of holding fast to traditional ways.

This combination of rawness and conservatism seems to be characteristic of other new societies in their early stages. Travelers' reports of the United States and Australia in their earlier days describe what seem to be the same phenomena; even placid New Zealand is described in these terms during its first century. Louis Hartz has offered an explanation in the suggestion that new societies are fragment societies, that is to say, their civilization and culture represent fragments broken off from Old World, principally European, civilization and culture that have to undergo great changes in a new environment; but precisely because of that, they are held onto almost desperately by the pioneering generations, who need them as a familiar anchor. While that is not an entirely satisfactory explanation, it does offer a

**251**

good starting point from which to understand the paradox of conservation and change in new societies where, on one hand, the frontier is all important and, on the other, stubborn conservatism seems to be a fact of life.

Israel's conservatism is not in support of an ancient tradition but in support of the new ways of Zionism. There is, of course, a very vocal ultra-Orthodox religious element in the population, which has fossilized the old traditions and vociferously opposes all change in the Jewish way of life. In fact, they have undergone changes hardly less great than those of their most secular counterparts. For example, their grandfathers and even their fathers made the rejection of the Hebrew language a cornerstone of their program. Today they all speak Hebrew, even if reluctantly. Nor, as any student of Jewish religious history will affirm, is their Judaism that of their immediate ancestors, even though they think that they have preserved every jot and title of the past. It is at a far remove from those who came before the ossification that took place in Eastern Europe in the late eighteenth and early nineteenth centuries and that led to the formation of contemporary Orthodoxy.

On the other hand, those who grew up with Zionist ways are often just as Orthodox—as desirous of preventing change in their way of life. Within one generation, what were considered by the Zionist founders to be experiments were engraved in stone. In many respects, that is a more disturbing situation, since it reflects the strong tendency toward conservatism inherent in Jewish political culture, which transforms even revolutionary ideas into unchangeable ordinances and ways in one or two generations.

Still, this very conservatism, which has made it so difficult to consider changing the institutions and practices of the Israeli polity, is an anchor on behalf of Israeli democratic republicanism, a bulwark against the anarchic tendencies that also flourish in Israeli society. Here the outside observer should not be fooled by the decibel level of Israeli politics. The tone of Israeli political debate does tend to be strident so much so that, taken by itself, the Israeli polity always gives the impression of being on the verge of collapsing or fracturing irrevocably. But the collapse does not happen because of the strong forces that propel Israelis toward unity. Both the stridency and the tendencies toward unity are part and parcel of Jewish political culture, which has now become Israeli. Few would argue for its aesthetic virtues, but it is important not to confuse aesthetic judgments with realistic assessments of the situation.

In some respects, a very high percentage of the founders of the state set out to create a raw society, principally the socialist founders, who rejected the cultivated elements of civilization as being bourgeois affectations, but also the ultra-Orthodox, who viewed them as secular distractions from the serious business of halachic living. Thus, rawness itself became part of the ideology, at least until the Sephardim and certain Ashkenazic groups such as the Jews from Hungary and the English-speaking world brought in other ideas, albeit with less Zionist legitimacy than the ideologies of the founders. As a result, Israel is no longer as raw as it once was, but it is raw enough.

What this book attempts to do is look beyond this rawness and the immediate manifestations of Israel's conservatism, to understand what has happened, and what is likely to happen, in the building of Israel as a new society. The discussion in the foregoing pages attempts to point up some of the larger factors affecting political stability and change in Israel today. It has concentrated on latent rather than manifest factors, because it is to the former that we must look to discover directions that seem hidden in a civil society whose conservatism with regard to political and governmental change is pronounced. In fact, it is only because the latent forces herein described have their roots in some of the most conservative aspects of Israeli civil society, namely, the Jewish political cultural component, that one is justified in suggesting that they will become more manifest in a variety of ways as time goes on.

## THE NEW TERRITORIAL DEMOCRACY

In the final analysis, contemporary Israel is a compound of ideological, sectorial, and territorial groupings. The first gave birth to the other two, but in turn gave way to the second as the original ideological motivations were transformed into issues of self-interest. Today, both are making way for the third. Even so, while the territorial dimension is likely to become increasingly important in Israel, the sectorial and ideological dimensions will remain because of the character of the Jewish people, who set the state's rhythm and who invariably are motivated by one ideology or another and often divided by different ideological trends. Since Jews, like all other people, have interests to be served, the sectorial dimension is also guaranteed. The only question is to what extent it is shaped by ideological and to what extent by territorial democracy.

In that connection, this book suggests that the place to look for the direction of political innovations in contemporary Israel is in the local arena, where, despite the many restraints placed upon local government, politics function somewhat freer from the constraints of the countrywide political system. Exploration in depth of the patterns of local politics, the relations between local politics and the central authorities, and the impact of local politics on the political system as a whole are items that should have high priority on any agenda for the study or reform of Israeli politics.

## PRUDENCE AND IDEOLOGY

The history of the Zionist enterprise and the Jewish state that has resulted from it reflects a combination of prudence and ideology, a combination already present in Israel's founding. The ideological underpinnings of the

Zionist movement and the competing ideologies within it were crucial in providing the motivating force for a seemingly impossible mission, while the prudence learned by Jews as a result of hard experience and sober assessment of earlier setbacks kept the enterprise together and on track. It would be too much to suggest that the Zionist revolution was like the American Revolution, a revolution of sober expectations. Quite to the contrary, the Zionist revolution was explicitly and deliberately messianic in every one of its variations. The Jews' "sober" leadership either rejected Zionism out of hand as promoting the pursuit of unobtainable goals, or backed down at crucial junctures in the history of the Zionist movement. Nevertheless, a very real measure of prudence became part and parcel of the movement, serving a vital need in restraining excesses of messianism.

It was this ability to overcome the passions generated by ideology and its accompanying rhetoric and to choose prudential courses of action that has enabled the movement to achieve what it has against great odds, but it is often a touch-and-go matter as to whether or not Israelis and their leadership will choose prudence or build policies on messianic visions, on the expectation that the real world will lend itself to their implementation. Fortunately, prudence has won in the end in each case to date, although not without great cost in some.

Indeed, Israel's major problems stem from those kinds of excesses. More often than not, the Jews' vices stem from carrying their virtues to excess. Jewish idealism has its roots in Jewish messianism, but extreme messianism is a Jewish disease. One of the pillars of the third Jewish commonwealth is a strong consensus on the part of the great bulk of its citizens to reject manifestations of extreme messianism for just that reason. The very future of the state depends upon the ability to retain that kind of prudential counterbalance to the periodic and inevitable messianic outbursts.

## JEWISH STATE AND JEWISH CONDITION

Few, if any, countries in the world have come in for the same measure of attention as has the still-quite-young state of Israel. Whether it be for praise or condemnation, admiration or blame, the state serves as a magnet for attention, in a way that Jews and their activities have since the beginning of Jewish existence. In this respect, as in so many others, Israel is both a mirror and a manifestation of the Jewish experience. In the foregoing pages, it has been suggested that Israel has two dimensions, as the modern state that it is and as the central expression of the Jewish experience in our times. An understanding of the interplay of these two dimensions in every aspect of Israeli life is necessary for an understanding of the state itself.

During the first years of Israel's existence as an independent state, that fact was not always recognized. Indeed, there were those (and there still are a few) who argued that the future of Israel inevitably would be detached from the Jewish past of its founders, for good or for ill. Even those who do not argue from that position have tended to analyze the political life of the new state as if that separation were already an accomplished fact, as if the state could be understood as having sprung full-blown out of the events of 1948 or perhaps out of those of the last years of the nineteenth century.

As Israel's still-brief history unfolds, it is becoming all the more clear that such is not the case. Israel, its political (and other) institutions, and the political (and other) behavior of its people must be understood within the context of Jewish history and culture. Not only is the state inseparable from the Jewish people, but its experience is the Jewish experience in outline and even in detail. That is not an argument for a parochial view of Israel—quite to the contrary. What is characteristic of the Jewish experience is that it is both cosmopolitan and local: Jews have been involved in all the great currents of the history of the Western world, while at the same time being wrapped up in the most intimate and sometimes petty details of Jewish survival. So, too, with Israel.

The land itself is a manifestation of this seemingly paradoxical combination. Located at the very crossroads of Europe, Asia, and Africa, the center of the ancient and modern world, it dominates the geographic communications network that links east and west, north and south. Jerusalem itself sits astride the great continental divide separating the Atlantic watershed from all others.

At the same time, the heart of the land of Israel is drained by the Jordan River, which, in turn, flows into the Dead Sea, which has no outlet. At the very crossroads of the greatest land mass on earth, there is a tiny pocket whose principal waters flow into no great ocean, not the Atlantic Ocean to the west or the Arabian Sea and Indian Ocean to the east, but into a relatively inconspicuous, self-contained body of water. Only its peripheries flow into those larger bodies.

Thus, the land of Israel is the paradigm of the people of Israel. Since the days of Abraham, who by all accounts was one of a class of traders who linked the civilizations of the fertile cresent, to the present, when Jews are prominent in the mass media wherever they have the opportunity to be, the Jewish people has found its way to the heart of every communications network; yet even as it has played a disproportionate role in world history as a result, its core has drained into itself, and only the peripheries have drained outward into the great ocean of humanity.

## A NEW SOCIETY IN AN OLD WORLD

As a result, modern Israel is a dual experiment. On one hand, it is one of the group of new societies founded from scratch in the modern era by settlers who came together out of choice to build new ways of life on what for them were virgin territories. All new societies are essentially experimental ones, on several levels. In the first place, they invariably begin as experiments.

Those who set the tone among their founders are seeking to build what John Winthrop refered to, in connection with Puritan New England, as a "city upon a hill," that is to say, a better society for themselves and a beacon for mankind that will offer a model for the rest of the world to follow as best it can. New societies are equally experimental, because they are the deliberate creations of humans whose survival depends upon the success of the experiment, however measured.

Israel is a new society in both these respects. Its founders were concerned not only with providing a haven for Jews but with building a model for humankind, echoing an old Jewish vision that most of them garbed in the socialist fashions of their times. Their effort is no less an experiment than that of any other new society, nor are its results any more certain.

Here the special Jewish dimension must be added. While modern Israel was the last of the modern new societies to be founded, the Jewish people is the first new society in history. The Bible can be read as the record of the creation of a new society some 3,000 years ago, with all the characteristics and aspirations of any new society. Indeed, the Biblical account makes ancient Israel the paradigmatic new society, the model for all those to follow. At the same time, 2,000 years of dispersion has so transformed the Jewish people that modern Israel is an experiment to test if the Jews are yet capable of building and maintaining a state of their own. This question is asked consciously or subconsciously by every Israeli, Jew or non-Jew, and lies behind every discussion of the present and future of the state.

What this volume additionally suggests is that the manner, direction, and style of political development in Israel will be rather unique within the Middle East, because of Israel's character as a new society. It will be comparable only to the political development of other new societies in the world. Obviously the implications of that, if true, are many, and the ramifications are likely to be very significant. To some extent, new societies are condemned to live lonely lives, in the sense that the communications gap between them and the majority of the world's civil societies—the old societies—is very great indeed. The impact of the loneliness is likely to be even greater in a new society, small in territory and population and located like an island in a sea of traditional or modernizing societies of a very different kind.

Every new society, because it is an experiment, has a certain tentative quality about it. By its very nature, it gives to questions as to whether it will long endure. Abraham Lincoln posed the question properly for the United States, whether "a nation conceived in liberty and dedicated to the proposition that all men are created equal . . . can long endure." Every generation of Americans must answer that question, whether a nation conceived on Jewish terms can long endure. For Israelis, too, the question is a recurring one.

# NOTES

### 1. The Covenantal Foundations of a New Society

1. The concept "new societies" is based in part on the work of Louis Hartz, which he presented in *The Founding of New Societies* (New York: Harcourt, Brace and World, 1964). Argentina, Chile, Uruguay, and Jamaica, which in some ways meet the primary objective criteria used in determining which are the world's new societies, may have to be added to this list. The author refrains from doing so because, though the surface evidence is mixed, he has strong reservations about them and has not studied them sufficiently to make even a tentative determination.

2. For an examination of mystique as future-oriented myth, see John T. Marcus, "The World Impact of the West: The Mystique and the Sense of Participation in History," in Henry A. Murray, ed., *Myth and Myth Making* (New York: George Braziller, 1960), pp. 221–39.

3. Alexis de Toqueville and Frederick Jackson Turner provide us with the classic picture of the United States in these terms, each in his own way, in *Democracy in America* and *The Frontier in American History* (New York: Holt, 1920) respectively. The picture is recast in contemporary social-science terms by Seymour Martin Lipset in *The First New Nation* (New York: Basic Books, 1963), and by Ray Allen Billington in *America's Frontier Heritage* (New York: Holt, Rinehart and Winston, 1967).

The country's contractual origins are well delineated by Andrew C. McLaughlin in *The Foundations of American Constitutionalism* (New York: Fawcett, 1961), and by Perry Miller, *Errand into the Wilderness* (Cambridge, Mass.: Harvard University Press, 1956). The roots of its ideology are examined by Yehoshua Arieli in *Individualism and Nationalism in American Ideology* (Cambridge, Mass.: Harvard University Press, 1964).

4. The failure of many of the leading Zionists to "notice" the Arabs has been well documented. Early Zionist literature, written outside the country, makes no reference to an indigenous population in Palestine that would have to be dealt with on a continuing basis. In making this assumption about the "emptiness" of the land, the Zionists merely reflected common European notions about non-European populations in that period. For typical expressions see Rufus Learsi, *Fulfillment: The Epic Story of Zionism* (New York: World Publishing Co., 1951), and Arthur Hertzberg, ed., *The Zionist Idea* (New York: Atheneum, 1969).

5. The term *"old-new" land* was used by Theodore Herzl himself as the title for his utopian novel (*Altneuland*, in the original German) describing his vision of life in a restored Jewish state. For a broad picture of Zionist thought as a modern ideological system, see Hertzberg, *The Zionist Idea*.

6. Horace M. Kallen delineates the relationship between Israel and its mystique in *Utopians at Bay* (New York: Theodore Herzl Foundation, 1958). For an Israeli view of the mystique, see, for example, David Ben-Gurion, *Rebirth and Destiny of Israel* (New York: Philosophical Library, 1954). Ronald Sanders discusses

257

the development of the mystique in Israel in *The View From Masada* (New York: Harper and Row, 1966).

7. The use of covenant forms to create political relationships was an ancient Near Eastern practice, as George E. Mendenhall has pointed out in "Covenant Forms in Israelite Tradition," *Biblical Archeologist* 17, no. 3 (July 1954): 50–76. The Israelites transformed the covenant principle from one that was used for quasi-feudal purposes between rulers or polities into one used for federal purposes within polities. See, for example, S. J. Mackenzie, *Faith and History in the Old Testament* (New York: Macmillan Co., 1963), pp. 40–53, and John Bright, *A History of Israel* (Philadelphia: Westminster Press, 1956).

8. While no one has directly discussed ancient Israel as a new society, Yehezkel Kaufman has laid the groundwork for such a discussion in his monumental *Toldot Ha Emunah Ha Yisraelit* (Jerusalem and Tel Aviv: Bailik and Dvir, 1937–1960), 4 vols., available in an abridged English version as *The Religion of Israel* (Chicago: University of Chicago Press, 1960), selected and translated by Moshe Greenberg. See also Henri Frankfort et al., *Before Philosophy* (London: Pelican Books, 1949), and Harry M. Orlinsky, *Ancient Israel* (Ithaca, N.Y.: Cornell University Press, 1954). Lincoln Steffens offers some suggestive, if unusual, confirmations of this hypothesis in "Moses in Red," reprinted in Ella Winter and Herbert Shapiro, eds., *The World of Lincoln Steffens* (New York: Hill and Wang, 1962). Some Zionist thinkers, beginning with Moses Hess, the best of them, did see ancient Israel as the first "nation" in the modern sense, thus coming close to the concept suggested here. Hertzberg, *The Zionist Idea*, discusses them in his introduction. See also Hans Kohn, *The Idea of Nationalism* (New York: Macmillan, Co., 1944), chap. 1.

9. Whether or not other new societies came into existence in the premodern world remains an unanswered question. To this writer, the possibility remains open. It may be that all or parts of Switzerland and the Netherlands would qualify, even as it is obvious that France or England would not. What is necessary is some conformity to the definition posited in this paper, especially in terms of immigration, emptiness, and mystique. See Salo W. Baron, *The Jewish Community* (Philadelphia: Jewish Publication Society, 1938–1942), 3 vols.; Daniel J. Elazar and Stuart A. Cohen, *The Jewish Polity: Jewish Political Organization from Biblical Times to the Present* (Bloomington: Indiana University Press, 1985); and Daniel J. Elazar, ed., *Kinship and Consent: The Jewish Political Tradition and Its Contemporary Uses* (Lanham, Md.; University Press of America and Jerusalem Center for Public Affairs, 1983).

10. The handful of non-Jews who became active Zionists did so for profoundly ideological reasons emerging from their understanding of Scripture and its demands upon them.

11. Theodore Herzl, *The Jewish State*, reprinted from *Der Südenstadt* and translated by Harry Zohn (New York: Herzl Press, 1970).

12. See, for example, David Ben-Gurion, "Earning a Homeland," in *Rebirth and Destiny of Israel*, pp. 3–6.

13. Theodore Herzl, *Altneuland—Old-New Land*, translated by Paula Arnold (Haifa: Haifa Publishing Co., 1960).

14. For the basic works of Ahad Ha'am, see Ahad Ha'am *Selected Essays*, translated by Leon Simon (Philadelphia: Jewish Publication Society of America, 1912).

15. See, for example, A. D. Gordon, "Labor the Core of the Matter," in *The Second Aliyah* (New York: Zionist Youth Council, 1955), pp. 29–35.

16. On Berl Katznelson, see Anita Shapira, *Berl* (Tel Aviv: Am Oved Publishers, 1980) (Hebrew).

17. A selection of Ben Borochov's work is available in Hertzberg, *The Zionist Idea*, pp. 355–66.

18. Cf. Vladimir (Ze'ev) Jabotinsky, "Evidence Submitted to the Palestine Royal Commission (1937)," in Hertzberg, *The Zionist Idea*, pp. 559–70.

19. Selections of both Pines's and Kook's writings can be found in Hertzberg, *The Zionist Idea*, pp. 409–31.

20. On Magnes, see Arthur Goren, *New York Jews and the Quest for Community* (New York: Columbia University Press, 1970), and Hertzberg, *The Zionist Idea*, pp. 443–49.

21. Moshe Maoz, *Changes in the Position of the Jewish Communities of Palestineal Syria in the Mid-Nineteenth Century* (Jerusalem, 1970), Paper presented for the International Seminar on the History of Palestine and Its Jewish Settlement during the Ottoman Period.

22. On the recruitment of Jewish settlers in the period, see Yaakov Elazar, *HaRova HaYehudi B'Yerushalim HaAtika* [The Jewish Quarter in the Old City of Jerusalem] (Jerusalem: Maariv Publishing, 1975) (Hebrew).

23. For a description of the development of Jerusalem in this pattern, see Zeev Vilnai, *Yerushalayim Birat Yisrael* (Jerusalem: Ahiever, 1960).

24. Agudat Shocherai HaGymnasia HaIvrit, 1962–63; Y. Press, *One Hundred Years in Jerusalem* (Jerusalem: R. Masis, 1964); and Shlomo Harmati, *Three Predecessors of Ben Yehuda* (Jerusalem: Yitzhat Ben Zui, 1978).

25. The chronological calculations used here are based on the theory developed by this writer regarding the generational rhythm of political life. See Daniel J. Elazar, *Toward a Generational Theory of American Politics* (Philadelphia: Center for the Study of Federalism, 1968); "The Generational Rhythm of American Politics," *American Politics Quarterly* 6, no. 1 (January 1978); and his Israel field notes.

26. On the First Aliyah, see Avraham Yaari, *The Goodly Heritage*, abridged and translated by Israel Schen (Jerusalem: Youth and Hachalutz, Department of the World Zionist Organization, 1958). On the moshavot, see D. Weintraub, M. Lissak, and Y. Azmon, *Moshava, Kibbutz, and Moshav* (Ithaca: Cornell University Press, 1969).

27. The articles of agreement of a number of the early colonies are preserved in their archives and displayed on appropriate occasions. Petah Tikvah maintains its original covenant on year-round display in its municipal museum. See also *Petah Tikvah Metoledot HaMoshavah V'haIr* (Petah Tikvah: City of Petah Tikvah Cultural Department, 1964).

28. Yosef Gorni summarizes and evaluates demographic, social, and political data regarding the Second Aliyah in a most comprehensive manner in his article "Changes in the Social and Political Structure of the Second Aliya between 1904 and 1940," in Daniel Caspi and Gedalia Yogev, eds., *Zionism: Studies in the History of the Zionist Movement and of the Jewish Community in Palestine* (Tel Aviv: Tel Aviv University and Massada Publishing Co., 1975), vol. 1, pp. 49–101.

29. Martin Buber makes a strong case for this claim in *Paths in Utopia* (New York: Macmillan Co., 1950). See, in particular, his epilogue.

30. David Ben-Gurion, "Jewish Labor: The Origin of Settlement," in Ben-Gurion's address, originally given in 1932, shows that the struggle continued even after Mapai, his party, had achieved political dominance within the yishuv, and reflects much of the bitterness associated with that struggle.

31. Schweid Eliezer, *Israel at the Crossroads*, translated by Alton Meyer Winters (Philadelphia: Jewish Publication Society of America, 1973).

32. Gorni, "Second Aliya." The Second Aliyah settlers were somewhat more ambivalent toward the kind of federative arrangements that their predecessors adopted, but even they favored a collectivist kind of federative structure, in line with their greater emphasis on socialist ideologies with manifest or latent centralizing tendencies. Shmuel Dayan, one of the founders of Degania, the first kvutzah (kib-

butz), and later of Nahalal, the first *moshav ovdim,* and the father of Moshe Dayan, provides "A Picture of the Second Aliyah" in retrospect, in *The Second Aliyah,* setting out his view of its achievements after its legend had been born and he had become one of its primary custodians.

Dayan attributes to the Second Aliyah the origins of institutions that did not emerge until the Third, including Kupat Holim (the Histadrut general sick fund), and Hamashbir (the Histadrut cooperative stores). He even mentions the publication of *Davar,* the Histadrut newspaper, which was not founded until 1925. In many respects, that is the legend at its best. On the other hand, in his speech "Jewish Labor: The Origin of Settlement," David Ben-Gurion took a somewhat more realistic view.

## 2. Foundings and Revolutions

1. The two major concretizations of the myth of the Second Aliyah, according to Yosef Gorni, were *Kovetz HaShomer* (the anthology of the Jewish self-defense organization), published in 1937, and *Sefer HaAliya HaShnia* [the Book of the Second Aliyah], published in 1947.

2. Alexander Aaronsohn, *With the Turks in Palestine* (Boston: Houghton Mifflin, 1916); Joseph Baratz, *A Village by the Jordan* (Tel Aviv: Press Department of Ichud Habonim, 1960); Ben Halpern, *The Idea of the Jewish State* (Cambridge, Mass.: Harvard University Press, 1969); and Elhanan Orren, "Settlement—The Basis of Independence: Settlement, Policy, and Defense in the Zionist Struggle, 1878–1949," pt. 1 in *Shdemot,* no. 21/22 (Winter 1984): pp. 18–19.

3. Alex Bein, *The Return to the Soil* (Jerusalem: Youth and Hechalutz Department, World Zionist Organization, 1952); Noah Lucas, *The Modern History of Israel* (London: Weidenfeld and Nicolson, 1974); Raphael Patai, ed., *Encyclopedia of Zionism and Israel,* vol. 2 (New York: Herzl Press and McGraw Hill, 1971), pp. 1114–16; and Muki Tsur, Tair Zebulun, and Hanina Porath, *Ka'an Al Pni Adama* [Here on the Soil] (Tel Aviv: Kibbutz HaMeuchad and Sifriat Hapoalim, 1980) (Hebrew).

4. Patai, *Encyclopedia of Zionism.*

5. Alain Greilsammer, *Des Communistes Israeliens* (Paris: Presses de la Foundation Nationale des Sciences Poliques, 1978); Giora Goldberg, "Adaptation to Competitive Politics: The Case of Israeli Communism," *Studies in Comparative Communism* 14, no. 4 (1981): 331–51; and Jacob Hen-Tov, *Communism and Zionism in Israel* (New Brunswick: Transaction Books, 1974).

6. Shlomo Avineri, "Israel in the Post-Ben Gurion Era," *Midstream* (September 1965): 16–32; and Charles Liebman and Eliezer Don-Yehiya, *Civil Religion in Israel: Traditional Religion and Political Culture in the Jewish State* (Bloomington: Indiana University Press, 1983).

7. This and the following elections are portrayed in Patai, *Encyclopedia of Zionism,* vol. 1, pp. 84–85; Dan Horowitz and Moshe Lissak, *The Origins of the Israeli Polity* (Chicago: Chicago University Press, 1978); and Anita Shapira, *Berl* (Tel Aviv: Am Oved Publishers, 1980) (Hebrew).

8. Eli Eliachar, *Living with the Jews* (London: Weidenfeld and Nicolson, 1984), and Menachem Freidman, *Hevrah ve HaDat: HaOrthodoxiya Halo Tzionit be Eretz Yisrael* (Jerusalem: Yad Yitzhak Ben Tzvi, 1978).

9. Peter Medding, *Mapai in Israel: Political Organization and Government in a New Society* (Cambridge: Cambridge University Press, 1976); Shapira, *Berl;* and Shabtai Tevet, *Retzach Arlosoroff* [The Arlozoroff Murder] (Jerusalem: Shocken, 1982).

10. Lucas, *History of Israel,* and Harry Viteles, *A History of the Cooperative Movement in Israel,* 7 vols. (London: Valentine Mitchell, 1966), vol. 1—*The Evolution of the Cooperative Movement.*

11. Yosef Gorni, "Changes in the Social and Political Structure of the Second

Aliyah between 1904 and 1940," in Daniel Caspi and Gedalia Yogev, eds., *Zionism* (Tel Aviv: Tel Aviv University and Massada Publishing Company, 1975), vol. 1, pp. 49–101.

12. Some students of Israeli politics have preferred to describe these as consociational arrangements following Arendt Lijphart, which can be found in "Consociational Democracy," *World Politics* 21 no. 2 (January 1969): 207–25. For this writer, consocialization, where it is embodied in firmly established institutions, is a form of federalism, since it involves the linkage of discrete entities into a new whole by compacting in such a way as to preserve their respective integrities while pursuing common goals. For an exposition of federal principles useful in understanding the discussion, see the articles on "Federalism" by Daniel J. Elazar, in the *International Encyclopedia of the Social Sciences* (1968), and Max Boehm, in the *Encyclopedia of the Social Sciences* (1931).

13. The pattern of institution building referred to here is described by S. N. Eisenstadt, in *Israeli Society* (London: Weidenfeld and Nicolson, 1967) and Leonard J. Fein, in *Politics in Israel* (Boston: Little, Brown and Co., 1967).

14. On urban development, see Erik Cohen, *The City in Zionist Ideology* (Jerusalem: Institute of Urban and Regional Studies of the Eliezer Kaplan School of Urban and Social Sciences, 1970), pp. 2–22, and "Development Towns—The Social Dynamic of 'Planted' Urban Communities in Israel," in S. Eisenstadt, R. Bar-Yosef, and C. Adler, eds., *Integration and Development in Israel* (Jerusalem: Israel Universities Press, 1970).

15. On the founding of the kibbutzim and the kibbutz movements, see Yosef Criden and Saadia Gelb, *The Kibbutz Experience: Dialogue in Kfar Blum* (New York: Schocken Books, 1976); Michael Curtis, "Utopia and the Kibbutz," in Michael Curtis and Mordecai Chertoff, eds., *Israel: Social Structure and Change* (New Brunswick: Transaction Books, 1973); David Patterson, "The First Fifty Years of Collective Settlement in Israel," *Jewish Journal of Sociology* 2 (1960): 42–55; and Melford E. Spiro, *Kibbutz: Venture in Utopia* (New York: Schocken Books, 1973).

16. The status of the Jewish community in Palestine was formalized in law in this manner under both the Ottoman and British regimes. The Palestine Orders in Council of 1922, 1923, and 1939 and the Jewish Communal (Knesset Israel) Ordinance of 1927 set the framework for the internal autonomy of the yishuv under the mandatory regime.

17. Liebman and Don-Yehiya, *Civil Religion*, and Daniel J. Elazar and Stuart A. Cohen, "Epoch 13—Hitagduyot," in *The Jewish Polity* (Bloomington: Indiana University Press, 1985).

### 3. Toward Territorial Democracy in Israel

1. On Israel's Declaration of Independence, see Yigal Aricha, *"Meggilat Ha'atzmaut-Hazon u'Metziut"* [The Scroll of Independence—Vision and Reality], unpublished study, Bar Ilan University Department of Political Studies, 1983, the most comprehensive work available on the subject; and Horace M. Kallan, *Utopians at Bay* (New York: Theodore Herzl Foundation, 1958).

2. See S. N. Eisenstadt, *Israeli Society* (London: Weidenfeld and Nicolson, 1967), pp. 294–95, and compare with the results of the elections to the subsequent Knessets. In turn, the larger parties have introduced a limited system of ethnic "ticket balancing" in the composition of the party lists that determine who actually is elected to the Knesset once the party's proportion of the total vote is established.

3. The Israeli experience can be better understood when placed in the context described by Robert K. Merton in *Social Theory and Social Structure*, 2d ed. (Glencoe, Ill.: Free Press, 1957), when it is borne in mind that in Israel the parties' role is reversed.

4. Nadav Safran describes the shift of party control from direct to indirect services in *The United States and Israel* (Cambridge, Mass.: Harvard University Press, 1967), pt. 3.

5. The political aspects of this subject are discussed in Leonard J. Fein, *Politics in Israel* (Little, Brown and Co., 1967).

6. Alan Arian has documented and analyzed this relationship in *Ideological Change in Israel* (Cleveland: Case Western Reserve University Press, 1968).

7. The transition in Massachusetts has been well analyzed by Perry Miller in *The New England Mind: The Seventeenth Century* (New York: Macmillan Co., 1939).

8. Unfortunately, the literature on territorial democracy is very limited. Orestes Brownson was apparently the first person to use the phrase, in *The American Republic* (1866). Russell Kirk has expanded upon it as a concept in "The Prospects for Territorial Democracy in America" in Robert A. Goldwin, ed., *A Nation of States* (Chicago: Rand McNally, 1963), and a revised version in the second edition of that volume (1972). This writer has commented on its role in American politics in *Federalism and the Community* (Pittsburgh: University of Pittsburgh, 1968). Certain aspects of the problem of the territorial organization of power have been well treated in Arthur Maas, ed., *Area and Power* (Glencoe, Ill.: Free Press, 1959).

9. A. Droyanab, ed., *Sefer Tel Aviv* [Tel Aviv Book], vol. 1 (Tel Aviv: Vaadat Sefer Tel Aviv in association with the Municipality of Tel Aviv-Yafo, 1936) (Hebrew); Arieh Yotfat, "Shishim Shnot Hitpatchutah shel Tel Aviv," in *Tel Aviv Yearbook, 1969* (Tel Aviv: Municipality of Tel Aviv-Yafo, 1970) (Hebrew), and "Pratim le-Toldot Tel Aviv," in *Tel Aviv Statistical Yearbook, 1983* (Tel Aviv: Center for Economic and Social Research and Municipality of Tel Aviv-Yafo, 1984).

10. Erik Cohen, in *The City in Zionist Ideology*, examines the problem of the city from the perspective of the Zionist founders and surveys the actual state of urban development in the country in those first generations. Cohen suggests that the shift away from concern with urban as well as rural settlement is also a product of the Third Aliyah revolution, with its strong ideological dimensions. All told, he provides a necessary corrective to the romantic view of rural Israel.

11. *Statistical Abstract of Israel* (Jerusalem: Central Bureau of Statistics, 1968). In a significant number of cities and towns, territorial neutrality has led to the development of ethnic neighborhoods, which, however, are unable to obtain direct local representation under the present electoral system. Perhaps as a result, ethnic ticket balancing is even more pronounced on the local level than in Knesset elections.

12. The study of local government in Israel is still in its infancy. No comprehensive study of the subject has been published, although one is presently in preparation at the Jerusalem Center for Public Affairs. Eisenstadt, *Israeli Society*, and Fein, *Politics in Israel*, have sections on local government. The most comprehensive work is that of Shevach Weiss, *HaShilton HaMekomi B'Yisrael: Reka Hukati VeSocio-Politi* [Local Government in Israel: Legal and Sociopolitical Background] (Tel Aviv: Am Oved, 1972). Emanuel Guttman provides a standard description of *The Politics of Israel Local Government* (Milano: Edizioni di Comunita, 1963). Moshe Gat provides a good selective bibliography, now dated. The structure and formal powers of local government are described in Yehoshua Freudenheim, *Government in Israel* (Dobbs Ferry, N.Y.: Oceana Publications, 1967), chap. 9. The Jerusalem Center for Public Affairs maintains extensive files on local government and intergovernmental relations in Israel, including bibliographies, research papers, and raw materials for further research, all part of its continuing study of the subject. Other prime sources include *Dvar HaShilton HaMekomi*, the journal of the Israel Union of Local Authorities, published between December 1950 and January 1965, and the reports of the state comptroller of Israel, which include individual reports on virtually every local authority in the country at intervals going back over three decades, as well as annual reports that deal with general problems of local government and state-local relations.

See also Eliezer Brutzkus, *Physical Planning in Israel* (Jerusalem: n.p., 1964); Zeev Meljon, ed., *Towns and Villages in Israel* (Tel Aviv: Union of Local Authorities in Israel, 1966); Dov Rosen, ed., *Seker Munitzipali* [Municipal Survey: Jewish Cities and Local Councils] (Jerusalem: Ministry of the Interior, 1968, 2d. ed., 1974), an electoral survey in Hebrew; and the annual statistical reports of the Israel Central Bureau of Statistics for local authorities, issued since 1964–1965. The studies of the Center for the Study of Rural Settlement (Rehovot) include some empirical material on regional councils.

13. Y. Gevirtz, *Rural Local Government in Israel* (International Seminar for Local Government Administration, 1962). Yehoshua Ben-Aryeh describes one of these "small republics" in *Emek HaYarden HaTichon* (Merhavia: Hakibbutz Hameuchad, 1965).

14. Weiss, *Local Government*, chap. 10. It should be noted that the recruitment and advancement of Sephardic Jews are not spread evenly throughout the system of local government. The older and larger cities have disproportionately fewer, while the new towns, with their mainly "new immigrant" populations, have disproportionately more.

15. Rosen, *Seker Munitzipali*, presents a complete picture of electoral activity at the local level from the first postindependence elections through 1973. The 1978 and 1983 data are available at the Jerusalem Center for Public Affairs.

The extent of this new independence from party discipline is reflected in the rise of "kalanterism," perhaps one of its worst manifestations, whereby members of the council who have supported the coalition holding power locally are persuaded or seduced into joining with one of the opposition factions to vote the sitting coalition out of office. The original "kalanterist," a Jerusalem city councilman named Kalanter, made his move in 1959. Since then the number of instances has grown considerably. In several cases, serious differences in approach to government were involved, though in most personal ambition has been the motivating force. The Knesset regularly debates this "problem," to them particularly serious because it weakens party control over local officials, but has not yet been able to devise an acceptable way to prevent it. By the same token, interparty agreements to avoid kalanterism, made at the headquarters level, have proved unenforceable in the localities.

16. The Biblical account of the transformation is provided in great detail in the Book of Joshua. See also Daniel J. Elazar, *The Book of Joshua as a Political Classic: A Commentary* (Jerusalem and Philadelphia: Jerusalem Center for Public Affairs, 1980).

17. See Arian, *Ideological Change in Israel*.

18. Published examples of the Israelis' rediscovery of their Zionist and Jewish connections are cited in Daniel J. Elazar, "The Rediscovered Polity: Selections from the Literature of Jewish Public Affairs, 1967–1968," *American Jewish Year Book, 1969*, vol. 70 (New York and Philadelphia: American Jewish Committee and Jewish Publication Society of America, 1968), pp. 172–24.

19. A good summary of the development of local self-government in the Arab towns is available in Ori Stendel, *Arab Villages in Israel and Judea-Samaria* (Jerusalem: Israel Economist, 1967). The best sources of specific data are the reports of the state comptroller for specific towns. See also Ernest Stock, *From Conflict to Understanding: Relations between Jews and Arabs in Israel since 1948* (New York: Institute of Human Relations Press, 1968).

20. Field records, Jerusalem Center Workshop in Local Government, 1974.

21. See Erika Spiegel, *New Towns in Israel* (Stuttgart and Bern: Karl Kramer Verlag, 1966). The two exceptions are Tel Aviv-Jaffa and Maalot-Tarshisha. The first was created immediately after the establishment of the state, partly for security reasons, and before a clear urbanization policy was established. The second represents a merger of two very weak local councils in an effort to create one viable one. In addition, Acco, Lod, Ramle, and Haifa have mixed populations dating from before

1948, and Jerusalem has been a mixed city since June 1967. More recently, Arabs have moved into the Jewish towns of these "twin" communities, in search of better housing conditions, sometimes against the wishes of some of the local population, which, of course, cannot restrict them in their right to do so.

## 4. The Compound Structure of the Israeli Polity

1. See Robert Gordis, "Democratic Origins in Ancient Israel—the Biblical *Edah*," in *Alexander Marx Jubilee Volume* (New York: Jewish Theological Seminary, 1950), and Moshe Weinfeld, "The Transition from Tribal Republic to Monarchy in Ancient Israel and Its Impression on Jewish Political History," in Daniel J. Elazar, ed., *Kinship and Consent* (Washington, D.C.: University Press of America, 1983).

2. For an overview of the Knesset, see Asher Zidon, *Knesset, the Parliament of Israel*, translated from the Hebrew by Aryeh Rubinstein and Gertrude Hirschler (New York: Herzl Press, 1967); and Asher Arian, *Politika ve-Mishtar be-Yisrael* [Politics and Government in Israel] (Tel Aviv: Zmora Bitan, 1985) (Hebrew).

3. Max Nurock, "The Etymology of Administration," in *Public Administration in Israel and Abroad*, no. 4 (1963): 38–50.

4. Arian, *Politika ve-Mishtar be-Yisrael*.

5. See Zvi Yaron, "Religion in Israel," *American Jewish Yearbook, 1976*, vol. 76 (New York and Philadelphia: American Jewish Committee and Jewish Publication Society of America, 1975), pp. 41–90, for a full examination of the social, intellectual, and political dimensions of the link, including the special problem of understanding the relationship between religion and state in Israel, the place of religion and religious ideas in the Zionist movement, the development of what might be termed a Jewish civil religion in Israel, the character of the religious establishment, the state of belief and Jewish consciousness among Israeli Jews, institutionalized forms of religious observance in the state, and the political role of the religious parties.

Simon Herman's "The Interweaving of Jewishness and Israeliness" and Shlomit Levi and Louis Gutmann's "Zionism and Jewishness of Israelis" present empirical studies of the interrelationship. Herman's study of Israeli high-school students and their parents in the post-Six Day War period is particularly revealing with regard to the attitudes of the younger generation and what we can expect in the future with regard to Israelis' Jewishness. He emphasizes the way in which Jewish ethnic identity is interwoven with Israeli identity in Israel, suggesting that the more Jewish one is, the more committed one is to Israel as a state and an enterprise. He then suggests that the more religious one is, the stronger one's Jewish identity is likely to be. Levi and Gutmann carry the argument a step further, to provide evidence that for non-Orthodox Jews, Zionism has become almost another branch of Judaism, the "faith of the fathers" for those Israeli Jews.

Charles Liebman and Eliezer Don-Yehiya have studied the way in which Jewish tradition has become the basis for an Israeli "civil religion," one that merges into traditional Judaism, (see their *Civil Religion in Israel* [Berkeley and Los Angeles: University of California Press, 1984]). Israel's civil religion is concerned with the infusion of all of civil life with transcendent meaning; in part it follows the Greco-Roman sense of civil religion as a religious prop for the regime.

6. See, inter alia, Moshe Davis, ed., *World Jewry and the State of Israel* (New York: Arno Press, 1977); Daniel J. Elazar, "Israel, American Jewry, and the Re-emergence of a World Jewish Polity," in *Annual of Bar Ilan University Studies in Judaica and the Humanities* 16–17 (1979); and Daniel J. Elazar and Stuart A. Cohen, *The Jewish Polity: The Constitutional Organization of the Jewish People from Biblical Times to the Present* (Bloomington: Indiana University Press, 1985).

7. Daniel J. Elazar and Alysa M. Dortort, eds., *Understanding the Jewish*

*Agency: A Handbook* (Jerusalem: Jerusalem Center for Public Affairs, 1984), and Ernest Stock, "Jewish Multi-country Associations," in *American Jewish Year Book, 1974-75*, vol. 75 (New York and Philadelphia: American Jewish Committee and Jewish Publication Society of America, 1974), pp. 571–97. Josef Lador-Laderer, "World Jewish Associations," in *Encyclopedia Judaica Yearbook* (Jerusalem: Keter, 1973), pp. 351–56.

8. Jacob Ettinger, *The Task of the Jewish National Fund* (The Hague: Jewish National Fund, 1981); Shimon Kushnir, *The Village Builder* (New York: Herzl Press, 1967); and Abraham Granovsky, *The Land Problem and the Future* (Jerusalem: Jewish National Fund, 1945).

9. Arye Globerson, *Higher Education and Employment—A Case Study of Israel* (Hampshire, England: Saxon House, 1978), and Max Rauch, "Higher Education in Israel" (Ph.D. diss., University of Southern California, 1971).

10. Elazar and Dortort, *Jewish Agency*. See also annual *Reports on Departments' Activities* (Jerusalem: World Zionist Organization).

11. Elazar and Dortort, *Jewish Agency*.

12. Jacob Landau, *The Arabs in Israel* (Oxford: Oxford University Press, 1969); Ian Lustick, "Israel's Arab Minority in the Begin Era," in Robert Freedman, ed., *Israel in the Begin Era* (New York: Praeger, 1982), and "Political Attitudes of Christian and Moslem Children," *European Journal of Social Psychology* 7, no. 3: 369–73; Ori Stendel, *The Minorities of Israel* (Jerusalem: Israel Economist, 1973); and Sammy Smooha, "Control of Minorities in Israel and Northern Ireland," *Comparative Studies in Society and History* 22 (April 1980): 256–80.

13. On the history of this effort, see, inter alia, research files of Avraham Landsman, Jerusalem Center for Public Affairs. Mr. Landsman was the Israel Ministry of the Interior official responsible for encouraging the municipalization of Arab villages in the 1950s.

14. Henry E. Baker, *The Legal System of Israel*, 2d ed. (Jerusalem: Israel Universities Press, 1968); Martin Edelman, "The Rabbinic Courts in the Evolving Political Culture of Israel," *Middle Eastern Studies* 16, no. 3: 145–66; and Hedva Porat-Martin, "Rabbinical and Civil Courts in Israel: A Dual Legal System in Action" (Ph.D. diss., University of California, 1979).

15. Baker, *Legal System*, and Meir Silverstone, "Personal Status in the Israel Legal System," *Public Administration in Israel and Abroad, 1971*, vol. 12, pp. 14–24.

16. Baker, *Legal System*; Landau, *Arabs in Israel*; Ian Lustick, *Arabs in the Jewish State* (Austin: University of Texas Press, 1980); and Silverstone, "Personal Status."

17. Eliezer Don-Yehiya, ed., *Conflict and Consensus in Jewish Politics* (Ramat Gan: Bar Ilan University Press, 1984); Charles Liebman and Eliezer Don-Yehiya, *Piety and Politics* (Bloomington: Indiana University Press, 1984); and Meir Silverstone, "The Israel Ministry of Religious Affairs and the Chief Rabbinate of Israel," *Public Administration in Israel and Abroad, 1973*, vol. 14, pp. 33–41.

18. Daniel J. Elazar, "The Compound Structure of Public Service Delivery Systems in Israel" (Beverly Hills: Sage Publications, 1977); Allon Gal, *Socialist Zionism* (Cambridge, Mass.: Schenkman, 1973); and Walter Laqueur, *A History of Zionism* (London: Weidenfeld and Nicolson, 1972).

19. For a thorough exploration of the politics of coalition formation, see Eliezer Don-Yehiya, "Religion and Coalition: The National Religious Party and Coalition Formation in Israel" in Asher Arian, ed., *The Elections in Israel, 1973* (Jerusalem: Jerusalem Academic Press, 1975), and "The Politics of Religious Parties in Israel," in Sam Lehman-Wilzig and Bernard Susser, *Public Life in Israel and the Diaspora* (Ramat Gan: Bar Ilan University Press, 1981).

20. Dan Horowitz and Moshe Lissak, *The Origins of the Israeli Party* (Chicago:

Chicago University Press, 1978), and Amnon Rubinstein, *From Herzl to Gush Emmunim and Back Again* (Tel Aviv: Schocken, 1980).

21. M. Bruno and Z. Zussman, "Exchange Rate Flexibility, Inflation, and Structural Change: Israel under Alternative Regimes," *Journal of Economic Development* 6 (1979): 483–514; Abba Lerner and Haim Ben Shachar, *The Economics of Efficiency and Growth-Lessons from Israel and the West Bank* (Cambridge, Mass.: Ballinger Publishing, 1975); Michael Michaely, *Israel* (New York: National Bureau of Economic Research, 1975); and Moshe Sanbar, *The Political Economy of Israel, 1948–1982* (Jerusalem: Jerusalem Center for Public Affairs, 1984).

22. Benjamin Akzin and Yehezkel Dror, *High Pressure Planning* (Syracuse, N.Y.: Syracuse University Press, 1966); Eric Cohen, "Development Towns—The Social Dynamics of 'Planted' Urban Communities in Israel," in S. Eisenstadt, R. Bar Yosef, and C. Adler, eds., *Integration and Development in Israel* (Jerusalem: Israel Universities Press, 1970); Elisha Efrat, "Aspects of Physical Planning in Israel," *Kidmah* 6, no. 21 (December 1980): 4–9; and Efraim Orni and Elisha Efrat, *Geography of Israel* (Jerusalem: Israel Universities Press, 1974).

23. Yosef Criden and Saadia Gelb, *The Kibbutz Experience—Dialogue in Kfar Blum* (New York: Schocken Books, 1976); Yosef Lanir, *Ba'ayot Tikshoret ve Minhal be Kibbutz ha-Gadol be Tkufateinu"* [Communication and Administrative Problems in the Contemporary Large Kibbutz] (Ramat Efal: Yad Tabenkin, 1979); and Dan Leon, *The Kibbutz: A New Way of Life* (Oxford: Pergamon Press, 1964).

24. E. Baldwin, *Differentiation and Cooperation in an Israeli Veteran Moshav* (Manchester: Manchester University Press, 1972); J. Ben-David, "The Kibbutz and the Moshav," in J. Ben-David, ed., *Agricultural Planning and Village Community in Israel* (Paris: UNESCO, 1964); David W. Brown, *Ideology and Political Relations in Israeli Immigrant Cooperatives (Moshavei Olim)* (Manchester: University of Manchester, 1974); *The Moshav Shitufi* (Tel Aviv: Afro-Asian Institute for Labor Studies and Cooperation in Israel, 1960); M. I. Klayman, *The Moshav in Israel: A Case Study of Institution Building for Agricultural Development* (New York: Praeger, 1970); and Emanuel Labes, "Moshav Life," in *Handbook of the Moshav* (Jerusalem: World Zionist Organization, 1962), pp. 12–29.

25. Yitzhak Gevirtz, "Agricultural Cooperatives in Regional Councils" and "Elections to Regional Councils," in *ISLGA*, vol. 1; F. M. Katz, N. Menuhin, and Hana Ludmer, *Regional Organization and Management of Development: Israel and Galilee Case Study*, Publication on Problems of Regional Development, no. 32 (Rehovot: Settlement Study Center, 1982); Dov Rosen, *Seker Munitzipali* [Municipal Survey: Jewish Cities and Local Councils] (Jerusalem: Ministry of the Interior, 1968) (Hebrew); B. Sharon, "Agudai Kolaleni le-Shituf Azori" [Federation for Overall Regional Cooperation], *Davar Shilton HaMakomi* (August–September 1968); R. Weitz, et al., *Regional Cooperation in Israel*, Publication on Problems of Regional Development, no. 1 (Rehovot Study Center, 1966); and E. Cohen and E. Leshem, *Survey of Regional Cooperation in Three Regions of Collective Settlements*, Publications on Problems of Regional Development, no. 2 (Rehovot Study Center, 1969).

26. Erik Cohen, *The City in Zionist Ideology* (Jerusalem: Institute of Urban and Regional Studies of the Eliezer Kaplan School of Urban and Social Sciences, 1970).

27. See David Ben-Gurion's speeches on pluralism in the 1930s and statism in the 1950s in *Rebirth and Destiny of Israel*, edited and translated under the supervision of Mordecai Nurock (New York: Philosophical Library, 1954).

28. Tom Bowder, *Army in the Service of the State* (Tel Aviv: University Publishing Projects, 1975); Edward Luttwak and Dan Horowitz, *The Israel Army* (London: Allen Lane, 1975); Amos Perlmutter, *Politics and the Military in Israel* (London: Frank Cass, 1978); and Zeev Schiff, *A History of the Israeli Army, 1870–1974* (San Francisco: Straight Arrow Books, 1974).

## 5. The Local Dimension in Israeli Politics

1. Shevach Weiss, "Local Government in Israel: A Study of Its Leadership" (Ph.D. diss., the Hebrew University of Jerusalem, 1968); Yehoshua Freudenheim, *Government in Israel* (Dobbs Ferry, N.Y.: Oceana Publications, 1967), chap. 9; Chaim Kalchheim, "Iryat Yerushaliyim ve Misradai ha Memshela Perek be Yechisai Giomlin ben HaShilton haMercazi le Vain HaShilton HaMekomi" [A Case of Relations between Central and Local Government Municipality of Jerusalem and the Government Ministries] (Ph.D. diss., the Hebrew University of Jerusalem, 1976) (Hebrew); Eliezer Don-Yehiya, *Sherutim Datiyim V'Politiqua: HaKamatan V'Irgunan shel HaMoetzot HaDatiot B'Yisrael* [*Religious Services and Politics: The Establishing and Organization of the Religious Councils in Israel*] (Ramat Gan and Jerusalem: Bar Ilan University Institute of Local Government and Jerusalem Center for Public Affairs, 1984); Fred Lazin, "Welfare Policy Formation in Israel: The Policy Role of the Local Agency," Paper delivered at the 1979 annual meeting of the American Political Science Association, Washington, D.C.; Daniel J. Elazar, "The Compound Structure of Public Service Delivery Systems in Israel," in Vincent Ostrom and Francis Pennel Bish, eds., *Comparing Urban Public Service Delivery Systems* (Beverly Hills: Sage Publications, 1977), pp. 47–82, and "Local Government as an Integrating Factor in Israeli Society," in Michael Curtis and Mordecai S. Chertoff, eds., *Israel: Social Structure and Change* (New Brunswick: Transaction Books, 1973), pp. 5–26.

2. Emanuel Guttman, *The Politics of Israel Local Government* (Milan: Edizioni di Communita, 1963) and *The Development of Local Government in Palestine* (New York: Columbia University, 1958); J. AvRazi, "History of Israel's Local Government," *International Seminar for Local Government Administration* (ISLGA), vol. 1 (Jerusalem: Ministry for Foreign Affairs Department for International Cooperation; Ministry of the Interior Department for Local Government—Israel Union of Local Authorities, 1962); Shmuel Steven Adler and Arie Hecht, "Local Autonomy in Israel," *Public Administration in Israel and Abroad* (1970), pp. 35–47; Matityahu Adler, "Local Government in Israel," *P.A. in Israel and Abroad* (1960), vol. 1, pp. 78–82.

3. Weiss, "Local Government"; Guttman, *Israel Local Government*; Elazar, "Delivery Systems"; and S. N. Eisenstadt, *Israeli Society* (London: Weidenfeld and Nicolson, 1967).

4. Harold F. Alderfer, *Local Government in Developing Countries* (New York: McGraw Hill, 1964); Marvin H. Bernstein, *The Politics of Israel: The First Decade of Statehood* (Princeton: Princeton University Press, 1957); W. Hoven and A. Van der Elshout, *Local Government in Selected Countries: Ceylon, Israel, Japan* (New York: United Nations, 1963); and Edwin Samuel, *British Traditions in the Administration of Israel* (London: Valentine Mitchell, 1957).

5. Erik Cohen, "Development Towns—The Social Dynamics of 'Planted' Urban Communities in Israel," in S. Eisenstadt, R. Bar-Yosef, and C. Adler, eds., *Integration and Development in Israel* (Jerusalem: Israel Universities Press, 1970); Myron J. Aronoff, "Development Towns in Israel," in Michael Curtis and Mordecai Chertoff, eds., *Israel: Social Structure and Change* (New Brunswick: Transaction Books, 1973); Erika Spiegel, *New Towns in Israel* (Stuttgart/Bern: Karl Kramer Verlag, 1966); Myron J. Aronoff, *Frontier Town: The Politics of Community-Building in Israel* (Manchester: Manchester University Press, 1973).

6. Mattiyahu Adler, "Central Government or Local Self-Government," *Hamihal, The Public Administrator's Quarterly in Israel* (1956); Yehezkel Dror and Emanuel Guttman, *The Government of Israel* (Jerusalem: The Hebrew University of Jerusalem, 1961); Kalcheim "Iryat Yerushaliyim"; Edwin Samuel, "Local Government in Israel," *Israel Youth Horizon*, no. 4 (November–December 1953); and Szewach Wiess, *Haifa; Mitziot, Mevucha ve Etgar* [Haifa: Reality, Confusion, and

Challenge] (Haifa: "Rentres," 1973) (Hebrew).

7. Wiess, "Local Government"; Guttman, *Israel Local Government;* Bernstein, *Politics of Israel;* Roy David Elston, *Israel: The Making of a Nation* (London: Oxford University Press, 1963); and Oscar Kraines, *Government and Politics in Israel* (Boston: Houghton, Mifflin Co., 1961).

8. Henry E. Baker, *Legal System of Israel* (Jerusalem: Israel Universities Press, 1968), pp. 153–59; Moshe Gat, *Nitonai Yesod leMivneh haRishiot haMekomiot* [Basic Data on the Structure of Local Authorities] (Ramat Gan: Bar Ilan University Institute of Local Government, 1976) (Hebrew); Zeev Meljon, *Towns and Villages* (Tel Aviv: Union of Local Authorities in Israel, 1966); and Dov Rosen, "The Amalgamation of Small Local Authorities in Israel," *Public Administration in Israel and Abroad, 1962,* vol. 3, pp. 59–70.

9. Efraim Torgovnik and Shevah Weiss, "Local Non-party Political Organizations in Israel," *Western Political Quarterly* 25 (June 1972): 305–22.

10. Lior Martins and Chaim Hoffman "Igudai 'Arim B'Yisrael" [Federations of Cities in Israel] (Jerusalem: Ministry of the Interior, 1981) (Hebrew).

11. M. Amiaz, "Iggudai HaAshiot HaMakomiot V'Hasherutim HaTechnim" [Federations of Local Authorities and Technical Services], *Davar HaShilton HaMakomi* (June–July 1971): 6–8 (Hebrew); and Zeev Meljon, "Union of Local Authorities," in *ISLGA,* vol. 1.

12. For a case study, see Aronoff, *Frontier Town.*

13. R. M. Kramer, *Community Development in Israel and the Netherlands* (Berkeley and Los Angeles: University of California Press, 1970); Robert A. Rosenbloom, "The Politics of the Neighborhood Movement," *South Atlantic Urban Studies* 4(1979):149–63.

14. Daniel J. Elazar et al., *Project Renewal: An Introduction to the Issues and Actors* (Jerusalem: Jerusalem Center for Public Affairs, 1980); Daniel J. Elazar, Paul E. King, and Orli HaCohen, *The Extent, Focus, and Impact of Diaspora Involvement in Project Renewal* (Jerusalem: Jerusalem Center for Public Affairs, 1983). This evaluation was commissioned by the International Evaluation Committee for Project Renewal on behalf of the Jewish Agency for Israel and the government of Israel; Naomi Carmon and Moshe Hill, eds., *Neighborhood Rehabilitation in Israel,* Research Report no. 1 (Haifa: Samuel Neaman Institute for Advanced Studies in Science and Technology—Technion-Israel Institute of Technology, 1979); Moshe Katzav, *Chevra V'Calcala B'Schunot* [Society and Economy in Project Renewal] (Ramat Gan: Bar Ilan University Institute of Local Government, 1983) (Hebrew); Ginni Walsh, "Is Renewal Renewing," *Israel Economist* (June 1982): 21–36.

15. *Reforma Municipalit be Arai Gush Dan* [Municipal Reform in the Dan Region], 8 vols. (Jerusalem: Ministry of the Interior, 1968) (Hebrew); *Shilton Mekomi Be Yisrael* (Jerusalem: State Commission for Local Government Affairs, 1981); Rosen, *Seker Munitzipali.* See also Internal Reports and Memoranda of the State Commission on Local Government (Sanbar Commission), 1978–1980.

16. Nezer Menuhin, "Concepts and Strategies for Analyzing and Handling Problems of Critical Region—The Land of the Galilee" (Ph.D. diss., Ramat Gan: Bar Ilan University, 1980) (Hebrew): S. M. Katz, N. Menuchin, and Hana Ludmer, *Regional Organization and Management of Development: Israel and Galilee Case Study,* Publication on Problems of Regional Development, no. 32 (Rehovot: Settlement Study Center, 1977).

17. Cf. Daniel J. Elazar, *Mearechet HaYachasim Ben HaReshuyot HaMekomiot V'Hashilton HaMerkazi B'Yisrael* [The System of Relations between the Local Authorities and the Central Government in Israel] (Ramat Gan: Bar Ilan University Institute of Local Government, 1983) (Hebrew); Kalchheim, "Iryat Yerushaliyim."

18. Cf. Daniel J. Elazar et al., *Project Renewal: The View from the Neighborhoods* (Jerusalem: Jerusalem Center for Public Affairs, 1979).

19. Cf. Asher Arian, ed., *The Elections in Israel, 1969* (Jerusalem: Jerusalem Academic Press, 1972); Daniel J. Elazar, "The Local Elections: Sharpening the Trend toward Territorial Democracy," in Asher Arian, ed., *The Elections in Israel, 1973* (Jerusalem: Jerusalem Academic Press, 1975); unpublished analysis of the 1978 local elections by Moshe Gat, files of the Jerusalem Center for Public Affairs; Avraham Lantzman, "The 1983 Israeli Municipal Elections: Mixed Trends and Minor Upsets," *Jerusalem Letter,* no. 68 (December 1983).

20. Cf. Shlomo Deshen, *Immigrant Voters in Israel* (Manchester: Manchester University Press, 1970), and Alex Weingrod, *Reluctant Pioneers—Village Development in Israel* (Ithaca: Cornell University Press, 1966).

21. It is a sign of that city's character that there is no good study of Tel Aviv. Lahat's role must be traced through the press coverage of his administration.

22. Weiss, *Haifa.*

23. Cf. Meron Benveniste, *Jerusalem: Polarized Community* (Jerusalem: West Bank Project, 1983); Henry Cattan, *Jerusalem* (London: Croom Helm, 1981); Saul Bernard Cohen, *Jerusalem Undivided* (New York: Herzl Press, 1980); Daniel J. Elazar and Simcha Werner, *The Reunification of Jerusalem* (forthcoming); Reuven Goldberg, "The Spatial Division of Internal Migration in Jerusalem, 1972–1978" (Master's thesis, the Hebrew University of Jerusalem, 1979); Annette Hochstein, *Metropolitan Trends in the Jerusalem Area* (Jerusalem: West Bank Project, 1983); and Joel Kramer, *Jerusalem, Problems and Prospects* (New York: Praeger, 1980).

## 6. Serving the Public in an Emergent Society

1. "Ideology and Economic Policy," *Israel Economist* (March 1982): 7–8, 18; David Kochav, "Israel's Defense Burden Grows despite the Peace with Egypt," *Jerusalem Letter,* no. 48 (10 June 1982); Assaf Razin, "Meshek Israel: 1983" [Israel Economy: 1983], *Rivon LeCalcala,* no. 119 (January 1984): 834–37 (Hebrew); and Benjamin Rubin, "The Political Economy of Israel in Early 1984: An Assessment," *Jerusalem Letter/Viewpoints,* no. 31 (11 March 1984).

2. *Local Government in Israel* (Jerusalem: State Commission for Local Government Affairs, 1981); Ometz Morag, *Mimoon HaMemshalah be-Yisrael: Hitpathut ve-Baayot* [Government Finance in Israel: Development and Problems] (Jerusalem: The Hebrew University of Jerusalem, 1967), chaps. 1 and 9 (Hebrew); Z. Meljon, *Local Government Finance in Israel* (Tel Aviv: Union of Local Authorities in Israel, 1969); Shevach Weiss, "Iyvatim Bshitat HaMimoun HaMunitsippalit" [Distortions in the System of Municipal Finance], *Dvar Shilton HaMakomi* (October/November 1974).

3. Myron J. Aronoff, *Frontier Town: The Politics of Community Building in Israel* (Manchester: Manchester University Press, 1974); Shlomo Deshen, *Immigrant Voters in Israel* (Manchester: Manchester University Press, 1970); Z. Gitelman, *Becoming Israelis: Political Resocialization of Soviet and American Immigrants* (New York: Praeger, 1982); Moshe Shokeid, *The Dual Heritage* (Manchester: Manchester University Press, 1971); and Judith T. Shuval, *Immigrants on the Threshold* (New York: Atherton Press, 1963).

4. Eva Etzion-Halevy, *Political Manipulation and Administrative Power—A Comparative Study* (London: Routledge and Kegan Paul, 1979) and *Political Culture in Israel* (New York: Praeger, 1977).

5. Deborah Bernstein, "Contradictions and Protests in the Process of Nation-Building: The Black Panthers of Israel: 1971–72 (Ph.D. diss., University of Sussex, 1976); Erik Cohen, "The Black Panthers and Israeli Society," *Jewish Journal of Sociology* 14, no. 1 (1972): 93–109; Eva Etzioni-Halevy, "Protest Politics in the Israeli Democracy," *Political Science Quarterly* 90 (1975); 497–520; David J. Schnall, *Radical Dissent in Contemporary Israeli Politics* (New York: Praeger, 1979); and Lilly Weissbrod, "Protest and Dissidence in Israel," in Myron A. Aronoff, *Cross Currents*

*in Israeli Culture and Politics* (New Brunswick: Transaction Books, 1984). Shlomo Deshen, "Social Organization and Politics in Israeli Urban Quarters," *Jerusalem Quarterly* 22 (1982): 21–37; Sam N. Lehman-Wilzig, "Public Protest and Systematic Stability in Israel: 1960–1979," in S. Lehman-Wilzig and B. Susser, eds., *Comparative Jewish Politics: Public Life in Israel and the Diaspora* (Ramat Gan: Bar Ilan University Press, 1981), and "Conflict and Communication: Public Protest in Israel, 1950–1982," in S. Cohen and E. Don-Yehiya, eds., *Comparative Jewish Politics*, vol. 2 (Ramat Gan: Bar Ilan University Press, 1984).

6. See, for example, David Pines and Oded Hochman, *Costs of Adjustment and the Spacial Pattern of a Growing, Open City* (Ramat Aviv: Tel Aviv University, 1980).

7. For example, Efraim Torgovnik, "Local Policy Determinants in a Centralist System," *Publius* 7, no. 2 (1977): 61–84, and "A Movement for Change in a State System," in H. Penniman, ed., *Israel at the Polls* (Washington, D.C.: American Enterprise Institute, 1979). Moshe Hazani, for example, has shown the negative impact of the unilateral intervention of the Ministry of Housing in one Israeli community, which theoretically is too small to plan its own housing (in Israel that is a function assumed by the central government in any case) but which undoubtedly would have done a better job than the bureaucratized intervention of a ministry whose plans at that time were primarily the products of theoretical considerations and current architectural styles, without significant reference to the site or community involved. Cf. Moshe Hazani, *Anatomia shel Kehillah: Shikum Memossad ke Neged Shikum Mekomi* [The Anatomy of a Local Community] (Ramat Gan: Bar Ilan University Institute of Local Government, 1976) (Hebrew), and "The Dinosaur and the Housing Problem," *Jerusalem Letter*, no. 31 (27 August 1980).

8. Cf. Steven E. Plaut, "Israel at an Economic Crossroads," *Midstream* 27, no. 5 (1983): 7–10; "Is Israel Economically Viable?" *Midstream* 28 (no. 1) (1982): 6–9; and "Kalkalat Tzad ha-Hertza be-HaMeshek ha-Israeli" [Supply Side Economics in the Israeli Economy], *Rivon LeCalcala*, no. 115 (December 1982): 372–77 (Hebrew).

9. Moshe Sanbar, *The Political Economy of Israel, 1948–1982* (Jerusalem: Jerusalem Center for Public Affairs, 1984).

10. Cf. Yosef Criden and Saadia Gelb, *The Kibbutz Experience: Dialogue in Kfar Blum* (New York: Schocken Books, 1976); and Saadia Gelb, "The Kibbutz in Israel, 1983–1984," *Jerusalem Letter/Viewpoints*, no. 35 (July 1984).

11. Giora Goldberg and Sam Lehman-Wilzig, "Religious Protest and Police Reaction in a Theo-democracy: Israel, 1950–1979," *Journal of Church and State* 25, no. 3 (1983): 491–505, and Yehuda Prag, "Training in the Israel Police," *Public Administration in Israel and Abroad, 1968*, vol. 9, pp. 85–90.

12. P. Elman, "The Israel Ombudsman: An Appraisal," *Israel Law Review* 10, no. 3 (1975): 293–323; Emanuel Guttman, "The Participation of Citizens in Political Life," *International Social Science Journal* 12, no. 1 (1960): 59–69; S. Levy, "The Cylindrical Structure of Political Involvement," *Social Indicators Research* 6, no. 4 (1979):41–64; David Nachmias and David Rosenbloom, *Citizens and Administrators in Israel* (New York: St. Martin's, 1978); and Yael Yishai, "Interest Groups in Israel," *Jerusalem Quarterly* 20 (1979): 36–48.

13. Walter I. Ackerman, "Back to School: A Look at Israeli Education," *Jerusalem Letter*, no. 23 (18 September 1979); J. S. Bentwich, *Education in Israel* (London; 1965); Rachel Elboin-Dror, "Conflict and Consensus in Educational Policy-making in Israel," *International Journal of Political Education* 4, no. 3: 219–32; Judith Tzivia Fine, "Education in an Israeli Immigrant Town" (Ph.D. diss., University of Pittsburgh, 1978); and Stephen Goldstein, "Free High School Education Comes to Israel," *Jerusalem Letter*, no. 9 (30 April 1978).

14. Walter I. Ackerman, "Reforming Israeli Education in Israel," in Michael Curtis and Mordechai S. Chertoff, eds., *Israel: Social Structure and Change* (New Brunswick: Transaction Books, 1973); Arnold Lewis, "Educational Policy and Social

Inequality," *Jerusalem Quarterly* 12 (Summer 1979): 101–111; Elad Peled, "The Hidden Agenda of Educational Policy in Israel: The Interrelationship between the Political System and the Educational System" (Ph.D. diss., Columbia University, 1979); Shimon Reshef, "National Aims and Education Policy," *Jerusalem Quarterly* 20 (Summer 1981): 97–104; and Hindy L. Schachter, "Educational Institutions and Political Coalition: The Case of Israel," *Comparative Educational Review* 16, no. 3 (October 1972): 462–73.

15. Elijah Bortniker, "Multiple Trends in Israel's Jewish Elementary School System: Investigation into the Origin, Development, and Present Status of Israel's School System and Its Political Subdivisions Known as 'Trends'" (Ph.D. diss., New York University, 1954); and Aharon F. Kleinburger, *Society, Schools, and Progress* (London: Pergamon Press, 1969).

16. Reyad Fahmi Al-Agha, "Arab-Jewish Public Education in Israel from 1948 to 1967 and Implications for Palestinian Arab Minority Education" (Ph.D. diss., University of Kansas, 1978); and S. N. Eisenstadt and Yochanan Peres, *Some Problems of Educating a National Minority: A Study of Israeli Education for the Arabs* (Washington, D.C.: U.S. Department of Health, Education, and Welfare, 1968).

17. Haim Gordon, "Realizing Martin Buber's Educational Philosophy: An Examination of Buber's Educational Thought and Its Relation to Kibbutz Education" (Ph.D. diss., George Peabody College for Teachers of Vanderbilt University, 1975); and Don Weintraub, Moshe Lissak, and Yael Azmon, *Moshava, Kibbutz and Moshav* (Ithaca: Cornell University Press, 1969).

18. The best study of this change is Eliezer Don-Yehiya, "Shituf ve-Conflict ben Machanot Politiim: HaMachanei HaDati ve Tnuat HaAvodat ve-Mashber Chinuch be-Yisrael" [Cooperation and Conflict between Political Camps: The Religious Camp and the Labor Movement and the Education Crisis in Israel] (Ph.D. diss., the Hebrew University of Jerusalem, 1977).

19. Fanny Ginor, "Analysis of Lower Income Groups in Israel," *Israel Year Book, 1975,* pp. 181–96; Eliezer D. Jaffe, "Reorganization of the Social Welfare Network in Israel: Proposed Conceptual Frameworks," *Jewish Journal of Sociology* 53, no. 4 (1977): 362–65; Fred Lazin, "The Effects of Administrative Linkages in Implementation: Welfare Policy in Israel," *Policy Sciences* 12 no. 2 (1980): 193–214; and Moshe Sanbar, "Social Aspects of Fiscal Policy in Israel," *International Problems* 16, nos. 3–4 (1977): 92–97.

20. Marian Lief Palley, *Planned Localism in Israeli Politics: A Case Study of the Community Centers Movement* (Jerusalem: Jerusalem Institute for Federal Studies, 1979).

21. The Society's journal, *Israel Land and Nature,* describes its activities.

## 7. Religion and the Polity

1. For an up-to-date review of the situation in the contemporary Middle East, see Michael Curtis, ed., *Religion and Politics in the Middle East* (Boulder: Westview, 1981), and Eliezer Goldman, "Religious Issues in Israel's Political Life" (Jerusalem: World Zionist Organization, 1964), pp. 84–94.

2. Two general overviews of the relationship between religion and state in Israel, from diametrically opposed perspectives, are S. Z. Abramov, *Perpetual Dilemma* (Rutherford, N.J.: Fairleigh Dickinson University Press, 1976), and Zvi Yaron, "Religion in Israel," *American Jewish Year Book, 1976* (New York and Philadelphia: American Jewish Committee and Jewish Publication Society of America, 1975), vol. 76, pp. 41–90.

3. Cf. Yaron, "Religion in Israel."

4. The definitive study of Israel's civil religion to date is that of Charles S. Liebman and Eliezer Don-Yehiya, *Civil Religions in Israel: Traditional Religion and*

*Political Culture in the Jewish State* (Berkeley and Los Angeles: University of California Press, 1983).

5. Cf. Daniel J. Elazar, "Religion and Politics in the Begin Era," in Robert C. Freedman, ed., *Israel in the Begin Era* (New York: Praeger, 1983).

6. Liebman and Don-Yehiya, *Civil Religion*.

7. See Daniel J. Elazar, "The New Sadducees," *Midstream* 24 (August–September 1978): 20–25.

8. Eliezer Don-Yehiya, "Secularization, Negation, and Integration: Concept of Traditional Judaism in Zionist Socialism," *Kivunim* 8 (Summer 1980): 29–46 (Hebrew).

9. Cf. Menachem Friedman, *Hevrah ve. HaDat: HaOrthodoxiya Halo Tzionit be Eretz Yisrael, 1918–1936* [Society and Religion: The Non-Zionist Orthodoxy in Israel, 1918–1936] (Jerusalem: Yad Yithak Ben Tzvi, 1978).

10. *Tefutsot Israel-HaTnua le Yahadut Mitkadmot ve HaTnua HaMesoratit* [Reform and Conservative Judaism] 21, no. 3 (Fall 1983) (Hebrew).

11. David Canaani, *HaAliyah HaShniyah ha-Ovedet ve-Yachasah la-Oat ve-la-Masoret* [The Second Working Aliyah and Its Attitude to Religion and Tradition] (Tel Aviv: Sifriat Hapoalim, 1976) (Hebrew).

12. Arthur Hertzberg, *The Zionist Idea* (Garden City, N.Y.: Doubleday, 1959), pp. 402–403.

13. Abramov, *Perpetual Dilemma* p. 71.

14. Friedman, *Hevrah ve HaDat*.

15. Abramov, *Perpetual Dilemma*.

16. Canaani, *HaAliyah HaShniyah;* Adin Steinsalz, "Religion in the State of Israel," *Judaism* 22, no. 2 (1973): 140–50; and Yaron, "Religion in Israel."

17. Abramov, *Perpetual Dilemma*.

18. Cf. Avraham Shapria, principal editor, *The Seventh Day: Soldiers' Talk about the Six Day War* (London: Steimatzky's Agency in association with Andre Deutsch, 1967), and *Shlemot*, the journal of the kibbutz movement.

19. Cf. Janet Aviad, *Return to Judaism* (Chicago: University of Chicago Press, 1983).

20. Cf. Daniel J. Elazar, "The New Sadduccees," *Midstream* 24, no. 7 (August/September 1975): 20–25. For further discussion of the three camps, see Daniel J. Elazar, "Toward a Renewed Zionist Vision," *Forum* 26 (1977): 52–69.

## 8. Ashkenazim and Sephardim

1. S. N. Eisenstadt, *The Absorption of Immigrants* (London: Routledge and Kegan Paul, 1954); Raphael Patai, *Israel between East and West*, 2d ed. (Westport, Conn.: Greenwood Publishing Co., 1970); and David Ben Gurion, *Rebirth and Destiny of Israel* (New York: Philosophical Library, 1954); Judith T. Shuval, *Immigrants on the Threshold* (New York: Prentice Hall, 1963); Sammy Smooha, *Israel: Pluralism and Conflict* (Berkeley and Los Angeles: California University Press, 1978); Nissim Rejwan, "The Two Israels: A Study in Europocentrism," *Judaism* 16, no. 1 (Winter 1967):97–108; Shlomo A. Deshen, "Political Ethnicity and Cultural Ethnicity in Israel during the 1960s," in Abner Cohen, ed., *Urban Ethnicity* (London: Tavistock), pp. 281–309; and Lee Dutter, "Eastern and Western Jews: Ethnic Divisions in Israeli Society," *Middle East Journal* 31, no. 4 (1977):451–68.

2. Zvi Ankori, "Origins and History of Ashkenazi Jewry, *Forum*, nos. 46/47 (Fall/Winter 1982), pp. 149–75; Daniel J. Elazar, "Sephardim and Ashkenazim: The Classic and Romantic Traditions in Jewish Civilization," *Judaism* 33, no. 2 (Spring 1984):33–39; and Abraham Joshua Heschel, *The Earth Is the Lord's* (New York and Philadelphia: Harper and Row and Jewish Publication Society of America, 1950).

3. These are not exact figures, since the classification used in the Israeli census is European/American-born (which includes the Sephardic Jews of the Balkans and southern Europe), Asian/African-born, and Israeli-born, and after the second generation, the statistics do not identify individuals by ancestry, so at best we have approximations.

4. J. M. Rosenfeld and E. Morris, "Socially Deprived Jewish Families in Israel," in A. Jarus et al. eds., *Children and Families in Israel: Some Mental Health Perspectives* (New York, 1970), pp. 427–64; Dov Weintraub and Associates, *Immigration and Social Change* (Jerusalem: Israel University Press, 1971); Fanny Ginor, *Socio-Economic Disparities in Israel. Part I: Development and Trends* (Tel Aviv: Tel Aviv University, n.d.); S. N. Eisenstadt, Rivka Bar Yosef, and Chaim Adler, eds., *Integration and Development in Israel* (Jerusalem: University Press, 1970).

5. See, for example, the articles by Amos Oz, "Has Israel Altered Its Vision?" *New York Times Magazine*, 11 July 1982, and Shlomo Avineri, "The Beirut Massacres and the Two Political Cultures of Israel," *International Herald Tribune*, 14 October 1982. Oz is a prominent Israeli novelist, kibbutz member, and left-wing intellectual. Avineri is a prominent political scientist and former director general of the foreign ministry under the previous Labor government.

6. Daniel J. Elazar, "Israel's New Majority," *Commentary* 75, no. 3 (March 1983): 33–39, and "A New Look at the Two Israels," *Midstream* 24, no.4 (March 1978): pp. 3–10.

7. Harry I. Shapiro, *The Jewish People: A Biological History* (Paris: UNESCO, 1960); Michael Inbar and Chaim Adler, *Ethnic Integration in Israel* (New Brunswick: Transaction Books, 1977).

8. My own extensive contacts and conversations convinced me of this fact beyond any shadow of a doubt. In fact, the only people whom I met who were less concerned were a group of Israelis originally from the English-speaking countries—presumably the most "Western" of all. Cf. Daniel J. Elazar, "Challenging Begin from Within: The Response of the Religious Parties and the Sephardim to the Beirut Massacre," *Jerusalem Letter*, no. 52 (7 October 1982), and David Clayman, "Israel in the Wake of the Beirut Massacre: Ten Days in Search of Answers," *Jerusalem Letter*, no. 53 (15 October 1982).

9. For a more complete discussion of this question, see Daniel J. Elazar, *The Sephardim Today* (New York: Rossel Books, forthcoming); and "Sephardim and Ashkenazim: The Classic and Romantic Traditions in Judaism," *Judaism* 33 (Spring 1984): 146–59; Yochanan Peres, "Ethnic Differences in Israel," *Megamoth* (January 1974); Judah Matras, *Social Change in Israel* (Chicago: Aldine, 1965).

10. See Elazar, "Israel's New Majority." These figures were calculated from the surveys conducted by the Israeli government and the Jewish Agency to identify neighborhoods for Project Renewal.

11. See *Kipuach Vtipuach*, vol. 2, Bibliography published by the Ministry of Education, Jerusalem, 1983.

12. Adler and Inbar, *Ethnic Integration*.

13. Daniel J. Elazar, *The Place of the Zionist Vision and the State of Israel in the Sephardic World* (Jerusalem: Study Circle on Diaspora Jewry under the auspices of the President of Israel, 1983); Michel Abitol, "Zionist Activity in North Africa Up to the End of the Second World War," *Pe'amim* 2 (1979): 65–91 (Hebrew); David Benveniste, *From Salonica to Jerusalem: My Life* (Jerusalem: Sephardic and Oriental Community Publications, 1981) (Hebrew); Israel Mishael, *Between Afghanistan and Eretz Israel*, edited by Issachar Katzir (Jerusalem: Sephardic Community Committee, 1981) (Hebrew); and Dan V. Segre, *A Crisis of Identity: Israel and Zionism* (Oxford: Oxford University Press, 1980).

14. Daniel J. Elazar, ed., *Kinship and Consent* (Ramat Gan: Turtledove Publish-

ing, 1981), and Daniel J. Elazar and Stuart Cohen, *The Jewish Polity* (Bloomington: Indiana University Press, 1985).

15. Daniel J. Elazar, "Local Government as an Integrating Factor in Israeli Society," in Michael Curtis and Mordecai Chertoff, eds., *Israel: Social Structure and Change* (New Brunswick: Transaction Books, 1973); Mark Iris and Avraham Shama, "Political Participation and Ethnic Conflict in Israel," in Gregory Mahler, ed., *Readings on the Israeli Political System: Structures and Processes* (Washington, D.C.: University Press of America, 1983); and Szewach Weiss, "Local Government in Israel: A Study of Its Leadership" (Ph.D. diss., the Hebrew University of Jerusalem, 1968). See also the Jerusalem Center for Public Affairs files on local government in Israel. In 1965, only 20 percent of the members of local councils in the large and medium-size cities (the older settlements) were drawn from among Sephardim, despite the fact that the latter constituted 60 percent of the population in that group. Even so, 37 percent of the deputy mayors of those cities were drawn from among them, up from 11 percent in 1955.

16. Shlomo Avineri, "Political Trends under the Begin Government," *Dissent* 27, no. 1: 27–35; Dan Caspi, Avraham Diskin, and Emanuel Guttman, eds., *The Roots of Begin's Success: The 1981 Elections* (London: Croom Helm, 1983); Louis Guttman, "The Vote, Yesterday and Today," *The Jerusalem Post* (26 August 1977); Hanna Herzog, "The Ethnic Lists in Election 1981: An Ethnic Political Identity?" in Asher Arian, ed., *The Election in Israel 1981* (Tel Aviv: Ramot Publishing Company, 1983); Michal Shamir and Asher Arian, "The Ethnic Vote in Israel's 1981 Elections," *Electoral Studies* 1, no. 3: 315–31.

17. Howard Penniman and Daniel J. Elazar, *Israel at the Polls, 1981* (Bloomington: Indiana University Press, 1985).

## 9. Israel, the Arabs, and the Territories

1. Yehoyada Haim, "Zionist Attitudes toward the Palestinian Arabs" (Ph.D. diss., Georgetown University, 1975); Ben Halpern, *The Idea of the Jewish State*, 2d ed. (Cambridge, Mass.: Harvard University Press, 1969): Albert M. Hyamson, *Palestine under the Mandate, 1920–1949* (London: Methuen, 1950); Howard Sachar, *A History of Israel: From the Rise of Zionism to Our Time* (Philadelphia: Jewish Publication Society of America, 1976); and Chana Sosevsky, "Attitudes of Zionist Intellectuals to the Arab Population in Palestine as Expressed in the Literature before the Young Turk Revolution of 1908" (Ph.D. diss., New York University, 1980).

2. Shlomo Avineri, ed., *Israel and the Palestinians: Reflections on the Clash of Two National Movements* (New York: St. Martin's Press, 1971); Esco Foundation for Palestine, Inc., *Palestine: A Study of Jewish, Arab, and British Policies*, 2 vols. (New Haven: Yale University Press, 1947); Neville J. Mandel, *The Arabs and Zionism before World War I* (Berkeley and Los Angeles: University of California Press, 1976); Moshe Maoz, ed., *Palestinian Arab Politics* (Jerusalem: Jerusalem Academic Press, 1975) and *Studies in Palestine during the Ottoman Period* (Jerusalem: Magnes Press, 1975); and Shmuel Sandler and Hillel Frisch, *Israel, The Palestinians, and the West Bank* (Lexington, Mass.: Lexington Books, 1984).

3. Theodore Herzl, *Altneuland—Old-New Land*, translated by Paula Arnold (Haifa: Haifa Publishing Co., 1960).

4. Ann Mosley Lesch, "The Frustration of a Nationalist Movement: Palestinian Arab Politics, 1917–1939" (Ph.D. diss., Columbia University, 1973); and Yehoshua Porat, *The Emergence of the Palestinian-Arab National Movement, 1918–1929* (London: Frank Cass, 1974) and *The Palestinian Arab National Movement, 1929–1939* (London: Frank Cass, 1978).

5. Personal interviews with Sephardic notables of the time and Eliahu Eliachar.

6. Adnan Mohammad Abu Ghazaleh, "Arab Cultural Nationalism in Palestine,

1919–1948" (Ph.D. diss., New York University, 1967); Walter Laquer, *A History of Zionism* (New York: Schocken Books, 1976); Oscar Rabinowicz, *Fifty Years of Zionism: A Historical Analysis of Dr. Weizmann's "Trial and Error"* (London: Anscombe, 1951).

7. It should be noted that HaShomer HaTzair, later the Mapam party, at the extreme left of the Labor Zionist camp, advocated a binational state by the mid-1920s and continued to do so until the 1940s. A major resolution to that effect was adopted formally at the founding conference of the Kibbutz Artzi HaShomer HaTzair in 1927. Mapam since has abandoned that position for a partitionist one, but with a confederal option.

8. David Ben-Gurion, "Jewish Labor: The Origin of Settlement," in *Rebirth and Destiny of Israel*, edited and translated under the supervision of Mordecai Nurock (New York: Philosophical Library, 1954); A. D. Gordon, "Labor the Core of the Matter" in *The Second Aliyah* (New York: Zionist Youth Council, 1955), pp. 29–35; and Anita Shapira, "The Struggle for 'Jewish Labor' in the Yishuv Period," in S. Cohen and E. Don-Yehiya, eds., *Comparative Jewish Politics—Vol. II: Conflict and Consensus in Jewish Political Life* (Ramat Gan: Bar Ilan University Press, 1984).

9. Berl Katznelson, the ideologist of Mapai, was a steadfast opponent of partition, and Ben-Gurion accepted it reluctantly. See Anita Shapira, *Berl* (Tel Aviv: Am Oved Publishers, 1980) (Hebrew).

10. Moshe Dayan, *Moshe Dayan: The Story of My Life* (New York: Williams Morrow and Co., 1976), and on Shimon Peres, see Matti Golan, *Shimon Peres: A Biography*, translated from the Hebrew by Ina Friedman (London: Weidenfeld and Nicolson, 1982).

11. Allon's original plan was based on the military technology of the Six Day War, which was still a generation behind that of the weaponry used in Vietnam. Moreover, it assumed a clear division of areas of Jewish and Arab settlement in the administered territories. The post-1967 years brought about a radical transformation of the military weaponry introduced to the Middle East, so that, rather than lagging behind, both sides came to possess and use the most advanced weapons systems in the world. New policies had to be designed with that fact in mind. Also, for reasons Allon rejected on a political level but was not entirely out of sympathy with on an emotional one, as the areas of Jewish settlement became increasingly intermixed with those of the Arab population, he recognized that, on a practical basis, those settlements would not be evacuated. Finally, and perhaps most important for him, the integration of the territories and their populations within the Israeli economy, which brought prosperity to both peoples, had to be taken into account. He concluded that the Allon Plan should be implemented with regard to separating Jewish and Arab territories, but that the two entities should be confederated somehow.

12. Menachem Begin, *The Revolt* (Jerusalem: Steimatsky, 1972); J. Schechtman and Y. Ben Ari, *History of the Revisionist Movement, Vol. I: 1925–1930* (Tel Aviv: Hadar, 1970); and Ya'akov Shavit, "The Attitude of the Revisionist Movement towards the Arab Nationalist Movement," *Forum* no. 30/31 (Summer 1971): 100–14.

13. Menachem Begin, *Self-Rule for Palestinian Arabs, Residents of Judea, Samaria, and the Gaza District Which Will Be Instituted upon the Establishment of Peace*, Knesset speech, 28/12/77.

14. Eliezer Don-Yehiya, "The Politics of the Religious Parties in Israel," in S. Lehman-Wilzig and B. Susser, eds., *Comparative Jewish Politics: Public Life in Israel and the Diaspora* (Ramat Gan: Bar Ilan University Press, 1981); Amnon Rubinstein, *MeHerzel ad Gush Emmunim U'behazarah* [From Herzl to Gush Emmunim and Back] (Jerusalem: Shocken, 1980); Harold Fisch, *The Zionist Revolution: A New Perspective* (London: Wiedenfeld and Nicolson, 1978); Eliezer Don-Yehiya, "Jewish Orthodoxy, Zionism, and the State of Israel," *Jerusalem Quarterly* 31 (1984): 10.

15. Ian Lustick, "Israel's Arab Minority in the Begin Era," in Robert Freedman,

ed., *Israel in the Begin Era* (New York: Praeger, 1982); and Moshe Shokeid, "Political Parties and the Arab Electorate in an Israeli City," in E. Marx, ed., *A Composite Portrait of Israel* (London: Academic Press, 1980).

16. Jacob M. Landau, *The Arabs in Israel: A Political Study* (Oxford: Oxford University Press, 1972), and "The Arab Vote," in D. Caspi, A. Diskin, and E. Guttman, eds., *The Roots of Begin's Success* (London: Croom Helm, 1983); Ian Lustick, *Arabs in the Jewish State: Israel's Control of a National Minority* (Austin: University of Texas Press, 1980); Sammy Smooha, *The Orientation and Politicization of the Arab Minority in Israel* (Haifa: Arab Jewish Center, 1980); and S. Smooha, and Ora Cibluski, *Social Research on Arabs in Israel, 1948–1977* (Ramat Gan: Turtledove, 1978).

17. For an overview of the emergence of a Palestinian identity, see Yehoshafat-Harkavy, "The Evolution of the Palestinian Movement," in George Gruen, ed., *The Palestinians in Perspective* (New York: Institute of Human Relations Press, 1982).

18. Gabriel Ben-Dor, ed., *The Palestinians and the Middle East Conflict* (Ramat Gan: Turtledove, 1978); Noam Chomsky, "Israeli Jews and Palestinian Arabs: Reflections on a National Conflict," *Holy Cross Quarterly* 5, no. 2 (1972): 7–23; Paul Y. Hammond and Sidney S. Alexander, eds., *Political Dynamics in the Middle East* (New York: American Elsevier Publishing Co., 1972); Yehoshafat Harkabi, *Arab Attitudes to Israel* (Jerusalem: Keter, 1972); Walter Laquer, ed., *The Israel-Arab Reader* (New York: Bantam Books, 1971); and Sandler and Frisch, *Israel, the Palestinians and the West Bank*.

19. Israel Kimshi, Benjamin Heyman, and Claud Gabriel, *Jerusalem, 1967–1975: A Socio-economic Survey* (Jerusalem: Hebrew University, Institute for Urban and Regional Studies, Jerusalem Studies Center, April 1976); David Shahar, "Trends in the Metropolitan Development of Jerusalem," in *Jerusalem, Discussion Paper no. 2* (Jerusalem: Jerusalem Research Institute, 1980), pp. 60–61; Saul B. Cohen, *Jerusalem Undivided* (New York: Herzl Press, 1980); Annette Hochstein, *Metropolitan Trends in the Jerusalem Area* (Jerusalem: West Bank Project, 1983).

20. Cf. Daniel J. Elazar, ed., *Governing Peoples and Territories* (Philadelphia: Institute for the Study of Human Issues, 1982).

21. Cf. Daniel J. Elazar, ed., *Judea, Samaria, and Gaza: Views on the Present and Future* (Washington, D.C.: American Enterprise Institute, 1982).

22. Cf. Daniel J. Elazar et al., *Handbook of Federal and Autonomy Arrangements* (forthcoming).

23. Cf. Sandler and Frisch, *Israel, the Palestinians and the West Bank*.

## 10. An Emergent Political Culture

1. The concept of political culture is discussed in Gabriel Almond and Sidney Verba, *The Civic Culture*, (Princeton: Princeton University Press, 1963); Lucian Pye and Sidney Verba, eds., *Political Culture* (Princeton: Princeton University Press, 1965); Daniel J. Elazar, *American Federalism: A View from the States* (New York: Thomas Y. Crowell, 1966), chap. 4; and *Political Culture, Workings Kits no. 1 and 2* (Philadelphia: Center for the Study of Federalism, Temple University, 1969). Leonard J. Fein presents one picture of Israel's political culture in chaps. 2 and 3 of *Politics in Israel* (Boston: Little, Brown and Co., 1967).

2. Almond and Verba, *Civic Culture*, discuss this subject political culture. See also Edward Banfield, *The Moral Basis of a Backward Society* (Glencoe, Illinois: Free Press, 1958).

3. See Gabriel A. Almond, "Comparative Political Systems," in *The Journal of Politics* 18 (1956):391–409, for suggestive comments on the political culture of continental Europe. An expanded exposition of his thesis can be found in Almond and Verba, *Civic Culture*.

4. The fullest discussions of Jewish political culture presently available are Daniel J. Elazar, ed., *Kinship and Consent: The Jewish Political Tradition and Its Contemporary Manifestations* (Washington: University Press of America and Center for Jewish Community Studies, 1982), and Daniel J. Elazar and Stuart A. Cohen, *The Jewish Polity: The Constitutional Organization of the Jewish People from Biblical Times to the Present* (Bloomington: Indiana University Press, 1985). The author has suggested ways in which it can be pursued in his bibliographic essays "The Pursuit of Community: The Literature of Jewish Public Affairs, 1965–1966," *American Jewish Year Book, 1967* (Philadelphia: American Jewish Committee and Jewish Publication Society of America, 1967), vol. 68; and his article "The Reconstitution of Jewish Communities in the Post-war Period," *Jewish Journal of Sociology* (December 1969) offers a good starting point for its investigation. See also Salo W. Baron, *The Jewish Community* (Philadelphia: Jewish Publication Society, 1942), 3 vols.; Irving Agus, "The Rights and Immunities of the Minority," in *Jewish Quarterly Review* 45: 120–29; Gedalia Alon, *Mekharim B'toldot Yisrael* [Research in Israeli History] (Tel Aviv, 1957–58), vol. 2, pp. 58–74; and Jacob Katz, *Tradition and Crisis* (New York: Free Press, 1961), chaps. 1–5.

5. The covenant, or federal, idea goes back to the very foundations of Jewish political culture in the Biblical period. The use of covenant forms to create political relationships was an ancient Near Eastern practice, as George E. Mendenhall has pointed out in "Covenant Forms in Israelite Tradition," *Biblical Archeologist* 17, no. 3 (July 1964): 50–76. The Israelites transformed the covenant principle from one that was used for quasi-feudal purposes between rules and polities into one used for federal purposes within polities. See, for example, S. J. Mackenzie, *Faith and History in the Old Testament* (New York: Macmillan Co., 1963), pp. 40–53, and John Bright, *A History of Israel* (Philadelphia: Westminster Press, 1956).

6. David Ben-Gurion, "Mission and Dedication," in *Rebirth and Destiny of Israel*, edited and translated from Hebrew under the supervision of Mordecai Nurock (New York: Philosophical Library, 1954).

7. Fein, *Politics in Israel*, describes the bureaucracy in chap. 5. An excellent description of the federal (in its social sense) character of the army is provided by S. L. A. Marshall in "Israel's Citizen Army," in *Swift Sword* (American Heritage Publishing Co., 1967), pp. 132–33. See also Amos Perlmutter, *Military and Politics in Israel* (New York: Frank Case and Co., 1969).

8. For a challenge to the myth, see Maurice Roumani, "Some Aspects of Socialization in the Israeli Army: The Case of Oriental Jews," in Ernest Krausz and Solomon Poll, eds., *On Ethnic and Religious Diversity in Israel* (Ramat Gan: Bar Ilan University, 1975), pp. 35–49.

9. Gerald Caiden, *Israel's Administrative Culture* (Berkeley: Institute of Governmental Studies, 1970).

10. See Yehoshua Freudenheim, *Government in Israel* (Dobbs Ferry, N.Y.: Oceana Publications, 1967). The situation of classic parliamentary democracies is portrayed in John C. Wahlke and Alex M. Dragnich, eds., *Government and Politics* (New York: Random House, 1966).

11. Amnon Rubinstein discusses this question in "Supreme Court vs. The Knesset," *Hadassah Magazine* 51, no. 7 (March 1970).

12. The Israeli press releases on their technical assistance programs are most revealing in this regard. The role of the sense of vocation in the first decade of statehood is presented well in Horace M. Kallen, *Utopians at Bay* (New York: Theodore Herzl Foundation, 1958).

13. This thesis is the product of the Workshop in Political Culture of the Jerusalem Center for Public Affairs which has explored Israel's political culture in some depth. See the reports of the workshop for treatments of the subject in detail.

14. This writer originally developed these political culture categories to explain

the political culture of the United States. He since has discovered that they are apparently universal, provided they are understood in light of the second dimension of the political-cultural matrix, namely, whether or not the overall culture is civic, statist, or subject. In the Israeli context, the three are dimensions of Israel's national-civic political culture, which is a synthesis of civic and statist elements. See Daniel J. Elazar, *American Federalism: A View from the States* (New York: Harper and Row, 1984), 3rd ed., chaps. 5 and 6; Daniel J. Elazar, *Cities of the Prairie* (New York: Basic Books, 1970), chap. 6; and Daniel J. Elazar, "Israel's Emerging Political Culture," Research proposal submitted to Ford Foundation, December 1983.

15. There is good reason to believe that the federal element is present in all of the new societies, derived, at least in part, from their origins as contractual partnerships. That is true even in those societies where no visible federal structure is involved. Contractual government, the constitutional diffusion of power, and negotiated collaboration seem to be characteristic of their polities. See Daniel J. Elazar, "Federalism," *International Encyclopedia of the Social Sciences* (New York: Macmillan Co., 1970), and *Studying the Civil Community* (Philadelphia: Center for the Study of Federalism, 1970).

16. For examples of these contracts, see Zelig Chinitz, *A Common Agenda* (Jerusalem: Jerusalem Center for Public Affairs, 1985), Appendix 1.

17. Cf. Daniel J. Elazar and Alysa Dortort, eds., *Understanding the Jewish Agency—A Handbook* (Jerusalem: Jerusalem Center for Public Affairs, 1984) and *The Extent, Focus, and Impact of Diaspora Involvement in Project Renewal—Four Reports* (Jerusalem: Jerusalem Center for Public Affairs, 1985).

18. The examples of these discussions are too numerous to cite. A good source for following the continued debate is *Forum*, published quarterly by the World Zionist Organization.

19. Gabriela Shalet, "General Comments on Contracts (General Part) Law, 1973," *Israel Law Review* 9, no. 2. (1974).

20. See Menachem Elon, *HaMishpat HaIvri: Toldotav, Mekorotav, Ekronotav* [Jewish Law: History, Sources, Principles] (Jerusalem: Magnes Press, 1978); Elliot Nelson Dorff and Arthur Rosett, *Materials on the Jewish Legal Tradition with Comparative Notes; Preliminary Edition* (Los Angeles: University of Judaism, 1976), classroom edition; Menachem Elon, *Principles of Jewish Law* (Jerusalem: Keter Publishing House, October 1974); Menachem Elon and Haim Cohn, eds., *Shenaton Ha-Mishpat Ha-Ivri* [Annual of the Institute for Research in Jewish Law] (Jerusalem: Institute for Research in Jewish Law, 1974– ); Nahum Rakover, *Sidrat Mehkarim VeSkirot BaMishpat HaIvri* [Series of Research and Reviews in Jewish Law] (Jerusalem: Ministry of Justice). This series includes such studies as *Al Shilton HaHok*, [On the Rule of Law] (1970), *Haganat HaSvivah*, [Environmental Protection] (1972), and other topics relevant to the use of traditional Jewish legal sources by the modern state; and Ze'ev Falk and Aaron Kirschenbaum, eds., *Dine Israel: An Annual of Jewish Law and Israeli Family Law* (Tel-Aviv, 5730– ).

## 11. The Impact of the Frontier

1. See Daniel J. Elazar, *Cities of the Prairie* (New York: Basic Books, 1970), chap. 1, and Daniel J. Elazar, et al., *Cities of the Prairie Revisited* (Lincoln: University of Nebraska Press, 1986), chap. 1.

2. Frederick Jackson Turner, *The Frontier in American History* (New York: Holt, 1920), and Ray Allen Billington, *America's Frontier Heritage* (New York: Holt, Rinehart and Winston, 1967).

3. Elazar, *Cities*. See particularly the bibliographic footnotes.

4. S. N. Eisenstadt, *Israeli Society* (London: Weidenfeld and Nicolson, 1967),

and M. Curtis and M. Chernoff, *Israel: Social Structure and Change* (New Brunswick: Transaction Books, 1973), offer good accounts of Israel's development that can be analyzed from the perspective of the frontier thesis; Shlomo Deshen, *Immigrant Voters in Israel—Parties and Congregations in a Local Election Campaign* (Manchester: Manchester University Press, 1970).

5. David Ben-Gurion, "The Key to Immigration" and "Unity and Independence," in *Rebirth and Destiny of Israel*, edited and translated from Hebrew under the supervision of Mordecai Nurock (New York: Philosophical Library, 1954).

6. Alexander Berler, a pioneer Israeli urban planner, discusses "Urban Growth in Israel: Changes in Time and Space, 1948–1967," in his *New Towns in Israel*, translated from Hebrew by Chana Shmorak (Jerusalem: Israel University Press, 1970). There he outlines the process of the emergence of the urban frontier and its growing importance, and considers the emergence of the metropolitan frontier. Arie S. Shachar looks at the development of town policy and its implementation from the national planning perspective in "Israel's Development Towns," in D. H. K. Amiram and A. Shachar, *Development Towns in Israel* (Jerusalem: The Hebrew University, 1969). In "Israel's New Frontier: The Urban Periphery," in M. Curtis and M. Chertoff, eds., *Israel: Social Structure and Change* (New Brunswick, Transaction Books, 1973), Judah Matras looks at the situation from a social perspective, emphasizing the impact of the frontier experience on the actual settlement of the development towns. Finally, in *Immigrant Voters in Israel* (Manchester University Press, 1970), Shlomo Deshen focuses on one particular development town, in this case Kiryat Gat (which he calls "Ayara"), which he studied in 1965 at more or less the climactic moment of the founding generation of the development towns. Deshen gives us a look at the problematics of integrating veteran Israelis and immigrants from the Islamic countries, and how social hierarchies developed that are presently of considerable influence in Israeli society.

7. Daniel J. Elazar, "The Local Elections: Sharpening the Trend toward Territorial Democracy," in Asher Arian, ed., *The Elections in Israel, 1973* (Jerusalem: Jerusalem Academic Press, 1975), and Avraham Lantzman, "The 1983 Israeli Municipal Elections: Mixed Trends and Minor Upsets," *Jerusalem Letter*, no. 68 (1 December 1983).

8. From field notes of Daniel J. Elazar and Bar Ilan University Institute of Local Government Urban Field Research Project in 1975.

9. Field notes, Daniel J. Elazar and Bar Ilan Institute of Local Government Field Research Projects, 1973–1984.

10. On Jerusalem, see Saul B. Cohen, *Jerusalem Undivided* (New York: Herzl Press, 1980); Meron Benveniste, *Jerusalem: Polarized Community* (Jerusalem: West Bank Project, 1983); Israel Kimchi, Benjamin Heyman, and Claud Gabriel, *Jerusalem, 1967–1975: A Socio-economic Survey* (Jerusalem: The Hebrew University, Institute for Urban and Regional Studies, Jerusalem Studies Center, April 1976); David Shahar, "Trends in the Metropolitan Development of Jerusalem," in *Jerusalem Discussion Paper no. 2* (Jerusalem: Jerusalem Research Institute, 1980); Annette Hochstein, *Metropolitan Trends in the Jerusalem Area* Jerusalem: West Bank Project, 1983); Joel L. Kramer, ed., *Jerusalem: Problems and Prospects* (New York: Praeger, 1980).

11. Uri Leviathan describes one dimension of this transformation in "The Industrial Process in Israeli Kibbutzim," in Curtis and Chertoff. *Israel*. For a description of the situation today on the kibbutz, see Saadia Gelb, "The Kibbutz in Israel Today," in *Jerusalem Letter #73* (Jerusalem: Jerusalem Center for Public Affairs, July 22, 1984), and Josef Lanir, *The Kibbutz as a Political System: Behavioral and Functional Aspects*, thesis toward the master's degree submitted to Bar-Ilan University (Ramat Gan, 1978).

12. Gelb, "The Kibbutz in Israel Today."

13. Arad and Kiryat Gat are two very different examples of development towns on the urban frontier. Myron J. Aronof studied Arad in its first decade and published the results of his work as *Frontier Town*, which highlights a number of aspects of the emerging Israeli political cultural synthesis, including the emergence of a civic, as distinct from political, life, the integration of Ashkenazic and Sephardic elements of the population, albeit with a certain consciousness of interethnic difference and even latent hostility, and the development of ways of bargaining and negotiation appropriate to the new society.

Arad remains the exception, however, While Kiryat Gat is not exactly typical, either—no single community is—it comes closer to reflecting the distance that still must be traveled before a synthesis emerges. The selections from Shlomo Deshen's *Immigrant Voters in Israel*, a study of the 1965 elections in Kiryat Gat, indicate the way in which the political parties serve both as synthesizing devices and as means for accommodating and thereby perpetuating ethnic and even cultural differences. Deshen points out how different the parties look from the grassroots perspective of a development town from the way they look from their central offices, and how they must adjust their campaigning to the grassroots realities, among which are these ethnic and cultural differences.

### 12. The Future of Israeli Politics

1. Martin Diamond, *The Democratic Republic* (Chicago: Rand McNally, 1966); Daniel J. Elazar, "Constitution-Making: A Pre-eminently Political Act," in Richard Simeon, ed., *Redesigning the State: The Politics of Constitutional Change* (Toronto: Macmillan Press, 1985); Andrew McLaughlin, *The Foundations of American Constitutionalism* (Greenwich, Conn.: Fawcett Publications, 1961) and *Confederation and the Constitution, 1783–1789* (New York: Collier Books, 1962).

2. John Adams, *A Defense of the Constitution of Government of the United States of America* (1780), and Edmund Burke, "Speech to the Electors of Bristol" (1774).

3. On the Torah as constitution and halachah as constitutional law, see Ervin Birnbaum, *The Politics of Compromise: State and Religion in Israel* (Rutherford, N.J.: Fairleigh Dickinson University Press, 1970); Menachem Elon, "The Sources and Nature of Jewish Law and Its Application in the State of Israel," *Israel Law Review* 3 (1968): 88–126, 416–57; Y. Gershoni, "The Torah of Israel and the State," *Tradition* 12, no. 3–4 (1972): 25-34; "Jewish Law in the State of Israel," in *Proceedings of the Rabbinical Assembly* 36 (1974); and Norman L. Zucker, *The Coming Crisis in Israel* (Cambridge, Mass.: MIT Press, 1973).

4. Elazar, "Constitution-Making."

5. Cf. Emanuel Rackman, *Israel's Emerging Constitution, 1948–1951* (New York: Columbia University Press, 1955); J. Albert, "Constitutional Adjudication without a Constitution: The Case of Israel," *Harvard Law Review* 82 (1969): 1245–65; Daniel J. Elazar, "A Time of Constitutional Milestones in the History of Israel," *Jerusalem Letter/Viewpoints*, no. 34 (12 June 1984); Eli Likhovski, "Can the Knesset Adopt a Constitution Which Will Be the 'Supreme Law of the Land,'" *Israel Law Review* 4 (1969): 61–69; and Meir Shamgar, "On the Written Constitution," *Israel Law Review* 9, no. 4 (October 1974).

6. David Ben-Gurion, "Laws or a Constitution," in *Rebirth and Destiny of Israel*, edited and translated from Hebrew under the supervision of Mordecai Nurock (New York: Philosophical Library, 1954), pp. 363–79.

7. Amnon Rubinstein, *HaMishpat Hakonstitutionali shel Medinat Yisrael* [The Constitutional Law of the State of Israel] (Jerusalem: Schocken, 1969) (Hebrew).

8. Yigal Aricha, "Megillat HaAtzmaot—Chazon ve-Mitziot" [Declaration of Independence—Vision and Reality] (unpublished manuscript, prepared for Bar Ilan University and Jerusalem Center for Public Affairs, 1983) (Hebrew).

9. Horace M. Kallen was the first to single out a number of the themes in the Declaration of Independence that deserve careful examination for what they reveal about the consensus upon which Israel is based and the definition of the state's vocation. He was the first to view the declaration as expressing Israel's turning away from "Europe's religiocultural" tradition toward a restoration of an "authentic image of the people of Israel." His comparison of the declaration with the Torah and the American Declaration of Independence is particularly useful for understanding the similarities and differences between the two new societies. Today, school children in Israel are beginning to study the declaration from similar perspectives. See Horace M. Kallen, *Utopians at Bay* (New York: Theodore Herzl Foundation, 1958).

10. S. Z. Abramov, *Perpetual Dilemma: Jewish Religion in the Jewish State* (Rutherford, N.J.: Fairleigh Dickinson University Press, 1976); Birnbaum, *Politics of Compromise;* S. Ginossar, "Who is a Jew: A Better Law? The Law of Return (Amendment no. 2), 1970," *Israel Law Review* 5 (1970): 264–67; S. Rosenne, "The Israel Nationality Law, 5712-1972 and the Law of Return, 5710-1950," *Journal du Droit International* 81, no. 5 (1954); Amnon Rubinstein, "Who's a Jew and Other Woes," *Encounter* (March 1971), pp. 84–93; M. Shava, "Comment on the Law of Return (Amendment no. 2), 5730-1970," *Tel Aviv University Studies in Law,* 1977, p. 140; and Z. Terlo, "The Immigration Laws of Israel—Some Future Problems," *Public Administration in Israel and Abroad* 7 (1967): 24.

11. S. N. Eisenstadt, *Israeli Society* (London: Weidenfeld and Nicolson, 1968).

12. On Knesset members as representatives of interest groups, see the author's interviews with members of the Knesset, 1968–69. Also, Lester Seligman, *Leadership in a New Nation: Political Development in Israel* (New York: Atherton Press, 1964), and Eric M. Uslander, *"The Lord Helps Those Who Help Their Constituents: Redeeming Promises in the Promised Land,"* (Paper presented at the Midwest Political Science Association Annual Meeting, Chicago, 1983).

13. See Myron Aronoff, *Frontier Town: The Politics of Community Building in Israel* (Manchester: Manchester University Press, 1974).

14. Ibid.; A. Cohen, *Vaadot Munitzipaliot be-Ayorot HaPituach* [Municipal Committees in Development Towns] (Jerusalem: Sociology Department of the Hebrew University of Jerusalem and the Public Council for Community Work, 1962); Daniel J. Elazar, "The Compound Structure of Public Service Delivery Systems," in V. Ostrom and F. Bish, eds., *Comparing Urban Public Service Delivery Systems* (Beverly Hills: Sage Publications, 1977); I. Katz, "The Local Authority and Its Committees," *ISLGA,* vol. 1; and Efraim Torgovnik and Szewach Weiss, "Local Non-party Political Organizations in Israel," *Western Political Quarterly* 25 (June 1972): 305–22.

15. Eliezer Don-Yehiya, *Sherutim Datiyim ve Politika: HaKamaton ve Irgunan shel HaMoetzot HaDatiot be Yisrael* [Religious Services and Politics: The Founding and Organization of Religious Councils in Israel] (Ramat Gan and Jerusalem: Bar Ilan University Institute of Local Government and Jerusalem Center for Public Affairs, 1984), and Meir Silverstone, "The Israel Ministry of Religious Affairs and the Chief Rabbinate of Israel," *Public Administration in Israel and Abroad,* 1973 14: 31–44.

16. Aronoff, *Frontier Town;* Eliahu Bilicky, *Creation and Struggle, Haifa Labor Council, 1921–1981* (Tel Aviv: Am Oved, 1981) (Hebrew); and Dorothy Wilner, *Nation Building and Community in Israel* (Princeton: Princeton University Press, 1969)

17. R. M. Kramer, *Community Development in Israel and the Netherlands* (Berkeley and Los Angeles: University of California Press, 1970), and Robert A. Rosenbloom, "The Politics of the Neighborhood Movement," *South Atlantic Urban Studies* 4 (1979): 149–63.

18. Cf. Daniel J. Elazar, *Cities of the Prairie* (New York: Basic Books, 1970).

19. Cf. Leonard J. Fein, *The Politics of Israel* (Boston: Little, Brown and Co., 1967); Nathan Yanai, *Party Leadership in Israel* (Philadelphia: Turtledove Publishing,

1981); Asher Arian, ed., *The Elections in Israel 1969* Jerusalem: Jerusalem Academic Press, 1973); *The Elections in Israel, 1977* (Jerusalem: Jerusalem Academic Press, 1980); Eisenstadt, *Israeli Society;* Peter Medding, "A Framework for the Analysis of Power in Political Parties," *Political Studies* 20 (1973): 76–96; Birnbaum, *Politics of Compromise;* Walter Laqueur, *A History of Zionism* (London: Weidenfeld and Nicolson, 1972); David Nachmias, "A Note on Coalition Payoffs in a Dominant Party System," *Political Studies* 21 (1973): 301–305; Amos Perlmutter, *Military and Politics in Israel* (New York: Praeger, 1969).

20. On this subject treated before the ascendancy of the Likud, see Amos Elon, *The Israelis: Founders and Sons* (New York: Holt, Rinehart and Winston, 1971).

21. See Shmuel Sandler, "The National Religious Party: Israel's Third Party," *Jerusalem Letter,* no. 24 (28 October 1979).

22. For more extensive treatment of this phenomenon, see Daniel J. Elazar, "Religion and Party Politics in the Begin Era," in *Israel in the Begin Era,* ed. Robert Freedman (New York: Praeger, 1982).

23. For an examination of this phenomenon, see Eliezer Don-Yehiya, "Concept of Traditional Judaism in Zionist Socialism," *Kivunim,* no. 8 (Summer 1980): 29–46 (Hebrew).

24. The most important study of this phenomenon to date is Charles S. Liebman and Eliezer Don-Yehiya, *The Civil Religion of Israel: Tradition, Judaism and Political Culture in the Jewish State* (Berkeley and Los Angeles: University of California Press, 1983). The two authors also published the following articles drawn from their book: "Symbol System of Zionist Socialism: An Aspect of Israeli Civil Religion," *Modern Judaism* 1, no. 2 (September 1981): 121–48; and "Zionist Ultranationalism and Its Attitude toward Religion," *Journal of Church and State* 23, no. 2 (1981): 259–64. See also Daniel J. Elazar, "Toward a Jewish Vision of Statehood for Israel," *Judaism* 27, no. 2 (Spring 1975): 233–44.

25. Moshe Sanbar, *The Political Economy of Israel, 1948–1983* (Jerusalem: Jerusalem Center for Public Affairs, July 1984).

26. David Kochav, *The Influence of Defense Expenditure on the Israeli Economy* (Jerusalem: Jerusalem Center for Public Affairs, August 1984).

27. Moshe Sanbar, "The Economic Significance of the Israeli-Egyptian Agreement: How the Peace Treaty Can Reduce Israel's Dependence," in *Viewpoints #6* (Jerusalem: Jerusalem Center for Public Affairs, March 1979), and "Peace as an Economic Challenge," in *Viewpoints #6* (Jerusalem: Jerusalem Center for Public Affairs, April 1979).

# INDEX

Adams, John, 231
Agudath Israel, 130–33, 136, 173; growth of, 246–47
Alkalai, Judah, 21
Allon, Yigal, 32, 171
Antisemitism: and Zionism, 18, 228
Arabs: Arab vote, 174, 241–42; and Labor camp, 160–71; as minority in Israel, 5, 55–56, 64, 68–71, 110, 167–68, 171, 173, 174; and partition of Palestine, 42; and Zionist settlements, 10, 11. *See also* Palestinians
Aridor, Yoram, 249–50
Ashkenazim: Ashkenazic culture, 150–53, 156–57, 159–61; Ashkenazic vote, 147–50, 156, 163–65; dependent on abroad, 11, 20; history of, 26–27, 146–47, 153–54; old settlers, 11, 19; and Religious camp, 33; school system, 112; in Supreme Rabbinical Council, 135–36; and Yemenite Jews, 24. *See also* Sephardim
Auster, Daniel, 44

Balfour Declaration, 29, 38, 43, 66, 130, 169
Begin, Menachem: and civil religion, 124; and Likud, 243–44; neo-Sadduceanism of, 144; and Palestinians, 176; Sephardic support for, 160, 164; and two cultures, 150; on West Bank, 172; on Zionist settlements, 15
Behar, Nissim, 20
Ben-Gurion, David, 24, 26, 31, 44, 74; and annexation of West Bank, 170; and army, 80–81, 133, 188–89; on collectivism, 214; on constitution, 232–33; on frontier experience, 209–10; and Labor camp, 34; and religion, 132, 139; statism *(mamlachtiut)* of, 45–46, 75, 80–81, 101, 186, 188–89, 204; on Zionist settlements, 14; "The Key to Immigration," 210; "Mission and Dedication," 188–89; "Unity and Independence," 210
Ben-Israel, Manasseh, 158
Ben-Jehuda, Eliezer, 20
Bentov, Mordekhai, 44
Ben-Zvi, Yitzehak, 26, 31, 44
Berligne, Eliyahu, 44
Bernstein, Fritz, 44
Bible, 81, 135; biblical studies, 200; and history of the Jewish people, 12, 54, 256; secularization of, 32

Borochov, Ber, 16, 18
Buber, Martin, 17
Burke, Edmund, 231

Caiden, Gerald, 189
Camp David Agreement, 249
Cohen, Rachel, 44
Collectivism, 30; civic aspect of, 193; and frontier experience, 212; *kvutzah*, 24, 35, 37; labor battalions, 35, 48; and metropolitan-technological frontier, 222; revolutionary, 30, 34–36; and rural-land frontier, 214. *See also Kibbutz;* Settlement
Communism: and Eastern European Jews, 39–40
Communist Party (Israel), 35; Arab vote for, 174, 241, 242
Communist Party (Palestine), 31

Dayan, Moshe, 32; and Arabs, 170–71
Declaration of the Establishment of the State of Israel, 41, 234, 235; text of, 42–45
Declaration of Independence (Israel), 123; constitutional status of, 30, 63, 232, 233, 234
Democracy: democratic republicanism, 237; ideological, 48, 52; pluralistic, 97; territorial, 48–50, 51–54, 55, 100, 241, 253
Democratic Movement for Change, 6, 202, 226
Diaspora, 181, 198; aid of, 20–21, 35, 113; and Jewish political culture, 187; Jewish self-definition in, 141; Sephardic, 157; transformations of, 209; and Zionism, 14, 66, 67
Dobkin, Eliyahu, 45

Egypt, 42, 249
Eldad, Israel, 160
Eretz Israel, 10, 17, 28, 158, 172, 178, 185, 192, 228; collectivism in, 48; elections in, 32–33; and establishment of the State of Israel, 41, 42–43; and *kibbutz*, 212; modernization of, 19–20; political organization of, 1, 26; rebuilding of, 29–30; settlement in, 15, 128, 132. *See also* Palestine
Eshkol, Levi, 249
Europe: Eastern European Jews, 11, 26–28, 31, 39–40, 45, 52, 151–53, 154, 159–60,

DANIEL J. ELAZAR is Professor of Politial Science at Temple University and Bar-Ilan University, and president of the Jewish Institute for Federal Studies. He has written numerous books on American, Jewish, and Israeli politics.